Food, Nutrition and Sports Performance III

As sport has become more professionalised over the last thirty years, so the role of nutrition in promoting health and performance has become ever more important to athletes who search for the extra edge to succeed in their respective sports. With the expansion in the provision of medical and scientific support services in elite sport, those who advise athletes have had to become adept at identifying those dietary strategies that will help them to outperform their competitors.

This book is structured in two parts. The first analyses the science that underpins the nutritional goals of athletes, with a focus on the implications for athletes during training, competition and recovery. The second looks more closely at the practical implications for different sport categories, i.e. those that focus on strength, power or endurance, and on weight category sports, team sports and winter sports.

This volume will be of value to sports dieticians and nutritionists and others involved in the care and support of athletes, as well as to those who take an interest in the subject of sport nutrition and competitive performance. Coaches and athletes will also find much of interest here.

This book is based on the proceedings of the third in a series of Consensus Conferences in Sports Nutrition organised under the auspices of the International Olympic Committee.

This book was originally published as a special issue of the *Journal of Sports Sciences*.

Ronald J. Maughan obtained his BSc (Physiology) and PhD from the University of Aberdeen, and held a lecturing position in Liverpool before returning to Aberdeen where he was based for almost 25 years. He is now a professor emeritus at Loughborough University, UK. He has published extensively in the scientific literature, and is on the editorial board of several international journals.

Susan M. Shirreffs is a scientist with GlaxoSmithKline.

Food, Nutrition and Sports Performance III

Edited by
Ronald J. Maughan and Susan M. Shirreffs

Routledge
Taylor & Francis Group

LONDON AND NEW YORK

First published 2013
by Routledge
2 Park Square, Milton Park, Abingdon, Oxon, OX14 4RN

Simultaneously published in the USA and Canada
by Routledge
711 Third Avenue, New York, NY 10017

Routledge is an imprint of the Taylor & Francis Group, an informa business

British Library Cataloguing in Publication Data
A catalogue record for this book is available from the British Library

ISBN 13: 978-0-415-62792-4

Typeset in Minion
by Taylor & Francis Books

Publisher's Note
The publisher would like to make readers aware that the chapters in this book may be referred to as articles as they are identical to the articles published in the special issue. The publisher accepts responsibility for any inconsistencies that may have arisen in the course of preparing this volume for print.

MIX
Paper from responsible sources
FSC® C018575
www.fsc.org

Printed and bound in Great Britain by MPG Printgroup

Contents

Citation Information

The chapters in this book were originally published in the *Journal of Sport Sciences*, volume 29, issue S1 (December 2011). When citing this material, please use the original page numbering for each article, as follows:

Editorial (now Foreword)
IOC Consensus Conference on Nutrition in Sport, 25–27 October 2010,
International Olympic Committee, Lausanne, Switzerland
R. J. Maughan and S. M. Shirreffs
Journal of Sport Sciences, volume 29, issue S1 (December 2011) pp. S1

IOC consensus statement on sports nutrition 2010
Journal of Sport Sciences, volume 29, issue S1 (December 2011)
pp. S3–S4

List of conference participants
Journal of Sport Sciences, volume 29, issue S1 (December 2011) pp. S5

Chapter 1
Energy availability in athletes
A. B. Loucks, B. Kiens and H. H. Wright
Journal of Sport Sciences, volume 29, issue S1 (December 2011)
pp. S7–S15

Chapter 2
Carbohydrates for training and competition
L. M. Burke, J. A. Hawley, S. H. S. Wong and A. E. Jeukendrup
Journal of Sport Sciences, volume 29, issue S1 (December 2011)
pp. S17–S27

Chapter 3
Dietary protein for athletes: From requirements to optimum adaptation
S. M. Phillips and L. J. C. van Loon
Journal of Sport Sciences, volume 29, issue S1 (December 2011)
pp. S29–S38

Chapter 4
Fluid and electrolyte needs for training, competition, and recovery
S. M. Shirreffs and M. N. Sawka
Journal of Sport Sciences, volume 29, issue S1 (December 2011)
pp. S39–S46

Chapter 5
Antioxidant and Vitamin D supplements for athletes: Sense or nonsense?
S. Powers, W. B. Nelson and E. Larson-Meyer
Journal of Sport Sciences, volume 29, issue S1 (December 2011)
pp. S47–S55

FOREWORD

IOC Consensus Conference on Nutrition in Sport, 25–27 October 2010, International Olympic Committee, Lausanne, Switzerland

The first Consensus Conference on Nutrition in Sport of the Medical Commission of the International Olympic committee was held in 1991 to review the evidence on the role of nutrition in supporting athletic performance and protecting the health of the athlete. This resulted in the preparation of a short consensus statement, a series of scientific papers published in the *Journal of Sports Sciences* and a booklet that was aimed at providing a summary of the practical information for athletes, coaches and other support staff. In 2003, a further Consensus Conference was held to update the information, and again the scientific papers were published as a special issue of the *Journal of Sports Sciences*. In addition to updating the published materials, this conference was captured in an audiovisual format that was made available on CD. The CD of the conference has been distributed widely and is still used as an effective teaching aid around the world. The Nutrition for Athletes booklet was completely revised and updated for the Games of 2004 in Athens and again for the Games of 2008 in Beijing. Further revisions were produced for the Winter Games of 2006 in Torino and 2010 in Vancouver, the Youth Olympic Games of 2010 in Singapore and the Commonwealth Games of 2010 in Delhi. Each of these booklets included information relevant to the specific competitive environment. In each case, every participant at these Games and all team officials were provided with a copy of the booklet.

Such has been the rate of new developments in the field of sports nutrition that a further conference was held in October 2010 at the IOC Offices in Lausanne, Switzerland. The 2010 Conference provided an opportunity for a complete review of the scientific evidence on the relationship between nutrition, performance and health in sport. The scientific papers that formed the basis of that review were presented at the Conference by leading experts in the field and were revised in the light of the discussions that took place. Those papers then entered the Journal's normal peer review process and are now published in this supplementary issue of the Journal. Papers from the previous two Consensus Conferences are among the most highly cited in the Journal, attracting considerable attention from the scientific community and providing a strong evidence base for the information provided to athletes.

Publication of these papers in this issue of the *Journal of Sports Sciences* will be followed by a revision of the Nutrition for Athletes booklet to ensure that sound, evidence-based information in the field of nutrition and hydration can be provided to athletes and support staff in the build-up to the 2012 Olympic Games in London.

The 2010 conference featured 12 presentations and involved a total of 28 participants, including both research scientists and sports dieticians, from many different countries. The first day of the conference was devoted to a comprehensive review of new developments in the science that underpins the practice of sports nutrition. The second day was devoted to the practical application of this information across a range of sports with different physical and nutritional demands. Each topic was addressed by a single speaker, and two nominated discussants for each session were given the opportunity to open the discussion. Each speaker circulated a manuscript in advance of the conference, allowing all delegates to prepare for a full and open discussion. These manuscripts, and the evidence on which they are based, have therefore been subjected to rigorous scrutiny.

The conference was supported by a generous grant from The Coca-Cola Company.

RONALD J. MAUGHAN AND
SUSAN M. SHIRREFFS

IOC consensus statement on sports nutrition 2010

Diet significantly influences athletic performance. All athletes should adopt specific nutritional strategies before, during and after training and competition to maximise their mental and physical performance. Evidence-based guidelines on the amount, composition, and timing of food intake have been defined to help athletes perform and train more effectively, with less risk of illness and injury. Athletes will benefit from the guidance of qualified sports nutrition professionals who can advise on their individual energy, nutrient and fluid needs and help develop sport-specific nutritional strategies for training, competition and recovery. Energy demands depend on the periodised training load and competition program, and will vary from day to day and across the season. A diet that provides adequate energy from a wide range of commonly available foods can meet the carbohydrate, protein, fat and micronutrient requirements of training and competition. An appropriate diet will help athletes reach an optimum body size and body composition to achieve greater success in their sport. Careful selection of nutrient-rich foods to reduce the risk of developing nutrient deficiencies that impair both health and performance is especially important when energy intake is restricted to reduce body and/or fat mass. During high-intensity training, particularly of long duration, athletes should aim to achieve carbohydrate intakes that meet the needs of their training programs and also adequately replace carbohydrate stores during recovery between training sessions and competitions. Dietary protein should be consumed in daily amounts greater than those recommended for the general population, but a varied diet that meets energy needs will generally provide protein in excess of requirements. Foods or snacks that contain high-quality proteins should be consumed regularly throughout the day as part of the day's total protein intake, and in particular soon after exercise, in quantities sufficient to maximise the synthesis of proteins, to aid in long-term maintenance or gain of muscle and bone and in the repair of damaged tissues. Ingestion of foods or drinks providing 15–25 g of such protein after each training session will maximise the synthesis of proteins that underpins these goals. For events lasting an hour or more, the athlete should aim to begin competition with body carbohydrate stores sufficient to meet their needs by consuming carbohydrate-rich foods in the hours and days beforehand. Ingestion of even small amounts of carbohydrate during exercise can enhance cognitive and physical performance in competition lasting one hour. As the duration of the event increases, so does the amount of carbohydrate needed to optimise performance. To achieve the relatively high rates of intake (up to 90 g/h) needed to optimise performance in events lasting more than about 3 hours, athletes should practise consuming carbohydrate during training to develop an individual strategy, and should make use of sports foods and drinks containing carbohydrate combinations that will maximise absorption from the gut and minimise gastrointestinal disturbances. Dehydration, if sufficiently severe, can impair performance in most events, particularly in warm and high-altitude environments. Athletes should be well hydrated before exercise and drink sufficient fluid during exercise to limit dehydration to less than about 2% of body mass. Chilled fluids may benefit performance in hot conditions. Athletes should not drink so much that they gain weight during exercise. Sodium should be included when sweat losses are high, especially when exercise lasts more than about 2 hours. During recovery from exercise, rehydration should include replacement of both water and salts lost in sweat. When athletes must compete in several events in a short time-period, strategies to enhance recovery of fluid and fuel are important. Low energy availability should be avoided, as it can impair performance and adaptation to training and may be harmful to brain, reproductive, metabolic and immune function, and to bone health. Dieting in young athletes should be discouraged. Robust immunity and reduced risk of infection can be achieved by consuming a varied diet adequate in energy and micronutrients, ensuring adequate sleep and limiting other life stress. Athletes should be particularly aware of their needs for calcium, iron and Vitamin D, but the use of large amounts of some micronutrients may be harmful. Athletes at risk of disordered eating patterns and reproductive disorders should be promptly referred to a qualified health professional for evaluation and treatment. The use of supplements does not compensate for poor food choices and an inadequate diet, but supplements that provide essential nutrients may be a short-term option when food intake or food choices are restricted due to travel or other factors. Vitamin D may be needed in supplemental form when sun exposure is inadequate. Of the many different dietary ergogenic aids available to athletes, a very small number may enhance performance for some athletes when used in accordance with current evidence under the guidance of a well-informed professional. Athletes contemplating the use of supplements and sports foods should consider their efficacy, their cost, the risk to health and performance, and the potential for a positive doping test. Supplement use in young athletes should be discouraged, and the focus should be on consuming a nutrient-rich, well-chosen diet to allow for growth while maintaining a healthy body composition. To enjoy all the benefits of sport, athletes, whether they compete at the elite level or exercise on a recreational basis, should adopt specific nutrition strategies that can optimise mental and physical performance and support good health.

Lausanne
27 October 2010

Conference participants

Hans Braun, Germany
Mark Davis, USA
Paul L. Greenhaff, UK
John A. Hawley, Australia
Peter Hespel, Belgium
Asker E. Jeukendrup, UK
Luc J.C. Van Loon, The Netherlands
Enette Larson-Meyer, USA
Nanna L. Meyer, USA
Stuart M. Phillips, Canada
Mike N. Sawka, USA
Gary Slater, Australia
Trent Stellingwerff, Switzerland
Stephen H.S. Wong, Hong Kong

Louise M. Burke, Australia
Marty Gibala, Canada
Nanci Guest, Canada
Christine Helle, Norway
Francis E. Holway, Argentina
Bente Kiens, Denmark
Anne B. Loucks, USA
Ron J. Maughan, UK
Jeni Pearce, UK
Scott Powers, USA
Susan M. Shirreffs, UK
Lawrence L. Spriet, Canada
Jorunn Sundgot-Borgen, Norway
Hattie H. Wright, South Africa

Energy availability in athletes

ANNE B. LOUCKS[1], BENTE KIENS[2], & HATTIE H. WRIGHT[3]

[1]*Department of Biological Sciences, Ohio University, Athens, Ohio, USA,* [2]*The Molecular Physiology Group, Department of Exercise and Sport Sciences, University of Copenhagen, Copenhagen, Denmark, and* [3]*Center of Excellence for Nutrition, Faculty of Health Sciences, North-West University, Potchefstroom, South Africa*

Abstract

This review updates and complements the review of energy balance and body composition in the Proceedings of the 2003 IOC Consensus Conference on Sports Nutrition. It argues that the concept of energy availability is more useful than the concept of energy balance for managing the diets of athletes. It then summarizes recent reports of the existence, aetiologies, and clinical consequences of low energy availability in athletes. This is followed by a review of recent research on the failure of appetite to increase *ad libitum* energy intake in compensation for exercise energy expenditure. The review closes by summarizing the implications of this research for managing the diets of athletes.

Introduction

In the 2003 IOC Consensus Conference on Sports Nutrition, evidence was presented that many athletes, most often female athletes, were deficient in energy, and especially energy in the form of carbohydrates, resulting in impaired health and performance (Loucks, 2004). It was emphasized, however, that energy balance is not the objective of athletic training whenever athletes seek to modify their body size and composition to achieve performance objectives. They then need to carefully manage their diet and exercise regimens to avoid compromising their health.

Distinctions between energy availability and energy balance

In the field of bioenergetics, the concept of energy availability recognizes that dietary energy is expended in several fundamental physiological processes, including cellular maintenance, thermoregulation, growth, reproduction, immunity, and locomotion (Wade & Jones, 2004). Energy expended in one of these processes is not available for others. Therefore, bioenergeticists investigate the effects of a particular metabolic demand on physiological systems in terms of energy availability. They define energy availability as dietary energy intake minus the energy expended in the particular metabolic demand of interest. In experiments investigating effects of cold exposure, for example, energy availability would be defined, quantified, and controlled as dietary energy intake minus the energy cost of thermogenesis.

Exercise training increases, and in endurance sports may double or even quadruple, the amount of energy expended in locomotion. In exercise physiology, therefore, energy availability is defined as dietary energy intake minus the energy expended in *exercise* (EA = EI – EEE). As the amount of dietary energy remaining after exercise training for all other metabolic processes, energy availability is an *input to* the body's physiological systems.

In the field of dietetics, the concept of energy balance has been the usual basis of research and practice. Defined as dietary energy intake minus *total* energy expenditure (EB = EI – TEE), energy balance is the amount of dietary energy added to or lost from the body's energy stores after the body's physiological systems have done all their work for the day. Thus energy balance is an *output from* those systems. For healthy young adults, $EB = 0 \text{ kcal} \cdot \text{day}^{-1}$ when $EA = 45 \text{ kcal} \cdot \text{kg FFM}^{-1} \cdot \text{day}^{-1}$ (where FFM = fat-free mass).

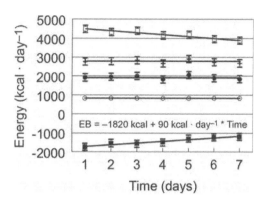

Figure 1. Negative energy balance rising at a rate of ≈ 90 kcal $\cdot$ day^{-1} as metabolic processes were suppressed while the energy intake (2770 kcal $\cdot$ day^{-1}), exercise energy expenditure (840 kcal $\cdot$ day^{-1}), and energy availability (2770 − 840 = 1930 kcal $\cdot$ day^{-1}) of eight lean, untrained men remained constant. EI (+) = energy intake, TEE ($\square$) = total energy expenditure, EEE (O) = exercise energy expenditure, EA ($\bullet$) = energy availability, EB ($\blacksquare$) = energy balance. Original figure based on data in Stubbs et al. (2004).

The contrast between energy availability and energy balance is illustrated in Figure 1, which shows data collected while eight lean, untrained men lived in a room calorimeter for a week (Stubbs et al., 2004). During that week, their energy intake (2770 kcal $\cdot$ day^{-1}), exercise energy expenditure (840 kcal $\cdot$ day^{-1}), and energy availability (2770 − 840 = 1930 kcal $\cdot$ day^{-1} $\approx$ 30 kcal $\cdot$ kg FFM^{-1} $\cdot$ day^{-1}) were constant. Meanwhile, the magnitude of their negative energy balance (2770 − 4500 = −1730 kcal $\cdot$ day^{-1} on Day 1) decreased towards zero at a rate of ~ 90 kcal $\cdot$ day^{-1} as various physiological processes slowed down. At this rate, they would have recovered EB = 0 kcal $\cdot$ day^{-1} (a pathological state of energy balance achieved by suppressing physiological systems) in 3 weeks, while remaining in severely low energy availability.

Undergraduate nutrition textbooks assert that energy requirements can be determined by measuring energy expenditure, but measures of energy expenditure contain no information about whether physiological systems are functioning in a healthy manner. Because physiological processes are suppressed by severely low energy availability, measurements of total or resting energy expenditure will underestimate a chronically undernourished athlete's energy requirements.

Therefore, because energy balance is an output from, rather than an input to, physiological systems, because it does not contain reliable information about energy requirements, and because it is not even the objective of athletic training, energy balance is not a useful concept for managing an athlete's diet.

Energy deficiency in athletes: Existence, aetiologies, and consequences

At the 2003 IOC Consensus Conference, the existence of widespread energy deficiency in athletes was still questioned. Since then, the IOC Medical Commission has published two position stands (Sangenis et al., 2005, 2006) and the American College of Sports Medicine (ACSM) has published a revised position stand (Nattiv, Loucks, Manore, Sundgot-Borgen, & Warren, 2007) on the "female athlete triad". In addition, a coaches' handbook on Managing the Female Athlete Triad developed by the co-chairs of the athlete interest group of the Academy of Eating Disorders has been published by the US National Collegiate Athletics Association (NCAA) (Sherman & Thompson, 2005). All four publications attribute the functional hypothalamic menstrual disorders and low bone mineral density found in many female athletes to energy deficiency, but the ACSM position stand differs from the other three in that it excludes disordered eating and eating disorders as necessary components of the triad. The ACSM emphasizes that athletes who expend large amounts of energy in prolonged exercise training can become energy deficient without eating disorders, disordered eating or even dietary restriction.

The ACSM identified three distinct origins of energy deficiency in athletes. The first is obsessive eating disorders with their attendant clinical mental illnesses. The second is intentional and rational but mismanaged efforts to reduce body size and fatness to qualify for and succeed in athletic competitions. This mismanagement may or may not include disordered eating behaviours such as fasting, diet pills, laxatives, diuretics, enemas, and vomiting that are entrenched parts of the culture and lore of some sports. The third is the inadvertent failure to increase energy intake to compensate for the energy expended in exercise. The percentages of cases of the female athlete triad originating from these three sources are unknown, but ACSM emphasized that any epidemiological study requiring the presence of an eating disorder or disordered eating for diagnosing cases of the triad (e.g. Schtscherbyna, Soares, de Oliveira, & Ribeiro, 2009) will underestimate its prevalence.

Sports vary greatly in the relative importance of various factors for competitive success. As they strive to achieve sport-specific mixes of these factors, athletes engage in different diet and exercise behaviours that impact energy availability. In endurance sports, prolonged exercise training greatly reduces energy availability, unless energy intake is increased to replace the energy expended in exercise. In sports where less energy is expended in training, dietary restriction may be a prominent part of the strategy for reducing energy availability to modify body size and composition.

Female athletes may also under-eat for reasons unrelated to sport. Around the world about twice as many young women as men *at every decile of body mass index* perceive themselves to be overweight (Wardle, Haase, & Steptoe, 2006). The disproportionate numbers actively trying to lose weight are even higher, and this disproportion *increases* as body mass index declines, so that almost nine times as many lean women as lean men are actively trying to lose weight! Indeed, more young female athletes report improvement of appearance than improvement of performance as a reason for dieting (Martinsen, Bratland-Sanda, Eriksson, & Sundgot-Borgen, 2010). Thus issues unrelated to sport may need to be addressed to persuade female athletes to eat appropriately.

The controversy about whether female athletes can increase glycogen stores as much as male athletes is instructive in this regard. An experiment in which participants consumed diets containing high and low percentages of carbohydrates found that women could not do so (Tarnopolsky, Atkinson, Phillips, & MacDougall, 1995). Subsequently, it was noted that the total energy intake (per kilogram of body weight) of the women in that study had been so low that the amount of carbohydrate they consumed on the high percent carbohydrate diet was no greater than the amount consumed by the men on the low percent carbohydrate diet. Later research showed that women could, indeed, load glycogen like men when they ate as much as men (per kilogram of body weight) (James et al., 2001; Tarnopolsky et al., 2001).

In the 2003 IOC Consensus Conference, the disruption of reproductive function at energy availabilities < 30 kcal $\cdot$ kg FFM$^{-1} \cdot$ day^{-1} was discussed in some detail and the low bone mineral density (BMD) found in amenorrhoeic athletes was represented as being mediated by oestrogen deficiency (Loucks, 2004). Since then, oestrogen-independent mechanisms by which low energy availability can reduce BMD have also been identified (Ihle & Loucks, 2004). As energy availability declines, the rate of bone protein synthesis declines along with insulin, which enhances amino acid uptake, in a linear dose–response manner. By contrast, the rate of bone mineralization declines abruptly as energy availability declines below 30 kcal $\cdot$ kg FFM$^{-1} \cdot$ day^{-1}, as do concentrations of insulin-like growth factor-1 and tri-iodothyronine. These effects occurred within 5 days of the onset of energy deficiency, and without a reduction in oestrogen concentration.

In older adults, fracture risk doubles for each reduction of one standard deviation below mean peak young adult BMD. In adolescents, fracture risk can rise even as BMD increases. Because BMD normally doubles during the decade of adolescence, a child entering adolescence with a high BMD relative to others of the same age can accrue bone mineral so slowly that adulthood is entered with a relatively low BMD. Because low BMD is an aetiological factor in stress fractures, anything that impairs bone mineral accrual during adolescence is undesirable. Unfortunately, this is exactly what was found in a study of 183 interscholastic competitive female athletes, of whom 93 were endurance runners and 90 were non-runners (Barrack, Rauh, & Nichols, 2010). The BMD z-scores were similar in runners and non-runners aged 13–15 years, but were significantly lower in runners than non-runners at 16–18 years of age.

Also questioned at the 2003 IOC Consensus Conference was whether energy deficiency and its clinical consequences were a problem among elite athletes. Since then a study of 50 British national or higher standard middle- and long-distance runners found BMD to be lower in amenorrhoeic runners and higher in eumenorrhoeic runners compared with European reference data (Gibson, Mitchell, Harries, & Reeve, 2004). The duration of eumenorrhoea was positively associated with spine BMD, and the rate of bone mineralization was reduced in the amenorrhoeic runners. Alone, the Eating Attitudes Test (EAT) is not clinically diagnostic for eating disorders, but in this study scores on the EAT classified one of 24 amenorrhoeic runners and none of nine oligomenorrhoeic runners as having an eating disorder, while eight amenorrhoeic runners and three oligomenorrhoeic runners were classified as practising disordered eating behaviours. This left 63% of the cases of amenorrhoea and 67% of the cases of oligomenorrhoea unaccounted for by the EAT test (Figure 2). Similarly, a low body mass index (< 18.5 kg $\cdot$ m^{-2}) failed to account for 67% of the cases of amenorrhoea and 67% of the cases of oligomenorrhoea (Figure 3). Another study diagnosed low BMD (z-score less than –1) in the lumbar spine of 34% and osteoporosis (z-score less than –2) in the radius of 33% of 44 elite British female endurance runners (Pollock et al., 2010). Reductions in BMD over time were associated with training volume. These findings led the authors to recommend that all female endurance athletes undergo dual-energy X-ray absorptiometry screening.

Ovarian function depends critically upon the frequency with which the pituitary gland secretes luteinizing hormone (LH) into the bloodstream, and LH pulsatility in exercising women depends on energy availability, rather than energy intake or energy expenditure separately (Loucks, Verdun, & Heath, 1998). Furthermore, exercise has no suppressive effect on LH pulsatility beyond the impact of its energy cost on energy availability (Loucks et al.,

1998). Reproductive function (Loucks & Thuma, 2003) and bone formation (Ihle & Loucks, 2004) are impaired abruptly and promptly below a threshold of energy availability (< 30 kcal $\cdot$ kg $FFM^{-1} \cdot day^{-1}$), which corresponds closely to resting metabolic rate. Figure 4 shows sleeping metabolic rate (SMR) measured by indirect calorimetry in young adult men ($n = 20$) and women ($n = 17$) (Westerterp, 2003). Sleeping metabolic rate is slightly less than resting metabolic rate by the small energy expendi-

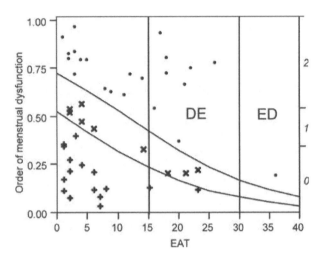

Figure 2. Logistic relationship between the order of menstrual dysfunction (right ordinate scale: 0 (+) = eumenorrhoea; 1 (×) = oligomenorrhoea; 2 (●) = amenorrhoea) and total EAT score ($P = 0.014$ for model). Left ordinate scale is a scale of probability. The right ordinate scale shows the proportions of participants in each category. DE = classified as disordered eating. ED = classified as eating disorder. Figure modified from Gibson et al. (2004).

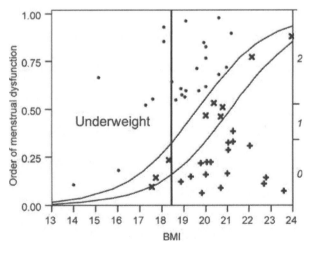

Figure 3. Logistic relationship between the order of menstrual dysfunction (right ordinate scale: 0 (+) = eumenorrhoea; 1 (×) = oligomenorrhoea; 2 (●) = amenorrhoea) and body mass index (BMI) ($P < 0.001$ for model). Left ordinate scale is a scale of probability. The right ordinate scale shows the proportions of participants in each category. BMI < 18.5 = underweight. Figure modified from Gibson et al. (2004).

ture associated with being awake. In Figure 4, the solid regression line relating sleeping metabolic rate to fat-free mass (SMR [MJ $\cdot$ day^{-1}] = 2.27 + 0.091 × FFM [kg]) has a significant y-intercept. The dashed line through the data and the origin has a slope of 30 kcal $\cdot$ kg $FFM^{-1} \cdot day^{-1}$. As Figure 4 shows, energy availabilities < 30 kcal $\cdot$ kg $FFM^{-1} \cdot day^{-1}$ provide less energy than is required for physiological systems in young adults to function at rest.

Observational and experimental data indicate that low energy availability also suppresses Type 1 immunity. The immune system mounts different defences against two types of pathogens. Type 1 defences are mounted against intracellular pathogens like viruses, while Type 2 defences are mounted against extracellular pathogens like bacteria. Endurance athletes frequently suffer upper respiratory tract infections (URTI) caused by viruses. A survey of all members of Swedish teams participating in the Olympic Games of 2002 and 2004 found that those participating in disciplines emphasizing leanness made more frequent attempts to lose weight, trained longer, and reported almost twice as many illnesses, primarily URTI, during the preceding 3 months (Hagmar, Hirschberg, Berglund, & Berglund, 2008). The results of a recent experiment challenge the hypothesis that Type 1 immunity in athletes might be suppressed by exercise itself (Lancaster et al., 2005). Participants expended 2200 kcal of energy by exercising for 2½ h at 65% of maximal oxygen uptake ($\dot{V}O_{2max}$). Replacing just 23% of this energy with carbohydrate reduced the suppression of Type 1 defences by an average of 65%. Thus, ingesting sufficient energy and nutrients is vital for supporting

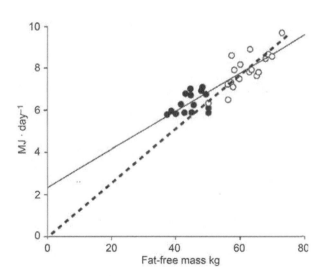

Figure 4. Sleeping metabolic rate plotted as a function of fat-free mass (FFM). ● = females; (○ = males. The solid regression line has a significant non-zero intercept. The dashed line is 30 kcal $\cdot$ kg $FFM^{-1} \cdot day^{-1}$. Figure modified from Westerterp (2003).

immune function, and even more so for immune-compromised individuals, such as those infected with HIV (Fenton & Silverman, 2008), whose resting energy expenditure is elevated (Mangili, Murman, Zampini, & Wanke, 2006). Therefore, HIV-infected athletes should take special care to reach their energy and nutrient needs.

Seventeen years have now passed since the first IOC Consensus Conference on Nutrition. Yet studies of energy intake and total energy expenditure continue to report that elite American figure skaters (Ziegler, Nelson, Barratt-Fornell, Fiveash, & Drewnowski, 2001), elite Kenyan runners (Fudge et al., 2006), and high-performance Canadian athletes in several sports (Lun, Erdman, & Reimer, 2009) train in substantial negative energy balance. Depending on the level of energy availability, such negative energy balance may either impair or benefit health and performance. In the current review period, two studies of elite athletes reported energy intake and exercise energy expenditure so that their average energy availability could be estimated. In the week before a race, the high percent carbohydrate diet of male Kenyan runners provided an energy availability of 34 kcal $\cdot$ kg FFM^{-1} $\cdot$ day^{-1} (Onywera, Kiplamai, Boit, & Pitsiladis, 2004). This energy availability may or may not have been appropriate depending on their athletic objectives at the time. If their performance in that particular race was less important than losing weight to improve performance in a later race, it was fine. However, no athletic objective would appear to justify professional male cyclists training for the Tour de France 6 months later at an energy availability of only 8 kcal $\cdot$ kg FFM^{-1} $\cdot$ day^{-1} (Vogt et al., 2005). Such observations indicate that the diet and exercise regimens of elite athletes range widely and are sometimes dangerously energy deficient.

Effects of prolonged exercise on hunger and energy intake

Eating disorders may be intractable, and weight and fat loss programmes may be challenging to manage effectively and safely, but these two origins of low energy availability in athletes are at least familiar to sports dietitians. The third origin, the suppression of appetite by prolonged exercise, appears to be less familiar. Neglect of appetite as an important factor in sports nutrition is indicated by the appearance of the word "appetite" only once (and then only in a discussion of fluid losses at high altitude) in the recently revised position stand on nutrition and athletic performance jointly adopted by the American Dietetic Association, the Dietitians of Canada, and the American College of Sports Medicine (Rodriguez, DiMarco, & Langley, 2009).

Some of the then available evidence that appetite is not a reliable indicator of energy needs in athletes was reviewed at the 2003 IOC Consensus Conference (Loucks, 2004). Shortly afterwards, the suppressive effect of prolonged exercise on *ad libitum* energy intake was clearly demonstrated by the experiment in which eight lean, untrained men expended ~ 840 kcal $\cdot$ day^{-1} by cycle ergometry as they lived in a room calorimeter for 7 days (Stubbs et al., 2004). During that week, their *ad libitum* energy intake was similar to another week in the room calorimeter when they did not exercise. This inadvertent failure to increase energy intake in compensation for exercise energy expenditure reduced their *ad libitum* energy availability by ~ 10 kcal $\cdot$ kg FFM^{-1} $\cdot$ day^{-1}.

The participants in that experiment actually performed the experiment four times, with and without exercise while consuming equally palatable 62% and 37% carbohydrate diets in a 2 × 2 cross-over design. Compared with weeks when the participants ate the 37% carbohydrate diet, their *ad libitum* energy intake declined by ~ 1000 kcal $\cdot$ day^{-1} on the 62% carbohydrate diet, reducing their *ad libitum* energy availability by ~ 16 kcal $\cdot$ kg FFM^{-1} $\cdot$ day^{-1}. Moreover, the suppressive effects of prolonged exercise and the high percent carbohydrate diet were additive. *Ad libitum* energy availability declined from ~ 47 kcal $\cdot$ kg FFM^{-1} $\cdot$ day^{-1} when the participants were sedentary on the 37% carbohydrate diet to ~ 21 kcal $\cdot$ kg FFM^{-1} $\cdot$ day^{-1} when they exercised on the 62% carbohydrate diet (Figure 5).

These findings in lean, untrained men exercising in a laboratory confirmed a previous report of a high

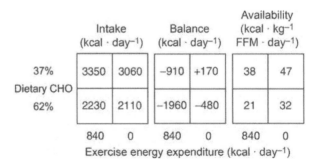

Figure 5. The *ad libitum* energy intake, energy balance, and energy availability of eight lean men living in a laboratory for 7 days during an experiment contrasting two diets (50% fat, 32% carbohydrate [CHO]; and 25% fat, 67% CHO) and two levels of exercise (840 and 0 kcal $\cdot$ day^{-1}) (data from Stubbs et al., 2004). Energy availability was estimated assuming 16% body fat. Appetite failed to match energy intake to activity-induced energy expenditure on either diet. Appetite also failed to drive energy intake on a low fat, high carbohydrate diet to match energy expenditure at either activity level. These effects were additive. Reproduced from Loucks (2007) with permission from Adis, a Wolters Kluwer business (© Adis Data Information BV 2007. All rights reserved).

percent carbohydrate diet suppressing *ad libitum* energy intake in 12 male and 13 female trained runners living at home (Horvath, Eagen, Fisher, Leddy, & Pendergast, 2000a; Horvath, Eagen, Ryer-Calvin, & Pendergast, 2000b). These runners ran 42 miles a week, expending ~ 600 kcal $\cdot$ day^{-1} for 31 days. They repeated this regimen three times while consuming equally palatable diets containing 42%, 55%, and 67% carbohydrate. As the percent carbohydrate content of the diet decreased, *ad libitum* energy availability increased from 27 to 34 and 39 kcal $\cdot$ kg FFM^{-1} $\cdot$ day^{-1} in the women and similarly from 27 to 37 and 42 kcal $\cdot$ kg FFM^{-1} $\cdot$ day^{-1} in the men. Endurance time at 80% $\dot{V}O_{2max}$ on a treadmill improved by 18% as the percent carbohydrate content of the diet was reduced from 67% to 55%. Interestingly, this reduction in percent carbohydrate content did not reduce the amount of carbohydrate consumed, because of the associated increase in *ad libitum* energy intake. The differences in *ad libitum* energy intake on the three diets had no effects on body weight or body fat (Figure 6). The mechanism by which a high percent carbohydrate diet suppresses appetite has yet to be

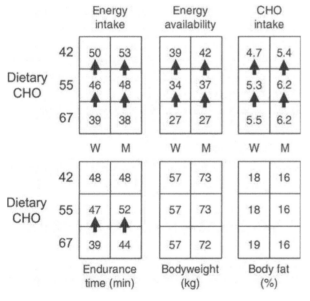

Figure 6. The *ad libitum* energy intake (kcal $\cdot$ kg FFM^{-1} $\cdot$ day,$^{-1}$), energy availability (kcal$\cdot$kg FFM^{-1} $\cdot$ day^{-1}), carbohydrate (CHO) intake (g $\cdot$ kg body weight^{-1} $\cdot$ day^{-1}), 80% maximal oxygen uptake endurance time, body weight and percent body fat of 12 female (W) and 13 male (M) endurance-trained runners living at home for 31 days during an experiment contrasting three diets (17% fat, 67% CHO; 31% fat, 55% CHO; and 44% fat, 43% CHO) (data from Horvath et al., 2000a, 2000b). Arrows indicate statistically significant differences. Increasing dietary fat from 17% to 31% (reducing dietary CHO from 67% to 55%) increased *ad libitum* energy intake enough to preserve carbohydrate intake and increased endurance performance by 18% without affecting body weight or body fat. Reproduced from Loucks (2007) with permission from Adis, a Wolters Kluwer business (© Adis Data Information BV 2007. All rights reserved).

investigated, but plausible factors include the greater bulk and fibre content (Mann et al., 2007) of carbohydrate-rich foods.

Recently, an even longer experiment simulating the microgravity in space confirmed the suppression of *ad libitum* energy intake by prolonged exercise (Bergouignan et al., 2010). In this experiment, eight healthy, lean, untrained women exercised in the prone position for 50 min at 40–80% $\dot{V}O_{2max}$ on alternate days during 60 days of bed rest while eight others did not exercise. *Ad libitum* energy balance was 0.7 MJ $\cdot$ day^{-1} lower in the women who exercised than in those who did not. Again, there were no differences in body weight between the two groups at any time during the 60-day study.

Evidence about the influence of gender on the suppression of *ad libitum* energy intake by prolonged exercise is conflicting. Some researchers have found the suppression in women to be greater (Staten, 1991) and others smaller (Stubbs et al., 2002a, 2002b) than that in men.

Investigators of the mechanisms that mediate the suppression of *ad libitum* energy intake by exercise recognize that appetite is comprised of two drives. Hunger, which urges us to begin eating, is stimulated by the orexigenic hormone ghrelin, whereas satiety, which leads us to stop eating, is stimulated by several anorexigenic hormones including peptide YY (PYY), glucagon-like peptide 1 (GLP-1), and pancreatic polypeptide (PP). Compared with placebo infusions, peripheral infusions of ghrelin and PYY at physiological concentrations alter food intake, with ghrelin increasing food intake at a single meal and cumulatively over 24 h by 28% (Wren et al., 2001) while PYY reduces it by 30% (Batterham et al., 2003).

A common experimental protocol for investigating these mechanisms has been to administer a standard dinner and breakfast followed by either a prolonged exercise bout or rest and then an *ad libitum* buffet lunch. One such study administered 60 min of exercise at 66% of maximum heart rate (Martins, Morgan, Bloom, & Robertson, 2007). The ~ 300 kcal of exercise energy expenditure was followed by an increase of only ~ 150 kcal in *ad libitum* energy intake. At lunchtime, hunger scores and concentrations of ghrelin were no higher after exercise than after rest, but PP was significantly increased after exercise.

Similar results have been found in one-day experiments on lean, untrained young men who performed 30 min of exercise at 50% and 75% of $\dot{V}O_{2max}$ (Ueda, Yoshikawa, Katsura, Usui, & Fujimoto, 2009), 90 min of exercise at 68% of $\dot{V}O_{2max}$ (King, Miyashita, Wasse, & Stensel, 2010), and a 450-kcal bout of resistance exercise (Ballard et al., 2009), and on healthy post-menopausal women who performed 2 h of exercise at 46% of $\dot{V}O_{2max}$ (Borer,

2010), as well as on male and female endurance trained runners who ran for 90 min at $\sim 60\%$ of $\dot{V}O_{2max}$ before a 10-km time-trial as fast as possible on a treadmill after 2 days of carbohydrate loading and a standardized 70% carbohydrate breakfast (Russel, Willis, Ravussin, & Larson-Meyer, 2009).

Other experiments have investigated individual differences in the effects of exercise training on *ad libitum* energy intake over a period of 12 weeks (King, Hopkins, Caudwell, Stubbs, & Blundell, 2008; King et al., 2009). These experiments on overweight and obese men and women confirmed the exercise-induced suppression of *ad libitum* energy intake mediated by suppressed hunger and increased satiety that had been found in shorter term experiments, but they also revealed a high degree of individual variability in weight and fat loss. When participants were retrospectively classified as compensators or non-compensators based on actual weight loss compared with the weight loss expected from exercise energy expenditure, *ad libitum* energy intake was found to have increased in the compensators and decreased in the non-compensators (King et al., 2008). Exercise induced a similar increase in satiety in both groups, which was even greater after 12 weeks of training than before, but compensators became progressively hungrier during the experiment (King et al., 2009).

Thus, findings in both trained and untrained male and female participants consistently demonstrate that a single bout of diverse forms of exercise acutely suppresses *ad libitum* energy intake and that exercise training chronically maintains the resulting energy deficiency for many weeks. This effect has been interpreted to be at least partially responsible for exercise-induced anorexia (Russel et al., 2009). Whether some female athletes become hungrier and increase *ad libitum* energy intake as their training progresses, and thereby avoid developing functional hypothalamic amenorrhoea (like overweight participants who do not lose weight on an exercise training programme), has yet to be investigated.

Implications for managing the diets of athletes

The studies of *ad libitum* energy intake cited above demonstrate that appetite is an unreliable indicator of energy requirements for athletes engaged in prolonged exercise training, just as thirst is an unreliable indicator of water requirements during a marathon race. Marathon runners are advised not to wait until they are thirsty before they begin drinking during a race. Similarly, athletes who engage in prolonged exercise training should be advised to eat by discipline, that is, to eat specific amounts of particular foods at planned times, instead of waiting until they are hungry and then eating only until they are satisfied.

The recommendation for athletes in endurance sports to consume a diet containing a high percentage of carbohydrates should also be reconsidered. The original evidentiary basis for this recommendation was the finding that high carbohydrate intake for a few days before a high-intensity endurance event increased glycogen storage and improved performance (Costill, 1988). It may be reasonable to expect endurance athletes to override their appetites to consume a high volume of a high percent carbohydrate diet for glycogen loading for a day or two as a pre-race tactic, but it may not be realistic to expect them to override the appetite-suppressive effects of both a high percent carbohydrate diet and prolonged exercise as a lifestyle. Meanwhile, research is needed to determine whether the suppression of *ad libitum* energy intake by a high percent carbohydrate diet can be ameliorated by increasing the proportion of refined carbohydrate in the diet (Mann et al., 2007).

The American Academy of Pediatrics (AAP, 2005), the IOC Medical Commission (Sangenis et al., 2005), and ACSM (Nattiv et al., 2007) have all recommended that national and international governing bodies of sports and athletic organizations put policies and procedures in place to eliminate potentially harmful weight loss practices of female athletes. Procedures and policies were not specified, because best practices may be sport-specific. These recommendations followed the establishment of such policies and procedures by the governing bodies of US men's collegiate wrestling in the late 1990s (Oppliger, Utter, Scott, Dick, & Klossner, 2006) and men's international ski jumping in 2004 (FIS, 2004). The procedures specified by NCAA Wrestling Rule 3 are expensive, intrusive for the athlete, labour-intensive for athletic trainers, and bureaucratic with local and national databases, but they seem to have been effective in reducing unhealthy weight loss behaviours and promoting competitive equity (Oppliger et al., 2006). Based on this success, a call has gone out for the International Judo Federation (IJF) to implement regulations to improve weight management behaviours among judo competitors, and for these regulations to be adopted by all National and Regional Federations (Artioli et al., 2010a).

By contrast, the International Ski Federation (FIS) employed a very different strategy for preventing excessive weight loss practices in ski jumpers (FIS, 2004). Instead of policing athlete behaviour, the FIS removed the motivation for ski jumpers to pursue excessive weight loss objectives. Ski jumpers have their height and weight measured at the top of the hill immediately before their jump, whereupon they are simply issued skis that are shorter or longer in proportion to their body mass index. Shorter skis reduce aerodynamic lift to compensate for the advantage a lighter jumper would otherwise gain, so that a jumper's success depends on their skill rather than their body weight. Adoption of this new rule reduced the percentage of underweight ski jumpers in the next World Cup competition from 23% to 8% (Muller, Groschl, Muller, & Sudi, 2006). Replacing body mass index with mass index (MI = body mass divided by the square of sitting height) has been proposed to further improve the rule (Muller, 2009).

Periodization of training may require a periodization of energy availability to achieve training objectives. Experimental evidence indicates that athletes should follow diet and exercise regimens that provide energy availabilities of 30–45 kcal · kg FFM^{-1} · day^{-1} while training to reduce body size or fatness. However, if athletes in other sports are like judo competitors, personal counselling of athletes by sports dietitians may not be the most effective way to moderate athlete behaviour to prevent excessive energy deficiency. Among seven different types of advisors for weight management behaviour, judo competitors ranked dietitians second to last, ahead only of physicians (Artioli et al., 2010b). The most influential advisor was the coach. In that context, a more effective way to modify athlete behaviour may be for sports dietitians and nutritionists to educate coaches, using workshops and handbooks that are specifically targeted at them, about the importance of energy availability and practical techniques for managing it.

References

AAP (2005). American Academy of Pediatrics Committee on Sports Medicine and Fitness: Promotion of healthy weight-control practices in young athletes. *Pediatrics, 116,* 1557–1564.

Artioli, G., Franchini, E., Nicastro, H., Sterkowicz, S., Solis, M. Y., & Lancha, A. H., Jr. (2010a). The need of a weight management control program in judo: A proposal based on the successful case of wrestling. *Journal of the International Society of Sports Nutrition, 7,* 15.

Artioli, G. G., Gualano, B., Franchini, E., Scagliusi, F. B., Takesian, M., Fuchs, M., et al. (2010b). Prevalence, magnitude, and methods of rapid weight loss among judo competitors. *Medicine and Science in Sports and Exercise, 42,* 436–442.

Ballard, T. P., Melby, C. L., Camus, H., Cianciulli, M., Pitts, J., Schmidt, S., et al. (2009). Effect of resistance exercise, with or without carbohydrate supplementation, on plasma ghrelin concentrations and postexercise hunger and food intake. *Metabolism, 58,* 1191–1199.

Barrack, M. T., Rauh, M. J., & Nichols, J. F. (2010). Cross-sectional evidence of suppressed bone mineral accrual among female adolescent runners. *Journal of Bone and Mineral Research, 25,* 1850–1857.

Batterham, R. L., Le Roux, C. W., Cohen, M. A., Park, A. J., Ellis, S. M., Patterson, M., et al. (2003). Pancreatic polypeptide reduces appetite and food intake in humans. *Journal of Clinical Endocrinology and Metabolism, 88,* 3989–3992.

Bergouignan, A., Momken, I., Schoeller, D. A., Normand, S., Zahariev, A., Lescure, B., et al. (2010). Regulation of energy balance during long-term physical inactivity induced by bed rest with and without exercise training. *Journal of Clinical Endocrinology and Metabolism, 95,* 1045–1053.

Borer, K. T. (2010). Nonhomeostatic control of human appetite and physical activity in regulation of energy balance. *Exercise and Sport Sciences Reviews, 38,* 114–121.

Costill, D. L. (1988). Carbohydrates for exercise: Dietary demands for optimal performance. *International Journal of Sports Medicine, 9,* 1–18.

Fenton, M., & Silverman, E. (2008). Medical nutrition therapy for human immunodeficiency virus (HIV) infection and acquired immunodeficiency syndrome (AIDS). In L. Mahan & S. Escott-Stump (Eds.), *Krause's food, nutrition and diet therapy* (pp. 1008–1016). Philadelphia, PA: W. B. Saunders.

FIS (2004). International Ski Federation World Congress, Miami, FL, USA.

Fudge, B. W., Westerterp, K. R., Kiplamai, F. K., Onywera, V. O., Boit, M. K., Kayser, B., et al. (2006). Evidence of negative energy balance using doubly labelled water in elite Kenyan endurance runners prior to competition. *British Journal of Nutrition, 95,* 59–66.

Gibson, J. H., Mitchell, A., Harries, M. G., & Reeve, J. (2004). Nutritional and exercise-related determinants of bone density in elite female runners. *Osteoporosis International, 15,* 611–618.

Hagmar, M., Hirschberg, A. L., Berglund, L., & Berglund, B. (2008). Special attention to the weight-control strategies employed by Olympic athletes striving for leanness is required. *Clinical Journal of Sports Medicine, 18,* 5–9.

Horvath, P. J., Eagen, C. K., Fisher, N. M., Leddy, J. J., & Pendergast, D. R. (2000a). The effects of varying dietary fat on performance and metabolism in trained male and female runners. *Journal of the American College of Nutrition, 19,* 52–60.

Horvath, P. J., Eagen, C. K., Ryer-Calvin, S. D., & Pendergast, D. R. (2000b). The effects of varying dietary fat on the nutrient intake in male and female runners. *Journal of the American College of Nutrition, 19,* 42–51.

Ihle, R., & Loucks, A. B. (2004). Dose–response relationships between energy availability and bone turnover in young exercising women. *Journal of Bone and Minereral Research, 19,* 1231–1240.

James, A. P., Lorraine, M., Cullen, D., Goodman, C., Dawson, B., Palmer, T. N., et al. (2001). Muscle glycogen super-compensation: Absence of a gender-related difference. *European Journal of Applied Physiology, 85,* 533–538.

King, J. A., Miyashita, M., Wasse, L. K., & Stensel, D. J. (2010). Influence of prolonged treadmill running on appetite, energy intake and circulating concentrations of acylated ghrelin. *Appetite, 54,* 492–498.

King, N. A., Caudwell, P. P., Hopkins, M., Stubbs, J. R., Naslund, E., & Blundell, J. E. (2009). Dual-process action of exercise on appetite control: Increase in orexigenic drive but improvement in meal-induced satiety. *American Journal of Clinical Nutrition, 90,* 921–927.

King, N. A., Hopkins, M., Caudwell, P., Stubbs, R. J., & Blundell, J. E. (2008). Individual variability following 12 weeks of supervised exercise: Identification and characterization of compensation for exercise-induced weight loss. *International Journal of Obesity (London), 32,* 177–184.

Lancaster, G. I., Khan, Q., Drysdale, P.T., Wallace, F., Jeukendrup, A. E., Drayson, M. T., et al. (2005). Effect of prolonged exercise and carbohydrate ingestion on type 1 and type 2 T lymphocyte distribution and intracellular cytokine production in humans. *Journal of Applied Physiology, 98,* 565–571.

Loucks, A. B. (2004). Energy balance and body composition in sports and exercise. *Journal of Sports Sciences, 22,* 1–14.

Loucks, A. B. (2007). Low energy availability in the marathon and other endurance sports. *Sports Medicine, 37,* 348–352.

Loucks, A. B., & Thuma, J. R. (2003). Luteinizing hormone pulsatility is disrupted at a threshold of energy availability in regularly menstruating women. *Journal of Clinical Endocrinology and Metabolism, 88,* 297–311.

Loucks, A. B., Verdun, M., & Heath, E. M. (1998). Low energy availability, not stress of exercise, alters LH pulsatility in exercising women. *Journal of Applied Physiology, 84,* 37–46.

Lun, V., Erdman, K. A., & Reimer, R. A. (2009). Evaluation of nutritional intake in Canadian high-performance athletes. *Clinical Journal of Sports Medicine, 19,* 405–411.

Mangili, A., Murman, D. H., Zampini, A. M., & Wanke, C. A. (2006). Nutrition and HIV infection: Review of weight loss and wasting in the era of highly active antiretroviral therapy from the Nutrition for Healthy Living cohort. *Clinical Infectious Diseases, 42,* 836–842.

Mann, J., Cummings, J. H., Englyst, H. N., Key, T., Liu, S., Riccardi, G., et al. (2007). FAO/WHO scientific update on carbohydrates in human nutrition: Conclusions. *European Journal of Clinical Nutrition, 61* (suppl. 1), S132–S137.

Martins, C., Morgan, L. M., Bloom, S. R., & Robertson, M. D. (2007). Effects of exercise on gut peptides, energy intake and appetite. *Journal of Endocrinology, 193,* 251–258.

Martinsen, M., Bratland-Sanda, S., Eriksson, A. K., & Sundgot-Borgen, J. (2010). Dieting to win or to be thin? A study of dieting and disordered eating among adolescent elite athletes and non-athlete controls. *British Journal of Sports Medicine, 44,* 70–76.

Muller, W. (2009). Determinants of ski-jump performance and implications for health, safety and fairness. *Sports Medicine, 39,* 85–106.

Muller, W., Groschl, W., Muller, R., & Sudi, K. (2006). Underweight in ski jumping: The solution of the problem. *International Journal of Sports Medicine, 27,* 926–934.

Nattiv, A., Loucks, A. B., Manore, M. M., Sundgot-Borgen, J., & Warren, M. P. (2007). American College of Sports Medicine Position Stand: The female athlete triad. *Medicine and Science in Sports and Exercise, 39,* 1867–1882.

Onywera, V. O., Kiplamai, F. K., Boit, M. K., & Pitsiladis, Y. P. (2004). Food and macronutrient intake of elite Kenyan distance runners. *International Journal of Sport Nutrition and Exercise Metabolism, 14,* 709–719.

Oppliger, R. A., Utter, A. C., Scott, J. R., Dick, R. W., & Klossner, D. (2006). NCAA rule change improves weight loss among national championship wrestlers. *Medicine and Science in Sports and Exercise, 38,* 963–970.

Pollock, N., Grogan, C., Perry, M., Pedlar, C., Cooke, K., Morrissey, D., et al. (2010). Bone-mineral density and other features of the female athlete triad in elite endurance runners: A longitudinal and cross-sectional observational study. *International Journal of Sport Nutrition and Exercise Metabolism, 20,* 418–426.

Rodriguez, N. R., DiMarco, N. M., & Langley, S. (2009). Position of the American Dietetic Association, Dietitians of Canada, and the American College of Sports Medicine: Nutrition and athletic performance. *Journal of the American Dietetic Association, 109,* 509–527.

Russel, R., Willis, K. S., Ravussin, E., & Larson-Meyer, E. D. (2009). Effects of endurance running and dietary fat on circulating ghrelin and peptide YY. *Journal of Sports Science and Medicine, 8,* 574–583.

Sangenis, P., Drinkwater, B. L., Loucks, A. B., Sherman, R. T., Sundgot-Borgen, J., & Thompson, R. A. (2005). International Olympic Committee Medical Commission Working Group on Women in Sport: Position Stand on the Female Athlete Triad. Retrieved from: http://multimedia.olympic.org/pdf/en_report_917_pdf

Sangenis, P., Drinkwater, B. L., Mountjoy, M., Constantini, N., Schamasch, P., Elwani, R., et al. (2006). IOC Consensus Statement: The Female Athlete Triad. *Medicine and Science in Tennis, 11,* 20.

Schtscherbyna, A., Soares, E. A., de Oliveira, F. P., & Ribeiro, B. G. (2009). Female athlete triad in elite swimmers of the city of Rio de Janeiro, Brazil. *Nutrition, 25,* 634–639.

Sherman, R., & Thompson, R. (2005). *Managing the female athlete triad: NCAA coaches handbook.* Indianapolis, IN: National Collegiate Athletic Association.

Staten, M. A. (1991). The effect of exercise on food intake in men and women. *American Journal of Clinical Nutrition, 53,* 27–31.

Stubbs, R. J., Hughes, D. A., Johnstone, A. M., Whybrow, S., Horgan, G. W., King, N., et al. (2004). Rate and extent of compensatory changes in energy intake and expenditure in response to altered exercise and diet composition in humans. *American Journal of Physiology: Regulatory, Integrative and Comparative Physiology, 286,* R350–R358.

Stubbs, R. J., Sepp, A., Hughes, D. A., Johnstone, A. M., Horgan, G. W., King, N., et al. (2002a). The effect of graded levels of exercise on energy intake and balance in free-living men, consuming their normal diet. *European Journal of Clinical Nutrition, 56,* 129–140.

Stubbs, R. J., Sepp, A., Hughes, D. A., Johnstone, A. M., King, N., Horgan, G. W., et al. (2002b). The effect of graded levels of exercise on energy intake and balance in free-living women. *International Journal of Obesity and Related Metabolic Disorders, 26,* 866–869.

Tarnopolsky, M. A., Atkinson, S. A., Phillips, S. M., & MacDougall, J. D. (1995). Carbohydrate loading and metabolism during exercise in men and women. *Journal of Applied Physiology, 78,* 1360–1368.

Tarnopolsky, M. A., Zawada, C., Richmond, L. B., Carter, S., Shearer, J., Graham, T., et al. (2001). Gender differences in carbohydrate loading are related to energy intake. *Journal of Applied Physiology, 91,* 225–230.

Ueda, S. Y., Yoshikawa, T., Katsura, Y., Usui, T., & Fujimoto, S. (2009). Comparable effects of moderate intensity exercise on changes in anorectic gut hormone levels and energy intake to high intensity exercise. *Journal of Endocrinology, 203,* 357–364.

Vogt, S., Heinrich, L., Schumacher, Y. O., Grosshauser, M., Blum, A., Konig, D., et al. (2005). Energy intake and energy expenditure of elite cyclists during preseason training. *International Journal of Sports Medicine, 26,* 701–706.

Wade, G. N., & Jones, J. E. (2004). Neuroendocrinology of nutritional infertility. *American Journal of Physiology: Regulatory, Integrative and Comparative Physiology, 287,* R1277–R1296.

Wardle, J., Haase, A. M., & Steptoe, A. (2006). Body image and weight control in young adults: International comparisons in university students from 22 countries. *International Journal of Obesity (London), 30,* 644–651.

Westerterp, K. (2003). Energy metabolism and body composition: General principles. *European Respiratory Monograph, 24,* 1–10.

Wren, A. M., Seal, L. J., Cohen, M. A., Brynes, A. E., Frost, G. S., Murphy, K. G., et al. (2001). Ghrelin enhances appetite and increases food intake in humans. *Journal of Clinical Endocrinology and Metabolism, 86,* 5992–5995.

Ziegler, P., Nelson, J. A., Barratt-Fornell, A., Fiveash, L., & Drewnowski, A. (2001). Energy and macronutrient intakes of elite figure skaters. *Journal of the American Dietetic Association, 101,* 319–325.

Carbohydrates for training and competition

LOUISE M. BURKE[1], JOHN A. HAWLEY[2], STEPHEN H. S. WONG[3], &
ASKER E. JEUKENDRUP[4]

[1]*Department of Sports Medicine, Australian Institute of Sport, Belconnen, ACT, Australia,* [2]*Exercise Metabolism Group,
School of Medical Sciences, RMIT University, Bundoora, Victoria, Australia,* [3]*Department of Sports Science and Physical
Education, The Chinese University of Hong Kong, Hong Kong SAR, The People's Republic of China, and* [4]*School of Sport and
Exercise Sciences, University of Birmingham, Birmingham, UK*

Abstract

An athlete's carbohydrate intake can be judged by whether total daily intake and the timing of consumption in relation to exercise maintain adequate carbohydrate substrate for the muscle and central nervous system ("high carbohydrate availability") or whether carbohydrate fuel sources are limiting for the daily exercise programme ("low carbohydrate availability"). Carbohydrate availability is increased by consuming carbohydrate in the hours or days prior to the session, intake during exercise, and refuelling during recovery between sessions. This is important for the competition setting or for high-intensity training where optimal performance is desired. Carbohydrate intake during exercise should be scaled according to the characteristics of the event. During sustained high-intensity sports lasting ~ 1 h, small amounts of carbohydrate, including even mouth-rinsing, enhance performance via central nervous system effects. While $30-60$ g $\cdot$ h^{-1} is an appropriate target for sports of longer duration, events > 2.5 h may benefit from higher intakes of up to 90 g $\cdot$ h^{-1}. Products containing special blends of different carbohydrates may maximize absorption of carbohydrate at such high rates. In real life, athletes undertake training sessions with varying carbohydrate availability. Whether implementing additional "train-low" strategies to increase the training adaptation leads to enhanced performance in well-trained individuals is unclear.

Introduction

During exercise, carbohydrate availability to the muscle and central nervous system can be compromised because the fuel cost of an athlete's training or competition programme exceeds endogenous carbohydrate stores. Provision of additional carbohydrate is important because carbohydrate availability limits the performance of prolonged (> 90 min) sub-maximal or intermittent high-intensity exercise and plays a permissive role in the performance of brief or sustained high-intensity work (Hargreaves, 1999). The 2003 IOC consensus meeting on sports nutrition provided a substantial focus on carbohydrate needs of athletes with the programme involving separate reviews on pre-exercise eating (Hargreaves, Hawley, & Jeukendrup, 2004), nutrition during exercise (Coyle, 2004), post-exercise recovery (Burke, Kiens, & Ivy, 2004), and training and nutrient interactions (Spriet & Gibala, 2004). This review will focus on areas in which the guidelines produced at that meeting should be updated.

Carbohydrate for daily refuelling and recovery

The restoration of muscle and liver glycogen is a fundamental goal of recovery between training sessions or competitive events, particularly when the athlete undertakes multiple workouts within a condensed time period. Table I summarizes guidelines for refuelling, incorporating recent refinements to our knowledge. In 2003 we identified the optimal timing and amount of carbohydrate intake for glycogen storage during early recovery, and whether strategies such as altering the timing, pattern, quality, and type of carbohydrate intake can promote better glycogen synthesis when total carbohydrate intake is below the amount needed for maximal glycogen storage. This will often be the case for female athletes and others who restrict energy intake to achieve

Table I. Updated guidelines for refuelling after exercise and in the athlete's everyday diet.

Well supported principles

- When it is important to train hard or with high intensity, daily carbohydrate intakes should match the fuel needs of training and glycogen restoration
- Targets for daily carbohydrate intake are usefully based on body mass (or proxy for the volume of active muscle) and exercise load. Guidelines can be suggested (Table II) but need to be fine-tuned according to the athlete's overall dietary goals and feedback from training
- Guidelines for carbohydrate intake should not be provided in terms of percentage contributions to total dietary energy intake
- When the period between exercise sessions is less than 8 h, athletes should consume carbohydrate as soon as practical after the first workout to maximize the effective recovery time between sessions. More importantly, in the absence of carbohydrate intake, refuelling is ineffective
- When carbohydrate intake is sub-optimal for refuelling, adding protein to a meal/snack will enhance glycogen storage (Figure 1)
- Early refuelling may be enhanced by a higher rate of carbohydrate intake, especially when consumed in frequent small feedings (Table II)
- During longer recovery periods (24 h) when adequate energy and carbohydrate is consumed, the types, pattern, and timing of carbohydrate-rich meals and snacks can be chosen according to what is practical and enjoyable
- Carbohydrate-rich foods with a moderate-to-high glycaemic index provide a readily available source of substrate for glycogen synthesis. This may be important when maximum glycogen storage is required in the hours after an exercise bout
- Nutrient-rich carbohydrate foods or other foods added to recovery meals and snacks can provide a good source of protein and other nutrients
- Adequate energy intake is needed to optimize glycogen storage; the restrained eating practices of some athletes interfere both with meeting targets for carbohydrate intake and optimizing glycogen storage from this intake
- Although there are small differences in glycogen storage across the menstrual cycle, females can store glycogen as effectively as male athletes if they consume adequate carbohydrate and energy
- Athletes should follow sensible practices regarding alcohol intake at all times, but particularly in the recovery period after exercise

Equivocal evidence – requiring further study

- Training in a glycogen-depleted or fasted state can enhance the adaptive responses to exercise stimulus and increases exercise capacity in previously untrained individuals. In real life, athletes undertake training sessions with varying carbohydrate availability. Whether implementing additional "train low" strategies enhances the performance of well-trained individuals is unclear

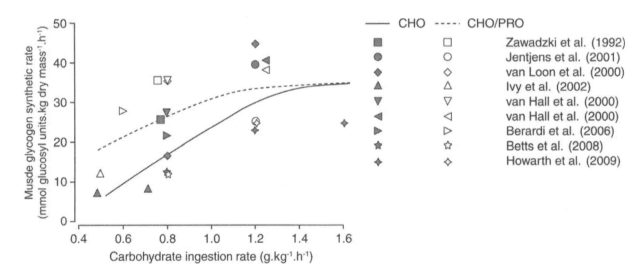

Figure 1. Reported rates of muscle glycogen resynthesis across nine studies that have compared muscle glycogen storage over >2–6 h post-exercise with varied rates of carbohydrate (CHO) intake, with or without co-ingestion of protein (PRO). This provides evidence that when CHO intake is below refuelling guidelines (<1.2 g.kg^{-1}.h^{-1}), the addition of protein ($\approx$20g) enhances glycogen synthesis. (adapted from Betts and Williams, 2010, with permission).

physique goals. Unfortunately, little further information is available.

Some opportunities exist, however, to enhance glycogen storage from a given amount of carbohydrate; these include use of high molecular weight glucose polymers (Piehl Aulin, Soderlund, & Hultman, 2000), co-ingestion of large amounts of caffeine (Pedersen et al., 2008), and prior creatine loading

(Robinson, Sewell, Hultman, & Greenhaff, 1999). Practical implications of these strategies may limit their use. For example, reliance on glucose polymer to provide a substantial energy intake reduces the nutrient density of the diet and may impair the athlete's ability to meet other nutritional goals. Meanwhile, side-effects associated with supplementation of large doses of caffeine (e.g. interference with sleep) or creatine (e.g. weight gain) may prevent these from being routinely used. Future research should attempt to identify the situations or individuals who might benefit from enhanced glycogen storage associated with these or other strategies in spite of the potential disadvantages. The dietary strategy of true value when energy restriction or poor appetite limit carbohydrate intake is to add protein. Despite earlier debate, it is now clear that this enhances glycogen storage when carbohydrate intake is suboptimal (Figure 1).

A key recommendation of the 2003 guidelines centred on the terminology to describe and advise athletes about the carbohydrate content of their eating plans or post-exercise diets. We proposed that a "high carbohydrate diet", particularly when judged as a percentage of energy intake, is a nebulous term that is poorly correlated to both the amount of carbohydrate actually consumed and the fuel requirements of an athlete's training or competition demands (Burke et al., 2004). Just as "energy availability" has been coined to define an athlete's energy intake in relation to the energy costs of their specific exercise programme, we now argue that "carbohydrate availability" is a preferable way to discuss carbohydrate intake. An athlete's carbohydrate status is best considered in terms of whether their total daily intake and the timing of its consumption in relation to exercise, maintains an adequate supply of carbohydrate substrate for the muscle and central nervous system ("high carbohydrate availability") or whether carbohydrate fuel sources are depleted or limiting for the daily exercise programme ("low carbohydrate availability").

Our continued approach to setting guidelines for daily carbohydrate intake is to consider the importance of achieving high carbohydrate availability, then estimate the carbohydrate cost of the specific exercise task. There is sound evidence that high carbohydrate availability is desirable in the competition setting where it may contribute to optimal performance (Hargreaves et al., 2004; Hawley, Schabort, Noakes, & Dennis, 1997; Temesi, Johnson, Raymond, Burdon, & O'Connor, 2011), but this may not always be the case for each training session. Estimations of the amount of carbohydrate required to replenish glycogen stores and to consume during exercise as a supplementary fuel source should consider the mass of the exercising musculature (using body weight as a proxy), with a sliding scale according to the training or competition energy cost (Table II). We have expanded the suggested work-based categories since the 2003 guidelines. Unfortunately, this is not underpinned by direct knowledge of the glycogen cost of the real-life exercise programmes undertaken by athletes; such data are surprisingly limited. Rather, it is driven by pragmatic feedback from sports nutritionists that previously stated targets were impractical for athletes who are large, follow energy-restricted diets, and/or undertake predominantly skill-based or low-intensity activities. Therefore, until a better model is proposed, it is sensible to increase the flexibility of guidelines for daily fuel requirements.

Another remodelling of key messages is that the athlete's needs are not static, but rather move between categories according to changes in the daily, weekly or seasonal goals and exercise commitments in a periodized training programme. We also note that it is useful to adjust an athlete's carbohydrate intake by strategically consuming meals/snacks providing carbohydrate and other nutrients around important exercise sessions. This allows nutrient and energy intake to track with the needs of the athlete's exercise commitments as well as specifically promoting the potential for high carbohydrate availability to enhance performance and recovery at key times.

Acute strategies to promote high carbohydrate availability for exercise

Manipulating nutrition and exercise in the hours and days prior to an important exercise bout allows an athlete to commence the session with glycogen stores that are commensurate with the estimated fuel costs of the event. In the absence of severe muscle damage, glycogen stores can be normalized with 24 h of reduced training and adequate fuel intake (Burke et al., 2004) (see Table II). Events of more than 90 min duration may benefit from higher glycogen stores (Hawley et al., 1997). The evolution of "carbohydrate loading" strategies illustrates how knowledge and practice in sports nutrition often develop. The first studies (Ahlborg et al., 1967) were undertaken in physically active rather than specifically trained individuals and used dietary extremes to achieve a maximal effect rather than nutritional manipulations that would be practical in the field. The glycogen supercompensation protocol derived from this era involved a period of depletion (3 days low carbohydrate + training) followed by a 3-day loading phase (taper + high carbohydrate intake). Today we recognize the importance of considering responses in highly trained individuals and according to the requirements of real sporting events. Subsequent studies around these issues have demonstrated that high glycogen concentrations can be achieved without a depletion phase (Sherman, Costill, Fink, & Miller, 1981) and with as little as 24–36 h of high carbohydrate intake/rest (Bussau, Fairchild, Rao, Steele, & Fournier 2002). Although it seems possible for the trained muscle to supercompensate glycogen with much less effort than previously thought, one study has found that very high elevations in muscle

Table II. Summary of guidelines for carbohydrate intake by athletes.

	Situation	Carbohydrate targets	Comments on type and timing of carbohydrate intake
DAILY NEEDS FOR FUEL AND RECOVERY: *these general recommendations should be fine-tuned with individual consideration of total energy needs, specific training needs, and feedback from training performance*			
Light	• Low-intensity or skill-based activities	$3-5$ g $\cdot$ kg^{-1} of athlete's body mass per day	• Timing of intake may be chosen to promote speedy refuelling, or to provide fuel intake around training sessions in the day. Otherwise, as long as total fuel needs are provided, the pattern of intake may simply be guided by convenience and individual choice
Moderate	• Moderate exercise programme (i.e. $\sim$1 h $\cdot$ day^{-1})	$5-7$ g $\cdot$ kg^{-1} $\cdot$ day^{-1}	
High	• Endurance programme (e.g. moderate-to-high intensity exercise of $1-3$ h $\cdot$ day^{-1})	$6-10$ g $\cdot$ kg^{-1} $\cdot$ day^{-1}	
Very high	• Extreme commitment (i.e. moderate-to-high intensity exercise of $>4-5$ h $\cdot$ day^{-1})	$8-12$ g $\cdot$ kg^{-1} $\cdot$ day^{-1}	• Protein- and nutrient-rich carbohydrate foods or meal combinations will allow the athlete to meet other acute or chronic sports nutrition goals
ACUTE FUELLING STRATEGIES: *these guidelines promote high carbohydrate availability to promote optimal performance in competition or key training sessions*			
General fuelling up	• Preparation for events <90 min exercise	$7-12$ g $\cdot$ kg^{-1} per 24 h as for daily fuel needs	• Athletes may choose compact carbohydrate-rich sources that are low in fibre/residue and easily consumed to ensure that fuel targets are met, and to meet goals for gut comfort or lighter "racing weight"
Carbohydrate loading	• Preparation for events >90 min of sustained/ intermittent exercise	$36-48$ h of $10-12$ g $\cdot$ kg^{-1} body mass per 24 h	
Speedy refuelling	• <8 h recovery between two fuel demanding sessions	$1.0-1.2$ g $\cdot$ kg^{-1} $\cdot$ h^{-1} for first 4 h then resume daily fuel needs	• There may be benefits in consuming small regular snacks
			• Compact carbohydrate-rich foods and drinks may help to ensure that fuel targets are met
Pre-event fuelling	• Before exercise >60 min	$1-4$ g $\cdot$ kg^{-1} consumed $1-4$ h before exercise	• The timing, amount, and type of carbohydrate foods and drinks should be chosen to suit the practical needs of the event and individual preferences/ experiences
			• Choices high in fat/protein/fibre may need to be avoided to reduce risk of gastrointestinal issues during the event
			• Low GI choices may provide a more sustained source of fuel for situations where carbohydrate cannot be consumed during exercise
During brief exercise	• <45 min	Not needed	
During sustained high-intensity exercise	• 45–75 min	Small amounts including mouth rinse	• A range of drinks and sports products can provide easily consumed carbohydrate
During endurance exercise including "stop and start" sports	• 1.0–2.5 h	$30-60$ g $\cdot$ h^{-1}	• Opportunities to consume foods and drinks vary according to the rules and nature of each sport
			• A range of everyday dietary choices and specialised sports products ranging in form from liquid to solid may be useful
			• The athlete should practice to find a refuelling plan that suits their individual goals including hydration needs and gut comfort
During ultra-endurance exercise	• >2.5–3.0 h	Up to 90 g $\cdot$ h^{-1}	• As above
			• Higher intakes of carbohydrate are associated with better performance
			• Products providing multiple transportable carbohydrates (glucose:fructose mixtures) will achieve high rates of oxidation of carbohydrate consumed during exercise

glycogen could not be repeated when a second protocol was undertaken immediately after a 48-h loading and glycogen-depleting exercise test (McInerney et al., 2005). Nevertheless, the well-trained athletes in this study were able to maintain performance on the successive endurance exercise protocols when a high carbohydrate diet was consumed between trials. Although laboratory studies provide evidence that exercise of more than 90 min duration can cause glycogen depletion, and thus benefit from strategies to supercompensate stores prior to the protocol (Hawley et al., 1997), more field research is needed to define the range of sporting events in which this might be of advantage. Sports-specific investigations have shown that carbohydrate loading can enhance performance of distance running ≥30 km (Karlsson & Saltin, 1971) and prolonged team games involving repeated high-intensity sprints such as ice hockey (Akermark, Jacobs, Rasmusson, & Karlsson, 1996) and soccer (Balsom, Wood, Olsson, & Ekblom, 1999). Current recommendations for pre-event carbohydrate intake are summarized in Table II and recognize the specificity of the needs and logistics of each sporting event, as well as the personal preferences and experience of the individual athlete.

Glycaemic index and exercise

The concept of the glycaemic index (GI) was first introduced in the early 1980s as a method of functionally ranking carbohydrate-rich foods, based on measured blood glucose responses to the intake of the test food compared with a reference food such as glucose or white bread (Jenkins et al., 1981). Although nutritional recommendations to improve exercise capacity and performance are often based on information related to the GI of carbohydrate sources, there is some debate about the consistency of the outcomes of implementing this advice.

Some studies focusing on the composition of a pre-exercise meal have provided evidence that a benefit exists in relation to metabolism and substrate utilization during subsequent exercise when low GI carbohydrate-rich foods are compared with a high GI meal (for a review, see Burke, 2010b). The primary benefit is that the attenuated post-prandial hyperglycaemia and hyperinsulinaemia of the low GI carbohydrate source reduces the suppression of free fatty acid oxidation that normally accompanies carbohydrate feeding, and possibly achieves better maintenance of plasma glucose concentrations and more sustained carbohydrate availability during exercise. However, although a few studies have reported enhanced endurance following the consumption of low GI carbohydrate sources in the pre-exercise meal (Thomas, Brotherhood, & Brand, 1991; Wong et al., 2008; Wu & Williams, 2009), most studies have failed

to find that metabolic differences arising from the GI of carbohydrates consumed before exercise translate into better exercise capacity or performance in subsequent exercise (for a review, see Burke, 2010b). Furthermore, when carbohydrate is ingested during endurance exercise, it negates the effect of glycaemic characteristics of the pre-exercise meals (Burke, Claassen, Hawley, & Noakes, 1998; Chen et al., 2009; Wong et al., 2009). Altering the GI of meals consumed before exercise may offer benefits for some situations (when it is difficult to consume carbohydrate during exercise) or individuals (those who are sensitive to a hyperinsulinaemic response to carbohydrate feedings). However, further research is needed before systematic manipulation of the GI of carbohydrate-rich foods in the athlete's diet can be recommended. In any case, like all aspects of the pre-event meal, the type, timing, and amount of carbohydrate in the competition menu needs to be individualized to the athlete's specific event, their gut comfort, and their individual preferences.

Carbohydrate intake during exercise

The consumption of carbohydrate immediately before and during exercise represents an effective strategy to provide an exogenous fuel source to the muscle and central nervous system. Reviews of this topic (Karelis, Smith, Passe, & Péronnet, 2010; Jeukendrup, 2011) identify a range of potential mechanisms by which supplementary carbohydrate during exercise can enhance performance. These include provision of an additional muscle fuel source when glycogen stores become depleted, muscle glycogen sparing, prevention of low blood glucose concentrations, and effects on the central nervous system. Given the potential for a variety of different, overlapping, and combined benefits on performance, and the variety of ways that fatigue or physiological limitations can manifest in different sports and exercise activities, it seems naive to think that a "one size fits all" recommendation for carbohydrate intake during exercise is sufficient. Yet it is only recently that guidelines were made available.

Both the 2003 IOC consensus view and the more recent ACSM position stand (2007) replaced relatively rigid guidelines of the American College of Sports Medicine (1996) with a more pragmatic approach to the different characteristics of each sport. Namely, for sports of more than 60 min duration in which fatigue would otherwise occur, athletes were encouraged to develop a personalized exercise nutrition plan that combined carbohydrate intake of $30–60 \text{ g} \cdot \text{h}^{-1}$ and adequate rehydration with the practical opportunities for intake during the event or session (Coyle, 2004). Opportunities for a more systematic approach to specific carbohydrate needs for different types of situations, however, were discouraged by prevailing beliefs, including the capping of the oxidation rate of exogenous carbohydrate at 60 g · h^{-1}, the concern that larger intakes might cause gastrointestinal distress, and the lack of evidence of a dose response to carbohydrate intake during exercise. Recent field and laboratory evidence supports an updating of this view.

Carbohydrate intake during prolonged exercise

Surveys of competitive to elite athletes have noted high ($\sim$90 g · h^{-1}) intakes of carbohydrate during exercise (Kimber, Ross, Mason, & Speedy, 2002; Saris, Van Erp-Baart, Brouns, Westerterp, & ten Hoor, 1989). These have been reported during endurance cycling events (Tour de France, Ironman triathlon) in which a relative ease of consuming foods and fluids while exercising combines with extreme fuel requirements, and where energy support may be an additional nutritional goal. Nevertheless, these observations have led to questions of whether it is the guidelines (30–60 g · h^{-1}) or athlete practices that are wrong.

Important answers come from a series of studies that systematically tracked the oxidation rates of various sources, forms, and combinations of carbohydrate consumed during exercise (Jeukendrup, 2010). The major finding from this body of work is that the rate limiting step in the oxidation of ingested carbohydrate is its intestinal absorption, with limits on absorption of glucose in its various forms by the sodium-dependent glucose transporter SGLT1 at $\sim$1 g · min^{-1}. However, when consumed in combination with a carbohydrate that is absorbed by a different transport mechanism (e.g. fructose, using GLUT5), rates of ingested carbohydrate can exceed 1.5 g · min^{-1} (Jentjens, Moseley, Waring, Harding, & Jeukendrup, 2004; Jentjens et al., 2006). The various interests of gastrointestinal comfort, opportunity to consume carbohydrate while exercising, and the high rates of exogenous carbohydrate oxidation required to maintain power output when glycogen becomes depleted, converge at a carbohydrate ingestion rate of $\sim$80–90 g · h^{-1}, at least when glucose and fructose are co-ingested in a 2:1 ratio (Jeukendrup, 2010). Athletic practice has both preceded and now benefited from these findings, since sports nutrition companies now produce a range of carbohydrate-containing fluids/gels/bars with this ratio of the so-called "multiple transportable carbohydrates". A variety of forms of these products, ranging from liquid to solid, appear to deliver high rates of carbohydrate (Pfeiffer, Stellingwerff, Zaltas, & Jeukendrup, 2010a, 2010b) and can be tolerated in the field (Pfeiffer, Stellingwerff, Zaltas, Hodgson, & Jeukendrup, 2011)

Added to the support for a revision of the guidelines for prolonged sporting activities, is emerging evidence of a dose–response relationship between carbohydrate intake and performance of events longer than 2.5 h in which the optimal rate of intake appears to be within the range of 60–90 g · h^{-1} (Smith et al., 2010a, 2010b). Finally, studies using multiple transportable carbohydrates have shown benefits to the performance of exercise activities of $\sim$3 h duration compared with the ingestion of glucose alone (Currell & Jeukendrup, 2008; Triplett, Doyle, Rupp, & Benardot, 2010). Therefore, new guidelines to promote individual experimentation with carbohydrate intakes of up to 90 g · h^{-1} in ultra-endurance sports are warranted (see Table II). We have provided these guidelines in absolute amounts, based on the evidence that there is little difference in the oxidation of exogenous carbohydrate according to body size/body mass (see Figure 2). Instead, factors such as the carbohydrate content of the habitual diet or intake during training sessions (Cox et al., 2010) may play a role in determining capacity for oxidizing carbohydrate ingested during exercise.

Carbohydrate intake in sports lasting $\sim$1 h

Sports involving $\sim$1 h of sustained or intermittent high-intensity exercise are not limited by the availability of muscle glycogen stores given adequate nutritional preparation. Therefore, evidence of enhanced performance when carbohydrate is consumed during a variety of such exercise protocols is perplexing (for a review, see Burke, Wood, Pyne, Telford, & Saunders, 2005). Findings of a lack of improvement of a 1-h cycling protocol with glucose *infusion* (Carter, Jeukendrup, Mann, & Jones, 2004b) but benefits from carbohydrate *ingestion* (Carter, Jeukendrup, & Jones, 2004a) created an intriguing hypothesis that the central nervous system might sense the presence of carbohydrate via receptors in the mouth and oral space, promoting an enhanced sense of well-being and improved pacing. This theory was subsequently confirmed by observations that simply rinsing the mouth with a carbohydrate solution can also enhance performance of the cycling bout (Carter et al., 2004a). A number of studies have now investigated this phenomenon, including several in which functional magnetic resonance imaging technology has tracked changes in various areas of the brain with carbohydrate mouth sensing (Chambers, Bridge, & Jones, 2009). In these studies, both sweet and non-sweet carbohydrates were shown to activate regions in the brain associated with reward and motor control.

There is now robust evidence that in situations when a high power output is required over durations of about 45–75 min, mouth rinsing or intake of very

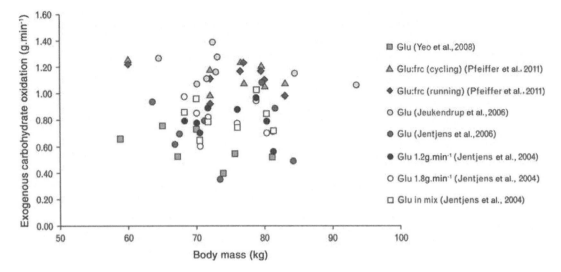

Figure 2. Results of peak oxidation rates of exogenous carbohydrate consumed during exercise versus body mass for individuals involved in a number of studies. These data show that there is no correlation between exogenous fuel use and body size, and suggest that guidelines for carbohydrate intake during exercise can be provided in absolute amounts rather than scaled to body mass (adapted from Jeukendrup et al., 2006, with permission). Glc = glucose, frc = fructose.

small amounts of carbohydrate play a largely non-metabolic role involving the central nervous system in enhancing performance by 2–3% (Jeukendrup & Chambers, 2010). Not all studies have reported this effect, however, possibly because a carbohydrate-rich pre-event meal is associated with a dampening of the effect (Beelen et al., 2009). These findings have been incorporated into updated guidelines for carbohydrate intake during exercise (Table II).

Train low/compete high – a new paradigm for training adaptations?

Although we have previously encouraged athletes to follow a training diet based on the fuel cost of their exercise load, evolving research into exercise and nutrient interactions has identified that an alternative approach might be of value. From a cellular perspective, training adaptations are the consequence of the accumulation of specific proteins required for sustaining energy metabolism during and after a series of exercise sessions (Hawley & Burke, 2010). However, it has been uncertain whether it is a lack or surplus of a substrate that triggers the training adaptation (Coyle, 2000). New molecular insights show that compared with high muscle glycogen content, an acute bout of (endurance) exercise commenced with low muscle glycogen results in a greater transcriptional activation of enzymes involved in carbohydrate metabolism (i.e. the AMP-activated protein kinase [AMPK], GLUT-4, hexokinase, and the pyruvate dehydrogenase [PDH] complex), and an increase in adaptive responses favouring fat metabolism (see Hawley & Burke, 2010; Hawley, Burke, Phillips, & Spriet,

2011). Based on convincing evidence of enhanced muscle markers of cellular signalling and metabolic adaptation following training in a low carbohydrate environment, a new concept of dietary periodization has been promoted whereby the athlete should "train low" to promote a greater training response, before switching to high carbohydrate availability for competition when optimal performance is required (Baar & McGee, 2008).

The watershed investigation of Hansen and colleagues (2005) provides apparent evidence to support such dietary periodization. The 10-week training study required previously sedentary men to train one leg with a "two a day" training protocol every second day, while the contralateral leg undertook the same workouts, spread over a daily training schedule (Hansen et al., 2005). Maximal power output increased equally in each leg, but the leg that trained twice-a-day, commencing 50% of its training sessions with a low glycogen concentration, showed greater increases in kicking endurance accompanied by greater maximal activity of an "aerobic" enzyme. These findings have significant scientific merit and possible application for exercise programmes targeting metabolic improvements and health outcomes. However, there are some caveats that must be applied in relation to sports performance.

The first problem is the misconception that all "train low" techniques require chronic adherence to a low carbohydrate diet. Exposure to a high-fat, low-carbohydrate diet causes differences in the metabolic outcomes associated with repeated exercise, both in short-term fat adaptation protocols (Burke & Hawley, 2002) and longer-term training studies (Helge, 2002). Although training on a high-fat diet is associated with an increased ability to oxidize fat during exercise and a decreased reliance on muscle glycogen utilization (Helge, Watt, Richter, Rennie, & Kiens, 2001; Burke et al., 2002), there are also indications that it can reduce the chronic adaptations to training (Helge, Richter, & Kiens, 1996) and impair carbohydrate utilization (Stellingwerff et al., 2006) and the ability to sustain high-intensity exercise performance (Havemann et al., 2006). Therefore, the more recent train low protocols have utilized a different approach to reducing carbohydrate availability for training. In fact, the protocol used in the primary study used the placement of training sessions rather than dietary manipulation to achieve low glycogen levels for specific workouts. Other ways to selectively reduce carbohydrate availability for training include exercising after an overnight fast, consuming water during prolonged workouts, withholding carbohydrate in the hours after exercise, and restricting carbohydrate below the fuel requirements of the training load (Burke, 2010a). Such protocols differ in the duration of exposure to a low carbohydrate environment as well as the focus on reducing endogenous and/or exogenous carbohydrate stores.

The second issue involves direct translation of research on exercise metabolism into the outcomes of sport or athletic performance. Characteristics that have been questioned include the transfer of information from previously untrained individuals to well-trained populations and the use of a "clamped" training programme (training at the same power-specific output for each session) compared with the principles of progressive overload and self-pacing that underpin the training programmes of athletes (Hawley & Burke, 2010). Further studies utilizing the "two a day training" model of low glycogen training (Hulston et al., 2010; Morton et al., 2009; Yeo et al., 2008), or manipulation of exogenous carbohydrate availability via the presence or absence of carbohydrate intake before and during exercise (De Bock et al., 2008; Cox et al., 2010; Nybo et al., 2009; Van Proeyen, Szlufcik, Nielens, Ramaekers, & Hespel, 2011), have been undertaken. Given the large number of study characteristics that can be manipulated, it is not surprising that the sparse literature has only just scratched the surface of the potential areas of interest and application. Nevertheless, there is consistent evidence that undertaking some exercise sessions with low glycogen/exogenous carbohydrate availability can enhance the metabolic adaptations associated with training, even in well-trained individuals.

It is important to recognize, however, that no sporting medals are awarded for the muscle with highest concentration of cellular signalling molecules or metabolic enzymes. Instead, victory goes to athletes who are the swiftest, highest, strongest or otherwise best able to perform in their event. Muscular adaptations achieved by training provide part of the process by which athletes improve their ability to perform. However, changes in muscle physiology are not, *per se*, a proxy for performance and currently there is no convincing evidence that train low strategies achieve an enhancement of performance over a conventional diet/training approach (Hawley & Burke, 2010). Furthermore, several disadvantages are associated with train low techniques, including an impairment of the ability to train at high intensities; this is not insignificant because it is a cornerstone of the principles of preparation for elite sport.

In summary, further research on this topic is needed, but a pragmatic commentary on practices in the field is that athletes already periodize the carbohydrate availability for their training sessions. By design or by accident, some workouts are undertaken with reduced carbohydrate availability (the second or third session of a day during high-volume periods, early morning sessions undertaken before breakfast, training during a period of energy restriction for weight loss) while others are undertaken with good carbohydrate support (quality sessions scheduled during lower volume periods, sessions undertaken after a meal). Thus the real question is not whether there is a role for dietary periodization with carbohydrate availability, but whether it should be exploited in a different way. For the moment, it makes sense to focus on good carbohydrate availability for sessions requiring high intensity or high levels of technique and skill, while noting that it is less important during lower intensity workouts or the conditioning sessions at the beginning of a season.

Summary and future directions for research

It is encouraging that even in areas that have benefited from nearly a decade of sports science research, new ideas continue to emerge and add value to the practice of sports nutrition. Quantitative and qualitative guidelines for carbohydrate intake over the day and in relation to exercise, based on our updated knowledge, are summarized in Tables I and II. Questions for future research include:

1. Can manipulation of nutrition characteristics promote better glycogen storage from a given carbohydrate intake, particularly in cases where energy restrictions or practical challenges cause sub-optimal carbohydrate intake.
2. Can strategies to "train low" with low availability of endogenous and/or exogenous carbohydrate availability be further incorporated into the periodized training programme to enhance

competition performance? In particular, researchers need to employ practical and sensitive measures of performance to determine whether metabolic differences in the muscle translate into functional changes that are worthwhile in determining the outcomes of sport.

3. Can a better understanding of the effects of carbohydrate on the central nervous system help us to exploit an ergogenic effect?

References

Ahlborg, B., Bergstrom, J., Brohult, J., Ekelund, L. G., Hultman, E., & Maschio, G. (1967). Human muscle glycogen content and capacity for prolonged exercise after different diets. *Forsvarsmedicin, 3*, 85–99.

Akermark, C., Jacobs, I., Rasmusson, M., & Karlsson, J. (1996). Diet and muscle glycogen concentration in relation to physical performance in Swedish elite ice hockey players. *International Journal of Sport Nutrition, 6*, 272–284.

American College of Sports Medicine (1996). Position stand: Exercise and fluid replacement. *Medicine and Science in Sports and Exercise, 28* (1), i–vii.

American College of Sports Medicine (2007). American College of Sports Medicine position stand: Exercise and fluid replacement. *Medicine and Science in Sports and Exercise, 39*, 377–390.

Baar, K., & McGee, S. L. (2008). Optimizing training adaptations by manipulating glycogen. *European Journal of Sport Science, 8*, 97–106.

Balsom, P. D., Wood, K., Olsson, P., & Ekblom, B. (1999). Carbohydrate intake and multiple sprint sports: With special reference to football (soccer). *International Journal of Sports Medicine, 20*, 48–52.

Beelen, M., Berghuis, J., Bonaparte, B., Ballak, S. B., Jeukendrup, A. E., & Van Loon, L. J. (2009). Carbohydrate mouth rinsing in the fed state: Lack of enhancement of time-trial performance. *International Journal of Sport Nutrition and Exercise Metabolism, 19*, 400–409.

Berardi, J. M., Price, T. B., Noreen, E. E., & Lemon, P. W. (2006). Postexercise muscle glycogen recovery enhanced with a carbohydrate-protein supplement. *Medicine and Science in Sports and Exercise, 38*, 1106–1113.

Betts, J. A., & Williams, C. (2010). Short-term recovery from prolonged exercise: Exploring the potential for protein ingestion to accentuate the benefits of carbohydrate supplements. *Sports Medicine, 40*, 941–959.

Betts, J. A., Williams, C., Boobis, L., & Tsintzas, K. (2008). Increased carbohydrate oxidation after ingesting carbohydrate with added protein. *Medicine and Science in Sports and Exercise, 40*, 903–912.

Burke, L. M. (2010a). Fueling strategies to optimize performance: Training high or training low? *Scandinavian Journal of Medicine and Science in Sports, 20* (suppl. 2), 11–21.

Burke, L. M. (2010b). Nutrition for recovery after competition and training. In L. M. Burke & V. Deakin (Eds.), *Clinical sports nutrition* (4th edn., pp. 358–392). Sydney, NSW: McGraw-Hill.

Burke, L. M., Claassen, A., Hawley, J. A., & Noakes, T. D. (1998). Carbohydrate intake during prolonged cycling minimizes effect of glycemic index of preexercise meal. *Journal of Applied Physiology, 85*, 2220–2226.

Burke, L. M., & Hawley, J. A. (2002). Effects of short-term fat adaptation on metabolism and performance of prolonged exercise. *Medicine and Science in Sports and Exercise, 34*, 1492–1498.

Burke, L. M., Hawley, J. A., Angus, D. J., Cox, G. R., Clark, S., Cummings, N. K. et al. (2002). Adaptations to short-term high-fat diet persist during exercise despite high carbohydrate availability. *Medicine and Science in Sports and Exercise, 34*, 83–91.

Burke, L. M., Kiens, B., & Ivy, J. L. (2004). Carbohydrates and fat for training and recovery. *Journal of Sports Sciences, 22*, 15–30.

Burke, L. M., Wood, C., Pyne, D. B., Telford, R. D., & Saunders, P. U. (2005). Effect of carbohydrate intake on half-marathon performance of well-trained runners. *International Journal of Sport Nutrition and Exercise Metabolism, 15*, 573–589.

Bussau, V. A., Fairchild, T. J., Rao, A., Steele, P. D., & Fournier, P. A. (2002). Carbohydrate loading in human muscle: An improved 1 day protocol. *European Journal of Applied Physiology, 87*, 290–295.

Carter, J. M., Jeukendrup, A. E., & Jones, D. A. (2004a). The effect of carbohydrate mouth rinse on 1-h cycle time trial performance. *Medicine and Science in Sports and Exercise, 36*, 2107–2111.

Carter, J. M., Jeukendrup, A. E., Mann, C. H., & Jones, D. A. (2004b). The effect of glucose infusion on glucose kinetics during a 1-h time trial. *Medicine and Science in Sports and Exercise, 36*, 1543–1550.

Chambers, E. S., Bridge, M. W., & Jones, D. A. (2009). Carbohydrate sensing in the human mouth: Effects on exercise performance and brain activity. *Journal of Physiology, 587*, 1779–1794.

Chen, Y. J., Wong, S. H., Chan, C. O., Wong, C. K., Lam, C. W., & Siu, P. M. (2009). Effects of glycemic index meal and CHO-electrolyte drink on cytokine response and run performance in endurance athletes. *Journal of Science and Medicine in Sport, 12*, 697–703.

Cox, G. R., Clark, S. A., Cox, A. J., Halson, S. L., Hargreaves, M., Hawley, J. A. et al. (2010). Daily training with high carbohydrate availability increases exogenous carbohydrate oxidation during endurance cycling. *Journal of Applied Physiology, 109*, 126–134.

Coyle, E. F. (2000). Physical activity as a metabolic stressor. *American Journal of Clinical Nutrition, 72*, 512S–520S.

Coyle, E. F. (2004). Fluid and fuel intake during exercise. *Journal of Sports Sciences, 22*, 39–55.

Currell, K., & Jeukendrup, A. E. (2008). Superior endurance performance with ingestion of multiple transportable carbohydrates. *Medicine and Science in Sports and Exercise, 40*, 275–281.

De Bock, K., Derave, W., Eijnde, B. O., Hesselink, M. K., Koninckx, E., Rose, A. J. et al. (2008) Effect of training in the fasted state on metabolic responses during exercise with carbohydrate intake. *Journal of Applied Physiology, 104*, 1045–1055.

Hansen, A. K., Fischer, C. P., Plomgaard, P., Andersen, J. L., Saltin, B., & Pedersen, B. K. (2005). Skeletal muscle adaptation: Training twice every second day vs. training once daily. *Journal of Applied Physiology, 98*, 93–99.

Hargreaves, M. (1999). Metabolic responses to carbohydrate ingestion: Effects on exercise performance. In D. R. Lamb & R. Murray (Eds.), *Perspectives in exercise science and sports medicine* (pp. 93–124). Carmel, IN: Cooper.

Hargreaves, M., Hawley, J. A., & Jeukendrup, A. E. (2004). Pre-exercise carbohydrate and fat ingestion: Effects on metabolism and performance. *Journal of Sports Sciences, 22*, 31–38.

Havemann, L., West, S., Goedecke, J. H., McDonald, I. A., St. Clair Gibson, A., Noakes, T. D. et al. (2006). Fat adaptation followed by carbohydrate-loading compromises high-intensity sprint performance. *Journal of Applied Physiology, 100*, 194–202.

Hawley, J. A., & Burke, L. M. (2010). Carbohydrate availability and training adaptation: Effects on cell metabolism. *Exercise and Sport Sciences Reviews, 38*, 152–160.

Hawley, J. A., Burke, L. M., Phillips, S. M., & Spriet, L. (2011). Nutritional modulation of training-induced skeletal muscle adaptation. *Journal of Applied Physiology, 110*, 834–845.

Hawley, J. A., Schabort, E. J., Noakes, T. D., & Dennis, S. C. (1997). Carbohydrate-loading and exercise performance: An update. *Sports Medicine, 24*, 73–81.

Helge, J. W. (2002). Long-term fat diet adaptation effects on performance, training capacity, and fat utilization. *Medicine and Science in Sports and Exercise, 34*, 1499–1504.

Helge, J. W., Richter, E. A., & Kiens, B. (1996). Interaction of training and diet on metabolism and endurance during exercise in man. *Journal of Physiology, 492*, 293–306.

Helge, J .W., Watt, P. W., Richter, E. A., Rennie, M. J., & Kiens, B. (2001). Fat utilization during exercise: Adaptation to a fat-rich diet increases utilization of plasma fatty acids and very low density lipoprotein-triacylglycerol in humans. *Journal of Physiology, 537*, 1009–1020.

Howarth, K. R., Moreau, N. A., Phillips, S. M., & Gibala, M. J. (2009). Coingestion of protein with carbohydrate during recovery from endurance exercise stimulates skeletal muscle protein synthesis in humans. *Journal of Applied Physiology, 106*, 1394–1402.

Hulston, C. J., Venables, M. C., Mann, C. H., Martin, C., Philp, A., Baar, K. et al. (2010). Training with low muscle glycogen enhances fat metabolism in well-trained cyclists. *Medicine and Science in Sports and Exercise, 42*, 2046–2055.

Ivy, J. L., Goforth, H. W., Damon, B. M., McCauley, T. R., Parsons, E. C., & Price, T. B. (2002). Early postexercise muscle glycogen recovery is enhanced with a carbohydrate-protein supplement. *Journal of Applied Physiology, 93*, 1337–1344.

Jenkins, D. J., Wolever, T. M., Taylor, R. H., Barker, H., Fielden, H., Baldwin, J. M. et al. (1981). Glycemic index of foods: A physiological basis for carbohydrate exchange. *American Journal of Clinical Nutrition, 34*, 362–366.

Jentjens, R. L., Moseley, L., Waring, R. H., Harding, L. K., & Jeukendrup, A. E. (2004). Oxidation of combined ingestion of glucose and fructose during exercise. *Journal of Applied Physiology, 96*, 1277–1284.

Jentjens, R. L., Underwood, K., Achten, J., Currell, K., Mann, C. H., & Jeukendrup, A. E. (2006). Exogenous carbohydrate oxidation rates are elevated after combined ingestion of glucose and fructose during exercise in the heat. *Journal of Applied Physiology, 100*, 807–816.

Jentjens, R. L., Van Loon, L. J. C., Mann, C. H., Wagenmakers, A. J. M., & Jeukendrup, A. E. (2001). Addition of protein and amino acids to carbohydrates does not enhance postexercise muscle glycogen synthesis. *Journal of Applied Physiology, 91*, 839–846.

Jeukendrup, A. E. (2010). Carbohydrate and exercise performance: The role of multiple transportable carbohydrates. *Current Opinion in Clinical Nutrition and Metabolic Care, 13*, 452–457.

Jeukendrup, A. E. (2011). Endurane sports: Marathon, triathlon, road cycling. Forthcoming in *Journal of Sports Sciences*.

Jeukendrup, A. E., & Chambers E. S. (2010). Oral carbohydrate sensing and exercise performance. *Current Opinion in Clinical Nutrition and Metabolic Care, 13*, 447–451.

Jeukendrup, A. E., Moseley L., Mainwaring G. I., Samuels, S., Perry, S., & Mann, C. H. (2006). Exogenous carbohydrate oxidation during ultraendurance exercise. *Journal of Applied Physiology, 100*, 1134–1141.

Karelis, A. D., Smith, J. W., Passe, D. H., & Péronnet, F. (2010). Carbohydrate administration and exercise performance: What are the potential mechanisms involved? *Sports Medicine, 40*, 747–763.

Karlsson, J., & Saltin, B. (1971). Diet, muscle glycogen, and endurance performance. *Journal of Applied Physiology, 31*, 203–206.

Kimber, N. E., Ross, J. J., Mason, S. L., & Speedy, D. B. (2002). Energy balance during an Ironman triathlon in male and female triathletes. *International Journal of Sport Nutrition and Exercise Metabolism, 12*, 47–62.

McInerney, P., Lessard, S. J., Burke, L. M., Coffey, V. G., Lo Giudice, S. L., Southgate, R. J. et al. (2005). Failure to repeatedly supercompensate muscle glycogen stores in highly trained men. *Medicine and Science in Sports and Exercise, 37*, 404–411.

Morton, J. P., Croft, L., Bartlett, J. D., MacLaren, D. P., Reilly, T., Evans, L. et al. (2009). Reduced carbohydrate availability does not modulate training-induced heat shock protein adaptations but does upregulate oxidative enzyme activity in human skeletal muscle. *Journal of Applied Physiology, 106*, 1513–1521.

Nybo, L., Pedersen, B., Christensen, B., Aagaard, P., Brandt, N., & Kiens, B. (2009). Impact of carbohydrate supplementation during endurance training on glycogen storage and performance. *Acta Physiologica, 197*, 117–127.

Pedersen, D. J., Lessard, S. J., Coffey, V. G., Churchley, E. G., Wootton, A. M., Ng, T. et al. (2008). High rates of muscle glycogen resynthesis after exhaustive exercise when carbohydrate is coingested with caffeine. *Journal of Applied Physiology, 105*, 7–13.

Pfeiffer, B., Stellingwerff, T., Zaltas, E., Hodgson, A. B., & Jeukendrup, A. E. (2011). Carbohydrate oxidation from a drink during running compared with cycling exercise. *Medicine and Science in Sports and Exercise, 43*, 327–334.

Pfeiffer, B., Stellingwerff, T., Zaltas, E., & Jeukendrup, A. E. (2010a). Oxidation of solid versus liquid carbohydrate sources during exercise. *Medicine and Science in Sports and Exercise, 42*, 2030–2037.

Pfeiffer, B., Stellingwerff, T., Zaltas, E., & Jeukendrup, A. E. (2010b). Carbohydrate oxidation from a carbohydrate gel compared to a drink during exercise. *Medicine and Science in Sports and Exercise, 42*, 2038–2045.

Piehl Aulin, K., Soderlund, K., & Hultman, E. (2000). Muscle glycogen resynthesis rate in humans after supplementation of drinks containing carbohydrates with low and high molecular masses. *European Journal of Applied Physiology, 81*, 346–351.

Robinson, T. M., Sewell, D. A., Hultman, E., & Greenhaff, P. L. (1999). Role of submaximal exercise in promoting creatine and glycogen accumulation in human skeletal muscle. *Journal of Applied Physiology, 87*, 598–604.

Saris, W. H. M., Van Erp-Baart, M. A., Brouns, F., Westerterp, K. R., & ten Hoor, F. (1989). Study on food intake and energy expenditure during extreme sustained exercise: The Tour de France. *International Journal of Sports Medicine, 10*, S26–S31.

Sherman, W. M., Costill, D. L., Fink, W. J., & Miller, J. M. (1981). Effect of exercise-diet manipulation on muscle glycogen and its subsequent utilisation during performance. *International Journal of Sports Medicine, 2*, 114–118.

Smith, J. W., Zachwieja, J. J., Horswill, C. A., Pascoe, D. D., Passe, D., & Ruby, B. C. (2010a). Evidence of a carbohydrate dose and prolonged exercise performance relationship. *Medicine and Science in Sports and Exercise, 42*, 84.

Smith, J. W., Zachwieja, J. J., Peronnet, F., Passe, D. H., Massicotte, D., & Lavoie, C. (2010b). Fuel selection and cycling endurance performance with ingestion of [13C]glucose: Evidence for a carbohydrate dose response. *Journal of Applied Physiology, 108*, 1520–1529.

Spriet, L. L., & Gibala, M. J. (2004). Nutritional strategies to influence adaptations to training. *Journal of Sports Sciences, 22*, 127–141.

Stellingwerff, T., Spriet, L. L., Watt, M. J., Kimber, N. E., Hargreaves, M., Hawley, J. A. et al. (2006). Decreased PDH activation and glycogenolysis during exercise following fat adaptation with carbohydrate restoration, *American Journal of Physiology: Endocrinology and Metabolism, 290*, E380–E388.

Temesi, J., Johnson, N. A., Raymond, J., Burdon, C. A., & O'Connor, H. T. (2011). Carbohydrate ingestion during endurance exercise improves performance in adults. *Journal of Nutrition, 141*, 890–897.

Thomas, D. E., Brotherhood, J. E., & Brand, J. C. (1991). Carbohydrate feeding before exercise: Effect of glycemic index. *International Journal of Sports Medicine, 12*, 180–186.

Triplett, D., Doyle, J. A., Rupp, J. C., & Benardot, D. (2010). An isocaloric glucose-fructose beverage's effect on simulated 100-km cycling performance compared with a glucose-only beverage. *International Journal of Sport Nutrition and Exercise Metabolism, 20*, 122–131.

Van Hall, G., Shirreffs, S. M., & Calbet, J. A. (2000). Muscle glycogen resynthesis during recovery from cycle exercise: No effect of additional protein ingestion. *Journal of Applied Physiology, 88*, 1631–1636.

Van Loon, L. J. C., Saris, W. H. M., Kruijshoop, M., & Wagenmakers, A. J. M. (2000). Maximizing postexercise muscle glycogen synthesis: Carbohydrate supplementation and the application of amino acid or protein hydrolysate mixtures. *American Journal of Clinical Nutrition, 72*, 106–111.

Van Proeyen, K., Szlufcik, K., Nielens, H., Ramaekers, M., & Hespel, P. (2000). Beneficial metabolic adaptations due to endurance exercise training in a fasted state. *Journal of Applied Physiology, 110*, 236–245.

Wong, S. H. S., Sui, P. M., Lok, A., Chen, Y. J., Morris, J., & Lam, C. W. (2008). Effect of the glycaemic index of pre-exercise carbohydrate meals on running performance. *European Journal of Sport Science, 8*, 23–33.

Wong, S. H. S., Chan, O. W., Chen, Y. J., Hu, H. L., Lam, C. W., & Chung, P. K. (2009). Effect of preexercise glycemic-index meal on running when CHO-electrolyte solution is consumed during exercise. *International Journal of Sport Nutrition and Exercise Metabolism, 19*, 222–242.

Wu, C. L., & Williams, C. (2009). A low glycemic index meal before exercise improves endurance running capacity in men. *International Journal of Sport Nutrition and Exercise Metabolism, 16*, 510–527.

Yeo, W. K., Paton, C. D., Garnham, A. P., Burke, L. M., Carey, A. L., & Hawley, J. A. (2008). Skeletal muscle adaptation and performance responses to once a day versus twice every second day endurance training regimens. *Journal of Applied Physiology, 105*, 1462–1470.

Zawadzki, K. M., Yaspelkis, B. B., & Ivy, J. L. (1992). Carbohydrate-protein complex increases the rate of muscle glycogen storage after exercise. *Journal of Applied Physiology, 72*, 1854–1859.

Dietary protein for athletes: From requirements to optimum adaptation

STUART M. PHILLIPS[1] & LUC J. C. VAN LOON[2]

[1]*Department of Kinesiology, Exercise Metabolism Research Group, McMaster University, Hamilton, Ontario, Canada and*
[2]*Department of Human Movement Sciences, NUTRIM School for Nutrition, Toxicology and Metabolism, Maastricht University Medical Centre, Maastricht, Netherlands*

Abstract

Opinion on the role of protein in promoting athletic performance is divided along the lines of how much aerobic-based versus resistance-based activity the athlete undertakes. Athletes seeking to gain muscle mass and strength are likely to consume higher amounts of dietary protein than their endurance-trained counterparts. The main belief behind the large quantities of dietary protein consumption in resistance-trained athletes is that it is needed to generate more muscle protein. Athletes may require protein for more than just alleviation of the risk for deficiency, inherent in the dietary guidelines, but also to aid in an elevated level of functioning and possibly adaptation to the exercise stimulus. It does appear, however, that there is a good rationale for recommending to athletes protein intakes that are higher than the RDA. Our consensus opinion is that leucine, and possibly the other branched-chain amino acids, occupy a position of prominence in stimulating muscle protein synthesis; that protein intakes in the range of $1.3–1.8$ g $\cdot$ kg^{-1} $\cdot$ day^{-1} consumed as 3–4 isonitrogenous meals will maximize muscle protein synthesis. These recommendations may also be dependent on training status: experienced athletes would require less, while more protein should be consumed during periods of high frequency/intensity training. Elevated protein consumption, as high as $1.8–2.0$ g $\cdot$ kg^{-1} $\cdot$ day^{-1} depending on the caloric deficit, may be advantageous in preventing lean mass losses during periods of energy restriction to promote fat loss.

Introduction

While the net rates of protein synthesis and degradation, collectively referred to as "turnover", are relatively high in humans, the net loss (synthesis minus breakdown) of amino acids is relatively low. For example, whole body protein breakdown might be 280 g $\cdot$ day^{-1} in a 70 kg male with 28–32 kg of skeletal muscle tissue. Whole body protein synthesis would be about 280 g $\cdot$ day^{-1} also; however, there are transient periods in which protein breakdown exceeds synthesis and in that time there is a net loss of amino acids necessitating the consumption of protein to replace losses. Those losses are typically about 40–60 g $\cdot$ day^{-1} for a sedentary person weighing 70–90 kg and it is debatable what the losses would be in athletes, be they aerobically trained or resistance trained. The current US and Canadian RDA and Australian RDI tell us that a daily protein intake somewhere between 0.75 and 0.80 g $\cdot$ kg^{-1} will meet the needs of about 98% of the population. The most recent American College

of Sports Medicine position stand (Gerovasili et al., 2009) on dietary practices for athletes recommends a protein intake of 1.2–1.7 g $\cdot$ kg^{-1} $\cdot$ day^{-1} for endurance- and resistance-trained athletes. All of the above recommendations are based on data from studies of nitrogen balance. From a physiological perspective, to be in nitrogen – or protein – balance means only that protein (nitrogen) intake is balanced by protein (nitrogen) loss. It is hard to imagine what variable an athlete or their coach might believe is associated with being in nitrogen balance, least of all performance. It is also well acknowledged that the nitrogen balance technique has serious technical drawbacks, which may result in requirements that are too low. The reader is referred to the most recent WHO/FAO/UNU technical report (Sakuma et al., 2009) for a detailed and in-depth discussion of the various drawbacks of the nitrogen balance approach.

Despite the technical problems of nitrogen balance, a number of studies have attempted to define what protein intakes would be required to achieve a state of nitrogen balance, and thus define an athletic protein requirement, in athletes (Friedman & Lemon, 1989; Lemon, Tarnopolsky, MacDougall, & Atkinson, 1992; Tarnopolsky, MacDougall, & Atkinson, 1988). Data from these studies leads to the conclusion that the protein needs of athletes can be as high as twice the RDA/RDI (Friedman & Lemon, 1989; Lemon et al., 1992; Tarnopolsky et al., 1988). At the same time, a number of longitudinal studies have reached the conclusion that exercise training in novices actually reduces protein utilization and requirements due to reduced activation of amino acid oxidation/catabolism in endurance athletes (McKenzie et al., 2000), or that resistance exercise induces a more efficient use of amino acids arising from muscle protein breakdown (Hartman, Moore, & Phillips, 2006; Moore et al., 2007). What is more important perhaps than debating what nitrogen balance means for an athlete is to look at protein from a functional perspective and to try and recognize that an "optimal" intake for athletes might exist that is not predicated on merely satisfying a minimal requirement and thus being in nitrogen balance. It is also recognized that such an intake is not easy to define. The function that athletes care most about is optimal performance in their sport of choice. Often improvements in performance will involve gaining muscle mass and potentially also losing fat mass, as a high lean-to-fat body weight ratio is desirable in several sports. With this framework in mind, we can look at specific situations where protein can act as a substrate for the synthesis of new muscle proteins, leading eventually to net muscle accretion or to the repair of excessive protein damage, and at strategies to aid in fat mass loss while still maintaining lean mass. Thus, the goal of this review is to provide some guidance as to what an athletic "optimal" protein intake might be.

The role of protein in training-induced adaptation

Muscle mass is normally fairly constant during adult life up to the fourth or fifth decade, when the slow process of sarcopenia is thought to begin (Evans, 1995). The maintenance of muscle mass is a balance between muscle protein synthesis (MPS) and muscle protein breakdown (MPB). The algebraic difference between MPS and MPB, to yield net muscle protein balance (NPB), is the operative variable determining gain or loss of muscle mass (Burd, Tang, Moore, & Phillips, 2009). Obviously, from the standpoint of obtaining an optimum adaptation, athletes look to maximize the adaptive responses to their training bouts by maximizing their NPB. This is accomplished through the synergistic action of both exercise and amino acid/protein ingestion to promote

increases in MPS (Moore, Phillips, Babraj, Smith, & Rennie, 2005; Moore et al., 2009b). The key processes underlying these adaptations, involving gene transcription, protein signalling, and translation initiation, are too complex and tangential to the main focus of this review; however, the reader is referred to several reviews on these topics for more in-depth discussion of these mechanisms (Hundal & Taylor, 2009; Mahoney & Tarnopolsky, 2005; Rennie, Wackerhage, Spangenburg, & Booth, 2004; Sarbassov et al., 2004).

Protein ingestion following exercise reduces indices of damage such as release of creatine kinase (Greer, Woodard, White, Arguello, & Haymes, 2007; Rowlands, Thorp, Rossler, Graham, & Rockell, 2007; Rowlands et al., 2008; Valentine, Saunders, Todd, & St. Laurent, 2008). How dietary protein ingestion might affect muscle damage is unknown. There is some indication that post-exercise protein feeding might support an enhanced performance (Cockburn, Stevenson, Hayes, Robson-Ansley, & Howatson, 2010; Rowlands et al., 2008; Saunders, Moore, Kies, Luden, & Pratt, 2009), but no plausible mechanism for this effect is readily available and not all data support such a conclusion (Cermak, Solheim, Gardner, Tarnopolsky, & Gibala, 2009; van Essen & Gibala, 2006). What cannot be ignored, however, is the fact that protein consumption is necessary for MPS to be stimulated to result in a positive NPB. Athletes engaged in resistance exercise would no doubt find benefit in repeated periods of positive protein balance to eventually allow for muscle protein accretion and subsequent hypertrophy to occur. It is less clear what benefit endurance-trained athletes may derive, but it is not unreasonable to suggest that mitochondrial protein synthesis would proceed at a higher rate with ingestion of protein versus no protein (Wilkinson et al., 2008). The supposition would then be that endurance athletes may experience a greater training-induced increase in mitochondrial volume and enhanced adaptation in response to training, but such a thesis has not been tested. A recent paper did find that immediate post-exercise supplementation with protein versus carbohydrate did result in greater improvements in peak oxygen uptake in older men (Robinson, Turner, Hellerstein, Hamilton, & Miller, 2011); however, how protein accomplished this is uncertain.

Protein serves both as a substrate and a trigger for adaptation after both resistance and aerobic exercise. If protein provision in close temporal proximity to exercise promotes a better adaptation (i.e. greater muscle mass gain or greater gains in oxidative capacity), then this would serve as a basis for a framework in which we can begin to discuss an optimum protein intake for athletes. There is evidence to support this concept in resistance training studies (Cribb & Hayes, 2006; Hartman et al., 2007; Holm et al., 2008), but not for aerobic-based training. However, inherent in the concept that protein consumption promotes training is the need to focus on protein intakes that create optimum adaptation rather than those tied merely to nitrogen balance. Viewed from this perspective, there are important messages for athletes in terms of quantity, timing, and quality of protein intake in relation to the training stimulus.

What quantity of protein should athletes consume?

The US Dietary Reference Intakes (DRI) specify a daily dietary protein intake for all individuals aged 19 years and older of $0.8 \text{ g} \cdot \text{kg}^{-1}$ (Institute of Medicine, 2005). This recommended dietary allowance (RDA) is cited as adequate for almost all persons. This amount of protein would be considered by many athletes as the amount to be consumed in a single meal, particularly for strength-trained athletes. There do exist, however, published data to suggest that individuals habitually performing resistance and/or endurance exercise require more protein than their sedentary counterparts (Friedman & Lemon, 1989; Lemon et al., 1992; Tarnopolsky et al., 1988, 1992). The RDA values for protein are clearly set at "the level of protein judged to be adequate … to meet the known nutrient needs for practically all healthy people" (Institute of Medicine, 2005). The RDA covers protein losses with margins for inter-individual variability and protein quality, but the notion of consumption of "extra" protein above these levels to cover increased needs due to physical activity is not considered.

Studies of protein requirements in athletes have shown an increased requirement for protein in strength-trained (Lemon et al., 1992; Tarnopolsky et al., 1988, 1992) and endurance-trained athletes (Friedman & Lemon, 1989; Meredith, Zackin, Frontera, & Evans, 1989; Tarnopolsky et al., 1988). Increased protein requirements for individuals engaging in resistive activities might be expected due to the need for "extra" dietary protein to synthesize new muscle or repair muscle damage. On the other hand, endurance exercise is associated with marked increases in leucine oxidation (McKenzie et al., 2000; Phillips, Atkinson, Tarnopolsky, & MacDougall, 1993), which would elevate overall requirements for protein (if other amino acids are also oxidized to an appreciable extent), or at least for leucine. The shortcomings of nitrogen balance have long been recognized, as the adequate protein intake is calculated from implausibly high retentions of nitrogen at high protein intakes (Hegsted, 1976;

Young, 1986; Young, Gucalp, Rand, Matthews, & Bier, 1987). This highlights the need for another approach to examining protein requirements; tracer-derived estimations of protein requirements are one alternative method. Using this approach, it was reported that consumption of a "low" protein diet ($0.86 \text{ g} \cdot \text{kg}^{-1} \cdot \text{day}^{-1}$) by a group of strength-trained athletes resulted in an accommodated state in which whole body protein synthesis was reduced compared with medium ($1.4 \text{ g} \cdot \text{kg}^{-1} \cdot \text{day}^{-1}$) and high ($2.4 \text{ g} \cdot \text{kg}^{-1} \cdot \text{day}^{-1}$) protein diets (Tarnopolsky et al., 1992). No difference was seen in whole body protein synthesis between the medium and high protein diets, but amino acid oxidation was elevated on the high protein diet, indicating that this protein intake was providing amino acids in excess of the rate at which they could be integrated into body proteins. It should be emphasized that these results do not mean that $1.4 \text{ g} \cdot \text{kg}^{-1} \cdot \text{day}^{-1}$ was required to cover dietary protein needs, but simply that $0.86 \text{ g} \cdot \text{kg}^{-1} \cdot \text{day}^{-1}$ was not sufficient to allow maximal rates of protein synthesis. It is not known what body proteins were being made at a sub-maximal rate at $0.86 \text{ g} \cdot \text{kg}^{-1} \cdot \text{day}^{-1}$, but if muscle protein synthesis was adversely affected then clearly these data would be of relevance to athletes.

A protein dose–response relationship was shown to exist following resistance exercise (Moore et al., 2009a). In this study, isolated egg protein was fed to young men in graded doses from 0 to 40 g after resistance exercise and MPS was measured. Muscle protein synthesis showed a graded increase from 0 to 20 g and despite doubling protein intake to 40 g, there was no difference in MPS. At the same time that the plateau in MPS was observed, the oxidation of leucine was significantly elevated over that seen at rest and following doses of 5 g and 10 g of protein. The conclusion from these data was that an intake of protein of ~20 g in larger men (85 kg) was sufficient to maximally stimulate MPS, but that higher intakes would not offer any further benefit and the excess amino acids were oxidized (Moore et al., 2009a). Interestingly, the dose of essential amino acids (EAA) in 20 g of egg protein (i.e. 8.3 g) that was found to maximally stimulate MPS was remarkably similar to that seen at rest, which was 10 g of EAA (Cuthbertson et al., 2005). These data (Moore et al., 2009a) suggest that an optimum quantity of protein to consume to maximally stimulate MPS after resistance exercise appears to be around 20–25 g of high-quality protein.

Recent data from Harber and colleagues (2010) suggest that feeding (a drink at $5 \text{ kcal} \cdot \text{kg}^{-1}$, which delivered for every 5 kcal: 0.83 g carbohydrate, 0.37 g protein, and 0.03 g fat) did not enhance mixed MPS after a 1 h cycle ride at ~72% of peak oxygen uptake; however, changes in mixed MPS may not capture the feeding-induced enhancement of mitochondrial protein synthesis. Thus, at this time a similar conclusion to that reached by Moore and colleagues on a maximally effective dose of protein is not available for those engaging in endurance exercise, but it would be prudent to measure not only mixed MPS but mitochondrial protein synthesis to isolate the potential effects of the exercise bout on that fraction.

Timing of protein consumption

Athletes have the choice of consuming protein before, during, and after exercise. There are different theories as to which period promotes an optimum adaptation, but in the case of resistance exercise almost all of them relate to the ability of protein to provide amino acid precursors to either support MPS or inhibit MPB. Protein consumption with respect to aerobic exercise focusing on peri-workout/event nutrition is backed by a theory that amino acids could support some energy-yielding pathways and/or attenuate muscle damage and enhance performance. Post-exercise protein consumption may enhance adaptation by also restoring glycogen, but it appears that this is the case only if inadequate carbohydrate is consumed (Jentjens, van Loon, Mann, Wagenmakers, & Jeukendrup, 2001) and this phenomenon will not be discussed here.

With respect to resistance exercise, some studies have shown that pre-exercise protein consumption can enhance MPS (Tipton et al., 2001) and others have shown no effect (Fujita et al., 2009; Tipton et al., 2006). Thus, at this time pre-exercise feeding appears unlikely to increase MPS and long-term gains in muscle mass. A number of training studies have used a combination of pre-exercise and post-exercise feeding to enhance gains in muscle mass (Burk, Timpmann, Medijainen, Vahi, & Oopik, 2009; Cribb & Hayes, 2006), so it is impossible to tell whether the pre-exercise meal imparted any benefit, since post-exercise meals are unequivocally beneficial (see below).

Consumption of protein during exercise may provide amino acids to "prime the pump". In other words, the amino acids present in the circulation during exercise may increase MPS and possibly suppress MPB to enhance protein balance either during or after the exercise bout. Only one study has examined peri-workout protein consumption with resistance exercise (Beelen et al., 2008). In this study, the ingestion of protein and carbohydrate did enhance MPS during the exercise bout and into early recovery, but this did not extend into the overnight fasted period.

A number of studies have provided endurance-trained athletes with protein during a workout to assess the impact of this macronutrient on metabolism and also on performance. Consumption of protein during endurance exercise results in an improved whole body protein balance during and after the exercise bout (Koopman et al., 2004), but the effects on MPS and MPB are not known. Some studies have shown that protein provision during exercise can enhance performance (Saunders et al., 2009; Valentine et al., 2008), but others have shown no performance effect (Cermak et al., 2009; van Essen & Gibala, 2006). Thus, there seems to be little reason to recommend the ingestion of protein during aerobic exercise for performance enhancement and there is no discernible benefit in terms of MPS or MPB.

It is axiomatic that provision of protein and/or amino acids to athletes in the post-exercise period, particularly after resistance exercise, stimulates MPS (for reviews, see Burd et al., 2009; Drummond, Dreyer, Fry, Glynn, & Rasmussen, 2009; Koopman, Saris, Wagenmakers, & van Loon, 2007b; Phillips, Tang, & Moore, 2009). As might be expected, the impact of resistance exercise is quite specific for synthesis of proteins in the myofibrillar protein fraction (Moore et al., 2009b). There are also reports that provision of protein after the performance of aerobic exercise stimulates MPS (Howarth, Moreau, Phillips, & Gibala, 2009; Levenhagen et al., 2001), particularly of the mitochondrial protein fraction (Wilkinson et al., 2008). While there is some debate about the "critical" nature of the timing of post-exercise protein consumption, a simple message may be that the earlier after exercise an athlete consumes protein the better. This conclusion may seem to gloss over a number of important studies showing, or not showing, the benefit of early post-exercise protein provision with respect to both stimulation of MPS and/or hypertrophy, but it emphasizes a principle that athletes would likely benefit from. That is, the sooner the recovery process following exercise can begin the better. So while a crucial "window of anabolic opportunity" is not, at least currently, well defined, it would make sense that protein provision should begin as soon as possible after exercise to promote recovery and possibly to enhance the rate of – or absolute level of – adaptation.

Protein source and quality

Protein quality is measured using a variety of indices but the most commonly accepted and understood index is the protein digestibility corrected amino acid score or PDCAAS. Using the PDCAAS, a number of proteins are classified as "high quality", meaning they have a PDCAAS score of 1.0 or are very close to 1.0. Unsurprisingly, animal-source proteins such as milk (and the constituent proteins of milk, casein and whey), egg, and most meats are high quality. Isolated soy protein, once the anti-nutritional components are removed, also has a PDCAAS score of 1.0. Use of the PDCAAS has been criticized, however, since scores are artificially truncated at 1.0 despite the fact that isolated milk proteins, casein, and whey proteins all have scores of ~1.2 (Phillips et al., 2009; Schaafsma, 2005). An obvious question, therefore, is whether there are any advantages to habitual consumption of these proteins in terms of promotion of recovery (increments in MPS and/or suppression of MPB or less muscle damage) and adaptation (greater muscle mass accretion or enhancement of oxidative capacity). In fact, evidence does exist to support the former thesis that milk proteins, for example, result in a greater stimulation of MPS after resistance exercise than the consumption of equivalent protein and macronutrient energy as isolated soy protein (Wilkinson et al., 2007). Practised over time, the habitual consumption of milk versus equivalent soy protein resulted in greater hypertrophy (Hartman et al., 2007). In addition, comparisons of the capacity of isonitrogenous quantities of soy, casein, and whey protein to stimulate MPS both at rest and following resistance exercise demonstrated the advantage of whey protein (Tang, Moore, Kujbida, Tarnopolsky, & Phillips, 2009). The reasons for the superiority of milk proteins over an ostensibly nutritionally equivalent protein such as isolated soy are not clear, but it appears that the amino acid leucine, possibly in conjunction with the other branched-chain amino acids (BCAA), could be critically important.

Leucine is a BCAA that can activate key signalling proteins resident in the protein kinase B-mammalian target of rapamycin (mTOR) pathway responsible for translation initiation. The effects of leucine have been shown *in vitro* (Atherton, Smith, Etheridge, Rankin, & Rennie, 2010) and *in vivo* (for reviews, see Drummond & Rasmussen, 2008; Drummond et al., 2009; Kimball & Jefferson, 2006a, 2006b). Milk proteins in particular are rich in leucine and this may explain part of their efficacy in stimulating MPS and promoting hypertrophy. Whey protein in particular is highly enriched in leucine, which appears to translate into a greater ability of this protein fraction to stimulate muscle growth, at least compared with soy (Phillips et al., 2009). However, if leucine content is such a significant factor in stimulating MPS, this does not explain the finding that whey protein was more effective than soy, which were both more effective than casein in stimulating MPS following resistance exercise when the leucine contents range from whey with the highest to soy with the lowest (Tang et al., 2009). A critically important observation in this study was the rate of appearance of leucine in the systemic circulation, which was most rapid following whey protein consumption, intermediate with soy protein, and very slow with casein (Tang et al., 2009). Thus, even though casein's leucine content is higher than that of soy, the digestion of casein, which clots in the stomach and so is slowly digested, slowed the appearance of leucine and prevented systemic leucine concentrations from increasing to a sufficient level to turn on MPS. This "leucine trigger" hypothesis for MPS is supported by other observations (Fouillet, Mariotti, Gaudichon, Bos, & Tome, 2002; Lacroix et al., 2006). Interestingly, Koopman and colleagues (2009) reported that partially hydrolysed casein protein improved the rate of MPS post-consumption versus the intact protein. Hydrolysis of casein in this case would allow a more rapid digestion and absorption of the protein and thus a more rapid leucinaemia and a more rapid overall aminoacidaemia, leading to enhanced MPS (Koopman et al., 2009). Thus, a higher leucine content and rapidly digested proteins may be a prudent choice for athletes to consume as the spike in blood leucine appears to be critically important in activating MPS. Sustaining MPS after the initial leucine-mediated activation may well be dependent on adequate provision of the other EAA and in particular the BCAA, which means that supplements of isolated leucine would likely be of little benefit over and above consumption of high-quality proteins, at least for athletes.

Changes in body composition with nutrition and exercise

The key variable determining weight loss is the relative energy deficit created by dietary energy restriction and/or increased energy expenditure. For athletes in particular, weight loss is often a desired goal, but an important question is whether certain patterns of macronutrient consumption can bring about a better "quality" of weight loss. In this sense, the quality of weight loss refers to loss of weight with the highest possible fat-to-lean ratio. In most situations, loss of inert mass as fat is the desired goal of athletes. However, it may be that on occasion an athlete needs to simply lose weight to make a particular weight class for example, and in this scenario it is clear that loss of lean mass would be a "sacrifice" that some athletes may be willing to make. It is also worth noting that a certain amount of skeletal muscle could be lost without much, or any, adverse affect on performance (Degoutte et al., 2006; Zachwieja et al., 2001), but this appears to depend on the rate of weight loss (Garthe, Raastad, Refsnes, Koivisto, & Sundgot-Borgen, 2011). Assuming, however, that fat mass reduction is what most athletes would desire during a period of weight loss with the realization that leanness can offer a competitive advantage, the question is whether there are optimal ratios of nutrients to consume to achieve this goal and also avoid nutritional deprivation.

The macronutrient composition of energy-restricted diets and the influence of these ratios on weight loss is controversial. Many popular weight-loss diets have set protein at $\sim 15\%$ of energy, $< 30\%$ lipids, and ~ 50–55% carbohydrates, with reductions in dietary fat and increases in dietary fibre being favoured. It is reasonable to reduce energy density with this ratio of macronutrients and promote weight loss in the short term, but low satiety and poor adherence over longer periods are common in people adhering to a diet with this ratio of macronutrients (Abete, Astrup, Martinez, Thorsdottir, & Zulet, 2010; Foreyt et al., 2009; Sacks et al., 2009). Generally speaking, on this diet the tissue composition of weight loss is 70–80% adipose and 20–30% lean tissue (almost exclusively skeletal muscle) (Weinheimer, Sands, & Campbell, 2010). Emerging evidence suggests that reducing the intake of dietary carbohydrates is a critically important step in promoting both greater weight loss and greater loss of body fat (Abete et al., 2010; Foreyt et al., 2009; Krieger, Sitren, Daniels, & Langkamp-Henken, 2006). The mechanisms underpinning this effect are uncertain but may relate to a lower daily blood glucose concentration and also lower daily insulin (Feinman & Fine, 2007). Insulin's primary functions as a hormone are to promote storage of blood glucose in skeletal muscle and adipose tissue and to inhibit lipolysis and promote triglyceride synthesis and storage rather than release (Feinman & Fine, 2007). Another proven strategy is to reduce not just the total quantity of carbohydrate but also to globally lower the glycaemic load of the diet by selecting low glycaemic-index (GI) carbohydrate sources (for a review, see Abete et al., 2010). However, following low carbohydrate, lower GI diets may be a problem for endurance athletes seeking to compete, since dietary carbohydrate intakes are recommended to be higher to allow a more rapid and full recovery of endogenous glycogen stores (Phillips, 2006). Thus, at the expense of carbohydrates, a higher protein or fat intake can obviously compromise performance. While lower total and relative carbohydrate diets appear effective, an important question is what macronutrient should replace the carbohydrate. Diets moderately high in protein and modestly restricted in carbohydrate and fat may have more beneficial effects on body weight homeostasis and associated metabolic variables (Abete et al., 2010; Feinman & Fine, 2007; Foreyt et al., 2009; Krieger et al., 2006; Layman, 2004). This review is aimed at rather moderate protein diets, but still almost twice that recommended by the RDA or RDI (20–30%

energy or intakes of 1.8–2.7 g protein $\cdot$ kg^{-1} $\cdot$ day^{-1}, at the expense of carbohydrates), and those with lower carbohydrates (within 40% energy or 3.6 g carbohydrate $\cdot$ kg^{-1} $\cdot$ day^{-1}).

Increasing dietary protein intake to values higher than commonly recommended has a beneficial effect on retention of lean mass during hypoenergetic periods of weight loss (Abete et al., 2010; Feinman & Fine, 2007; Foreyt et al., 2009; Krieger et al., 2006; Layman, 2004). Meta-analyses of trials (Krieger et al., 2006) have shown that higher protein, at the expense of carbohydrate, improves the amount of fat loss and preserves lean tissue. Importantly for athletes, the weight loss-induced decrement in lean mass can be offset by performance of resistive exercise (Layman et al., 2005; MacKenzie, Hamilton, Murray, Taylor, & Baar, 2009; Mettler, Mitchell, & Tipton, 2010). Several studies have shown a synergism between resistance exercise and higher protein content of the diet in terms of enhancing the retention of lean mass during hypoenergetic periods (Layman et al., 2005; MacKenzie et al., 2009; Mettler et al., 2010). Other mechanisms that have been proposed for why protein is an effective substitution for dietary carbohydrate have to do with protein's satiety-promoting effects, which appear to be greater than those of carbohydrate and fat. A comprehensive review of satiety and weight loss is not possible, however. In addition, the thermogenic effect of protein consumption has long been known to be the greatest of all macronutrients.

Other nutrients

The addition of other nutrients to protein may enhance the metabolic effectiveness of protein in either stimulating MPS or suppressing MPB. An important point is that resistance-trained athletes may be less concerned about restoration of muscle glycogen as a goal as opposed to endurance-trained athletes. Nonetheless, an important question, even for resistance-trained athletes, is whether carbohydrate, through insulin, mediates a greater rise in MPS or suppression of MPB, To date three studies have addressed this question and none found that the addition of smaller (20–40 g) or larger (90–120 g) amounts of carbohydrate resulted in enhanced rates of MPS or, at least from whole body measures, suppression of MPB (Glynn et al., 2010; Koopman et al., 2007a). Even when twice as much carbohydrate (50 g as maltodextrin) is added to a sufficient quantity of protein (25 g of whey) there is no further stimulation of MPS or suppression of MPB. Collectively, these findings indicate that so long as protein intake is sufficient, carbohydrate does little to augment post-exercise protein turnover (Glynn et al., 2010; Koopman et al., 2007; Sancak et al.,

2010). When viewed from a broad perspective, athletes recovering from exercise would have to serve four "masters": hydration, restoration of metabolized carbohydrate, restoration/repair of damaged proteins, and remodelling proteins. Viewed in this light, protein consumed in a liquid form concurrently with carbohydrate would provide an optimum "package" of nutrients to achieve these goals. Bovine fluid milk would likely represent such a package of nutrients and when consumed as a post-exercise "recovery" drink has been shown to augment lean mass gain (for a review, see Phillips et al., 2009). As far as rehydration is concerned, milk has also been shown to be equivalent or better than water and isotonic sports drinks in terms of restoring fluid balance (Shirreffs, Watson, & Maughan, 2007; Watson, Love, Maughan, & Shirreffs, 2008). A number of studies have also shown that when consumed after exercise, flavoured versions of milk (e.g. chocolate), which most often contain added carbohydrate as a simple sugar, can enhance subsequent exercise performance (Karp et al., 2006; Thomas, Morris, & Stevenson, 2009) and reduce indices of muscle damage (Gilson et al., 2010). It appears that milk, and its flavoured varieties, would be an entirely reasonable and cost-effective alternative to supplements to enhance recovery and enhance performance.

Summary

- Protein consumption can enhance rates of MPS and possibly lower rates of MPB, thus improving muscle NPB. The improvement in NPB appears to accumulate to promote greater protein retention in the case of resistance exercise and may enhance training-induced adaptations with endurance training, although the latter has yet to be tested.
- A dose of protein that appears to maximally stimulate MPS appears to be in the range of 20–25 g, although this estimate may be lower for lighter athletes (i.e. <85 kg).
- Protein may act as more than simply substrate to supply the building blocks for protein synthesis and may be an important trigger to affect phenotypic changes induced by exercise. Leucine in particular occupies a prominent position and may well be critical in enhancing protein-mediated recovery and adaptation as detailed above.
- The rate of digestion of purportedly nutritionally equivalent proteins affects the response of MPS and this appears to be linked to the amplitude and the rate of rise in blood leucine to activate key signalling proteins and turn on MPS.
- The optimum timing for protein ingestion to promote the most favourable recovery and adaptation is after exercise. While data do not yet exist to define exactly how long a theoretical "window of anabolic opportunity" exists, it is safest to state that athletes who are interested in performance need to consume protein as soon as possible after exercise.
- To optimize the ratio of fat-to-lean tissue mass loss during hypoenergetic periods, athletes are advised to ensure that they lower their carbohydrate intake to $\sim 40\%$ of their energy intake (with an emphasis on consumption of lower GI carbohydrates), which usually means no more than 3–$4 \text{ g} \cdot \text{kg}^{-1} \cdot \text{day}^{-1}$, and increase their protein intake to ~ 20–30% of their energy intake or ~ 1.8–$2.7 \text{ g} \cdot \text{kg}^{-1} \cdot \text{day}^{-1}$. Consideration of how low carbohydrate intake should go would be dictated by how much exercise performance may be compromised by consuming lower than recommended carbohydrates. By engaging in resistance exercise during a hypoenergetic dieting period, athletes will also provide a markedly anabolic stimulus to retain muscle protein. All of the aforementioned strategies will, however, result in less absolute weight loss than if protein is not increased and resistive exercise is not performed, which may be important for some athletes.
- There appears to be no evidence to recommend the addition of carbohydrate to protein sources to optimize the anabolic environment for MPS. For endurance-trained athletes, the same recommendation will quite likely enhance the restoration of glycogen, which may be an important consideration.
- An economical, practical, and efficacious beverage for athletes to consume after exercise is milk, particularly flavoured milk that contains added simple sugar. For the athlete who suffers from lactose maldigestion, there are a number of practical options such as pre-treated lactose reduced milk. This beverage provides fluid that is better retained than water and isotonic sport drinks, carbohydrate to restore muscle glycogen, and high-quality proteins to repair and facilitate adaptive changes in protein synthesis.

References

Abete, I., Astrup, A., Martinez, J. A., Thorsdottir, I., & Zulet, M. A. (2010). Obesity and the metabolic syndrome: Role of different dietary macronutrient distribution patterns and specific nutritional components on weight loss and maintenance. *Nutrition Reviews, 68,* 214–231.

Atherton, P. J., Smith, K., Etheridge, T., Rankin, D., & Rennie, M. J. (2010). Distinct anabolic signalling responses to amino acids in C2C12 skeletal muscle cells. *Amino Acids, 38,* 1533–1539.

Beelen, M., Tieland, M., Gijsen, A. P., Vandereyt, H., Kies, A. K., Kuipers, H. et al. (2008). Coingestion of carbohydrate and protein hydrolysate stimulates muscle protein synthesis during exercise in young men, with no further increase during subsequent overnight recovery. *Journal of Nutrition, 138*, 2198–2204.

Burd, N. A., Tang, J.E., Moore, D. R., & Phillips, S. M. (2009). Exercise training and protein metabolism: Influences of contraction, protein intake, and sex-based differences. *Journal of Applied Physiology, 106*, 1692–1701.

Burk, A., Timpmann, S., Medijainen, L., Vahi, M., & Oopik, V. (2009). Time-divided ingestion pattern of casein-based protein supplement stimulates an increase in fat-free body mass during resistance training in young untrained men. *Nutrition Research, 29*, 405–413.

Cermak, N. M., Solheim, A. S., Gardner, M. S., Tarnopolsky, M. A., & Gibala, M. J. (2009). Muscle metabolism during exercise with carbohydrate or protein-carbohydrate ingestion. *Medicine and Science in Sports and Exercise, 41*, 2158–2164.

Cockburn, E., Stevenson, E., Hayes, P. R., Robson-Ansley, P., & Howatson, G. (2010). Effect of milk-based carbohydrate-protein supplement timing on the attenuation of exercise-induced muscle damage. *Applied Physiology, Nutrition and Metabolism, 35*, 270–277.

Cribb, P. J., & Hayes, A. (2006). Effects of supplement timing and resistance exercise on skeletal muscle hypertrophy. *Medicine and Science in Sports and Exercise, 38*, 1918–1925.

Cuthbertson, D., Smith, K., Babraj, J., Leese, G., Waddell, T., Atherton, P. et al. (2005). Anabolic signaling deficits underlie amino acid resistance of wasting, aging muscle. *FASEB Journal, 19*, 422–424.

Degoutte, F., Jouanel, P., Begue, R. J., Colombier, M., Lac, G., Pequignot, J. M. et al. (2006). Food restriction, performance, biochemical, psychological, and endocrine changes in judo athletes. *International Journal of Sports Medicine, 27*, 9–18.

Drummond, M. J., Dreyer, H. C., Fry, C. S., Glynn, E. L., & Rasmussen, B. B. (2009). Nutritional and contractile regulation of human skeletal muscle protein synthesis and mTORC1 signaling. *Journal of Applied Physiology, 106*, 1374–1384.

Drummond, M. J., & Rasmussen, B. B. (2008). Leucine-enriched nutrients and the regulation of mammalian target of rapamycin signalling and human skeletal muscle protein synthesis. *Current Opinion in Clinical Nutrition and Metabolic Care, 11*, 222–226.

Evans, W. J. (1995). What is sarcopenia? *Journals of Gerontology-Series A: Biological Sciences and Medical Sciences, 50* (Spec. No.), 5–8.

Feinman, R. D., & Fine, E. J. (2007). Nonequilibrium thermodynamics and energy efficiency in weight loss diets. *Theoretical Biology and Medical Modelling, 4*, 27.

Foreyt, J. P., Salas-Salvado, J., Caballero, B., Bullo, M., Gifford, K. D., Bautista, I. et al. (2009). Weight-reducing diets: Are there any differences? *Nutrition Reviews, 67* (suppl. 1), S99–S101.

Fouillet, H., Mariotti, F., Gaudichon, C., Bos, C., & Tome, D. (2002). Peripheral and splanchnic metabolism of dietary nitrogen are differently affected by the protein source in humans as assessed by compartmental modeling. *Journal of Nutrition, 132*, 125–133.

Friedman, J. E., & Lemon, P. W. (1989). Effect of chronic endurance exercise on retention of dietary protein. *International Journal of Sports Medicine, 10*, 118–123.

Fujita, S., Dreyer, H. C., Drummond, M. J., Glynn, E. L., Volpi, E., & Rasmussen, B. B. (2009). Essential amino acid and carbohydrate ingestion before resistance exercise does not enhance postexercise muscle protein synthesis. *Journal of Applied Phyiology, 106*, 1730–1739.

Garthe, I., Raastad, T., Refsnes, P. E., Koivisto, A., & Sundgot-Borgen, J. (2011). Effect of two different weight-loss rates on body composition and strength and power-related performance in elite athletes. *International Journal of Sports Nutrition and Exercise Metabolism, 21*, 97–104.

Gerovasili, V., Stefanidis, K., Vitzilaios, K., Karatzanos, E., Politis, P., Koroneos, A. et al. (2009). Electrical muscle stimulation preserves the muscle mass of critically ill patients: A randomized study. *Critical Care, 13*, R161.

Gilson, S. F., Saunders, M. J., Moran, C. W., Moore, R. W., Womack, C. J., & Todd, M. K. (2010). Effects of chocolate milk consumption on markers of muscle recovery following soccer training: A randomized cross-over study. *Journal of the International Society of Sports Nutrition, 7*, 19.

Glynn, E. L., Fry, C. S., Drummond, M. J., Dreyer, H. C., Dhanani, S., Volpi, E. et al. (2010). Muscle protein breakdown has a minor role in the protein anabolic response to essential amino acid and carbohydrate intake following resistance exercise. *American Journal of Physiology: Regulatory, Integrative, and Comparative Physiology, 299*, R533–R540.

Greer, B. K., Woodard, J. L., White, J. P., Arguello, E. M., & Haymes, E. M. (2007). Branched-chain amino acid supplementation and indicators of muscle damage after endurance exercise. *International Journal of Sports Nutrition and Exercise Metabolism, 17*, 595–607.

Harber, M. P., Konopka, A. R., Jemiolo, B., Trappe, S. W., Trappe, T. A., & Reidy, P. T. (2010). Muscle protein synthesis and gene expression during recovery from aerobic exercise in the fasted and fed states. *American Journal of Physiology: Regulatory, Integrative, and Comparative Physiology, 299*, R1254–R1262.

Hartman, J. W., Moore, D. R., & Phillips, S. M. (2006). Resistance training reduces whole-body protein turnover and improves net protein retention in untrained young males. *Applied Physiology, Nutrition and Metabolism, 31*, 557–564.

Hartman, J. W., Tang, J. E., Wilkinson, S. B., Tarnopolsky, M. A., Lawrence, R. L., Fullerton, A. V. et al. (2007). Consumption of fat-free fluid milk after resistance exercise promotes greater lean mass accretion than does consumption of soy or carbohydrate in young, novice, male weightlifters. *American Journal of Clinical Nutrition, 86*, 373–381.

Hegsted, D. M. (1976). Balance studies. *Journal of Nutrition, 106*, 307–311.

Holm, L., Olesen, J. L., Matsumoto, K., Doi, T., Mizuno, M., Alsted, T. J. et al. (2008). Protein-containing nutrient supplementation following strength training enhances the effect on muscle mass, strength, and bone formation in postmenopausal women. *Journal of Applied Physiology, 105*, 274–281.

Howarth, K. R., Moreau, N. A., Phillips, S. M., & Gibala, M. J. (2009). Coingestion of protein with carbohydrate during recovery from endurance exercise stimulates skeletal muscle protein synthesis in humans. *Journal of Applied Physiology, 106*, 1394–1402.

Hundal, H. S., & Taylor, P. M. (2009). Amino acid transceptors: Gate keepers of nutrient exchange and regulators of nutrient signaling. *American Journal of Physiology: Endocrinology and Metabolism, 296*, E603–E613.

Institute of Medicine (2005). *Dietary reference intakes for energy, carbohydrate, fiber, fat, fatty acids, cholesterol, protein, and amino acids.* Washington, DC: National Academies Press.

Jentjens, R. L., van Loon, L. J., Mann, C. H., Wagenmakers, A. J., & Jeukendrup, A. E. (2001). Addition of protein and amino acids to carbohydrates does not enhance postexercise muscle glycogen synthesis. *Journal of Applied Physiology, 91*, 839–846.

Karp, J. R., Johnston, J. D., Tecklenburg, S., Mickleborough, T. D., Fly, A. D., & Stager, J. M. (2006). Chocolate milk as a post-exercise recovery aid. *International Journal of Sports Nutrition and Exercise Metabolism, 16*, 78–91.

Kimball, S. R., & Jefferson, L. S. (2006a). New functions for amino acids: Effects on gene transcription and translation. *American Journal of Clinical Nutriton, 83*, 500S–507S.

Kimball, S. R., & Jefferson, L. S. (2006b). Signaling pathways and molecular mechanisms through which branched-chain amino acids mediate translational control of protein synthesis. *Journal of Nutrition, 136*, 227S–231S.

Koopman, R., Beelen, M., Stellingwerff, T., Pennings, B., Saris, W. H., Kies, A. K. et al. (2007a). Coingestion of carbohydrate with protein does not further augment postexercise muscle protein synthesis. *American Journal of Physiology: Endocrinology and Metabolism, 293*, E833–E842.

Koopman, R., Crombach, N., Gijsen, A. P., Walrand, S., Fauquant, J., Kies, A. K. et al. (2009). Ingestion of a protein hydrolysate is accompanied by an accelerated *in vivo* digestion and absorption rate when compared with its intact protein. *American Journal of Clinical Nutrition, 90*, 106–115.

Koopman, R., Pannemans, D. L., Jeukendrup, A. E., Gijsen, A. P., Senden, J. M., Halliday, D. et al. (2004). Combined ingestion of protein and carbohydrate improves protein balance during ultra-endurance exercise. *American Journal of Physiology: Endocrinology and Metabolism, 287*, E712–E720.

Koopman, R., Saris, W. H., Wagenmakers, A. J., & van Loon, L. J. (2007b). Nutritional interventions to promote post-exercise muscle protein synthesis. *Sports Medicine, 37*, 895–906.

Krieger, J. W., Sitren, H. S., Daniels, M. J., & Langkamp-Henken, B. (2006). Effects of variation in protein and carbohydrate intake on body mass and composition during energy restriction: A meta-regression. *American Journal of Clinical Nutrition, 83*, 260–274.

Lacroix, M., Bos, C., Leonil, J., Airinei, G., Luengo, C., Dare, S. et al. (2006). Compared with casein or total milk protein, digestion of milk soluble proteins is too rapid to sustain the anabolic postprandial amino acid requirement. *American Journal of Clinical Nutrition, 84*, 1070–1079.

Layman, D. K. (2004). Protein quantity and quality at levels above the RDA improves adult weight loss. *Journal of the American College of Nutrition, 23*, 631S–636S.

Layman, D. K., Evans, E., Baum, J. I., Seyler, J., Erickson, D. J., & Boileau, R. A. (2005). Dietary protein and exercise have additive effects on body composition during weight loss in adult women. *Journal of Nutrition, 135*, 1903–1910.

Lemon, P. W., Tarnopolsky, M. A., MacDougall, J. D., & Atkinson, S. A. (1992). Protein requirements and muscle mass/strength changes during intensive training in novice body-builders. *Journal of Applied Physiology, 73*, 767–775.

Levenhagen, D. K., Gresham, J. D., Carlson, M. G., Maron, D. J., Borel, M. J., & Flakoll, P. J. (2001). Postexercise nutrient intake timing in humans is critical to recovery of leg glucose and protein homeostasis. *American Journal of Physiology: Endocrinology and Metabolism, 280*, E982–E993.

MacKenzie, M. G., Hamilton, D. L., Murray, J. T., Taylor, P. M., & Baar, K. (2009). mVps34 is activated following high-resistance contractions. *Journal of Physiology, 587*, 253–260.

Mahoney, D. J., & Tarnopolsky, M. A. (2005). Understanding skeletal muscle adaptation to exercise training in humans: Contributions from microarray studies. *Physical Medicine and Rehabilitation Clinics of North America, 16*, 859–873, vii.

McKenzie, S., Phillips, S. M., Carter, S. L., Lowther, S., Gibala, M. J., & Tarnopolsky, M. A. (2000). Endurance exercise training attenuates leucine oxidation and BCOAD activation during exercise in humans. *American Journal of Physiology: Endocrinology and Metabolism, 278*, E580–E587.

Meredith, C. N., Zackin, M. J., Frontera, W. R., & Evans, W. J. (1989). Dietary protein requirements and body protein metabolism in endurance-trained men. *Journal of Applied Physiology, 66*, 2850–2856.

Mettler, S., Mitchell, N., & Tipton, K. D. (2010). Increased protein intake reduces lean body mass loss during weight loss in athletes. *Medicine and Science in Sports and Exercise, 42*, 326–337.

Moore, D. R., Del Bel, N. C., Nizi, K. I., Hartman, J. W., Tang, J. E., Armstrong, D. et al. (2007). Resistance training reduces fasted- and fed-state leucine turnover and increases dietary nitrogen retention in previously untrained young men. *Journal of Nutrition, 137*, 985–991.

Moore, D. R., Phillips, S. M., Babraj, J. A., Smith, K., & Rennie, M. J. (2005). Myofibrillar and collagen protein synthesis in human skeletal muscle in young men after maximal shortening and lengthening contractions. *American Journal of Physiology: Endocrinology and Metabolism, 288*, E1153–E1159.

Moore, D. R., Robinson, M. J., Fry, J. L., Tang, J. E., Glover, E. I., Wilkinson, S. B. et al. (2009a). Ingested protein dose response of muscle and albumin protein synthesis after resistance exercise in young men. *American Journal of Clinical Nutrition, 89*, 161–168.

Moore, D. R., Tang, J. E., Burd, N. A., Rerecich, T., Tarnopolsky, M. A., & Phillips, S. M. (2009b). Differential stimulation of myofibrillar and sarcoplasmic protein synthesis with protein ingestion at rest and after resistance exercise. *Journal of Physiology, 597*, 897–904.

Phillips, S. M. (2006). Dietary protein for athletes: From requirements to metabolic advantage. *Applied Physiology, Nutrition and Metabolism, 31*, 647–654.

Phillips, S. M., Atkinson, S. A., Tarnopolsky, M. A., & MacDougall, J. D. (1993). Gender differences in leucine kinetics and nitrogen balance in endurance athletes. *Journal of Applied Physiology, 75*, 2134–2141.

Phillips, S. M., Tang, J. E., & Moore, D. R. (2009). The role of milk- and soy-based protein in support of muscle protein synthesis and muscle protein accretion in young and elderly persons. *Journal of the American College of Nutrition, 28*, 343–354.

Rennie, M. J., Wackerhage, H., Spangenburg, E. E., & Booth, F. W. (2004). Control of the size of the human muscle mass. *Annual Review of Physiology, 66*, 799–828.

Robinson, M. M., Turner, S. M., Hellerstein, M. K., Hamilton, K. L., & Miller, B. F. (2011).Long-term synthesis rates of skeletal muscle DNA and protein are higher during aerobic training in older humans than in sedentary young subjects but are not altered by protein supplementation. *FASEB Journal* (DOI: 10.1096/fj.11-186437).

Rowlands, D. S., Rossler, K., Thorp, R. M., Graham, D. F., Timmons, B. W., Stannard, S. R. et al. (2008). Effect of dietary protein content during recovery from high-intensity cycling on subsequent performance and markers of stress, inflammation, and muscle damage in well-trained men. *Applied Physiology, Nutrition and Metabolism, 33*, 39–51.

Rowlands, D. S., Thorp, R. M., Rossler, K., Graham, D. F., & Rockell, M. J. (2007). Effect of protein-rich feeding on recovery after intense exercise. *International Journal of Sport Nutrition and Exercise Metabolism, 17*, 521–543.

Sacks, F. M., Bray, G. A., Carey, V. J., Smith, S. R., Ryan, D. H., Anton, S. D. et al. (2009). Comparison of weight-loss diets with different compositions of fat, protein, and carbohydrates. *New England Journal of Medicine, 360*, 859–873.

Sakuma, K., Watanabe, K., Hotta, N., Koike, T., Ishida, K., Katayama, K. et al. (2009). The adaptive responses in several mediators linked with hypertrophy and atrophy of skeletal muscle after lower limb unloading in humans. *Acta Physiologica (Oxford), 197*, 151–159.

Sancak, Y., Bar-Peled, L., Zoncu, R., Markhard, A. L., Nada, S., & Sabatini, D. M. (2010). Ragulator-Rag complex targets mTORC1 to the lysosomal surface and is necessary for its activation by amino acids. *Cell, 141*, 290–303.

Sarbassov, D. D., Ali, S. M., Kim, D. H., Guertin, D. A., Latek, R. R., Erdjument-Bromage, H. et al. (2004). Rictor, a novel binding partner of mTOR, defines a rapamycin-insensitive and raptor-independent pathway that regulates the cytoskeleton. *Current Biology, 14*, 1296–1302.

Saunders, M. J., Moore, R. W., Kies, A. K., Luden, N. D., & Pratt, C. A. (2009). Carbohydrate and protein hydrolysate coingestions improvement of late-exercise time-trial performance. *International Journal of Sport Nutrition and Exercise Metabolism, 19*, 136–149.

Schaafsma, G. (2005). The Protein Digestibility-Corrected Amino Acid Score (PDCAAS) – a concept for describing protein quality in foods and food ingredients: A critical review. *Journal of AOAC International, 88*, 988–994.

Shirreffs, S. M., Watson, P., & Maughan, R. J. (2007). Milk as an effective post-exercise rehydration drink. *British Journal of Nutrition, 98*, 173–180.

Tang, J. E., Moore, D. R., Kujbida, G. W., Tarnopolsky, M. A., & Phillips, S. M. (2009). Ingestion of whey hydrolysate, casein, or soy protein isolate: Effects on mixed muscle protein synthesis at rest and following resistance exercise in young men. *Journal of Applied Physiology, 107*, 987–992.

Tarnopolsky, M. A., Atkinson, S. A., MacDougall, J. D., Chesley, A., Phillips, S., & Schwarcz, H. P. (1992). Evaluation of protein requirements for trained strength athletes. *Journal of Applied Physiology, 73*, 1986–1995.

Tarnopolsky, M. A., MacDougall, J. D., & Atkinson, S. A. (1988). Influence of protein intake and training status on nitrogen balance and lean body mass. *Journal of Applied Physiology, 64*, 187–193.

Thomas, K., Morris, P., & Stevenson, E. (2009). Improved endurance capacity following chocolate milk consumption compared with two commercially available sport drinks. *Applied Physiology, Nutrition and Metabolism, 34*, 78–82.

Tipton, K. D., Elliott, T. A., Cree, M. G., Aarsland, A. A., Sanford, A. P., & Wolfe, R. R. (2006). Stimulation of net muscle protein synthesis by whey protein ingestion before and after exercise. *American Journal of Physiology: Endocrinology and Metabolism, 292*, E71–E76.

Tipton, K. D., Rasmussen, B. B., Miller, S. L., Wolf, S. E., Owens-Stovall, S. K., Petrini, B. E. et al. (2001). Timing of amino acid-carbohydrate ingestion alters anabolic response of muscle to resistance exercise. *American Journal of Physiology: Endocrinology and Metabolism, 281*, E197–E206.

Valentine, R. J., Saunders, M. J., Todd, M. K., & St. Laurent, T. G. (2008). Influence of carbohydrate-protein beverage on cycling endurance and indices of muscle disruption. *International Journal of Sport Nutrition and Exercise Metabolism, 18*, 363–378.

Van Essen, M., & Gibala, M. J. (2006). Failure of protein to improve time trial performance when added to a sports drink. *Medicine and Science in Sports and Exercise, 38*, 1476–1483.

Watson, P., Love, T. D., Maughan, R. J., & Shirreffs, S. M. (2008). A comparison of the effects of milk and a carbohydrate-electrolyte drink on the restoration of fluid balance and exercise capacity in a hot, humid environment. *European Journal of Applied Physiology, 104*, 633–642.

Weinheimer, E. M., Sands, L. P., & Campbell, W. W. (2010). A systematic review of the separate and combined effects of energy restriction and exercise on fat-free mass in middle-aged and older adults: Implications for sarcopenic obesity. *Nutrition Reviews, 68*, 375–388.

Wilkinson, S. B., Phillips, S. M., Atherton, P. J., Patel, R., Yarasheski, K. E., Tarnopolsky, M. A. et al. (2008). Differential effects of resistance and endurance exercise in the fed state on signalling molecule phosphorylation and protein synthesis in human muscle. *Journal of Physiology, 586*, 3701–3717.

Wilkinson, S. B., Tarnopolsky, M. A., MacDonald, M. J., Macdonald, J. R., Armstrong, D., & Phillips, S. M. (2007). Consumption of fluid skim milk promotes greater muscle protein accretion following resistance exercise than an isonitrogenous and isoenergetic soy protein beverage. *American Journal of Clinical Nutrition, 85*, 1031–1040.

Young, V. R. (1986). Nutritional balance studies: Indicators of human requirements or of adaptive mechanisms? *Journal of Nutrition, 116*, 700–703.

Young, V. R., Gucalp, C., Rand, W. M., Matthews, D. E., & Bier, D. M. (1987). Leucine kinetics during three weeks at submaintenance-to-maintenance intakes of leucine in men: Adaptation and accommodation. *Human Nutrition Clinical Nutrition, 41*, 1–18.

Zachwieja, J. J., Ezell, D. M., Cline, A. D., Ricketts, J. C., Vicknair, P. C., Schorle, S. M. et al. (2001). Short-term dietary energy restriction reduces lean body mass but not performance in physically active men and women. *International Journal of Sports Nutrition, 22*, 310–316.

Fluid and electrolyte needs for training, competition, and recovery

SUSAN M. SHIRREFFS[1] & MICHAEL N. SAWKA[2]

[1]*School of Sport, Exercise and Health Sciences, Loughborough University, Loughborough, UK and* [2]*Thermal and Mountain Medicine Division, US Army Research Institute of Environmental Medicine, Natick, Massachusetts, USA*

Abstract

Fluids and electrolytes (sodium) are consumed by athletes, or recommended to athletes, for a number of reasons, before, during, and after exercise. These reasons are generally to sustain total body water, as deficits (hypohydration) will increase cardiovascular and thermal strain and degrade aerobic performance. Vigorous exercise and warm/hot weather induce sweat production, which contains both water and electrolytes. Daily water (4–10 L) and sodium (3500–7000 mg) losses in active athletes during hot weather exposure can induce water and electrolyte deficits. Both water and sodium need to be replaced to re-establish "normal" total body water (euhydration). This replacement can be by normal eating and drinking practices if there is no urgency for recovery. But if rapid recovery (<24 h) is desired or severe hypohydration (>5% body mass) is encountered, aggressive drinking of fluids and consuming electrolytes should be encouraged to facilitate recovery for subsequent competition.

Fluids and electrolytes for hydration

Hypohydration can degrade aerobic exercise performance, and increase physiological strain and perceived exertion during exercise in temperate, warm/hot environments. Normally, total body water (TBW) is ~60% of weight, so a 72 kg athlete has a total body water of ~43 L (Institute of Medicine, IOM, 2005). Total body water per unit lean body mass is relatively constant (~74%) across age, sex, and race (IOM, 2005). Total body water is distributed between the intracellular fluid volume (65% TBW) and extracellular fluid volume (35% TBW), with the ~15 L extracellular fluid volume including ~3 L plasma volume (IOM, 2005). Therefore, it is important to remember that the easily assessed plasma volume provides a relatively small portion of the extracellular fluid volume. Given the normal day-to-day variation in body water content, hypohydration or hyperhydration probably starts once the body water content exceeds the normal euhydration window of approximately ± 0.2–0.5% of body mass (Adolph, 1943; Adolph & Dill, 1938). Water loss and intake can be episodic, so body water fluctuates (Sawka, Cheuvront, & Carter, 2005; Sawka et al.,

2007). Assessment of hydration status is not straightforward, although various measures are in common use and serial measures of body weight and urine specific gravity provide useful tools for athletes (Cheuvront et al., 2010a). Plasma osmolality provides the "best" physiological index of hydration status from sweat losses (Cheuvront et al., 2010a); other methods either require serial measures or are very invasive or very variable or invalid (Cheuvront et al., 2010a; IOM, 2005). It should be noted that plasma osmolality will not be a sensitive marker of hypohydration induced by diuretics, cold or high-altitude exposure, as they induce an iso-osmotic hypovolaemia, for which there is no valid biomarkers.

Daily water losses occur from respiration, urinary/faecal and sweat losses, but during physical exercise and exposure to heat stress, sweat loss is the largest potential source of water loss (IOM, 2005; Sawka et al., 2005). In exercise, hypohydration most commonly occurs when sweat loss is not replaced, but it can also occur as a result of fluid restriction that may be unintentional or be planned as part of a strategy to lose weight. With sweat loss, substantial quantities of electrolytes, in particular sodium can be lost. Sweat sodium is hypotonic relative to plasma, so sweat-mediated hypohydration will act to increase plasma osmolality but decrease plasma volume (IOM, 2005). Since sodium is the primary cation for the intracellular fluid space, its replacement is critical for re-establishing total body water (Nose, Mack, Shi, & Nadel, 1988). Regardless of the mode of water loss responsible for inducing body water deficits, fluid loss will occur both in the intracellular and extracellular fluid compartments (Costill, Coté, & Fink, 1976) and reduce plasma (blood) volume. Figure 1 provides the relationship of plasma volume reductions (from euhydration) relative to hypohydration level from sweat dehydration and diuretic administration (Cheuvront et al., 2010c). It should be noted, however, that since diuretics induce solute loss, the loss of extracellular fluid and plasma is greater. In addition, as mentioned above, diuretics induce an iso-osmotic hypovolaemia rather than the hypertonic hypovolaemia associated with sweat-induced hypohydration.

Hypohydration may occur prior to exercise or may result from fluid loss during exercise. The former may be deliberate in an aim to reduce body mass in weight category sports, or may be inadvertent due to failure to ingest sufficient fluid to match ongoing losses. This is likely to be of concern to athletes competing in weight category sports. There are, however, some indications that many athletes may begin both training and competition in a state of fluid deficit. Analysis of samples collected from elite football (soccer) players before training revealed that a significant number had urine osmolality values that were consistent with hypohydration (Shirreffs, Sawka, & Stone, 2006). Perhaps more surprisingly, samples collected from players before a competitive game revealed that 8 of the 20 outfield players had a urine osmolality in excess of 900 mOsmol · kg^{-1} when they arrived for the game (Maughan, Watson,

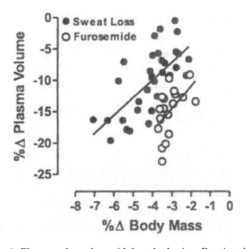

Figure 1. Plasma volume loss with hypohydration. Reprinted from Cheuvront et al. (2010) with the permission of the American Physiological Society.

Evans, Broad, & Shirreffs, 2007b). This evidence is mostly in the form of measures of urine osmolality or specific gravity made on athletes in these situations. Only when exercise duration exceeds ~ 60 min and when the ambient temperature is high, is it likely that fluid deficits during exercise will reach levels that are likely to have an effect on performance.

Hydration and performance

The influence of hydration status on aerobic performance and to a lesser extent cognitive performance has been studied widely, and consensus statements have been published in recent years (IOM, 2005; Sawka et al., 2007). It is agreed that hypohydration will degrade aerobic performance (IOM, 2005; Sawka et al., 2007), but there is active debate regarding the mechanisms responsible (Cheuvront et al., 2010c; Sawka & Noakes, 2007).

Hypohydration increases heat storage and reduces one's ability to tolerate exercise-induced heat strain (IOM, 2005; Sawka et al., 2007). The increased heat storage is mediated by reduced sweating rate and reduced skin blood flow for a given core temperature (Sawka et al., 2007). The reduced ability to tolerate exercise-heat strain is likely due to an inability to sustain the required cardiac output and a reduction in maximal aerobic power thus increasing the relative exercise intensity (Cheuvront, Carter, Castellani, & Sawka, 2005). Hypohydration that exceeds 2% of body mass loss ($\sim 3\%$ TBW) consistently degrades aerobic performance in temperate and warm/hot environments. Kenefick and colleagues demonstrated that hypohydration degrades time-trial performance to a greater extent with increasing heat stress (Kenefick, Cheuvront, Palombo, Ely, & Sawka, 2010). Their participants performed cycle ergometer exercise for 30 min at a constant intensity (50% $\dot{V}O_{2max}$) followed by a time-trial (total work completed in 15 min). Four groups of participants completed euhydration and hypohydration (-4% body mass) trials during compensable heat stress in 10°C, 20°C, 30°C, and 40°C environments. Therefore, the environments had a modest effect on core temperature (38.4–38.9°C) but induced step-wise increments (by ~ 3°C from 25°C to 36°C) in skin temperature. Figure 2 presents the percent decrement time-trial performance from euydration at each skin temperature. When skin temperature was > 29°C, time-trial performance was degraded by $\sim 1.6\%$ for each additional 1°C increase in skin temperature. Kenefick and colleagues' (2010) physiological data showed that a combination of high skin blood flow with plasma (blood) volume reductions via cardiovascular strain appeared to mediate the performance degradations. In addition, Castellani et al. (2010) recently demonstrated that

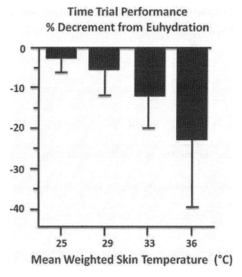

**Time Trial Performance
% Decrement from Euhydration**

Figure 2. The percent decrement in time-trial performance from euydration at each skin temperature. Reprinted from Sawka et al. (In Press); data from Kenefick et al. (2010). Reprinted with the permission of the American Physiological Society.

hypohydration markedly degrades aerobic performance at high altitude, and suggested that the systemic vasodilation from hypoxia and plasma (blood) volume from hypohydration act together to accentuate performance decrements.

The general conclusions that have been drawn for sweating-induced dehydration are that:

- Body water reductions in excess of 2% of body mass consistently degrade aerobic performance (IOM, 2005; Sawka et al., 2007), particularly in environments that are warmer (thus increasing skin temperature and skin blood flow requirements) (Cheuvront, Carter, Haymes, & Sawka, 2006; Kenefick et al., 2010): the warmer the environment, the greater the aerobic performance degradation (Kenefick et al., 2010), and the greater the water deficit, the greater the aerobic performance degradation (Sawka, Francesconi, Young, & Pandolf, 1984). Gigou and colleagues performed a meta-analytic review on studies of pre-exercise hypohydration, and concluded that hypohydration induced prior to exercise reduces mean power output by 3.2% relative to control trials where hydration was maintained (Gigou, Lamontagne-Lacasse, & Goulet, 2010). They further concluded that pre-exercise hypohydration of 3% or more of body mass impairs endurance performance.
- Reductions in body mass in the order of 1–2% appear generally not to degrade aerobic performance when the exercise duration is less than 90 min and the environment is temperate (20–21°C) (Cheuvront, Carter, & Sawka, 2003).

- Reductions in body mass in the order of 3–4% do not degrade muscular strength (Greiwe et al., 1998), jumping ability (Cheuvront et al., 2010b) or anaerobic performance (Cheuvront et al., 2006) but can degrade high-intensity endurance (Judelson et al., 2007). Reductions of 2–3% are associated with a deterioration in the ability to execute sport-specific skills (Baker, Dougherty, Chow, & Kenney, 2007; Devlin, Fraser, Barras, & Hawley, 2001; Dougherty, Baker, Chow, & Kenney, 2006). Baker et al. (2007) reported that basketball players attempted fewer shots and were less able to make shots linked with movement (e.g. lay-up) when dehydration had risen to 3% of normal body mass, and shooting was further impaired at a 4% deficit.
- Reductions in body mass in the order of 2–3% appear to have no significant effect on sprint running performance – that is, when body mass is "carried" (Judelson et al., 2007).
- Mild to moderate dehydration (up to 3% body mass loss), without heat stress, is unlikely to be associated with reductions in cognitive function, psychomotor function, mood, and mental readiness (Adams et al., 2008; Leibowitz, Abernethy, Buskirk, Bar-Or, & Hennessy, 1972; Szinnai, Schachinger, Arnaud, Linder, & Keller, 2005)
- High levels of hypohydration (more than 3% body mass loss), or more moderate levels combined with heat stress, may influence cognitive function, mood, and mental readiness (Cian et al., 2000; Cian, Barraud, Melin, & Raphel, 2001; Sharma, Sridharan, Pichan, & Panwar, 1986).

As discussed, body mass is related to total body water because lean body mass is consistently about 74% water. Therefore, fatter individuals will have a smaller total body water and a given weight reduction (body mass) from water loss will incur a greater reduction in total body water or represent a more severe hypohydration. In addition, as discussed above, aerobic performance will be more likely to be degraded at higher skin temperatures, and aerobic tasks are affected more than strength and power tasks. Therefore, since athletes vary in body composition, heat acclimation state (influencing skin temperature), and events vary in aerobic/non-aerobic components, it is likely that considerable variability will be observed for hypohydration-mediated sports performance degradation in real-life situations. However, these are general conclusions and some individuals may find their performance is influenced more or less than that suggested here for a given water deficit. In addition, the smallest performance changes that can currently be identified in research studies are greater than what might be a meaningful impact in a competitive event.

It is also important to recognize that the artificial environment of some laboratory studies may introduce confounding factors. In a study by Robinson et al. (1995), for example, the conclusion was that fluid ingestion during exercise did not sustain performance in a cycling time-trial. However, the participants in this study were required to drink very large volumes: 629 ml cool flavoured water 5 min before the start of exercise and a further 215 ml every 10 min for the first 40 min of exercise. Perhaps unsurprisingly, the participants reported extreme abdominal discomfort, which may well have accounted for the lack of a beneficial effect of fluid intake.

Comparisons of studies on fluid provision are complicated by differences in the composition of drinks provided, and few studies include both water control and no-drink control treatments. Other variables include differences in the exercise test, participant training status, heat acclimation status, environmental conditions, nutritional status, the drinking schedule, and the temperature of drinks. Many studies, perhaps especially those in which relatively untrained individuals are required to perform in time-trials where pace judgement is of critical importance, are compromised by the absence of appropriate familiarization trials.

Taking all of the available information together would suggest that where performance is crucial, the scientific data can be used as a guide but each individual will need to establish their own individual response to changes in hydration status.

Hydration and perceived exertion and subjective feelings

The impact of hypohydration on cognitive performance has been reviewed extensively (IOM, 2005) and the impact is not clear-cut.

The subjective sensation of effort is increased during exercise if hypohydration is allowed to develop. Moran and colleagues reported that perception of effort, as assessed using the Borg scale, was closely related to the degree of hypohydration (Moran, Montain, & Pandolf, 1988). An exercise intensity that was rated at 13.4 ± 0.5 ("somewhat hard") when participants were dehydrated by 1.1% of body mass was rated at 17.6 ± 0.3 ("very hard") when dehydration reached 4.2%, thus there is clearly an association between the development of hyperthermia and the subjective sensation of effort. Galloway and Maughan (1997) reported a progressively higher subjective sensation of effort as ambient temperature increased from 4°C to 31°C. This effect was apparent early in exercise and may account at

least in part for the slower pace adopted by experienced runners when required to exercise in hot environments (Tucker, Rauch, Harley, & Noakes, 2004). In addition, hypohydration might increase thermal discomfort during exercise heat stress (Cheuvront et al., 2010c).

The increased sensation of effort when exercising in a dehydrated state is clearly important for the athlete, as it is likely to lead to a reduction in performance (Cheuvront et al., 2010c). It may, however, be of greater relevance in those who exercise for health reasons: an increased sensation of effort may be a factor in the early termination of an exercise session and is also likely to discourage long-term adherence to an exercise programme.

Consumption of fluids and electrolytes for hydration

In 2003, the International Olympic Committee held its second Consensus Conference on nutrition for sport. When considering the recommendations for drinking for hydration reasons, the following statement was included (Consensus Statement, 2004):

> Sufficient fluid should be consumed during exercise to limit dehydration to less than about 2% of body mass ... Sodium should be included when sweat losses are high, especially if exercise lasts more than about 2 h. Athletes should not drink so much that they gain weight during exercise. During recovery from exercise, rehydration should include replacement of both water and salts lost in sweat.

In addition, and specifically from the two key papers that covered the topic of hydration (Coyle, 2004; Shirreffs, Armstrong, & Cheuvront, 2004a), the following conclusions were drawn:

> Sodium should be included in fluids consumed during exercise if the exercise lasts more than 2 h. It should also be included in fluids consumed by individuals in any event who lose more than 3–4 g of sodium in their sweat. (Coyle, 2004)

> After exercise that has resulted in body mass loss due to sweat loss, water and sodium should be consumed in a quantity greater than those in the losses to optimize recovery of water and electrolyte balance. (Shirreffs et al., 2004a)

The evidence on which these comments were based can be found within the cited papers and will not be discussed further here. And now, some 7–8 years later, these conclusions remain sound and more recent reviews of the topic have arrived at similar conclusions (e.g. Sawka et al., 2007).

In addition, Montain and colleagues (Montain, Cheuvront, & Sawka, 2006) performed a mathematical model of sodium consumption and drinking behaviour on plasma sodium, and demonstrated that overdrinking (relative to sweating) is the primary factor mediating hyponatraemia and that consumption of "sports beverages" containing sodium can delay its development. There has been no new emerging evidence to suggest that any electrolyte other than the already identified sodium has a significant role in hydration before, during or after exercise. *Before exercise*, sodium containing fluids, or foods containing sodium, can help retain any water consumed to establish euhydration prior to the start of exercise when this is desired (Sawka et al., 2007). *During exercise*, sodium consumption along with water is recommended when exercise duration is more than 2 h or when significant amounts of sodium losses (3–4 g) are likely to occur (Coyle, 2004), or when the volume of drink consumed is large enough that it may cause a significant reduction in plasma sodium concentration (Vrijens & Rehrer, 1999). *After exercise*, replacement of sodium and restoration of sodium balance is a prerequisite for an effective restoration and maintenance of euhydration (Shirreffs, Taylor, Leiper, & Maughan, 1996), and no other electrolytes have been shown to play a significant role in this. However, research in the last few years has re-emphasized the importance of not having too rapid a rehydration after exercise if a diuresis is to be avoided and euhydration is to be achieved and maintained. The slowing of the appearance into the circulation of the rehydration fluid can be achieved by the drinking pattern (Kovacs, Schmahl, Denden, & Brouns, 2002) or by delaying the gastric emptying of the drink from the stomach into the intestine by, for example, increasing the carbohydrate content of the drink (Evans, Shirreffs, & Maughan, 2009a, 2009b).

Fluids and electrolytes for thermoregulation

An increase in body core temperature is a common response to exercise, unless the intensity is low and/or the exercise is taking place in a cool environment. An elevated body temperature may be related to early fatigue or a reduction in the intensity at which exercise is performed (Gonzalez-Alonso et al., 1999; Nielsen et al., 1993; Tatterson, Hahn, Martin, & Febbraio, 2000); however, no study has independently examined the role of core temperature as skin temperature has covaried (Cheuvront et al., 2010c). As demonstrated by Ely et al. (Ely, Cheuvront, Kenefick, & Sawka, 2009) for euhydrated individuals and by Kenefick et al. (2010) for hypohydrated

individuals, a high skin temperature (with a modest rise in core temperature) will markedly degrade aerobic performance. It is likely that both a high skin temperature and high core temperature will increase skin blood flow requirements to displace blood from the central circulation and therefore reduce cardiac filling, and thus stroke volume and possibly cardiac output. The hypovolaemia (reduced plasma/blood volume) further contributes to decreased cardiac filling and an inability to achieve a high maximal cardiac output.

The effect of the ingested fluid temperature on the rise in core temperature during 2 h of recumbent cycling at 51% peak in a temperate environment of 26°C with relative humidity of 40% was investigated by Wimer et al. (Wimer, Lamb, Sherman, & Swanson, 1997). Compared with ingesting 1350 ml of water at 38°C, the ingestion of 1350 ml of drinks at 0.5°C attenuated the rise in rectal temperature. This observation was subsequently confirmed by Lee and Shirreffs (2007), who found that, compared with ingesting a litre of flavoured water at 50°C, the acute ingestion of the same volume of the same drink at 10°C during 90 min of cycling at 53% peak in a moderate environment (25°C, relative humidity 61%) attenuated the rise in rectal temperature. However, when drinks at 10°C and 50°C were consumed in four smaller aliquots of 400 ml each at intervals during 90 min cycling at 50% peak in a similar moderate environment (25°C, relative humidity 60%), the absolute rise in core temperature by the end of exercise was similar with both drinks (Lee, Shirreffs, & Maughan, 2008a).

A recent review of the literature (Burdon, O'Connor, Gifford, & Shirreffs, 2010a) concluded that ingestion of cold drinks may attenuate an exercise-induced rise in core temperature and improve exercise performance in the heat (by 10%), but this was based on only four studies (Lee & Shirreffs, 2007; Lee, Shirreffs, & Maughan, 2008a, 2008b; Mundel, Bunn, Hooper, & Jones, 2007) and the findings of these studies were mixed. Since this review, further research into exercise performance has been conducted (Burdon et al., 2010b; Ross et al., 2011; Siegel et al., 2010; Stanley, Leveritt, & Peake, 2010). Siegel and colleagues (2010) investigated the effect of ice slurry ingestion (at –1°C) on thermoregulatory responses and submaximal running time in the heat. Approximately 600 ml of the ice slurry or cold water (at 4°C) was consumed before running to exhaustion in a hot environment. Running time was longer after consuming ice slurry (50.2 min) compared with cold water (40.7 min). Ross and colleagues (2011) investigated the efficacy of combining external and internal cooling techniques on performance of a cycling time-trial in a hot and humid environment. The internal and external cooling was achieved by combining ingestion of a sports drink ice slurry (approximately 1 L) with cold towel application to the torso and legs. The combined internal/external cooling was associated with a 3% increase in power (~ 8 W) and 1.3% improvement in performance time ($\sim 1{:}06$ min) compared to a control trial when ad libitum ingestion of cold water (4°C) was allowed. Burdon and colleagues (2010b) investigated the effects of consuming approximately 1.7 L of a cold (4°C) compared with an approximately thermoneutral sports drink on performance in the heat. The drinks were consumed during 90 min of steady-state exercise prior to a 15 min performance test. Significant improvements (4.9%) in performance were observed with cold drink ingestion. Finally, Stanley and colleagues (2010) found no difference in cycling exercise performance in hot, humid conditions when either an ice-slush drink (at -0.8°C) or a drink at 18.4°C was consumed in the rest period between 75 min of steady-state cycling and a performance trial. These recent studies provide additional weight and validity to the previous conclusions drawn from research in this area.

Consumption of fluids and electrolytes for thermoregulation

Hypohydration reduces sweating and skin blood flow responses, thus increasing both core and skin temperature. The mechanisms responsible for this are increased plasma osmolality and reduced plasma (blood volume), both of which are related to the magnitude of hypohydration (IOM, 2005; Sawka et al., 2005, Fortney et al., 1984). Since sodium is the primary cation for extracellular fluid, the sodium deficits need to be replaced to re-establish extracellular fluid and total body water.

It might be expected, therefore, that ingestion of sufficient fluid to prevent a marked rise in serum osmolality or minimize plasma volume reduction will sustain thermoregulatory and thus cardiovascular support for exercise. Therefore, the replacement of both water and electrolytes is essential to sustain performance.

Heat, hydration, and the brain

It has long been known that the brain plays an important role in the sensation of effort during exercise (Bainbridge, 1919). The mechanisms that underpin this, however, have remained elusive and are generally relegated to a "black box" phenomenon that might be related to a high central (brain) temperature degrading brain function and reducing the drive to exercise (Nielsen et al., 1993). However, there is some evidence to suggest that the mechanism by which this might operate may be related to

changes in the permeability of the blood–brain barrier induced by hyperthermia and/or dehydration (Maughan, Shirreffs, & Watson, 2007a). A fixed period of exercise results in elevation of the serum concentration of a brain-specific protein, $S100\beta$, if the exercise takes place in the heat but not when the same exercise is performed in a temperate environment (Watson, Shirreffs, & Maughan, 2005). However, two recent studies have not supported the concept that heat stress (Cheuvront et al., 2008) or hypohydration (Castellani et al., 2010) increase $S100\beta$ during exercise. Therefore, it is unclear if there is an increase in the permeability of the blood–brain barrier to relatively large protein molecules with exercise-heat stress. In a further study, Watson and colleagues showed that the provision of sufficient fluid during prolonged exercise in a warm environment to limit the rise in plasma osmolality that was observed in a trial where no fluid was given was effective in preventing a rise in serum $S100\beta$ (Watson, Black, Clark, & Maughan, 2006).

Conclusions

Hypohydration and hyperthermia can negatively influence the physiological responses to exercise and aerobic exercise performance. These effects can, however, be reduced by consumption of appropriate fluids and electrolytes (sodium).

Note

The opinions or assertions contained herein are the private views of the authors and are not to be construed as official or as reflecting the views of the US Army or the US Department of Defense. Any citations of commercial organizations and trade names in this report do not constitute an official Department of the Army endorsement of approval of the products or services of these organizations.

References

Adams, G. E., Carter, R., III, Cheuvront, S. N., Merullo, D. J., Castellani, J. W., Lieberman, H. R. et al. (2008). Hydration effects on cognitive performance during military tasks in temperate and cold environments. *Physiology and Behavior*, 93, 748–756.

Adolph, E. F. (1943). *Physiological regulations.* Lancaster, PA: Jacques Cattell Press.

Adolph, E. F., & Dill, D. B. (1938). Observations on water metabolism in the desert. *American Journal of Physiology*, 123, 369–378.

Baker, L. B., Dougherty, K. A., Chow, M., & Kenney, W. L. (2007). Progressive dehydration causes a progressive decline in basketball skill performance. *Medicine and Science in Sports and Exercise*, 39, 1114–1123.

Bainbridge, F. A. (1919). *The physiology of muscular exercise.* London: Longmans.

Burdon, C., O'Connor, H., Gifford, J., & Shirreffs, S. M. (2010a). Influence of beverage temperature on exercise performance in the heat: A systematic review. *International Journal of Sports Nutrition and Exercise Metabolism*, 20, 166–174.

Burdon, C., O'Connor, H., Gifford, J., Shirreffs, S., Chapman, P., & Johnson, N. (2010b). Effect of drink temperature on core temperature and endurance cycling performance in warm, humid conditions. *Journal of Sports Sciences*, 28, 1147–1156.

Castellani, J. W., Muza, S. R., Cheuvront, S. N., Sils, I. V., Fulco, C. S., Kenefick, R. W. et al. (2010). Effect of hypohydration and altitude exposure on aerobic exercise performance and altitude sickness. *Journal of Applied Physiology*, 109, 1792–1800.

Cheuvront, S. N., Carter, R., III, Castellani, J. W., & Sawka, M. N. (2005). Hypohydration impairs endurance exercise performance in temperate but not cold air. *Journal of Applied Physiology*, 99, 1972–1976.

Cheuvront, S. N., Carter, R., III, Haymes, E. M., & Sawka, M. N. (2006). Moderate hypohydration and hyperthermia do not affect anaerobic exercise performance. *Medicine and Science in Sports and Exercise*, 38, 1093–1097.

Cheuvront, S. N., Carter, R., III, & Sawka, M. N. (2003). Fluid balance and endurance exercise performance. *Current Sports Medicine Reports*, 2, 202–208.

Cheuvront, S. N., Chinevere, T. D., Ely, B. R., Kenefick, R. W., Goodman, D. A., McClung, S. P. et al. (2008). Serum S-100β response to exercise-heat strain before and after acclimation. *Medicine and Science in Sports and Exercise*, 40, 1477–1482.

Cheuvront, S. N., Ely, B. R., Kenefick, R. W., & Sawka, M. N. (2010a). Biological variation and diagnostic accuracy of dehydration assessment markers. *American Journal of Clinical Nutrition*, 92, 565–573.

Cheuvront, S. N., Kenefick, R. W., Ely, B. R., Harman, E. A., Castellani, J. W., Frykman, P. N. et al. (2010b). Hypohydration reduces vertical ground reaction impulse but not jump performance. *European Journal of Applied Physiology*, 109, 1163–1170.

Cheuvront, S. N., Kenefick, R. W., Montain, S. J., & Sawka, M. N. (2010c). Mechanisms of aerobic performance impairment with heat stress and dehydration. *Journal of Applied Physiology*, 109, 1989–1995.

Cian, C., Barraud, P. A., Melin, B., & Raphel, C. (2001). Effects of fluid ingestion on cognitive function after heat stress or exercise-induced dehydration. *International Journal of Psychophysiology*, 42, 243–251.

Cian, C., Koulmann, N., Barraud, P. A., Raphel, C., Jimenez, C., & Melin, B. (2000). Influence of variation in body hydration on cognitive function: Effect of hyperhydration, heat stress and exercise-induced dehydration. *Journal of Psychophysiology*, 14, 29–36.

Consensus Statement (2004). IOC consensus statement on sports nutrition 2003. *Journal of Sports Sciences*, 22, x.

Costill, D. L., Coté, R., & Fink, W. (1976). Muscle water and electrolytes following varied levels of dehydration in man. *Journal of Applied Physiology*, 40, 6–11.

Coyle, E. F. (2004). Fluid and fuel intake during exercise. *Journal of Sports Sciences*, 22, 39–55.

Devlin, L. H., Fraser, S. F., Barras, N. S., & Hawley, J. A. (2001). Moderate levels of hypohydration impair bowling accuracy but not bowling velocity in skilled cricket players. *Journal of Science and Medicine in Sport*, 4, 179–187.

Dougherty, K. A., Baker, L. B., Chow, M., & Kenney, W. L. (2006). Two percent dehydration impairs and six percent carbohydrate drink improves boys' basketball skills. *Medicine and Science in Sports and Exercise*, 38, 1650–1658.

Ely, B., Cheuvront, S. N., Kenefick, R. W., & Sawka, M. N. (2009). Aerobic performance is degraded, despite mild hyperthermia, in hot environments. *Medicine and Science in Sports and Exercise*, 42, 135–141.

Evans, G. H., Shirreffs, S. M., & Maughan, R. J. (2009a). Post-exercise rehydration in man: The effects of osmolality and carbohydrate content of ingested drinks. *Nutrition*, 25, 905–913.

Evans, G. H., Shirreffs, S. M., & Maughan, R. J. (2009b). Post-exercise rehydration in man: The effects of carbohydrate content and osmolality of drinks ingested *ad libitum*. *Applied Physiology, Nutrition and Metabolism*, 34, 785–793.

Fortney, S. M., Wenger, C. B., Bove, J. R., & Nadel, E. R. (1984). Effect of hyperosmolality on control of blood flow and sweating. *Journal of Applied Physiology*, 57, 1688–1695.

Galloway, S. D. R., & Maughan, R. J. (1997). Effects of ambient temperature on the capacity to perform prolonged cycle exercise in man. *Medicine and Science in Sports and Exercise*, 29, 1240–1249.

Gigou, P.-Y., Lamontagne-Lacasse, M., & Goulet, E. D. B. (2010). Meta-analysis of the effects of pre-exercise hypo-hydration on endurance performance, lactate threshold and $\dot{V}O_{2max}$. *Medicine and Science in Sports and Exercise*, 42 (suppl.), 361–362.

Gonzalez-Alonso, J., Teller, C., Andersen, S. L., Jensen, F. B., Hyldig, T. M., & Nielsen, B. (1999). Influence of body temperature on the development of fatigue during prolonged exercise in the heat. *Journal of Applied Physiology*, 86, 1032–1039.

Greiwe, J. S., Staffey, K. S., Melrose, D. R., Narve, M. D., & Knowlton, R. G. (1998). Effects of dehydration on isometric muscular strength and endurance. *Medicine and Science in Sports and Exercise*, 30, 284–288.

Institute of Medicine (IOM) (2005). Water. In *Dietary reference intakes for water, potassium, sodium, chlordie, and sulfate* (pp. 73–185). Washington, DC: National Academies Press.

Judelson, D. A., Maresh, C. M., Anderson, J. M., Armstrong, L. E., Casa, D. J., Kraemer, W. J. et al. (2007). Hydration and muscular performance: Does fluid balance affect strength, power and high-intensity endurance? *Sports Medicine*, 37, 907–921.

Kenefick, R. W., Cheuvront, S. N., Palombo, L. J., Ely, B. R. & Sawka, M. N. (2010). Skin temperature modifies impact of hypohydration on aerobic performance. *Journal of Applied Physiology*, 109, 79–86.

Kovacs, E. M., Schmahl, R. M., Denden, J. M., & Brouns, F. (2002). Effect of high and low rates of fluid intake on post-exeircse rehydration. *International Journal of Sport Nutrition and Exercise Metabolism*, 12, 14–23.

Leibowitz, H. W., Abernethy, C. N., Buskirk, E. R., Bar-Or, O., & Hennessy, R. T. (1972). The effect of heat stress on reaction time centrally and peripherally presented stimuli. *Human Factors*, 14, 155–160.

Lee, J. K. W., & Shirreffs, S. M. (2007). The influence of drink temperature on thermoregulatory responses during prolonged exercise in a moderate environment. *Journal of Sport Sciences*, 25, 975–985.

Lee, J. K. W., Shirreffs, S. M., & Maughan, R. J. (2008a). The influence of serial feeding of drinks at different temperatures on thermoregulatory responses during prolonged exercise. *Journal of Sports Sciences*, 26, 583–590.

Lee, J. K. W., Shirreffs, S. M., & Maughan, R. J. (2008b). Cold drink ingestion improves exercise endurance capacity in the heat. *Medicine and Science in Sports and Exercise*, 40, 1637–1644.

Maughan, R. J., Shirreffs, S. M., & Watson, P. (2007a). Exercise, heat, hydration and the brain. *Journal of the American College of Nutrition*, 26, 604S–612S.

Maughan, R. J., Watson, P., Evans, G. H., Broad, N., & Shirreffs, S. M. (2007b). Water balance and salt losses in competitive football. *International Journal of Sport Nutrition and Exercise Metabolism*, 17, 583–594.

Montain, S. J., Cheuvront, S. N., & Sawka, M. N. (2006). Exercise associated hyponatremia: Quantitative analysis to understand the aetiology. *British Journal of Sports Medicine, 40*, 98–106.

Moran, D. S., Montain, S. J., & Pandolf, K. B. (1998). Evaluation of different levels of hydration using a new physiological strain index. *American Journal of Physiology: Regulatory, Integrative and Comparative Physiology, 275*, R854–R860.

Mundel, T., Bunn, S. J., Hooper, P. L., & Jones, D. A. (2007). The effects of face cooling during hyperthermic exercise in man: Evidence for an integrated thermal, neuroendocrine and behavioural response. *Experimental Physiology, 92*, 187–195.

Nielsen, B., Hales, J. R., Strange, S., Christensen, N. J., Warberg, J., & Saltin, B. (1993). Human circulatory and thermoregulatory adaptations with heat acclimation and exercise in a hot, dry environment. *Journal of Physiology, 460*, 467–485.

Nose, H., Mack, G. W., Shi, X. R., & Nadel, E. R. (1988). Involvement of sodium retention hormones during rehydration in humans. *Journal of Applied Physiology, 65*, 332–336.

Robinson, T. A., Hawley, J. A., Palmer, G. S., Wilson, G. R., Gray, D. A., Noakes, T. D. et al. (1995). Water ingestion does not improve 1-h cycling performance in moderate ambient temperatures. *European Journal of Applied Physiology and Occupational Physiology, 71*, 153–160.

Ross, M. L., Garvican, L. A., Jeacocke, N. A., Laursen, P. B., Abbiss, C. R., Martin, D. T. et al. (2011). Novel pre-cooling strategy enhances time trial cycling in the heat. *Medicine and Science in Sports and Exercise, 43*, 123–133.

Sawka, M. N., Burke, L. M., Eichner, E. R., Maughan, R. J., Montain, S. J., & Stachenfeld, N. S. (2007). American College of Sports Medicine position stand: Exercise and fluid replacement. *Medicine and Science in Sports and Exercise, 39*, 377–390.

Sawka, M. N., Cheuvront, S. N. & Carter, R. (2005). Human water needs. *Nutrition Reviews, 63*, S30–S39.

Sawka, M. N., Francesconi, R. P., Young, A. J., & Pandolf, K. B. (1984). Influence of hydration level and body fluids on exercise performance in the heat. *Journal of the American Medical Association, 252*, 1165–1169.

Sawka, M. N., Leon, L. R., Montain, S. J., & Sonna, L. A. (in press). Integrated physiological mechanisms of exercise performance, adaptation, and maladaptation to heat stress. *Comprehensive Physiology.*

Sawka, M. N., & Noakes, T. D. (2007). Contrasting perspectives in exercise science and sports medicine: Does dehydration impair exercise performance? *Medicine and Science in Sports and Exercise, 39*, 1209–1217.

Sharma, V. M., Sridharan, K., Pichan, G., & Panwar, M. R. (1986). Influence of heat stress-induced dehydration on mental functions. *Ergonomics, 29*, 791–799.

Shirreffs, S. M., Armstrong, L. E., & Cheuvront, S. N. (2004a). Fluid and electrolyte needs for preparation and recovery from training and competition. *Journal of Sports Sciences, 22*, 57–63.

Shirreffs, S. M., Sawka, M. N., & Stone, M. (2006). Water and electrolyte needs for football training and match-play. *Journal of Sports Sciences, 24*, 699–707.

Shirreffs, S. M., Taylor, A. J., Leiper, J. B., & Maughan, R. J. (1996). Post-exercise rehydration in man: Effects of volume consumed and sodium content of ingested fluids. *Medicine and Science in Sports and Exercise, 28*, 1260–1271.

Siegel, R., Mate, J., Brearley, M. B., Watson, G., Nosaka, K., & Laursen, P. B. (2010). Ice slurry ingestion increases core temperature capacity and running time in the heat. *Medicine and Science in Sports and Exercise, 42*, 717–725.

Stanley, J., Leveritt, M., & Peake, J. M. (2010). Thermoregulatory responses to ice-slush beverage ingestion and exercise in the heat. *European Journal of Applied Physiology, 110*, 1163–1173.

Szinnai, G., Schachinger, H., Arnaud, M. J., Linder, L., & Keller, U. (2005). Effect of water deprivation on cognitive-motor performance in healthy men and women. *American Journal of Physiology: Regulatory, Integrative and Comparative Physiology, 289*, R275–R280.

Tatterson, A. J., Hahn, A. G., Martin, D. T., & Febbraio, M. A. (2000). Effects of heat stress on physiological responses and exercise performance in elite cyclists. *Science and Medicine of Sport, 3*, 186–193.

Tucker, R., Rauch, L., Harley, Y. X. R., & Noakes, T. D. (2004). Impaired exercise performance in the heat is associated with an anticipatory reduction in skeletal muscle recruitment. *Pflugers Archives, 448*, 422–430.

Vrijens, D. M., & Rehrer, N. J. (1999). Sodium-free fluid ingestion decreases plasma sodium during exercise in the heat. *Journal of Applied Physiology, 86*, 1847–1851.

Watson, P., Black, K. E., Clark, S. C., & Maughan, R. J. (2006). Exercise in the heat: Effect of fluid ingestion on blood–brain barrier permeability. *Medicine and Science in Sports and Exercise, 38*, 2118–2124.

Watson, P., Shirreffs, S. M., & Maughan, R. J. (2005). Blood–brain barrier integrity may be threatened by exercise in a warm environment. *American Journal of Physiology: Regulatory, Integrative and Comparative Physiology, 288*, R1689–R1694.

Wimer, G. S., Lamb, D. R., Sherman, W. M., & Swanson, S. C. (1997). Temperature of ingested water and thermoregulation during moderate-intensity exercise. *Canadian Journal of Applied Physiology, 22*, 479–493.

Antioxidant and Vitamin D supplements for athletes: Sense or nonsense?

SCOTT POWERS[1], W. BRADLEY NELSON[1], & ENETTE LARSON-MEYER[2]

[1]Department of Applied Physiology and Kinesiology, University of Florida, Gainesville, Florida, USA and [2]Family and Consumer Sciences, University of Wyoming, Laramie, Wyoming, USA

Abstract

The idea that dietary supplements can improve athletic performance is popular among athletes. The use of antioxidant supplements is widespread among endurance athletes because of evidence that free radicals contribute to muscle fatigue during prolonged exercise. Furthermore, interest in vitamin D supplementation is increasing in response to studies indicating that vitamin D deficiency exists in athletic populations. This review explores the rationale for supplementation with both antioxidants and vitamin D and discusses the evidence to support and deny the benefits of these dietary supplements. The issue of whether athletes should use antioxidant supplements remains highly controversial. Nonetheless, at present there is limited scientific evidence to recommend antioxidant supplements to athletes or other physically active individuals. Therefore, athletes should consult with their health care professional and/or nutritionist when considering antioxidant supplementation. The issue of whether athletes should supplement with vitamin D is also controversial. While arguments for and against vitamin D supplementation exist, additional research is required to determine whether vitamin D supplementation is beneficial to athletes. Nevertheless, based upon the growing evidence that many athletic populations are vitamin D deficient or insufficient, it is recommended that athletes monitor their serum vitamin D concentration and consult with their health care professional and/or nutritionist to determine if they would derive health benefits from vitamin D supplementation.

Introduction

Many athletes are interested in using dietary supplements because of the perception that these additives can improve athletic performance (Huang, Johnson, & Pipe, 2006; Maughan, Depiesse, & Geyer, 2007). Although many diverse dietary supplements are available, the use of antioxidant supplements is common among endurance athletes because of evidence that free radicals promote muscle fatigue during prolonged exercise. Moreover, interest in vitamin D supplementation has increased recently due to reports suggesting that vitamin D deficiency exists in some athletes, particularly those that participate in indoor sports (e.g. basketball) (Constantini, Arieli, Chodick, & Dubnov-Raz, 2010; Halliday et al., 2011; Lehtonen-Veromaa et al., 1999; Lovell, 2008). Furthermore, recent reviews on vitamin D and muscle performance suggest that vitamin D deficiency impairs muscular performance and that vitamin D supplementation can potentially improve athletic performance (Bartoszewska, Kamboj, & Patel, 2010). Collectively, these reports have increased the awareness of the need for vitamin D among athletes and stimulated interest in supplementation.

This review discusses the rationale for supplementation with antioxidants and vitamin D, and highlights the evidence to support (or deny) the benefits of these dietary supplements.

Antioxidants and the athlete

The following sections provide an overview of both free radicals and antioxidants. We also discuss the physiological link between free radicals and muscle fatigue during exercise. Finally, we present arguments both for and against antioxidant supplementation in athletes. We begin with an introduction to free radicals.

Overview of free radicals and antioxidants

Free radicals (hereafter referred to as radicals) are molecules (or fragments of molecules) that contain one or more unpaired electrons in their outer orbital (Halliwell & Gutteridge, 2007). An unpaired electron results in molecular instability, thus radicals are highly reactive molecules that can promote oxidative damage to cellular components (i.e. proteins, lipids, and DNA). This radical-induced damage is commonly referred to as "oxidative stress" and oxidation of cellular constituents can lead to cell dysfunction and, in extreme cases, cell death. Also, note that the label "reactive oxygen species" (ROS) is a general term that refers not only to oxygen-centred radicals but also includes non-radical but reactive derivatives of oxygen (e.g. hydrogen peroxide) (Halliwell & Gutteridge, 2007). The damaging effects of reactive oxygen species can be negated in cells by antioxidants and in the context of this review, antioxidants will be defined as any substance that significantly delays or prevents oxidative damage of a target molecule (Halliwell & Gutteridge, 2007).

It is well established that physical exercise results in increased radical and ROS production in active skeletal muscles. Indeed, several reports indicate that exercise-induced radical production is responsible for oxidative damage to cells and contributes to muscular fatigue during prolonged exercise (Powers & Jackson, 2008). The source of muscle ROS production during exercise remains an active area of research and a highly debated topic. Historically, it has been believed that mitochondria are the dominant source of ROS production in contacting skeletal muscles. However, growing evidence suggests that mitochondria are not an important source of reactive oxygen species in exercising muscles and that xanthine oxidase or NADPH-oxidase may play a more important role in exercise-induced ROS production in muscle (Powers & Jackson, 2008).

Given that cells produce radicals, it is not surprising that all cells contain an endogenous antioxidant system composed of both enzymatic and non-enzymatic antioxidants. Moreover, dietary antioxidants (e.g. vitamin C and vitamin E) cooperate with the endogenous antioxidant defence systems to form a united antioxidant network in muscle fibres. This cooperative interaction between endogenous antioxidants and dietary antioxidants has fuelled the argument that antioxidant supplementation will boost the muscle fibre's ability to scavenge reactive oxygen species and protect against exercise-induced oxidative damage.

Radicals contribute to skeletal muscle fatigue

Muscle fatigue is commonly defined as a reduction in the ability of a muscle to generate force. Exercise-induced muscle fatigue is a multi-factorial process and the specific causes of fatigue can vary widely. Nonetheless, growing evidence indicates that radical production in skeletal muscles contributes to fatigue during prolonged submaximal exercise (i.e. events lasting > 30 min) (Reid, 2008). As mentioned previously, ROS production increases in contracting skeletal muscles and low levels of reactive oxygen species play an essential role in the regulation of muscle force production. Although a low level of reactive oxygen species in skeletal muscle is required for optimum force production, excessive reactive oxygen species can induce oxidative damage to muscle proteins and diminish muscle force production. Indeed, well-controlled animal studies indicate that scavenging radicals via antioxidants can protect skeletal muscles against oxidative damage and also delay fatigue during prolonged submaximal exercise (Powers & Jackson, 2008; Reid, 2008). In contrast, antioxidant scavengers are not effective in delaying muscle fatigue in animals performing high-intensity exercise (Powers & Jackson, 2008; Reid, 2008).

Do radicals contribute to exercise-induced muscular fatigue in humans? The answer to this question remains a matter of debate, but a growing number of studies suggest that acute administration of the antioxidant N-acetylcysteine delays human muscle fatigue during prolonged submaximal exercise. Specifically, N-acetylcysteine is a thiol-based antioxidant and its administration can delay muscular fatigue in humans during submaximal exercise tasks (e.g. electrically stimulated limb muscle, voluntary cycling exercise, and repetitive handgrip exercise) (Kelly, Wicker, Barstow, & Harms, 2009; Matuszczak et al., 2005; McKenna et al., 2006; Reid, Stokic, Koch, Khawli, & Leis, 1994). At present, it is unclear whether N-acetylcysteine retards human muscle fatigue during exercise close to or above maximum oxygen uptake (e.g. 85–90% $\dot{V}O_{2max}$) (Kelly et al., 2009; Medved et al., 2003; Medved, Brown, Bjorksten, & McKenna, 2004). In contrast to the findings that acute N-acetylcysteine administration can delay muscle fatigue during prolonged submaximal exercise, there is little evidence that other more commonly used antioxidant supplements (e.g. beta carotene, vitamin E, and/or vitamin C) can improve human exercise performance (Powers, DeRuisseau, Quindry, & Hamilton, 2004). Based upon current evidence, it appears that N-acetylcysteine supplementation can increase performance during prolonged exercise in humans, but there is limited evidence to support the concept that supplementation with vitamin C, vitamin E or beta carotene can improve human performance.

The fact that working skeletal muscles produce radicals has motivated many athletes to use antioxidant supplements in hopes of preventing exercise-induced radical damage and/or muscular fatigue. However, whether or not antioxidant supplements are helpful or harmful to the athlete remains a highly debated topic. We next summarize the arguments for and against antioxidant supplementation in athletes and other physically active individuals.

Arguments to support antioxidant supplementation in athletes

Advocates of antioxidant supplementation in athletes provide three primary arguments in favour of this practice. First, supporters argue that rigorous exercise training results in increased production of reactive oxygen species in skeletal muscles, thus antioxidant supplements are required to protect muscle fibres against oxidative damage (Schroder, Navarro, Mora, Galiano, & Tramullas, 2001; Schroder, Navarro, Tramullas, Mora, & Galiano, 2000). Supporters also argue that most common antioxidant supplements are not toxic even at relatively high levels of supplementation. Therefore, antioxidant supplementation is not likely to do harm and, in theory, antioxidant supplementation has the potential to be beneficial. Nonetheless, the merit of this statement continues to be debated among investigators in the field of redox biology and skeletal muscle.

A second argument to support antioxidant supplementation for athletes is that radicals have been shown to promote muscle fatigue in some types of exercise (Reid, 2008). Indeed, the evidence that some antioxidants (i.e. *N*-acetylcysteine) can improve human endurance performance provides motivation for many athletes to enrich their diets with antioxidants supplements. Many supplement companies have used the scientific reports that *N*-acetylcysteine improves performance and delays fatigue to encourage athletes to supplement with antioxidants. Indeed, the possibility that antioxidant supplementation can delay fatigue and improve endurance performance remains one of the strongest arguments in favour of antioxidant supplementation.

Finally, there is one circumstance that clearly supports the use of antioxidant supplements in athletes. Specifically, dietary recall studies reveal that some athletes do not consume a well-balanced diet, and therefore these individuals can be deficient in antioxidant intake. This is a reasonable supposition that is supported by studies investigating the nutritional habits of specific athletic populations (Machefer et al., 2007; Rankinen et al., 1998; Schroder et al., 2000). Therefore, for athletes that do not consume a well-balanced diet, antioxidant supplementation appears reasonable to bring them to the recommended levels of key antioxidant vitamins.

Arguments against antioxidant supplementation in athletes

Several lines of reasoning argue against antioxidant supplementation. First, although prolonged and/or intense exercise can promote oxidative stress in the active muscles, it is important to recognize that exercise-induced oxidative stress is a transient phenomenon and there is no evidence that exercise-induced radical production in skeletal muscle is detrimental to human health. Furthermore, regular exercise training promotes increased enzymatic and non-enzymatic antioxidants in muscle fibres resulting in improved endogenous protection against exercise-mediated oxidative damage (Criswell et al., 1993; Powers, Nelson, & Hudson, 2010). Therefore, this increase in endogenous antioxidants may be sufficient to protect against excessive exercise-induced oxidative damage and antioxidant supplementation is not required. Moreover, if an athlete maintains a diet that meets energy needs and is nutritionally well balanced, it is feasible that the athlete does not require supplementary antioxidants above those contained in the diet.

Perhaps the strongest argument against antioxidant supplementation for athletes and other active individuals is that emerging evidence indicates antioxidant supplementation may impair muscle function or retard some important exercise-induced adaptations in skeletal muscle (Coombes et al., 2001; McClung et al., 2010). For example, growing evidence indicates that exercise-induced production of reactive oxygen species serves as a signal to promote the expression of numerous skeletal muscle proteins, including antioxidant enzymes, mitochondrial proteins, and heat shock proteins (Hamilton et al., 2003; Powers & Jackson, 2008; Sen, 2001). Furthermore, two recent reports indicate that antioxidant supplementation with high levels of vitamins E and C (i.e. ~16 times higher than the recommended dietary allowance for adults) can blunt the training adaptation to exercise (Gomez-Cabrera et al., 2008; Ristow et al., 2009). These recent developments call for a very careful analysis of the use of antioxidants in athletes engaged in training.

A final argument against antioxidant supplementation in athletes is that the available data do not support the concept that antioxidant supplementation is beneficial to human health. For example, a meta-analysis of 68 randomized antioxidant supplement trials (total of 232,606 human participants) concluded that dietary supplementation with beta carotene, vitamin A, and vitamin E does not improve health outcomes and may increase mortality (Bjelakovic, Nikolova, Gluud, Simonetti, & Gluud, 2007). These authors also concluded that the roles of vitamin C and selenium on human mortality are unclear and require further study before a recommendation can be rendered.

Summary and conclusions: Antioxidant supplementation in athletes

The question of whether athletes should use antioxidant supplements remains an important and highly debated topic. Arguments for and against antioxidant supplementation exist and additional research will be required to firmly establish whether antioxidant supplementation is beneficial or harmful to athletes. However, at present there is limited scientific evidence to recommend antioxidant supplements to athletes or other physically active individuals. In fact, the current evidence suggests that athletes should use caution when considering supplementation with high doses of antioxidants. Therefore, based on the available evidence, we conclude that athletes should not use antioxidant supplements but should focus on consuming a well-balanced, energetically adequate diet that is rich in antioxidant-containing foods (i.e. whole grains, fruits, vegetables, nuts, and seeds).

Vitamin D and the athlete

Here we provide an introduction to the biochemical functions of vitamin D and discuss the arguments for and against vitamin D supplementation in athletes. We also consider calcium intake and supplementation in the context of vitamin D. We begin with an overview of the health benefits of vitamin D.

Overview of vitamin D

Vitamin D is not technically a vitamin but is a group of secosteroids that have endocrine and paracrine functions. Although vitamin D is found in the diet, physiological need can be met through endogenous synthesis upon exposure of the skin to ultraviolet-B radiation (UV-B, 290–315 nm). Ultraviolet-B exposure initiates a series of metabolic reactions that result in the conversion of 7-dehydrocholesterol, present in the membrane of epidermal and dermal cells, into vitamin D3 (cholecalciferol) (Holick, 2004). Endogenous vitamin D3 and vitamins D2 (ergocalciferol) and D3 obtained from the diet are subsequently hydroxylated to 25(OH)D, which is the main circulating or storage form. Further conversion to the biologically active form, 1,25-dihydroxyvita-min D ($1,25(OH)_2D$) by the kidney occurs under the direction of parathyroid hormone when serum calcium or phosphorus concentrations are low (Holick, 2004).

Vitamin D is essential for maintaining normal calcium metabolism and a major purpose of vitamin D is to increase intestinal calcium absorption. Research, for example, has found that only 10–15% dietary calcium is absorbed in the vitamin D-deficient state, whereas 30–35% is absorbed when vitamin D status is sufficient (Heaney, Dowell, Hale, & Bendich, 2003; Holick, 2004). Adequate vitamin D and calcium are also essential for bone health (Panda et al., 2004). Low calcium intake (Myburgh, Hutchins, Fataar, Hough, & Noakes, 1990) together with reduced vitamin D status (Ruohola et al., 2006) have been associated with decreased bone density and increased risk for stress fractures, particularly in amenorrhoeic athletes (Wolman, Clark, McNally, Harries, & Reeve, 1992).

Aside from this classic function, vitamin D also regulates the expression of over 1000 genes in a variety of tissues (Cannell, Hollis, Sorenson, Taft, & Anderson, 2009). Furthermore, vitamin D has been shown to be an important regulator of inflammation and immunity, partially via up-regulation of immune proteins and anti-inflammatory cytokines and down-regulation of inflammatory cytokines (Larson-Meyer & Willis, 2010). In skeletal muscle, vitamin D has been reported to play an important role in calcium handling, protein synthesis, and muscle cell proliferation/growth (Ceglia, 2009; Hamilton, 2010).

Recent reviews conclude that vitamin D deficiency is at epidemic levels for all age groups worldwide (Holick, 2004; Willis, Peterson, & Larson-Meyer, 2008; Zittermann, 2003). Importantly, vitamin D deficiency has been linked to numerous disorders including osteoporosis, several types of cancer, hypertension, and autoimmune diseases (Cannell, Hollis, Zasloff, & Heaney, 2008; Holick, 2004; Larson-Meyer & Willis, 2010; Zittermann, 2003) and increased risk of stress fracture (Ruohola et al., 2006) and season illness (Halliday et al., 2011).

Sources of vitamin D and calcium

The newly revised recommended dietary allowance (RDA) for vitamin D in adults is 600 IU (Ross, Taylor, Yaktine, & Del Valle, 2010). Several minutes (5–30) of direct sun exposure several times a week between 10.00 and 14.00 h on the arms and legs during spring, summer, and fall is often adequate to prevent vitamin D deficiency in young adults (Holick, 2007). In fact, vitamin D produced from skin exposure is the predominant source of circulating vitamin D in humans (Cannell et al., 2008). However, vitamin D can also be supplied via the diet from limited natural sources, including fatty fish, egg yolks, and sun-dried mushrooms. Although some countries, including the USA and Canada, add vitamin D to milk, margarine, ready-to-eat cereals, and other selected products, the modern diet in most of the world lacks sufficient vitamin D. This suggests that when sun exposure is limited, vitamin D status is likely to be compromised.

In contrast to vitamin D, the RDA for calcium (i.e. 1000 mg for adults aged 19–50 years, 1200 mg for adults older than 50 years, and 1300 mg for children younger than 18 years) can easily be obtained from the diet. Athletes can meet calcium requirements by including several servings of dairy products or 8–10 servings of calcium-containing plant foods daily (Messina, Melina, & Mangels, 2003). Non-dairy foods that are rich in well-absorbable calcium include sardines, low-oxalate green leafy vegetables (broccoli, kale, Chinese cabbage and collard, mustard, and turnip greens), calcium-set tofu, fortified soy and rice milks, textured vegetable protein, tahini, certain legumes, fortified orange juice, and blackstrap molasses (Messina et al., 2003). Laboratory studies have determined that the calcium bioavailability of most of these foods is comparable to cow's milk, which has a fractional absorption of about 32% (Weaver, Proulx, & Heaney, 1999; Zhao, Martin, & Weaver, 2005). The exceptions include soymilk fortified with tricalcium phosphate, most legumes, nuts, and seeds, which have a fractional absorption in the range of 17–24% (Zhao et al., 2005). Foods such as spinach, Swiss chard, beet greens, and rhubarb are not well-absorbed sources of calcium due to their high oxalate or phytate content. Athletes not meeting their calcium intake may consider calcium plus vitamin D supplementation as a short-term option but should work towards consumption of calcium-rich foods daily.

Assessment of vitamin D status

Clinically, the inactive form of circulating vitamin D, 25(OH)D, is used as a measure of vitamin D status. The definition of the optimum serum concentration of vitamin D, however, remains controversial. Nonetheless, most experts agree that a serum 25(OH)D concentration below 50 nmol $\cdot$ L^{-1} (20 ng $\cdot$ mL^{-1}) indicates deficiency, while a concentration below 80 nmol $\cdot$ L^{-1} (32 ng $\cdot$ mL^{-1}) should be considered insufficient (Larson-Meyer & Willis, 2010; Willis et al., 2008). While 25(OH)D concentrations between 100–250 nmol $\cdot$ L^{-1} (40-100 ng $\cdot$ mL^{-1}) are considered optimal (Cannell & Hollis, 2008; Hollis, 2005), there is little scientific evidence to support what is deemed as optimal (Larson-Meyer & Willis, 2010). In fact, the new US RDA for vitamin D was based only on bone health with the assumption that 25(OH)D concentrations > 50 nmol $\cdot$ L^{-1} are adequate (Ross et al., 2010). However, the newly revised RDA of 600 IU is below the 800–2200 IU recommended by researchers (Cannell & Hollis, 2008; Heaney, 2005; Holick, 2007) to optimize overall health and maintain serum 25(OH)D concentrations in the sufficient to optimal range. Overall, the lack of scientific agreement regarding the serum concentrations of vitamin D that are deemed optimal for health and physical performance remains an impediment for sports nutritionists.

Due to vitamin D's classic role in calcium homeostasis and its impact on skeletal muscle, several important questions regarding vitamin D status in athletes have emerged. For example, how many athletes are low in vitamin D? Do athletes need to supplement with vitamin D and can vitamin D supplementation improve performance? In the following sections we provide arguments both for and against vitamin D supplementation in athletes.

Arguments to support vitamin D supplementation

Two major arguments exist to support vitamin D supplementation in athletes. First, accumulating evidence suggests that athletes may be as much at risk for vitamin D deficiency as is the general population. Second, emerging evidence suggests that supplementation with vitamin D may improve health and athletic performance. A summary of these two suppositions follows.

Contrary to the large number of studies regarding vitamin D deficiency in the general population, limited studies have investigated vitamin D status in athletic populations. Nonetheless, a growing number of studies suggest that many athletes are at risk for vitamin D deficiency (Table I). In general, the athletes at greatest risk for vitamin D insufficiency and deficiency are those participating in indoor sports, those residing at higher latitudes (with less opportunity for sun exposure all year round), and those with dark-pigmented skin. For example, a study of Israeli athletes reported that ~94% of basketball players and dancers suffered from vitamin D insufficiency (defined as 25(OH)D < 75 nmol $\cdot$ L^{-1}) (Constantini et al., 2010). In the same study, 48% of outdoor athletes were vitamin D insufficient. Similarly, a study investigating serum 25(OH)D concentrations in Australian elite female gymnasts reported that ~33% of the athletes were vitamin D insufficient (25(OH)D < 50 nmol $\cdot$ L^{-1}) (Lovell, 2008). In another study of East German female gymnasts, 37% of the athletes were found to be vitamin D deficient (25(OH)D < 25 nmol $\cdot$ L^{-1}) (Bannert, Starke, Mohnike, & Frohner, 1991).

Evidence also exists that some outdoor athletes may be at risk for vitamin D deficiency. For example,

Table I. Examples of investigations indicating that many athletic populations suffer from insufficient blood concentrations of vitamin D as indicated by serum concentrations of 25(OH)D.

Study		Prevalence of low serum 25(OH)D
Constantini et al. (2010)		80% of indoor athletes[a] <75 nmol $\cdot$ L^{-1}
		48% of outdoor athletes[b] <75 nmol $\cdot$ L^{-1}
Hamilton et al. (2010)		91% of athletes[c] <50 nmol $\cdot$ L^{-1}
Lovell (2008)		33% of athletes[d] <50 nmol $\cdot$ L^{-1}
Bannert et al. (1991)		37% of athletes[e] <25 nmol $\cdot$ L^{-1}
Halliday et al. (2011)	Fall	9.8% of athletes[f] >50 nmol $\cdot$ L^{-1} but <80 nmol $\cdot$ L^{-1}
		2.4% of athletes[f] <50 nmol $\cdot$ L^{-1}
	Winter	60.6% of athletes[e] >50 nmol $\cdot$ L^{-1} <80 nmol $\cdot$ L^{-1}
		3% of athletes[f] <50 nmol $\cdot$ L^{-1}
	Spring	16% of athletes[f] >50 nmol $\cdot$ L^{-1} <80 nmol $\cdot$ L^{-1}
		4% of athletes[f] <20 nmol $\cdot$ L^{-1}
Lehtonen-Veromaa et al. (1999)	Winter	67.7% of athletes[g] <37.5 nmol $\cdot$ L^{-1}
	Summer	1.6% of athletes[g] <37.5 nmol $\cdot$ L^{-1}

[a]Males and females aged 10–30 years, Israel; dancing, basketball, swimming, Tae Kwon Do, judo, gymnastics, table tennis.
[b]Males and females aged 10–30 years, Israel; tennis, soccer, running, triathlon, sailing.
[c]Males aged 13–45 years, Qatar; professional-junior level sports in soccer, soccer referees, track and field, handball, shooting, squash, cycling, martial arts, body building.
[d]Females aged 10–17 years, Australia; elite gymnasts.
[e]Male and females aged 8–27 years, East Germany; competitive gymnasts.
[f]Males and females ≥18 years, USA; collegiate level football, soccer, cross-country/track AND field, cheerleading/dance, wrestling, swimming, basketball.
[g]Females aged 9–15 years, Finland; runners, dancers, non-athletes.

a study of young Finnish runners reported that $\sim68\%$ were vitamin D deficient during the winter; however, by the end of summer blood concentrations of vitamin D increased to sufficient concentrations (Lehtonen-Veromaa et al., 1999). Another example of a seasonal variation in vitamin D concentration of athletes residing at higher latitudes has been reported in the USA. Similar to the Finnish study, most athletes evaluated did not exhibit insufficient serum 25(OH)D concentrations during early fall and spring months but blood 25(OH)D concentrations were markedly lower and insufficient in the winter months (Halliday et al., 2011). Finally, a recent study performed in Qatar reported that $\sim91\%$ of the athletes evaluated were 25(OH)D deficient (<50 nmol $\cdot$ L^{-1}) (Hamilton, Grantham, Racinais, & Chalabi, 2010). These findings are somewhat surprising given that Qatar is a relatively sunny location (latitude $\sim25°30'$N). The authors report, however, that the majority of outdoor training was completed after sunset because of the environmental heat and social factors in Qatar. The results indicate that simply living in a sunny environment does not ensure adequate vitamin D synthesis. Indeed, clothing, regular sunscreen use, skin pigmentation, ageing, time of day of training, season, cloud cover, and latitude can dampen the effect of sun on vitamin D production by compromising the quantity of UV-B radiation absorbed by the skin.

The second major argument used to support vitamin D supplementation in athletes is that vitamin D supplementation may improve athletic perfor-

mance (in those who are deficient). The belief that vitamin D (or UV-B exposure) can positively impact athletic performance has an extensive history. For example, long before reports were published detailing the prevalence of low vitamin D among athletes, it was believed the exposure to UV-B radiation was ergogenic. In the late 1920s, German swimmers were irradiated with UV radiation from a sunlamp prior to athletic competition (Cannell, 2009). By the 1960s, the literature contained numerous reports that UV-B radiation could improve athletic performance (Cannell, 2009). Coinciding with these observations, a report suggested that distance running performance is improved during summer compared with winter months (Hiruta, Ishida, & Miyamura, 1990; Kristal-Boneh, Froom, Harari, Malik, & Ribak, 2000; Svedenhag & Sjodin, 1985). Together, these observations have led to speculation that vitamin D supplementation improves athletic performance.

Although the aforementioned studies have provided fuel for the concept that low vitamin D concentrations may impair athletic performance, the literature contains limited experimental studies that demonstrate a positive benefit of vitamin D supplementation on athletic performance in athletes. Nonetheless, two recent studies evaluated the relationship between muscle strength and or power in British and Chinese adolescent girls (Foo et al., 2009; Ward et al., 2009), who were mostly vitamin D deficient. These studies found a significant positive correlation between serum 25(OH)D concentrations and jumping height and velocity, muscle force, muscle power, (Ward et al., 2009), and hand grip strength (Foo et al., 2009). Another study indirectly linked to long-term performance benefits found that 8 weeks of supplementation with 800 IU of vitamin D plus 2000 mg calcium in female Navy recruits reduced the incidence of stress fracture (Lappe et al., 2008). Taken together, these studies are consistent with the concept that athletes deficient in vitamin D could benefit from vitamin D supplementation.

Arguments against vitamin D supplementation

Arguments against vitamin D supplementation in athletes are focused on two issues: (1) lack of scientific evidence to support that vitamin D is ergogenic; and (2) risk of vitamin D toxicity. In regard to the strength of the scientific evidence to support the case that vitamin D supplementation improves athletic performance, the lack of well-designed supplementation trials in athletes means that a clear answer is not available.

In reference to the concern over vitamin D toxicity, it should be recognized that vitamin D is a fat-soluble vitamin and that excessive intake by over-zealous athletes who feel "more is better" could result in toxicity (defined as a serum 25(OH)D concentration > 375 nmol $\cdot$ L^{-1} in the presence of hypercalcaemia). Vitamin D toxicity can result in nausea, vomiting, poor appetite, constipation, weakness, and weight loss (Chesney, 1989), as well as lead to mental confusion, cardiac rhythm irregularities (Favus & Christakos, 1996), and calcification of soft tissues. However, it is important to mention that intoxication from excess supplementation is extremely rare, and that most of the reported toxicity cases were due to inadvertent ingestion of excessively high supplemental doses many of which were due to manufacturer error (Klontz & Acheson, 2007). Doses of 10,000 IU $\cdot$ day^{-1} for up to 5 months have not been shown to cause toxicity (Vieth, 2004). According to the new "tolerable upper limit" for Vitamin D, daily doses of vitamin D up to 4000 IU $\cdot$ day^{-1} have been established as safe in almost all populations (Ross et al., 2010), but less is known concerning habitual supplementation > 4000 IU $\cdot$ day^{-1}.

An important final point – worthy of further research – is that there may be significant individual differences in the response of vitamin D supplementation to the rise in 25(OH)D concentrations. Provocative evidence suggests that these differences are related to common genetic variants in vitamin D binding protein (VDBP). This prtoein binds to vitamin D and its metabolites and carries them to target tissues (Foo et al., 2009). This is potentially important to athletes because it is not known how VDBP variants influence toxicity or performance responses to supplementation.

Summary and conclusions: Vitamin D supplementation in athletes

The question of whether vitamin D supplementation should be recommended for athletes remains controversial. There are proponents for and against vitamin D supplementation and additional research is essential to establish whether vitamin D supplementation is beneficial to athletes. Currently, there is little scientific evidence that vitamin D supplementation improves performance in athletes that are not vitamin D deficient. Nonetheless, based upon the evidence that many athletic populations are vitamin D deficient or insufficient, it is recommended that athletes monitor their serum vitamin D concentration and consult with their health care professional and/or nutritionist to determine if they would derive health benefits from vitamin D supplementation. On the other hand, all athletes should strive to consume the RDA for calcium.

References

Bannert, N., Starke, I., Mohnike, K., & Frohner, G. (1991). Parameters of mineral metabolism in children and adolescents in athletic training. *Kinderarztliche Praxis, 59* (5), 153–156.

Bartoszewska, M., Kamboj, M., & Patel, D. R. (2010). Vitamin D, muscle function, and exercise performance. *Pediatric Clinics of North America, 57*, 849–861.

Bjelakovic, G., Nikolova, D., Gluud, L. L., Simonetti, R. G., & Gluud, C. (2007). Mortality in randomized trials of antioxidant supplements for primary and secondary prevention: Systematic review and meta-analysis. *Journal of the American Medical Association, 297*, 842–857.

Cannell, J. (2009). More vitamin D questions and answers. *Vitamin D Council Newsletter.* Retrieved 21 February, 2009, from http://www.vitamindcouncil.org

Cannell, J. J., & Hollis, B. W. (2008). Use of vitamin D in clinical practice. *Alternative Medicine Review, 13* (1), 6–20.

Cannell, J. J., Hollis, B. W., Sorenson, M. B., Taft, T. N., & Anderson, J. J. (2009). Athletic performance and vitamin D. *Medicine and Science in Sports and Exercise, 41*, 1102–1110.

Cannell, J. J., Hollis, B. W., Zasloff, M., & Heaney, R. P. (2008). Diagnosis and treatment of vitamin D deficiency. *Expert Opinion on Pharmacotherapy, 9*, 107–118.

Ceglia, L. (2009). Vitamin D and its role in skeletal muscle. *Current Opinion in Clinical Nutrition and Metabolic Care, 12*, 628–633.

Chesney, R. W. (1989). Vitamin D: Can an upper limit be defined? *Journal of Nutrition, 119* (suppl.), 1825–1828.

Constantini, N. W., Arieli, R., Chodick, G., & Dubnov-Raz, G. (2010). High prevalence of vitamin D insufficiency in athletes and dancers. *Clinical Journal of Sport Medicine, 20*, 368–371.

Coombes, J. S., Powers, S. K., Rowell, B., Hamilton, K. L., Dodd, S. L., Shanely, R. A. et al. (2001). Effects of vitamin E and alpha-lipoic acid on skeletal muscle contractile properties. *Journal of Applied Physiology, 90*, 1424–1430.

Criswell, D., Powers, S., Dodd, S., Lawler, J., Edwards, W., Renshler, K. et al. (1993). High intensity training-induced changes in skeletal muscle antioxidant enzyme activity. *Medicine and Science in Sports and Exercise, 25*, 1135–1140.

Favus, M. J., & Christakos, S. (1996). *Primer on the metbolic bone diseases and disorders of mineral metabolism* (3rd edn.). Philadelphia, PA: Lippincott-Raven.

Foo, L. H., Zhang, Q., Zhu, K., Ma, G., Trube, A., Greenfield, H. et al. (2009). Relationship between vitamin D status, body composition and physical exercise of adolescent girls in Beijing. *Osteoporosis International, 20*, 417–425.

Gomez-Cabrera, M. C., Domenech, E., Romagnoli, M., Arduini, A., Borras, C., Pallardo, F. V. et al. (2008). Oral administration of vitamin C decreases muscle mitochondrial biogenesis and hampers training-induced adaptations in endurance performance. *American Journal of Clinical Nutrition, 87*, 142–149.

Halliday, T., Peterson, N., Thomas, J., Kleppinger, K., Hollis, B., & Larson-Meyer, D. (2011). Vitamin D status relative to diet, lifestyle, injury and illness in college athletes. *Medicine and Science in Sports and Exercise, 43*, 335–343.

Halliwell, B., & Gutteridge, J. (2007). *Free radicals in biology and medicine* (4th edn.). Oxford: Oxford University Press.

Hamilton, B. (2010). Vitamin D and human skeletal muscle. *Scandinavian Journal of Medicine and Science in Sports, 20*, 182–190.

Hamilton, B., Grantham, J., Racinais, S., & Chalabi, H. (2010). Vitamin D deficiency is endemic in Middle Eastern sportsmen. *Public Health Nutrition, 13*, 1528–1534.

Hamilton, K. L., Staib, J. L., Phillips, T., Hess, A., Lennon, S. L., & Powers, S. K. (2003). Exercise, antioxidants, and HSP72: Protection against myocardial ischemia/reperfusion. *Free Radical Biology and Medicine, 34*, 800–809.

Heaney, R. P. (2005). The vitamin D requirement in health and disease. *Journal of Steroid Biochemistry and Molecular Biology, 97*, 13–19.

Heaney, R. P., Dowell, M. S., Hale, C. A., & Bendich, A. (2003). Calcium absorption varies within the reference range for serum 25-hydroxyvitamin D. *Journal of the American College of Nutrition, 22*, 142–146.

Hiruta, S., Ishida, K., & Miyamura, M. (1990). Seasonal variations of ventilatory response to hypercapnia at rest. *Japanese Journal of Physiology, 40*, 753–757.

Holick, M. F. (2004). Sunlight and vitamin D for bone health and prevention of autoimmune diseases, cancers, and cardiovascular disease. *American Journal of Clinical Nutrition, 80* (suppl.), 1678S–1688S.

Holick, M. F. (2007). Vitamin D deficiency. *New England Journal of Medicine, 357*, 266–281.

Hollis, B. W. (2005). Circulating 25-hydroxyvitamin D levels indicative of vitamin D sufficiency: Implications for establishing a new effective dietary intake recommendation for vitamin D. *Journal of Nutrition, 135*, 317–322.

Huang, S. H., Johnson, K., & Pipe, A. L. (2006). The use of dietary supplements and medications by Canadian athletes at the Atlanta and Sydney Olympic Games. *Clinical Journal of Sport Medicine, 16*, 27–33.

Kelly, M. K., Wicker, R. J., Barstow, T. J., & Harms, C. A. (2009). Effects of *N*-acetylcysteine on respiratory muscle fatigue during heavy exercise. *Respiratory Physiology and Neurobiology, 165*, 67–72.

Klontz, K. C., & Acheson, D. W. (2007). Dietary supplement-induced vitamin D intoxication. *New England Journal of Medicine, 357*, 308–309.

Kristal-Boneh, E., Froom, P., Harari, G., Malik, M., & Ribak, J. (2000). Summer–winter differences in 24 h variability of heart rate. *Journal of Cardiovascular Risk, 7*, 141–146.

Lappe, J., Cullen, D., Haynatzki, G., Recker, R., Ahlf, R., & Thompson, K. (2008). Calcium and vitamin D supplementation decreases incidence of stress fractures in female navy recruits. *Journal of Bone and Mineral Research, 23*, 741–749.

Larson-Meyer, D. E., & Willis, K. S. (2010). Vitamin D and athletes. *Current Sports Medicine Reports, 9*, 220–226.

Lehtonen-Veromaa, M., Mottonen, T., Irjala, K., Karkkainen, M., Lamberg-Allardt, C., Hakola, P. et al. (1999). Vitamin D intake is low and hypovitaminosis D common in healthy 9- to 15-year-old Finnish girls. *European Journal of Clinical Nutrition, 53*, 746–751.

Lovell, G. (2008). Vitamin D status of females in an elite gymnastics program. *Clinical Journal of Sport Medicine, 18*, 159–161.

Machefer, G., Groussard, C., Zouhal, H., Vincent, S., Youssef, H., Faure, H. et al. (2007). Nutritional and plasmatic antioxidant vitamins status of ultra endurance athletes. *Journal of the American College of Nutrition, 26*, 311–316.

Matuszczak, Y., Farid, M., Jones, J., Lansdowne, S., Smith, M. A., Taylor, A. A. et al. (2005). Effects of *N*-acetylcysteine on glutathione oxidation and fatigue during handgrip exercise. *Muscle and Nerve, 32*, 633–638.

Maughan, R. J., Depiesse, F., & Geyer, H. (2007). The use of dietary supplements by athletes. *Journal of Sports Sciences, 25* (suppl. 1), S103–S113.

McClung, J. M., Deruisseau, K. C., Whidden, M. A., Van Remmen, H., Richardson, A., Song, W. et al. (2010). Over-expression of antioxidant enzymes in diaphragm muscle does not alter contraction-induced fatigue or recovery. *Experimental Physiology, 95*, 222–231.

McKenna, M. J., Medved, I., Goodman, C. A., Brown, M. J., Bjorksten, A. R., Murphy, K. T., et al. (2006). *N*-acetylcysteine attenuates the decline in muscle Na$^+$,K$^+$-pump activity and delays fatigue during prolonged exercise in humans. *Journal of Physiology, 576*, 279–288.

Medved, I., Brown, M. J., Bjorksten, A. R., Leppik, J. A., Sostaric, S., & McKenna, M. J. (2003). *N*-acetylcysteine infusion alters blood redox status but not time to fatigue during intense exercise in humans. *Journal of Applied Physiology, 94*, 1572–1582.

Medved, I., Brown, M. J., Bjorksten, A. R., & McKenna, M. J. (2004). Effects of intravenous *N*-acetylcysteine infusion on time to fatigue and potassium regulation during prolonged cycling exercise. *Journal of Applied Physiology, 96*, 211–217.

Messina, V., Melina, V., & Mangels, A. R. (2003). A new food guide for North American vegetarians. *Journal of the American Dietetic Association, 103*, 771–775.

Myburgh, K. H., Hutchins, J., Fataar, A. B., Hough, S. F., & Noakes, T. D. (1990). Low bone density is an etiologic factor for stress fractures in athletes. *Annals of Internal Medicine, 113*, 754–759.

Panda, D. K., Miao, D., Bolivar, I., Li, J., Huo, R., Hendy, G. N. et al. (2004). Inactivation of the 25-hydroxyvitamin D 1alpha-hydroxylase and vitamin D receptor demonstrates independent and interdependent effects of calcium and vitamin D on skeletal and mineral homeostasis. *Journal of Biological Chemistry, 279*, 16754–16766.

Powers, S. K., DeRuisseau, K. C., Quindry, J., & Hamilton, K. L. (2004). Dietary antioxidants and exercise. *Journal of Sports Sciences, 22*, 81–94.

Powers, S. K., & Jackson, M. J. (2008). Exercise-induced oxidative stress: Cellular mechanisms and impact on muscle force production. *Physiological Reviews, 88*, 1243–1276.

Powers, S., Nelson, W. B., & Hudson, M. B. (2010). Exercise-induced oxidative stress in humans: Cause and consequences. *Free Radical Biology and Medicine*. DOI:10.1016/j.freeradbiomed.2010.12.009

Rankinen, T., Lyytikainen, S., Vanninen, E., Penttila, I., Rauramaa, R., & Uusitupa, M. (1998). Nutritional status of the Finnish elite ski jumpers. *Medicine and Science in Sports and Exercise, 30*, 1592–1597.

Reid, M. B. (2008). Free radicals and muscle fatigue: Of ROS, canaries, and the IOC. *Free Radical Biology and Medicine, 44*, 169–179.

Reid, M. B., Stokic, D. S., Koch, S. M., Khawli, F. A., & Leis, A. A. (1994). N-acetylcysteine inhibits muscle fatigue in humans. *Journal of Clinical Investigation, 94*, 2468–2474.

Ristow, M., Zarse, K., Oberbach, A., Kloting, N., Birringer, M., Kiehntopf, M. et al. (2009). Antioxidants prevent health-promoting effects of physical exercise in humans. *Proceedings of the National Academy of Sciences of the United States of America, 106*, 8665–8670.

Ross, A. C., Taylor, C. L., Yaktine, A. L., & Del Valle, H. B. (2010). *Dietary reference intakes for calcium and vitamin D.* Washington, DC: National Academies Press.

Ruohola, J. P., Laaksi, I., Ylikomi, T., Haataja, R., Mattila, V. M., Sahi, T. et al. (2006). Association between serum 25(OH)D concentrations and bone stress fractures in Finnish young men. *Journal of Bone and Mineral Research, 21*, 1483–1488.

Schroder, H., Navarro, E., Mora, J., Galiano, D., & Tramullas, A. (2001). Effects of alpha-tocopherol, beta-carotene and ascorbic acid on oxidative, hormonal and enzymatic exercise stress markers in habitual training activity of professional basketball players. *European Journal of Nutrition, 40*, 178–184.

Schroder, H., Navarro, E., Tramullas, A., Mora, J., & Galiano, D. (2000). Nutrition antioxidant status and oxidative stress in professional basketball players: Effects of a three compound antioxidative supplement. *International Journal of Sports Medicine, 21*, 146–150.

Sen, C. K. (2001). Antioxidants in exercise nutrition. *Sports Medicine, 31*, 891–908.

Svedenhag, J., & Sjodin, B. (1985). Physiological characteristics of elite male runners in and off-season. *Canadian Journal of Applied Sport Sciences, 10*, 127–133.

Vieth, R. (2004). Why the optimal requirement for Vitamin D3 is probably much higher than what is officially recommended for adults. *Journal of Steroid Biochemistry and Molecular Biology, 89–90, 89–90*, 575–579.

Ward, K. A., Das, G., Berry, J. L., Roberts, S. A., Rawer, R., Adams, J. E. et al. (2009). Vitamin D status and muscle function in post-menarchal adolescent girls. *Journal of Clinical Endocrinology and Metabolism, 94*, 559–563.

Weaver, C. M., Proulx, W. R., & Heaney, R. (1999). Choices for achieving adequate dietary calcium with a vegetarian diet. *American Journal of Clinical Nutrition, 70* (suppl.), 543S–548S.

Willis, K. S., Peterson, N. J., & Larson-Meyer, D. E. (2008). Should we be concerned about the vitamin D status of athletes? *International Journal of Sport Nutrition and Exercise Metabolism, 18*, 204–224.

Wolman, R. L., Clark, P., McNally, E., Harries, M. G., & Reeve, J. (1992). Dietary calcium as a statistical determinant of spinal trabecular bone density in amenorrhoeic and oestrogen-replete athletes. *Bone and Mineral, 17*, 415–423.

Zhao, Y., Martin, B. R., & Weaver, C. M. (2005). Calcium bioavailability of calcium carbonate fortified soymilk is equivalent to cow's milk in young women. *Journal of Nutrition, 135*, 2379–2382.

Zittermann, A. (2003). Vitamin D in preventive medicine: Are we ignoring the evidence? *British Journal of Nutrition, 89*, 552–572.

Dietary supplements for athletes: Emerging trends and recurring themes

R. J. MAUGHAN[1], P. L. GREENHAFF[2], & P. HESPEL[3]

[1]School of Sport, Exercise and Health Sciences, Loughborough University, Loughborough, UK, [2]School of Biomedical Sciences, University of Nottingham Medical School, Nottingham, UK and [3]Faculty of Kinesiology and Rehabilitation Sciences, Katholieke Universiteit Leuven, Leuven, Belgium

Abstract

Dietary supplements are widely used at all levels of sport. Changes in patterns of supplement use are taking place against a background of changes in the regulatory framework that governs the manufacture and distribution of supplements in the major markets. Market regulation is complicated by the increasing popularity of Internet sales. The need for quality control of products to ensure they contain the listed ingredients in the stated amount and to ensure the absence of potentially harmful substances is recognized. This latter category includes compounds prohibited under anti-doping regulations. Several certification programmes now provide testing facilities for manufacturers of both raw ingredients and end products to ensure the absence of prohibited substances. Athletes should carry out a cost–benefit analysis for any supplement they propose to use. For most supplements, the evidence is weak, or even completely absent. A few supplements, including caffeine, creatine, and bicarbonate, are supported by a strong research base. Difficulties arise when new evidence appears to support novel supplements: in recent years, β-alanine has become popular, and the use of nitrate and arginine is growing. Athletes seldom wait until there is convincing evidence of efficacy or of safety, but caution is necessary to minimize risk.

Supplement use

Assessing the prevalence of dietary supplement use by athletes is complicated by the various definitions of what constitutes a supplement. For most purposes, sports drinks, energy bars, gels, and other sports foods are excluded from the definition of supplements, although the use of these products is widespread in sport. Dietary supplements are used by a large proportion of the general population, and the available evidence suggests that the rate of use is even higher among athletes (Huang, Johnson, & Pipe, 2006). The pattern of use varies between sports and with the level of competition. Tscholl and colleagues (Tscholl, Alonso, Dolle, Junge, & Dvorak, 2010) reported a rate of use of 1.7 supplement products per athlete, on the basis of analysis of almost 4000 doping control declarations from elite track and field athletes, but noted that the final ranking in the championships was unrelated to the quantity of reported supplements taken. A similar analysis at the 2002 and 2006 FIFA World Cups revealed a rate of use of 1.3 supplements per player per match in 2006 compared with 0.7 supplements per player per match in 2002 (Tscholl, Junge, & Dvorak, 2008). Even among recreational gym users, a large survey revealed that 37% used one or more dietary supplements (Goston & Correia, 2010).

Most athletes are aware that the use of some supplements can bring benefits that include improved adaptations to training that lead to performance enhancement, and the potential for preservation of good health (Maughan, Depiesse, & Geyer, 2007). Surveys show that athletes have many reasons for using supplements and some of those most commonly cited are listed in Table I. A recent study of 310 male and female athletes competing in the track and field World Championships showed that 83% of males and 89% of females were using one or more dietary supplements (F. Depiesse, unpublished data). The reasons these athletes gave for using supplements were:

- to aid recovery from training: 71%
- for health: 52%

Table I. Categories of dietary supplements commonly used by athletes.

- Promote tissue growth, repair, and adaptation to training
- Promote fat loss
- Enhance energy supply (including muscle buffering)
- Promote immune function and resistance to illness/infection
- Central nervous system stimulant effects
- Promote joint health
- Promote general health
- Sports drinks, energy bars, etc.

- to improve performance: 46%
- to prevent or treat an illness: 40%
- to compensate for a poor diet: 29%

These reasons raise some questions. Dietary supplement manufacturers are not permitted to claim that supplements can prevent or treat illness unless there is valid proof of such an effect, and this is invariably absent. If an athlete is concerned about a poor diet, it makes more sense to improve the quality of the diet than to try to compensate for this by the use of supplements.

It is less clear, however, that athletes fully understand the limitations to the claims made for many of the supplements that they use. They are also likely to be unaware of the negative consequences that may arise from the use of some supplements or from the inappropriate use of supplements that may be helpful in some circumstances, but detrimental to performance in others (Braun et al., 2009).

Supplement regulation

Although there are undoubted benefits for some consumers of dietary supplements, there is also the potential for some negative outcomes. Regulation of the dietary supplements market varies greatly between countries, and Internet sales often mean that athletes have access to supplements of uncertain origin. Inevitably, the United States represents the largest market and the Dietary Supplements Health and Education Act of 1994 (DSHEA) passed by the US Congress has meant that nutritional supplements that do not claim to diagnose, prevent or cure disease are not subject to regulation by the Food and Drugs Administration (FDA) in the same way as food ingredients are not subject to the stringent regulations that are applied to the pharmaceutical industry. From this it follows that there is not the same requirement to prove product purity and claimed benefits or to show safety with acute or chronic administration. The DSHEA included a legal definition of a "new dietary ingredient" and a requirement that a notification of intention to market a new ingredient be made to the FDA before its use in dietary supplements. However, the very many dietary ingredients on sale at the time of the Act were exempted under a "grandfather" clause, even though there was little or no evidence as to the efficacy and safety of many of these compounds. Furthermore, many supplements contain a complex mixture of various substances, the interaction of which is entirely unknown.

It is well recognized that there are problems with the quality of some of the dietary supplements on sale, but the options open to those responsible for food safety are limited by the legislation that applies. The FDA has used its powers to prevent the marketing of a number of new ingredients (McGuffin & Young, 2004) and to recall products where there is evidence of harm or where there are infringements of labelling or other standards. The FDA can also encourage companies selling products that are deemed unsafe or inappropriate to undertake voluntary recalls of such products. There have also been a number of cases where the FDA has issued public warnings over the safety of supplements or where these products have been withdrawn from sale because of links to adverse health effects: these include a widespread ban on the use of the herb kava in 2003 (Nutraingredients, 2003) and an FDA warning on hydroxycut products in May 2009 because of a number of serious adverse effects on liver function, including one death (FDA, 2009). In September 2010, the manufacturers announced a voluntary nationwide recall of "Off Cycle II Hardcore", a product containing 3,17-keto-etiocholtriene (an aromatase inhibitor), which was marketed as a dietary supplement (FDA, 2010). Although described by the manufacturers as a voluntary recall of the product, this was a direct response to notification by the FDA that this compound did not qualify as a new dietary ingredient.

It is not unusual to find cases of poor hygiene in the manufacture, storage, and provision of foodstuffs to the general public, so it should not be surprising that some dietary supplement manufacturers fail to follow good manufacturing practice. Some supplement products have been shown to contain impurities (lead, broken glass, animal faeces, etc.) because of poor quality control during manufacture or storage. The risk of gastrointestinal upset because of poor hygiene during the production and storage of products is a concern to athletes. At best, this may be nothing more than a minor inconvenience, but it may cause the athlete to miss a crucial competition. Recent reports have documented several cases of serious adverse effects on health resulting from the use of dietary supplements containing undeclared anabolic steroids, so it is clear that some products on the market remain unsafe (Krishnan, Feng, & Gordon, 2009).

Quality control

Where the content of active ingredients in a supplement is variable, this is likely to be due to poor quality control during the manufacturing process. There is also evidence, however, that some products do not to contain an effective dose of expensive ingredients listed on the label, and in some cases the active ingredient is entirely absent and the product contains only inexpensive materials. Even relatively inexpensive ingredients may be absent or present in only trivial amounts, as reported by Harris and colleagues (Harris, Almada, Harris, Dunnett, & Hespel, 2004) in the case of a creatine product. This has been interpreted by some as a cost-saving exercise by manufacturers. A rather sophisticated chemical analysis is required to identify the contents of a supplement, so there is no way for athletes to know what is in any of these products.

Cost–benefit analysis

Athletes who take supplements often have no clear understanding of the potential effects of the supplements they are using, but it is clear that supplements should be used only after a careful cost–benefit analysis has been conducted. On one side of the balance are the rewards, the most obvious of which is an improved performance in sport, and on the other side lie the costs and the risks. For several of the supplements used by athletes, there is good evidence of a benefit for some athletes in some specific circumstances (Maughan et al., 2007). In addition, athletes may respond very differently to a given supplement, with some exhibiting a beneficial effect while others experience a negative effect on performance. Hence supplements are often used in an inappropriate way, and athletes conceivably may benefit from professional advice by a qualified sports dietician before using any supplements. Such advice, however, is not readily available to all athletes.

Vitamin and mineral supplements are generally perceived as being harmless, and the one-a-day multivitamin tablet is seen as an insurance policy "just in case". Many herbal products are also used, even though there is little or no evidence to support their claimed benefits. The fact that most of these supplements enjoy only brief periods of popularity before disappearing from the marketplace suggests that any benefits perceived by athletes are not strong enough to warrant continued use or recommendation to friends and colleagues. Although these supplements are mostly benign, this is not always the case. Routine iron supplementation, for example, can do more harm than good, and the risk of iron toxicity is very real for some consumers (Papanikolaou & Pantopoulos, 2005). Mettler and Zimmermann (2010) assessed iron status in 170 recreational runners participating in the Zurich marathon, and found that functional iron deficiency was present in 5 (3.9%) and 11 (25.5%) male and female runners; however, iron overload was found in 19 of 127 (15.0%) men but only 2 of 43 women (4.7%).

Can a supplement cause a positive doping test?

The biggest concern for athletes who are liable to testing for the use of drugs that are prohibited in sport is the possibility that a supplement may contain something that will result in a positive doping test (Maughan, 2005). Recent evidence suggests that these concerns may apply to some foods as well as to supplements (Braun, Geyer, & Koehler, 2008). Only a very small number of individuals are tested for evidence of the use of doping agents, but these are invariably the most successful performers. For these athletes, a failed drugs test may mean the loss of medals won or records set, as well as temporary suspension from competition. It also leads to damage to the athlete's reputation and perhaps to permanent loss of employment and income. Where there has been deliberate cheating, such penalties seem entirely appropriate, but it is undoubtedly true that some failed doping tests can be attributed to the innocent ingestion of dietary supplements. The strict liability principle applied by the World Anti-Doping Agency (WADA) does not distinguish between deliberate cheating and inadvertent doping, so athletes must accept personal responsibility for all supplements (and medications) that they use.

Many published studies show that contamination of dietary supplements with prohibited substances is common (Maughan, 2005). A wide range of stimulants, steroids, and other agents that are included on WADA's prohibited list have been identified in otherwise innocuous supplements. These instances are quite distinct from the legitimate sale of some of these substances, as their presence is not declared on the product label; in some cases, these adulterated products are even labelled as being safe for use by athletes. In some but not all cases, the extraneous additions have actions that are linked to the intended use of the product. Thus anabolic agents have been found in supplements sold as muscle growth promoters, stimulants in herbal tonics, and anorectic agents in herbal weight loss supplements. These observations suggest that this is either a deliberate act to add active ingredients to otherwise ineffective products or that the managers have allowed some mixing of separate products at the manufacturing facility. This might occur in the preparation of the raw ingredients or in the formulation of the finished product. In some cases, the amount of supplement present may be high, even higher than the normal therapeutic dose. Geyer and colleagues (Geyer, Bredehoft, Marek, Parr, & Schanzer, 2002) purchased a "body building" supplement in England and upon analysis found it to contain methandieneone (commonly known as Dianabol) in an amount substantially higher than the therapeutic dose. This drug was present in high amounts, enough to have an anabolic effect, but also enough to produce serious side-effects, including liver toxicity and carcinogenicity. Unlike many of the earlier cases involving cases of steroids related to nandrolone and testosterone, these are not trivial levels of contamination, which raises the probability of deliberate adulteration of the product with the intention of producing a measurable effect on muscle strength and muscle mass. The prospect of adverse health effects at these high doses also raises real concerns.

Can you guarantee a supplement is safe?

In spite of these problems, it remains true that the majority of dietary supplements are safe and will not result in either health problems or violations of the doping code. It is equally true, however, that a problem remains in that a significant minority of the products on sale to athletes carry such risks. Many attempts are being made to address these problems, but there is not at present any way in which a particular product can be guaranteed to be free of any risks. This is in part due to the extremely small amounts of some substances that may cause a positive doping outcome. Ingestion of 19-norandrostenedione, a prohibited substance and precursor of nandrolone, will result in the appearance in the urine of 19-norandrosterone, the diagnostic metabolite. If the urinary concentration of 19-norandrosterone exceeds 2 ng · nl^{-1}, a doping offence is deemed to have occurred. The addition of as little as 2.5 μg of 19-norandrostenedione to a supplement can result in a urinary concentration of 19-norandrosterone in excess of this threshold in some, but not all, individuals (Watson, Judkins, Houghton, Russell, & Maughan, 2009). This effect is transient, and it can be seen from Figure 1 that even when a larger dose (10 μg) of steroid is administered, it is likely that only the first or second urine sample after ingestion will contain enough of the steroid metabolites to give a positive test: this means that an athlete who ingests this may or may not test positive, depending on when the sample is collected in relation to consumption of the supplement. The amount of steroid added is close to the limits of detection of the analytical methods currently applied to the analysis of dietary supplements, and there is no certainty that analysis of the finished product would have detected this.

The very small amounts of extraneous doping agents that have been reported to be present in many supplements – perhaps in as many as one in four of those selected for testing – will have no effect on physiological function, even though they may result in a positive doping test (Table II) (Geyer et al., 2004). In the absence of any physiological effect, there is no obvious reason for the deliberate addition of these compounds. It seems likely that their presence is due to accidental contamination at some stage of the manufacture, storage or distribution of

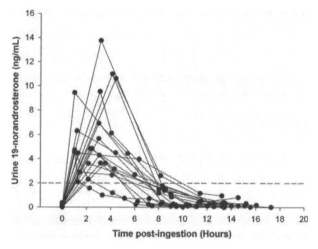

Figure 1. Individual values for urinary concentrations of 19-norandrosterone in 18 individuals after ingestion of a supplement to which 10 μg of 19-norandrostenedione had been added. Each point represents a separate urine sample. All participants produced at least one sample with a value above the WADA threshold for a doping test (2 ng · ml^{-1}). All values had returned below the WADA threshold within 10 h of ingestion of the steroid. Adapted from Watson et al. (2009).

Table II. Results of the analysis of dietary supplements for anabolic agents carried out for the International Olympic Committee by the Cologne Doping Laboratory (Geyer et al., 2004).

Country	No. tested	No. "positive"	Percent "positive"
Netherlands	31	8	25.8
Austria	22	5	22.7
UK	37	7	18.9
USA	240	45	18.8
Italy	35	5	14.3
Spain	29	4	13.8
Germany	129	15	11.6
Belgium	30	2	6.7
France	30	2	6.7
Norway	30	1	3.3
Switzerland	13	0	0
Sweden	6	0	0
Hungary	2	0	0
Total	634	94	14.8

Note: For each country where supplements were purchased, the table shows the number of samples tested, the number that contained prohibited steroids, and the fraction of the total this accounts for.

the raw ingredients or of the finished product. This may be due to cross-contamination of production lines where prohibited substances are processed alongside dietary supplements or due to poor quality control in the production of raw ingredients.

Various efforts are being made to address the problems and to minimize the risk of inadvertent doping by athletes by identifying products that athletes may use with confidence. There can be no absolute guarantee that any product is entirely safe, but such programmes do help the athlete to manage the risk. Because of the strict liability principle that applies in doping cases, inadvertent ingestion of a prohibited substance through use of a contaminated dietary supplement does not absolve the athlete of guilt. Athletes contemplating the use of dietary supplements should consider very carefully whether the potential benefits outweigh the risks of a doping offence that might bring an end to their career.

Supplements that may benefit some athletes

Of the many hundreds or even thousands of supplements on sale to athletes, only a few are supported by strong evidence for positive effects on health or performance and by evidence of absence of harm (Table III). The picture, however, continues to evolve as new evidence emerges, and many supplements experience short periods of popularity before falling out of favour. The scientific evidence often appears to have little impact on sales, thus by implication there is little incentive for those selling supplements to support scientific evaluation of their products. Several reports, for example, have indicated that glucosamine and chondroitin have little or no positive effect on joint pain in arthritis (Sawitzke, Shi, & Finco, 2008; Wandel et al., 2010), yet sales continue to be strong.

For a few supplements, there is good evidence from several well-controlled laboratory studies and also positive responses from athletes. It is clearly impossible to provide an overview of the many hundreds of different supplements used by athletes, and we will focus on only two to highlight some of the issues involved: the use of creatine supplements, where the evidence base is strong, both from a physiological and a performance perspective, and where there is a relatively long history of use, and the use of nitrate and L-arginine, which is novel and where the evidence base is small but convincing.

Creatine supplements: Benefits and risks

Creatine monohydrate is one of the most popular dietary supplements among strength and power athletes and is also widely used in team sports. Although there are reports of sporadic use by athletes over many years, it has become popular only since about 1992. Creatine is a natural guanidine compound and is a normal component of the diet, occurring in relatively high amounts ($3–7$ g $\cdot$ kg^{-1}) in skeletal muscle, so that meat and fish are the major dietary sources (Walker, 1979). Some of the body's creatine content is hydrolysed to creatinine at a fairly constant rate and about 2 g is lost in the urine each day. This can be replaced from dietary sources or by

Table III. Nutritional supplements with good evidence for improvements in exercise performance.

Supplement	Ergogenic effects	Underlying physiological effects
Alkalinizing agents (sodium bicarbonate) (sodium citrate)	Improves anaerobic endurance performance	Increases pre-exercise pH Increases extracellular buffer capacity
L-Arginine	Improves aerobic endurance exercise performance	Increases plasma nitrite concentration Reduces oxygen consumption during submaximal exercise
Beta-alanine	Improves aerobic and anaerobic endurance performance	Increases muscle carnosine content Improves intra-myocellular buffer capacity
Caffeine	Improves endurance exercise performance Improves reaction time	Reduces perception of fatigue Increases central drive by central adenosine receptor inhibition
Creatine	Improves performance in strength and power events Improves intermittent sprint performance Stimulates the effects of resistance training	Increases muscle free creatine and phosphorylcreatine content Stimulates muscle phosphorylcreatine resynthesis Facilitates muscle relaxation Stimulates muscle anabolism
Nitrate	Improves aerobic endurance exercise performance	Increases plasma nitrite concentration Reduces oxygen consumption during submaximal exercise Reduces the ATP cost of muscle force production Inhibits the fall in muscle phosphorylcreatine content during contractions

Note: The effects of water, electrolytes, carbohydrates, and protein/amino acid intake in exercise performance and training are addressed in other papers in this issue. Note that the number of published studies on the effects of L-arginine and nitrate is small, but the data seem convincing.

synthesis from amino acid precursors. A variety of synthetic creatine supplements have been developed, including creatine malate, creatine pyruvate, creatine citrate, creatine-magnesium chelate, creatine ethyl ester, and many more. Marketing claims for these compounds include better solubility and stability in solution, improved absorption and bioavailability, increased muscle uptake, and greater performance enhancement compared with creatine monohydrate. Where these alternatives have been investigated, however, no benefit has been reported (Spillane et al., 2009; Van Schuylenbergh, Van Leemputte, & Hespel, 2003).

About two-thirds of the total muscle creatine content is in the form of creatine phosphate, or phosphorylcreatine, with the remainder present in equilibrium amounts as free creatine. The muscle phosphorylcreatine content is relatively high and is usually seen as a store of high-energy phosphates that serves to prevent large decreases in the cellular ATP, and corresponding increases in ADP when energy demand is high. The phosphorylcreatine–creatine system also has an important role in acid–base balance during high-intensity exercise, as absorption of a proton during the creatine kinase reaction promotes activation of key enzymes in glycogenolysis (glycogen phosphorylase and phosphofructokinase) and buffers the hydrogen ions produced in glycolysis, thus delaying the development of intracellular acidosis.

There is now a very substantial body of evidence to support the view that supplementation of the diet with creatine monohydrate can increase the skeletal muscle creatine content (Harris, Soderlund, & Hultman, 1992), and improve performance and recovery during a variety of different exercise models (Bemben & Lamont, 2005). A classical creatine loading regimen consists of an initial loading phase of 15–20 g per day for 4–7 days followed by a maintenance dose of 2–5 g per day (Terjung et al., 2000). This contrasts with the typical daily intake from the diet for non-vegetarians of about 1 g per day, although some strength athletes who are focused on a high protein intake and achieve that by a high intake of animal protein sources may achieve high intakes from the diet. However, there are some data to indicate that the effects of creatine supplementation may fade during supplementation beyond 2 months (Derave, Eijnde, & Hespel, 2003). It is now known that insulin can stimulate short-term muscle creatine accumulation in humans above that seen with creatine alone (Steenge, Lambourne, Casey, MacDonald, & Greenhaff, 1998). Insulin infusion is clearly impractical, but combining 5 g of creatine with 95 g of simple carbohydrates has been shown to increase muscle creatine content to a greater extent than is seen with creatine alone (Green, Hultman,

MacDonald, Sewell, & Greenhaff, 1996). Similar effects are seen when creatine is combined with mixtures of carbohydrate and protein or amino acids (Pittas, Hazell, Simpson, & Greenhaff, 2010). Practically this indicates that creatine ingestion in conjunction with a meal containing carbohydrates and protein is more effective than ingestion on an empty stomach. Furthermore, exercise *per se* also promotes muscle creatine uptake during supplementation (Robinson, Sewell, Hultman, & Greenhaff, 1999).

Many different types of exercise performance have been studied, including strength, power, single and repeated sprints, and endurance, with exercise modes that include cycling, running, and swimming. It is well established that creatine supplementation can enhance power output during short maximal sprints (Terjung et al., 2000), and the effect may be even more evident when repeated sprints are preformed with short recovery periods (Casey, Constantin-Teodosiu, Howell, Hultman, & Greenhaff, 1996; Greenhaff, Casey, Short, Harris, & Söderlund, 1993; Hespel et al., 2001; Vandenberghe et al., 1996, 1997; Van Leemputte, Vandenberghe, & Hespel, 1999). This effect is also observed in multiple-sprint endurance exercise events such as football and other team sports (Cox, Mujika, Tumilty, & Burke, 2002). Furthermore, several studies have shown that creatine supplementation can potentiate the gains in fat-free mass and muscle force and power output that accompany resistance training (Hespel et al., 2001; Kreider et al., 1998; Maganaris & Maughan, 1998; Vandenberghe et al., 1997; Volek et al., 1999). There is also some evidence that creatine supplementation can facilitate recovery of muscle volume and functional capacity following muscle atrophy induced by leg immobilization (Hespel et al., 2001). Given the high incidence of musculoskeletal injury and consequent muscle disuse atrophy in athletes, creatine supplementation may be a worthwhile option to enhance post-injury rehabilitation and thereby speed return to training and competition. The mechanism of actions for these effects on muscle mass is not entirely clear (Louis et al., 2003a, 2003b; Louis, Van Beneden, Dehoux, Thissen, & Francaux, 2004). The increased training load that can be sustained with creatine supplementation, however, may be responsible at least in part for improved muscle mass and function (Kreider, 2003).

Creatine has also been shown to have effects on muscle glycogen storage. This may be important because although creatine supplementation appears to have no effect on endurance performance, muscle glycogen availability is a principal determinant of endurance exercise performance, and its depletion corresponds with the development of muscle fatigue

(Bergström, Hermansen, Hultman, & Saltin, 1967). A short period of "carbohydrate loading" can supercompensate muscle glycogen stores by over 100% within 48–72 h (Bergström & Hultman, 1966). As a result, substantial improvements in subsequent endurance exercise performance ("time to fatigue") of about 50% can be expected (Bergström et al., 1967). Supplementation with creatine in combination with a high-carbohydrate diet can augment post-exercise muscle glycogen storage during a conventional "carbohydrate loading" regimen in humans, and is of a magnitude that could be expected to produce a significant improvement in endurance exercise performance (~ 150 mmol $\cdot$ kg^{-1} dry muscle; Robinson et al., 1999). However, it should be emphasized that there is no evidence that such a performance benefit will result from the addition of creatine to high-carbohydrate meals to acutely increase muscle glycogen content. In addition, the probable gain in body weight due to such a creatine plus carbohydrate loading regimen may be detrimental to performance in many endurance competitions.

The safety of creatine supplementation is frequently questioned, but those studies that have been conducted do not confirm any cause for concern. The increase in body mass that often accompanies creatine supplementation may be desirable for many athletes, but may be problematic for those in weight-category or weight-sensitive sports. According to a report from the French Agency for Food Safety (AFFSA, 2001), about one-third of the published studies show no significant variations in weight; the other two-thirds show increases of 0.8–2.9%, at the most, in body weight, achieved in the first few days, with no subsequent alteration. The news media contain frequent anecdotal reports of muscle cramps, and occasionally more severe dysfunction, that are ascribed to creatine supplementation, but these are usually found on later investigation to be without substance. There are also warnings of the dangers of renal and hepatic failure as a result of high-dose creatine supplementation, but those long-term studies that have been carried out do not confirm these concerns (Kreider et al., 2003). It is widely accepted that it would be wise for those with established renal disease or those at risk for renal dysfunction (diabetes, hypertension, impaired glomerular filtration rate) to avoid creatine supplementation.

The French Agency for Food Safety (AFFSA, 2001) issued an opinion on the use of creatine supplements that included a warning of the risk of mutagenic and carcinogenic effects. This report attracted much attention, but the dangers have not been supported by any subsequent research. There is potential for the presence of two compounds, dicyandiamide and dihydrotriazine, that may occur

as by-products during the chemical synthesis from sarcosine and cyanamide. Both of these may be harmful to health, but in 2004 the European Food Safety Authority (EFSA) published an opinion on the use of creatine monohydrate as a food supplement and identified it as being safe within the dosage limits described here. It should be acknowledged that the safety and the regulatory status of the many different creatine derivatives that are currently on sale to athletes are unknown at the present time.

Dietary nitrate

Depending on the sports discipline, about 5–30% of the energy turnover during exercise is used to do useful work, with the remainder appearing directly as heat. Thus, even a small increase in the efficiency of muscle contraction may be of major significance for exercise performance. Increasing the efficiency of muscle contraction would allow a greater work output for the same oxygen cost. Athletes may experience a small increase in efficiency – as measured by a reduction in the oxygen cost of a standardized exercise task – in response to prolonged intensive training. Ingestion of large doses of nitrate (NO_3^-, about 0.1 mmol of sodium nitrate per kilogram of body mass, or 300–400 mg per day), either in the form of pure sodium nitrate (Larsen, Ekblom, Sahlin, Lundberg, & Weitzberg, 2007; Larsen, Weitzberg, Lundberg, & Ekblom, 2010; Vanhatalo et al., 2010) or beetroot juice (Bailey et al., 2009; Bailey et al., 2010a) in young healthy individuals rapidly increases plasma nitrite (NO_2^-) concentration about 2–3 fold, and this elevated nitrite concentration can be maintained for at least 2 weeks (Vanhatalo et al., 2010). Increased plasma nitrite stimulates the production of nitric oxide (NO). Nitric oxide is an important physiological signalling molecule that is implicated in, among other things, regulation of muscle blood flow and mitochondrial respiration. There is some interesting recent information to demonstrate that either acute or short-term ingestion of nitrate allows the same power output to be achieved with a lower rate of oxygen consumption. Thus, Larsen et al. (2007) found a significant reduction in the oxygen cost of submaximal cycling exercise, corresponding to an increase in mechanical efficiency, from $19.7 \pm 1.6\%$ to $21.1 \pm 1.3\%$, due to oral intake of sodium nitrate. Recent evidence from the same laboratory has identified a mechanism for this effect by showing that nitrate supplementation reduced the expression of ATP/ADP translocase, a protein involved in proton conductance within the mitochondria (Larsen et al., 2011). This resulted in a better oxidative phosphorylation efficiency (P/O ratio) in isolated mitochondria. They also showed that the improved mitochondrial P/O ratio correlated to the reduction in oxygen cost during exercise.

These effects on the mitochondria have implications for exercise performance, and dietary nitrate supplementation reduces maximal oxygen consumption while maintaining power output in maximal exercise (Larsen et al., 2010). Meanwhile, investigators in another laboratory reported the same effects could be achieved with dietary sources of nitrate. Volunteers were fed a placebo or 500 ml of beetroot juice (beetroot, spinach, and a few other vegetables have a high nitrate content) per day for 6 days, the beetroot juice providing 5.5 mmol of nitrate per day (Bailey et al., 2009). This study confirmed the reduction in the oxygen cost of submaximal exercise and also showed that during very intense exercise, the time to exhaustion was extended after ingestion of the beetroot juice (675 ± 203 s) relative to the placebo trial (583 ± 145 s). In a subsequent study, the same authors (Bailey et al., 2010a) showed that beetroot juice supplementation for 6 days attenuated the reduction in muscle phosphorylcreatine concentration during exercise and increased endurance time from 586 ± 80 s after placebo treatment to 734 ± 109 s. This was accompanied by an apparent reduction in the ATP cost of muscle force production. They have also shown (Lansley et al., 2011) that the effects of beetroot juice supplementation on blood pressure and the oxygen cost of walking and running were not observed when nitrate-depleted beetroot juice was given.

Another pathway to stimulate the production of nitric oxide is the stimulation of endogenous nitric oxide synthesis from L-arginine. Interestingly, a recent study showed acute high-dose L-arginine supplementation (3 days, 6 g per day) to yield similar effects on exercise-induced oxygen consumption as the ingestion of dietary nitrate (Bailey et al., 2010b).

The total number of studies showing performance benefits from nitrate supplementation is small and they have involved only a few participants, but the data look impressive. Concerns have been raised as to the safety of high doses of dietary nitrate and nitrite (Derave & Taes, 2009), echoing earlier concerns about a possible role in the development of cancers (Archer, 2002), but athletes have not awaited further studies to confirm the efficacy or safety of such supplements, and the use of beetroot juice is becoming increasingly popular in endurance events. Evidence is certainly increasing to indicate that nitrate is an essential component of the diet and has a range of beneficial effects on health (Archer, 2002; Gilchrist et al., 2010; McKnight et al., 1999). However, the dose–response curve is entirely unknown, and overdosing conceivably may be health damaging, as with all nutrients consumed in excess.

Therefore, further studies are sure to follow rapidly and will either confirm or refute these findings with regard to both efficacy and safety.

Conclusions

The use of dietary supplements is widespread in sport, as it is in the general population. Athletes should be aware that few supplements can match the extravagant health and performance claims that are often made for them. A few supplements may have something to offer in terms of health protection or performance enhancement, but supplement use cannot compensate for poor food choices and an inadequate diet. The risk of an adverse outcome, especially a positive doping test, remains real, and the risks of supplement use must be balanced against the potential rewards.

References

AFFSA (2001). Opinion of the French Agency for Food Safety and report on the assessment of the risks of creatine on the consumer and of the veracity of the claims relating to sports performance and the increase of muscle mass. Retrieved from: http://www.afssa.fr/Documents/NUT-Ra-Creatine.pdf (accessed 20 September 2010).

Archer, D. L. (2002). Evidence that ingested nitrate and nitrite are beneficial to health. *Journal of Food Protection, 65*, 872–875.

Bailey, S. J., Fulford, J., Vanhatalo, A., Winyard, P. G., Blackwell, J. R., DiMenna, F. J. et al. (2010a). Dietary nitrate supplementation enhances muscle contractile efficiency during knee-extensor exercise in humans. *Journal of Applied Physiology, 109*, 135–148.

Bailey, S. J., Winyard, P. G., Vanhatalo, A., Blackwell, J. R., DiMenna, F. J., Wilkerson, D. P. et al. (2009). Dietary nitrate supplementation reduces the O_2 cost of low-intensity exercise and enhances tolerance to high-intensity exercise in humans. *Journal of Applied Physiology, 107*, 1144–1155.

Bailey, S. J., Winyard, P. G., Vanhatalo, A., Blackwell, J. R., DiMenna, F. J., Wilkerson, D. P. et al. (2010b). Acute L-arginine supplementation reduces the O_2 cost of moderate-intensity exercise and enhances high-intensity exercise tolerance. *Journal of Applied Physiology, 109*, 1394–1403.

Bemben, M. G., & Lamont, H. S. (2005). Creatine supplementation and exercise performance: Recent findings. *Sports Medicine, 35*, 107–125.

Bergström, J., Hermansen, L., Hultman, E., & Saltin, B. (1967). Diet, muscle glycogen and physical exercise. *Acta Physiologica Scandinavica, 71*, 140–150.

Bergström, J., & Hultman, E. (1966). Muscle glycogen synthesis after exercise: An enhancing factor localized to the muscle cells in man. *Nature, 210*, 309–310.

Braun, H., Geyer, H., & Koehler, K. (2008). Meat products as potential doping traps? *International Journal of Sport Nutrition and Exercise Metabolism, 18*, 539–542.

Braun, H., Koehler, K., Geyer, H., Kleinert, J., Mester, J., & Schänzer, W. (2009). Dietary supplement use among elite young German athletes. *International Journal of Sport Nutrition and Exercise Metabolism, 19*, 97–109.

Casey, A., Constantin-Teodosiu, D., Howell, S., Hultman, E., & Greenhaff, P. L. (1996). Creatine ingestion favorably affects performance and muscle metabolism during maximal exercise in humans. *American Journal of Physiology: Endocrinology and Metabolism, 271*, E31–E37.

Cox, G., Mujika, I., Tumilty, D., & Burke, L. (2002). Acute creatine supplementation and performance during a field test simulating match play in elite female football players. *International Journal of Sports Nutrition and Exercise Metabolism, 12,* 33–46.

Derave, W., Eijnde, B. O., & Hespel, P. (2003). Creatine supplementation in health and disease: What is the evidence for long-term efficacy? *Molecular and Cellular Biochemistry, 244,* 49–55.

Derave, W., & Taes, Y. (2009). Beware of the pickle: Health effects of nitrate intake. *Journal of Applied Physiology, 107,* 1677.

EFSA (2004). Opinion of the Scientific Panel on Food Additives, Flavourings, Processing Aids and Materials in Contact with Food on a request from the Commission related to creatine monohydrate for use in foods for particular nutritional uses. *The EFSA Journal, 36,* 1–6.

FDA (2009). Warning on Hydroxycut products. Retrieved from: http://www.fda.gov/ForConsumers/ConsumerUpdates/ucm152152.htm (accessed 15 September 2010).

FDA (2010). Voluntary nationwide recall. Retrieved from: http://www.fda.gov/Safety/Recalls/ucm226109.htm (accessed 18 September 2010).

Geyer, H., Bredehoft, M., Marek, U., Parr, M. K., & Schanzer, W. (2002). Hohe Dosen des Anabolikums Metandienon in Nahrungserganzungsmitteln. *Deutsche Apotheke Zeitung, 142,* 29.

Geyer, H., Parr, M. K., Mareck, U., Reinhart, U., Schrader, Y., & Schänzer, W. (2004). Analysis of non-hormonal nutritional supplements for anabolic-androgenic steroids – results of an international study. *International Journal of Sports Medicine, 25,* 124–129.

Gilchrist, M., Winyard, P. G., & Benjamin, N. (2010). Dietary nitrate – good or bad? *Nitric Oxide: Biology and Chemistry, 22*(Suppl. 1), 104–109.

Goston, J. L., & Correia, M. I. T. D. (2010). Intake of nutritional supplements among people exercising in gyms and influencing factors. *Nutrition, 26,* 604–611.

Green, A. L., Hultman, E., MacDonald, I. A., Sewell, D. A., & Greenhaff, P. L. (1996). Carbohydrate feeding augments skeletal muscle creatine accumulation during creatine supplementation in man. *American Journal of Physiology: Endocrinology and Metabolism, 27,* E821–E826.

Greenhaff, P. L., Casey, A., Short, A. H., Harris, R., & Söderlund, K. (1993). Influence of oral creatine supplementation on muscle torque during repeated bouts of maximal voluntary exercise in man. *Clinical Science, 84,* 565–571.

Harris, R. C., Almada, A. L., Harris, D. B., Dunnett, M., & Hespel, P. (2004). The creatine content of Creatine Serum™ and the change in the plasma concentration with ingestion of a single dose. *Journal of Sports Sciences, 22,* 851–857.

Harris, R. C., Soderlund, K., & Hultman, E. (1992). Elevation of creatine in resting and exercised muscle of normal subjects by creatine ingestion. *Clinical Science, 83,* 367–374.

Hespel, P., Op't Eijnde, B., Van Leemputte, M., Ursø, B., Greenhaff, P., Labarque, V. et al. (2001). Oral creatine supplementation facilitates the rehabilitation of disuse atrophy and alters the expression of muscle myogenic factors in humans. *Journal of Physiology, 536,* 625–633.

Huang, S. H., Johnson, K., & Pipe, A. L. (2006). The use of dietary supplements and medications by Canadian athletes at the Atlanta and Sydney Olympic Games. *Clinical Journal of Sports Medicine, 16,* 27–33.

Kreider, R. B. (2003). Effects of creatine supplementation on performance and training adaptations. *Molecular and Cellular Biochemistry, 244,* 89–94.

Kreider, R. B., Ferreira, M., Wilson, M., Grinstaff, P., Plisk, S., Reinardy, J. et al. (1998). Effects of creatine supplementation on body composition, strength, and sprint performance. *Medicine and Science in Sports and Exercise, 30,* 73–82.

Kreider, R. B., Melton, C., Rasmussen, C. J., Greenwood, M., Lancaster, S., Cantler, E. C. et al. (2003). Long-term creatine supplementation does not significantly affect clinical markers of health in athletes. *Molecular and Cellular Biochemistry, 244,* 95–104.

Krishnan, P. V., Feng, Z. Z., & Gordon, S. C. (2009). Prolonged intrahepatic cholestasis and renal failure secondary to anabolic androgenic steroid-enriched dietary supplements. *Journal of Clinical Gastroenterology, 43,* 672–675.

Lansley, K. E., Winyard, P. G., Fulford, J., Vanhatalo, A., Bailey, S. J., Blackwell, J. R. et al. (2011). Dietary nitrate supplementation reduces the O_2 cost of walking and running: A placebo-controlled study. *Journal of Applied Physiology, 110,* 591–600.

Larsen, F. J., Ekblom, B., Sahlin, K., Lundberg, J. O., & Weitzberg, E. (2007). Effects of dietary nitrate on oxygen cost during exercise. *Acta Physiologica, 191,* 59–66.

Larsen, F. J., Schiffer, T. A., Bourniquet, S., Sahlin, K., Ekblom, B., Lundberg, J. O. et al. (2011). Dietary inorganic nitrate improves mitochondrial efficiency in humans. *Cell Metabolism, 13,* 149–159.

Larsen, F. J., Weitzberg, E., Lundberg, J. O., & Ekblom, B. (2010). Dietary nitrate reduces maximal oxygen consumption while maintaining work performance in maximal exercise. *Free Radicals in Biology and Medicine, 48,* 342–347.

Louis, M., Poortmans, J. R., Francaux, M., Berre, J., Boisseau, N., Brassine, E. et al. (2003a). No effect of creatine supplementation on human myofibrillar and sarcoplasmic protein synthesis after resistance exercise. *American Journal of Physiology: Endocrinology and Metabolism, 285,* E1089–E1094.

Louis, M., Poortmans, J. R., Francaux, M., Hultman, E., Berre, J., Boisseau, N. et al. (2003b). Creatine supplementation has no effect on human muscle protein turnover at rest in the postabsorptive or fed states. *American Journal of Physiology: Endocrinology and Metabolism, 284,* E764–E770.

Louis, M., Van Beneden, R., Dehoux, M., Thissen, J. P., & Francaux, M. (2004). Creatine increases IGF-I and myogenic regulatory factor mRNA in C(2)C(12) cells. *FEBS Letters, 557,* 243–247.

Maganaris, C. N., & Maughan, R. J. (1998). Creatine supplementation enhances maximum voluntary isometric force and endurance capacity in resistance trained men. *Acta Physiologica Scandinavica, 163,* 279–287.

Maughan, R. J. (2005). Contamination of dietary supplements and positive drugs tests in sport. *Journal of Sports Sciences, 23,* 883–889.

Maughan, R. J., Depiesse, F., & Geyer, H. (2007). The use of dietary supplements by athletes. *Journal of Sports Sciences, 25,* S103–S113.

McGuffin, M., & Young, A. L. (2004). Premarket notifications of new dietary ingredients – a ten-year review. *Food and Drug Law Journal, 59,* 229–244.

McKnight, G. M., Duncan, C. W., Leifert, C., & Golden, M. H. (1999). Dietary nitrate in man: Friend or foe? *British Journal of Nutrition, 81,* 349–358.

Mettler, S., & Zimmermann, M. B. (2010). Iron excess in recreational marathon runners. *European Journal of Clinical Nutrition, 64,* 490–494.

Nutraingredients (2003). South Africa issues kava recall. Retrieved from: http://www.nutraingredients.com/Regulation/South-Africa-issues-kava-recall (accessed 15 September 2010).

Papanikolaou, G., & Pantopoulos, K. (2005). Iron metabolism and toxicity. *Toxicology and Applied Pharmacology, 202,* 199–211.

Pittas, G., Hazell, M. D., Simpson, E. J., & Greenhaff, P. L. (2010). Optimization of insulin-mediated creatine retention during creatine feeding in humans. *Journal of Sports Sciences, 28,* 67–74.

Robinson, T. M., Sewell, D. A., Hultman, E., & Greenhaff, P. L. (1999). Role of submaximal exercise in promoting creatine and glycogen accumulation in human skeletal muscle. *Journal of Applied Physiology, 87,* 598–604.

Sawitzke, A. D., Shi, H., & Finco, M. F. (2008). The effect of glucosamine and/or chondroitin sulfate on the progression of knee osteoarthritis: A report from the Glucosamine/Chondroitin Arthritis Intervention Trial. *Arthritis and Rheumatism, 58,* 3183–3191.

Spillane, M., Schoch, R., Cooke, M., Harvey, T., Greenwood, M., & Kreider, R. et al. (2009). The effects of creatine ethyl ester supplementation combined with heavy resistance training on body composition, muscle performance, and serum and muscle creatine levels. *Journal of the International Society for Sports Nutrition,* (DOI: 10.1186/1550-2783-6-6).

Steenge, G. R., Lambourne, J., Casey, A., MacDonald, I. A., & Greenhaff, P. L. (1998). Stimulatory effect of insulin on creatine accumulation in human skeletal muscle. *American Journal of Physiology: Endocrinology and Metabolism, 275,* E974–E979.

Terjung, R. L., Clarkson, P. M., Eichner, E. R., Greenhaff, P. L., Hespel, P., Israel, R. G. et al. (2000). The physiological and health effects of oral creatine supplementation. *Medicine and Science in Sports and Exercise, 32,* 706–717.

Tscholl, P., Alonso, J. M., Dolle, G., Junge, A., & Dvorak, J. (2010). The use of drugs and nutritional supplements in top-level track and field athletes. *American Journal of Sports Medicine, 38,* 133–140.

Tscholl, P., Junge, A., & Dvorak, J. (2008). The use of medication and nutritional supplements during FIFA World Cups 2002 and 2006. *British Journal of Sports Medicine, 42,* 725–730.

Vandenberghe, K., Gillis, N., Van Leemputte, M., Van Hecke, P., Vanstapel, F., & Hespel, P. (1996). Caffeine counteracts the ergogenic action of muscle creatine loading. *Journal of Applied Physiology, 80,* 452–457.

Vandenberghe, K., Goris, M., Van Hecke, P., Van Leemputte, M., Vangerven, L., & Hespel, P. (1997). Long-term creatine intake is beneficial to muscle performance during resistance training. *Journal of Applied Physiology, 83,* 2055–2063.

Vanhatalo, A., Bailey, S .J., Blackwell, J. R., DiMenna, F. J., Pavey, T. G., Wilkerson, D. P. et al. (2010). Acute and chronic effects of dietary nitrate supplementation on blood pressure and the physiological responses to moderate-intensity and incremental exercise. *American Journal of Physiology: Regulatory, Integrative and Comparative Physiology, 299,* R1121–R1131.

Van Leemputte, M., Vandenberghe, K., & Hespel, P. (1999). Shortening of muscle relaxation time after creatine loading. *Journal of Applied Physiology, 86,* 840–844.

Van Schuylenbergh, R., Van Leemputte, M., & Hespel, P. (2003). Effects of oral creatine-pyruvate supplementation in cycling performance. *International Journal of Sports Medicine, 24,* 144–150.

Volek, J. S., Duncan, N. D., Mazzetti, S. A., Staron, R. S., Putukian, M., Gómez, A. L. et al. (1999). Performance and muscle fiber adaptations to creatine supplementation and heavy resistance training. *Medicine and Science in Sports and Exercise, 31,* 1147–1156.

Walker, J. B. (1979). Creatine: Biosynthesis, regulation, and function. *Advances in Enzymology, 50,* 177–242.

Wandel, S., Juni, P., Tendal, B., Nuesch, E., Villiger, P. M., Welton, N. J. et al. (2010). Effects of glucosamine, chondroitin, or placebo in patients with osteoarthritis of hip or knee: Network meta-analysis. *British Medical Journal, 341,* c4675.

Watson, P., Judkins, C., Houghton, E., Russell, C., & Maughan, R. J. (2009). Supplement contamination: Detection of nandrolone metabolites in urine after administration of small doses of a nandrolone precursor. *Medicine and Science in Sports and Exercise, 41,* 766–772.

Nutrition guidelines for strength sports: Sprinting, weightlifting, throwing events, and bodybuilding

GARY SLATER[1] & STUART M. PHILLIPS[2]

[1]School of Health and Sport Sciences, Faculty of Science, Health and Education, University of the Sunshine Coast, Maroochydore, Queensland, Australia, and [2]Exercise Metabolism Research Group, Department of Kinesiology, McMaster University, Hamilton, Canada

Abstract

Strength and power athletes are primarily interested in enhancing power relative to body weight and thus almost all undertake some form of resistance training. While athletes may periodically attempt to promote skeletal muscle hypertrophy, key nutritional issues are broader than those pertinent to hypertrophy and include an appreciation of the sports supplement industry, the strategic timing of nutrient intake to maximize fuelling and recovery objectives, plus achievement of pre-competition body mass requirements. Total energy and macronutrient intakes of strength-power athletes are generally high but intakes tend to be unremarkable when expressed relative to body mass. Greater insight into optimization of dietary intake to achieve nutrition-related goals would be achieved from assessment of nutrient distribution over the day, especially intake before, during, and after exercise. This information is not readily available on strength-power athletes and research is warranted. There is a general void of scientific investigation relating specifically to this unique group of athletes. Until this is resolved, sports nutrition recommendations for strength-power athletes should be directed at the individual athlete, focusing on their specific nutrition-related goals, with an emphasis on the nutritional support of training.

Introduction

The ability to generate explosive muscle power and strength is critical to success in Olympic weightlifting and powerlifting, as well as throwing events, including javelin, discus, shot put and hammer, plus sprints (100–200 m) in track and field. Consequently, athletes competing in these events will typically incorporate some form of generic resistance exercise into their overall training programme despite sport-specific training varying markedly.

Athletics competitors participating in throwing events typically undertake periodized training programmes that aim to develop maximum strength and power of the major muscle groups using a range of modalities such as plyometric exercises, sprinting, power lifts, Olympic lifts and weighted throwing drills to complement technical throwing training. Periodization of resistance training typically involves a transition from high-volume, high-force, low-velocity movements requiring less coordination characteristic of traditional powerlifting (Hoffman, Cooper, Wendell, & Kang, 2004) to more explosive, lower-force, low-repetition training using Olympic lifts in preparation for competition (Judge, Moreau, & Burke, 2003). The focus on explosive Olympic lifts over more traditional strength-based lifting results in more favourable power and strength gains (Hoffman et al., 2004), derived primarily from neural rather than skeletal muscle hypertrophy adaptations (Folland & Williams, 2007).

Consequently, this style of training enhances traits important to athletic development and is common among other explosive athletics disciplines like sprinting and jumping events (Lambert & Flynn, 2002), and is increasingly being incorporated into the training practices of powerlifters (Swinton, Lloyd, Agouris, & Stewart, 2009).

Unlike other sports that use resistance exercise to complement sport-specific training, powerlifting, Olympic lifting, and bodybuilding use resistance training as a primary mode of training. While Olympic and powerlifting athletes are primarily concerned with enhancing power and strength respectively, bodybuilding training primarily aims to induce skeletal muscle hypertrophy. Consequently, the training programmes of bodybuilders are unique, typically of greater volume than those of other athletes, using higher repetition ranges with multiple sets per muscle group and little rest between sets (Lambert & Flynn, 2002).

Given the disparity between sport-specific training programmes of strength-power athletes and their subsequent metabolic implications, this paper will focus on the nutritional implications of resistance training among strength-power athletes. The sport of bodybuilding will also be addressed given the focus on resistance exercise in overall training programme prescription.

Training nutrition

Nutrition plays an important role in three aspects of training nutrition for strength-power athletes: fuelling of sport-specific and strength training, recovery from this training, and the promotion of training adaptations, including skeletal muscle hypertrophy. Resistance exercise requires a high rate of energy supply, derived from both the phosphagen energy systems and glycogenolysis (Lambert & Flynn, 2002; Tesch, Colliander, & Kaiser, 1986), the contribution being dependent upon the relative power output, the work-to-rest ratio, and muscle blood flow (Tesch et al., 1986). The source of fatigue during resistance exercise is likely multi-factorial, including neuromuscular (Hakkinen, 1993) and peripheral metabolic factors such as a decline in intramuscular pH (MacDougall et al., 1999), the latter being somewhat dependent on the intensity and volume of training undertaken as well as the time point within a resistance training session. Metabolic fatigue during the earlier part of a workout may be due at least partially to reductions in phosphagen energy system stores and mild acidosis, while subsequent fatigue may result more from acidosis and impaired energy production from glycogenolysis (MacDougall et al., 1999).

A summary of the reported dietary intake of adult strength-power athletes in training is presented in Tables I and II. Investigations including athletes acknowledging the use of anabolic steroids have been omitted as steroid use has been shown to influence dietary practices (Kleiner, Calabrese, Fiedler, Naito, & Skibinski, 1989). Investigations focusing on the pre-competition dietary practices of bodybuilders have also been omitted due to the range of novel interventions undertaken acutely before competition to maximize muscularity, including adjustments in sodium, fluid, and carbohydrate intake (Kleiner, Bazzarre, & Litchford, 1990; Walberg-Rankin, Edmonds, & Gwazdauskas, 1993).

Given the extreme muscularity of these individuals and the association between muscle mass and total energy expenditure (Schulz & Schoeller, 1994), it is not surprising that these athletes have generous energy intakes. However, when expressed relative to body mass the energy intakes of strength-power athletes are generally unremarkable relative to those reported for athletes in other sports (Burke et al., 2003) but lower than current strength athlete guidelines of $\sim$185–210 kJ $\cdot$ kg^{-1} body mass (Manore, Barr, & Butterfield, 2000). This likely reflects the fact that taller and/or more muscular individuals have lower resting and total energy requirements relative to body mass (Heymsfield et al., 2009). Thus, consideration may need to be given to the allometric scaling of traditional sports nutrition guidelines for macronutrients among larger athletes to reflect their lower relative energy requirements. Consideration should also be given to the distribution of nutrient intake, with a paucity of information available on daily distribution of nutrient intake (Burke et al., 2003; van Erp-Baart, Saris, Binkhorst, Vos, & Elvers, 1989), making it difficult to infer compliance with guidelines relating to key periods of nutrient intake, specifically before, during, and after exercise.

Carbohydrate

A single resistance training session can result in reductions in muscle glycogen stores of as much as 24–40% (Koopman et al., 2006; MacDougall et al., 1999; Pascoe, Costill, Fink, Robergs, & Zachwieja, 1993; Tesch et al., 1986), the amount of depletion depending on the duration, intensity, and overall work accomplished during the session. Higher-repetition, moderate-load training characteristic of programming prescribed to promote skeletal muscle hypertrophy results in the greatest reductions in muscle glycogen stores (Pascoe et al., 1993), an effect most pronounced in type II fibres (Koopman et al., 2006). Reductions in muscle glycogen stores have been associated with performance impairment in both isokinetic torque (Jacobs, Kaiser, & Tesch, 1981) and isoinertial resistance training capacity (Leveritt & Abernethy, 1999), although this effect is not always evident (Mitchell, DiLauro, Pizza, & Cavender, 1997) and possibly dependent on the method used to induce a state of glycogen depletion. Nonetheless, it is conceivable that impaired training or competition performance could occur in any session or event that relied on rapid and repeated glycogen breakdown.

Given that resistance training is merely one component of the overall training programme of sprints and throwing event athletes, and that the skeletal muscle damage that accompanies resistance training (Gibala et al., 2000) impairs muscle glycogen resynthesis (Zehnder, Muelli, Buchli, Kuehne, & Boutellier, 2004), it would seem pertinent to

Table I. Reported dietary intake of energy and macronutrients among adult male strength and power athletes during training (unless otherwise stated) since 1980.

Sport	Population	Body mass (kg)	Energy		Carbohydrate		Protein		Fat		Survey method	Reference
			MJ	kJ·kg⁻¹	g	g·kg⁻¹	g	g·kg⁻¹	g	% E		
Throwing	Elite (n=6)	109	22.4 ± 2.9	205 ± 25	450 ± 52	4.1 ± 0.5	265 ± 44	2.4 ± 0.4	277 ± 97	47 ± 16	3–5 day weighed diary	Chen et al. (1989)
Sprinting	National level (n=20)	96	14.6 ± 3.3	152 ± 36	375	3.9	160	1.7 ± 0.9	158	41 ± 5	7 day diary	Faber et al. (1990)
	National team (n=2)	104	15.0 ± 2.8	145 ± 20	429 ± 81	4.1 ± 0.6	134 ± 2	1.3 ± 0.1	119 ± 8	30 ± 4	3 day diary	Sugiura et al. (1999)
	National level (n=10)	67	11.1 ± 1.5	167 ± 33	340 ± 57	5.1 ± 1.0	102 ± 20	1.5 ± 0.4	90 ± 16	30 ± 3	3 day diary	Sugiura et al. (1999)
Weightlifting	Elite (n=10)	80	19.2 ± 2.5	238 ± 25	431 ± 96	5.4 ± 1.2	257 ± 47	3.2 ± 0.6	205 ± 33	40 ± 7	3–5 day weighed diary	Chen et al. (1989)
	International (n=7)	76	12.8	167	320	4.2	97	1.3	134	39	4–7 day diary	van Erp-Baart et al. (1989)
	National and collegiate (n=28)		15.2 ± 3.9		392		161		160	39 ± 6	3 day diary	Grandjean (1989)
	National team (n=15)	95	31.4	330	764	8	295	3.1	380	45	3 day semi-weighed diary	Heinemann & Zerbes (1989)
Bodybuilding	National level (n=19)	84	15.2 ± 5.0	181 ± 50	399 ± 143	4.8	156 ± 42	1.9 ± 0.6	155 ± 62	39 ± 4	7 day diary	Burke et al. (1991)
	Competitive (n=76)	82	15.0 ± 4.2	183	320 ± 132	3.9	200 ± 79	2.4	157 ± 50	39	7 day diary	Faber et al. (1986)
	Elite (n=6)	80	20.1 ± 0.2	251	592	7.4 ± 0.3	224	2.7 ± 0.1	174	32	7 day diary	Tarnopolsky et al. (1988)
	International Competitive (n=7)	87	13.7	157	424	4.9	201	2.5	118	32	4–7 day diary	van Erp-Baart et al. (1989)
	Training	91	15.0 ± 4.9	165	457 ± 148	5	215 ± 59	2.4	110 ± 71	26 ± 12	3 day diary	Heyward et al. (1989)
	Competition	86	9.8 ± 1.1	113	365 ± 76	4.2	163 ± 59	1.9	32 ± 18	13 ± 8		
	Competitive (n=20)	77	15.4 ± 4.4	200	532	6.9	165	2.1	120	29 ± 7	4 day diary	Giada et al. (1996)
	International (n=7)	85	12.4 ± 1.5	145	369 ± 70	4.3	144 ± 41	1.7	95 ± 12	28	4 day diary	Maestu et al. (2010)

Table II. Reported dietary intake of energy and macronutrients among adult female strength and power athletes during training (unless otherwise stated) since 1980.

Sport	Population	Body mass (kg)	Energy		Carbohydrate		Protein		Fat		Survey method	Reference
			MJ	kJ·kg⁻¹	g	g·kg⁻¹	g	g·kg⁻¹	g	% E		
Throwing	Elite (n = 6)	84	18.6 ± 3.1	222 ± 38	386 ± 57	4.6 ± 0.7	208 ± 28	2.5 ± 0.3	230 ± 14	47 ± 21	3–5 day weighed diary	Chen et al. (1989)
Sprinting	National level (n = 10)	83	9.3 ± 2.0	112 ± 28	269	3.2	94	1.1 ± 0.3	95	38 ± 6	7 day diary	Faber et al. (1990)
	National team (n = 8)	67	11.0 ± 2.4	167 ± 39	336 ± 68	5.1 ± 1.1	93 ± 23	1.4 ± 0.4	94 ± 24	32 ± 3	3 day diary	Sugiura et al. (1999)
	National level (n = 11)	54	10.0 ± 2.2	191 ± 46	305 ± 79	5.8 ± 1.6	89 ± 25	1.7 ± 0.5	86 ± 17	33 ± 4	3 day diary	Sugiura et al. (1999)
Bodybuilding	International (n = 4)	56	6.2	110	196	3.5	112	2.0	47	28	4–7 day diary	van Erp-Baart et al. (1989)
	Competitive (n = 12)	58	6.8 ± 2.3	118	208 ± 60	3.6	102 ± 30	1.8	42 ± 30	21 ± 9	3 day diary	Heyward et al. (1989)
	Training Competition	52	6.1 ± 2.7	117	261 ± 112	5.0	77 ± 57	1.5	15 ± 7	10 ± 3	3 day diary	
	Collegiate (n = 4)	58	9.1 ± 3.6	156	290 ± 124	5.0	99 ± 44	1.7	69 ± 44	28.1	3 day diary	Lamar-Hildebrand et al. (1989)

encourage strength-trained athletes to maintain a moderate carbohydrate intake. Guidelines proposing an intake within the range of 6 g · kg⁻¹ body mass for male strength athletes (Lambert & Flynn, 2002) and possibly less for females (Volek, Forsythe, & Kraemer, 2006) have been advocated. Dietary survey literature relating to strength athletes suggests lifters and throwers typically report carbohydrate intakes of 3–5 g · kg⁻¹ body mass, while bodybuilders maintain daily intakes equivalent to 4–7 g · kg⁻¹ body mass, independent of gender (Tables I and II). While this may appear low relative to endurance athletes (Burke, Cox, Culmmings, & Desbrow, 2001), conclusive evidence of benefit from maintaining a habitual high carbohydrate intake among strength athletes remains to be confirmed. Given the lower relative energy expenditure of larger athletes and their requirements for other nutrients, plus the impact of adjusting carbohydrate on total energy intake, recommendations for carbohydrate intake at strategic times, including before, during and after exercise, may be more applicable for the strength athlete, ensuring carbohydrate availability is optimized at critical time points. Thus we would consider a range of daily carbohydrate intakes between 4 and 7 g · kg⁻¹ body mass as reasonable for these athletes depending on their phase of training.

Protein

Strength-trained athletes have advocated high protein diets for many years. While debate continues on the need for additional protein among resistance-trained individuals, general guidelines now recommend athletes undertaking strength training ingest approximately twice current recommendations for protein of their sedentary counterparts or as much as 1.6–1.7 g protein · kg⁻¹ · day⁻¹ (Phillips, 2004). Given the relatively wide distribution of protein in the meal plan and increased energy intake of athletes, it should not be surprising to learn that the majority of strength-trained athletes easily achieve these increased protein needs (Tables I and II). Exceeding the upper range of protein intake guidelines offers no further benefit and simply promotes increased amino acid catabolism and protein oxidation (Moore et al., 2009). Furthermore, there is evidence that an intense period of resistance training reduces protein turnover and improves net protein retention, thus reducing relative dietary protein requirements of experienced resistance-trained athletes (Hartman, Moore, & Phillips, 2006).

Simply contrasting an athlete's current daily protein intake against guidelines does not address if protein intake has been optimized to promote gains in muscle mass or optimize repair of damaged tissues. Rather, consideration should be given to other dietary factors, including total energy intake (Calloway & Spector, 1954), the daily distribution of protein intake, especially as it relates to training, and the source of dietary protein (Tang & Phillips, 2009). While there is very little information available on the eating patterns of strength athletes, available literature suggests the majority of daily protein intake is ingested at main meals, with little consideration for between-meal intake, presumably inclusive of pre- and post-training snacks (Burke et al., 2003). Thus, rather than focusing on total daily intake, athletes are encouraged to consume rapidly digested protein meals/snacks in close proximity to their exercise bout, especially during and after exercise (Phillips & Van Loon, 2011). Less is known about the impact of protein distribution in the meal plan outside of the acute period before and/or after exercise (<3 h). There is some evidence to suggest that protein breakdown may be less with a wider distribution of daily protein intake compared with an acute daily bolus of protein (Arnal et al., 2000). However, given that muscle protein synthesis becomes refractory to persistent aminoacidemia (Bohe, Low, Wolfe, & Rennie, 2001), Moore and colleagues (2009) suggest the ingestion of 20 g of high biological value protein (8–10 g essential amino acids) no more than 5–6 times daily may result in maximal stimulation of muscle protein synthesis.

Fat

The dietary fat intake of strength-power athletes reported in Tables I and II is generally higher than that recommended for healthy individuals (Zello, 2006), and often derived from sources rich in saturated fat (Chen et al., 1989; Faber, Benade, & van Eck, 1986; Faber, Spinnler-Benade, & Daubitzer, 1990; Giada et al., 1996), presumably from an emphasis on animal foods in the pursuit of a higher protein intake (Chen et al., 1989). While the acute health implications of such dietary practices on blood lipid profiles is not immediately evident (Faber et al., 1986, 1990; Giada et al., 1996), it may explain in part the lower dietary carbohydrate intakes reported among strength-power athletes. Given that isoenergetic substitution of fat for carbohydrate has a favourable effect on nitrogen balance (Richardson, Wayler, Scrimshaw, & Young, 1979), it is tempting to advocate a reduction in dietary fat intake, especially for those individuals exceeding current guidelines for fat intake. However, consideration must be given to the practical implication of substituting a high-energy density macronutrient with a lower energy macronutrient and the impact this may have on energy balance, especially among strength-power athletes with very high energy needs. Conversely, there may be situations in which a higher

intake of foods rich in unsaturated fats may be advocated for strength-power athletes struggling to achieve energy needs because of an emphasis on the selection of lower energy density foods in the meal plan.

Pre-exercise and during exercise

Athletes are encouraged to pay particular attention to dietary intake in the hours before exercise, based on the assumption that pre-exercise nutritional strategies can influence exercise performance. While this is a widely accepted practice before endurance exercise to enhance work capacity (Hargreaves, Hawley, & Jeukendrup, 2004), evidence is also emerging for a beneficial role of acute carbohydrate ingestion prior to strength training. For example, Lambert and colleagues (Lambert, Flynn, Boone, Michaud, & Rodriguez-Zayas, 1991) reported that supplemental carbohydrate ingestion before and during resistance exercise ($1 \text{ g} \cdot \text{kg}^{-1}$ before, $0.5 \text{ g} \cdot \text{kg}^{-1}$ during) increased total work capacity, a response that has been replicated elsewhere (Haff et al., 1999, 2001). However, not all investigations show benefit with acute carbohydrate ingestion (Haff et al., 2000; Kulik et al., 2008); we propose that the ergogenic potential for carbohydrate ingestion is most likely to be observed when undertaking resistance training of long duration and high volume. At present, a specific recommendation for an optimum rate or timing of carbohydrate ingestion for strength-power athletes before and during any given training session cannot be determined. As with all athletes, strength-power athletes should be encouraged to initiate training in a euhydrated state given that even moderate hypohydration can impair resistance-training work capacity (Kraft et al., 2010).

Recently, there has been interest in the co-ingestion of carbohydrate and essential amino acids both before and during resistance exercise, presumably to increase substrate availability and thus exercise performance, promote a more anabolic hormonal environment (Bird, Tarpenning, & Marino, 2006a, 2006b), stimulate muscle protein synthesis (Tipton et al., 2001), and/or reduce indices of muscle damage and soreness (Bird et al., 2006b; Saunders, Kane, & Todd, 2004). While initial research had suggested a greater muscle protein synthetic response to resistance training when nutritional support was provided before compared with after resistance exercise (Tipton et al., 2001), this has not been replicated elsewhere (Fujita et al., 2009; Tipton et al., 2007). Consequently, current guidelines advocate protein ingestion at a time that coincides with maximal stimulation of muscle protein synthesis, which is after exercise (Burd, Tang, Moore, & Phillips, 2009).

Recovery

Given that resistance training typically forms only one component of an athlete's training schedule, recovery strategies shown to enhance restoration of muscle glycogen stores such as post-exercise carbohydrate ingestion should be routinely implemented following resistance training. General sports nutrition guidelines advocate the ingestion of carbohydrate at a rate of 1.0–1.2 $g \cdot kg^{-1}$ body mass in the immediate post-exercise period (Burke, Kiens, & Ivy, 2004). However, this has no influence on muscle protein metabolism (Koopman et al., 2007). In contrast, post-exercise dietary protein ingestion results in an exacerbated elevation in muscle protein synthesis with a concomitant minor suppression in muscle protein breakdown, resulting in a positive net protein balance (Phillips, Tang, & Moore, 2009). The ingestion of ~ 20 g of high biological value protein after resistance exercise appears to be sufficient to maximally stimulate muscle protein synthesis, with amounts in excess of this merely promoting protein oxidation (Moore et al., 2009). Thus the combined ingestion of carbohydrate and protein acutely following resistance training results in more favourable recovery outcomes, including restoration of muscle glycogen stores and muscle protein metabolism, than the ingestion of either nutrient alone (Miller, Tipton, Chinkes, Wolf, & Wolfe, 2003). Post-exercise protein ingestion also lowers carbohydrate intake requirements in the acute recovery period, with an energy-matched intake of 0.8 $g \cdot kg^{-1} \cdot h^{-1}$ carbohydrate plus 0.4 $g \cdot kg^{-1} \cdot h^{-1}$ protein resulting in similar muscle glycogen resynthesis over 5 h as 1.2 $g \cdot kg^{-1} \cdot h^{-1}$ carbohydrate alone following intermittent exercise (van Loon, Saris, Kruijshoop, & Wagenmakers, 2000), with a similar response evident following resistance exercise (Roy & Tarnopolsky, 1998). Preliminary evidence also suggests the post-exercise co-ingestion of carbohydrate and protein may reduce muscle damage often seen in strength-trained athletes (Cockburn, Stevenson, Hayes, Robson-Ansley, & Howatson, 2010); whether such a change has a functional benefit is unclear.

The muscle soreness common among strength-power athletes following heavy eccentric loading or novel training sessions is associated with adverse athletic outcomes (Cheung, Hume, & Maxwell, 2003). A number of nutrition interventions have been trialled to minimize the soreness, including fish oils (Lenn et al., 2002), branched-chain amino acids (Jackman, Witard, Jeukendrup, & Tipton, 2010; Matsumoto et al., 2009; Sharp & Pearson, 2010; Shimomura et al., 2010), and protease supplements (Beck et al., 2007; Buford et al., 2009; Miller, Bailey, Barnes, Derr, & Hall, 2004). While there is some evidence of reduced soreness as a result of consumption of branched-chain amino acid and protease supplementation, it may be premature to recommend these as strategies to overcome muscle soreness.

Supplementation practices

Supplement use is reported to be higher among athletes than their sedentary counterparts, with particularly high rates of supplement use among weightlifters and bodybuilders (Sobal & Marquart, 1994). The high prevalence of supplement use among bodybuilders (Brill & Keane, 1994), Olympic weightlifters (Burke, Gollan, & Read, 1991), track and field athletes (Froiland, Koszewski, Hingst, & Kopecky, 2004; Nieper, 2005; Ronsen, Sundgot-Borgen, & Maehlum, 1999), and those who frequent commercial gymnasia (Morrison, Gizis, & Shorter, 2004; Sheppard, Raichada, Kouri, Stenson-Bar-Maor, & Branch, 2000) is not unexpected, given the range of products targeted at this market (Grunewald & Bailey, 1993; Philen, Ortiz, Auerbach, & Falk, 1992). While multi-vitamin and mineral supplements are very popular among all athletes, other products such as protein powders and specific amino acid supplements, caffeine, and creatine monohydrate are also frequently used by strength-trained athletes (Brill & Keane, 1994; Goston & Correia, 2010; Morrison et al., 2004; Nieper, 2005; Sheppard et al., 2000).

Recognizing the nutritional value of food sources of protein and essential amino acids, creatine monohydrate is the only supplement that has been reported to enhance skeletal muscle hypertrophy and functional capacity in response to resistance training (Hespel & Derave, 2007). However, liquid meal supplements rich in carbohydrate and protein may be valuable in the post-exercise period to boost total energy and specific nutrient intake at a time when the appetite is often suppressed (Cribb & Hayes, 2006). There is also evidence of enhanced muscular strength with acute caffeine ingestion (Warren, Park, Maresca, McKibans, & Millard-Stafford, 2010). An excellent review of issues relating to supplement use by athletes is presented elsewhere (Maughan, Greenhaff, & Hespel, 2011).

Strength-trained athletes continue to seek supplement information from readily accessible sources including magazines, fellow athletes, and coaches (Froiland et al., 2004; Nieper, 2005; Sheppard et al., 2000). Consequently, the accuracy of information provided may vary, leaving the athlete vulnerable to inappropriate and/or ineffective supplementation protocols. The presence of muscle dysmorphia, a body dysmorphic disorder characterized by a preoccupation with a sense of inadequate muscularity common among bodybuilders, may also influence supplementation practices and lead to anabolic steroid use (Hildebrandt, Schlundt, Langenbucher, & Chung, 2006).

Competition

Competition demands of strength sports are typically characterized by explosive single efforts where athletes are typically given a designated number of opportunities to produce a maximal performance, with significant recovery between each effort. Consequently, muscle energy reserves are unlikely to be challenged, even in the face of challenging environmental conditions of competitions like the summer Olympic Games (Peiser & Reilly, 2004). Consequently, nutrition priorities remain with more general goals like optimizing gastrointestinal tract comfort and preventing weight gain during the competition taper.

Olympic weightlifting, powerlifting, and bodybuilding are unique among strength-power sports in that competition is undertaken via weight categories or, on occasion, by height class in bodybuilding. As such, these athletes are vulnerable to the acute weight loss practices common to other weight category sports such as acute food/fluid restriction, resulting in a state of glycogen depletion and hypohydration (Kiningham & Gorenflo, 2001). While performance is typically compromised in sports requiring a significant contribution from aerobic and/or anaerobic energy metabolism, activities demanding high power output and absolute strength are less likely to be influenced by acute weight loss (Fogelholm, 1994). Furthermore, the weigh-in is typically undertaken 2 h before a weightlifting competition, affording athletes an opportunity to recover, at least partially, from any acute weight loss strategies undertaken prior to competition. The body mass management guidelines for wrestlers issued by the American College of Sports Medicine (ACSM) would appear applicable to Olympic weightlifters also (Oppliger, Case, Horswill, Landry, & Shelter, 1996).

Given the association between lower body fat percentages and competitive success, bodybuilders typically adjust their training and diet several weeks out from competition in an attempt to decrease body fat while maintaining/increasing muscle mass. While a compromise in muscle mass has been observed when attempting to achieve the extremely low body fat percentages desired for competition (Heyward, Sandoval, & Colville, 1989; Withers et al., 1997), this is not always the case (Bamman, Hunter, Newton, Roney, & Khaled, 1993; Maestu, Eliakim, Jurimae, Valter, & Jurimae, 2010; van der Ploeg et al., 2001). The performance implications of any skeletal muscle loss are unknown given the subjective nature of bodybuilding competition. Among female

bodybuilders such dietary restrictions are often associated with compromised micronutrient intake (Heyward et al., 1989; Lamar-Hildebrand, Saldanha, & Endres, 1989) and menstrual dysfunction (Walberg & Johnston, 1991), presumably because energy availability falls below the threshold of ~ 30 kcal $\cdot$ kg^{-1} fat free mass $\cdot$ day^{-1} required to maintain normal endocrine regulation of the menstrual cycle (Loucks, Kiens, & Wright, 2011).

If catabolism of muscle protein is experienced by an Olympic weightlifter or powerlifter as they attempt to "make weight" for competition, a compromise in force-generating capacity (Bamman et al., 1993), and thus weightlifting performance, is at least theoretically possible. To avoid this situation, consideration should be given to the amount of weight loss required and thus the specified weight category as well as nutritional strategies proven to assist with maintenance of lean body mass during weight loss, such as a relative increase in dietary protein intake (Mettler, Mitchell, & Tipton, 2010). Allocating sufficient time to achieve the specified weight-category limit without severe energy restriction will also be critical with possible consideration given to the strategic use of acute weight-loss strategies in the final 24–48 h before weigh-in. This may include the use of low-residue, low-volume meal plans as well as moderation of fluid intake, which in combination can induce a 2–3% body mass loss without promoting the health risks associated with other acute weight-loss strategies. However, as with any pre-competition strategy, this approach should be trialled in training with the support of suitably qualified sports science and/or sports medicine professionals to assess both tolerance and the amount of weight loss achieved. An excellent review of issues relating to body mass management of elite athletes is presented elsewhere (Sundgot-Borgen & Garthe, 2011).

Physique

Within the lifting events, physique traits influence performance in several ways. While the expression of strength has a significant neural component, lifting performance is closely associated with skeletal muscle mass (Brechue & Abe, 2002). Excluding the open weight category, weightlifters also tend to have low body fat, enhancing development of strength per unit body mass (Keogh, Hume, Pearson, & Mellow, 2007). Successful weightlifters also have a higher sitting height to stature ratio with shorter limbs, creating a biomechanical advantage (Keogh, Hume, Pearson, & Mellow, 2009). An association between physique traits and competitive success in the Olympic throwing events has been recognized for some time, with successful athletes being heavier and taller than their counterparts (Khosla, 1968) and growing in size at a rate well in excess of population secular trends (Norton & Olds, 2001). In contrast to other strength sports, body-building is unique in that competitive success is judged purely on the basis of the size, symmetry, and definition of musculature. Not surprisingly, body-builders are the most muscular of all the strength athletes (Huygens et al., 2002). Successful body-builders have lower body fat, yet are taller and heavier with wider skeletal proportions, especially the ratio of biacromial to bi-iliocristal breadths (Fry, Ryan, Schwab, Powell, & Kraemer, 1991).

While it is reasonable to presume that the nutritional focus of strength-power athletes remains with skeletal muscle hypertrophy throughout the year, in reality this is rarely the case, except perhaps during the "off-season" for bodybuilders or specified times of the annual macrocycle of other strength-power athletes. Furthermore, significant changes in body mass among bodybuilders, Olympic weightlifters, and powerlifters will likely influence the weight category they compete in and those they compete against. Thus the intention to promote skeletal muscle hypertrophy must be given serious consideration by athletes and their coaches before being implemented.

Conclusions

Nutrition plays a number of important roles for athletes competing in sports where the expression of explosive power and strength are critical to competitive success. While total energy intake of strength-power athletes tends to be greater than that of endurance-focused athletes, intake relative to body mass is often unremarkable, with less known about distribution of nutrient intake over the day. Strength-power athletes will benefit from a greater focus on the strategic timing of nutrient intake before, during, and after exercise to assist them in optimizing resistance training work capacity, recovery, and body composition. Strength and power athletes create unique challenges for the nutrition service provider given their reliance on readily accessible sources of information, susceptibility to sports supplement marketing, potentially distorted body image and challenges associated with achieving a specified weight category in some sports, plus the general void of scientific investigation in recent years relating specifically to this unique group of athletes.

References

Arnal, M. A., Mosoni, L., Boirie, Y., Houlier, M. L., Morin, L., Verdier, E. et al. (2000). Protein feeding pattern does not affect protein retention in young women. *Journal of Nutrition, 130*, 1700–1704.

Bamman, M. M., Hunter, G. R., Newton, L. E., Roney, R. K., & Khaled, M. A. (1993). Changes in body composition, diet, and strength of bodybuilders during the 12 weeks prior to competition. *Journal of Sports Medicine and Physical Fitness, 33*, 383–391.

Beck, T. W., Housh, T. J., Johnson, G. O., Schmidt, R. J., Housh, D. J., Coburn, J. W. et al. (2007). Effects of a protease supplement on eccentric exercise-induced markers of delayed-onset muscle soreness and muscle damage. *Journal of Strength and Conditioning Research, 21*, 661–667.

Bird, S. P., Tarpenning, K. M., & Marino, F. E. (2006a). Effects of liquid carbohydrate/essential amino acid ingestion on acute hormonal response during a single bout of resistance exercise in untrained men. *Nutrition, 22*, 367–375.

Bird, S. P., Tarpenning, K. M., & Marino, F. E. (2006b). Liquid carbohydrate/essential amino acid ingestion during a short-term bout of resistance exercise suppresses myofibrillar protein degradation. *Metabolism, 55*, 570–577.

Bohe, J., Low, J. F., Wolfe, R. R., & Rennie, M. J. (2001). Latency and duration of stimulation of human muscle protein synthesis during continuous infusion of amino acids. *Journal of Physiology, 532* (Pt 2), 575–579.

Brechue, W. F., & Abe, T. (2002). The role of FFM accumulation and skeletal muscle architecture in powerlifting performance. *European Journal of Applied Physiology, 86*, 327–336.

Brill, J. B., & Keane, M. W. (1994). Supplementation patterns of competitive male and female bodybuilders. *International Journal of Sport Nutrition, 4*, 398–412.

Buford, T. W., Cooke, M. B., Redd, L. L., Hudson, G. M., Shelmadine, B. D., & Willoughby, D. S. (2009). Protease supplementation improves muscle function after eccentric exercise. *Medicine and Science in Sports and Exercise, 41*, 1908–1914.

Burd, N. A., Tang, J. E., Moore, D. R., & Phillips, S. M. (2009). Exercise training and protein metabolism: Influences of contraction, protein intake, and sex-based differences. *Journal of Applied Physiology, 106*, 1692–1701.

Burke, L. M., Cox, G. R., Culmmings, N. K., & Desbrow, B. (2001). Guidelines for daily carbohydrate intake: Do athletes achieve them? *Sports Medicine, 31*, 267–299.

Burke, L. M., Gollan, R. A., & Read, R. S. (1991). Dietary intakes and food use of groups of elite Australian male athletes. *International Journal of Sport Nutrition, 1*, 378–394.

Burke, L. M., Kiens, B., & Ivy, J. L. (2004). Carbohydrates and fat for training and recovery. *Journal of Sports Sciences, 22*, 15–30.

Burke, L. M., Slater, G., Broad, E. M., Haukka, J., Modulon, S., & Hopkins, W. G. (2003). Eating patterns and meal frequency of elite Australian athletes. *International Journal of Sport Nutrition and Exercise Metabolism, 13*, 521–538.

Calloway, D. H., & Spector, H. (1954). Nitrogen balance as related to caloric and protein intake in active young men. *American Journal of Clinical Nutrition, 2*, 405–412.

Chen, J. D., Wang, J. F., Li, K. J., Zhao, Y. W., Wang, S. W., Jiao, Y. et al. (1989). Nutritional problems and measures in elite and amateur athletes. *American Journal of Clinical Nutrition, 49* (5 suppl.), 1084–1089.

Cheung, K., Hume, P., & Maxwell, L. (2003). Delayed onset muscle soreness: Treatment strategies and performance factors. *Sports Medicine, 33*, 145–164.

Cockburn, E., Stevenson, E., Hayes, P. R., Robson-Ansley, P., & Howatson, G. (2010). Effect of milk-based carbohydrate-protein supplement timing on the attenuation of exercise-induced muscle damage. *Applied Physiology, Nutrition, and Metabolism, 35*, 270–277.

Cribb, P. J., & Hayes, A. (2006). Effects of supplement timing and resistance exercise on skeletal muscle hypertrophy. *Medicine and Science in Sports and Exercise, 38*, 1918–1925.

Faber, M., Benade, A. J., & van Eck, M. (1986). Dietary intake, anthropometric measurements, and blood lipid values in weight training athletes (body builders). *International Journal of Sports Medicine, 7,* 342–346.

Faber, M., Spinnler-Benade, A. J., & Daubitzer, A. (1990). Dietary intake, anthropometric measurements and plasma lipid levels in throwing field athletes. *International Journal of Sports Medicine, 11,* 140–145.

Fogelholm, M. (1994). Effects of bodyweight reduction on sports performance. *Sports Medicine, 18,* 249–267.

Folland, J. P., & Williams, A. G. (2007). The adaptations to strength training: Morphological and neurological contributions to increased strength. *Sports Medicine, 37,* 145–168.

Froiland, K., Koszewski, W., Hingst, J., & Kopecky, L. (2004). Nutritional supplement use among college athletes and their sources of information. *International Journal of Sport Nutrition and Exercise Metabolism, 14,* 104–120.

Fry, A. C., Ryan, A. J., Schwab, R. J., Powell, D. R., & Kraemer, W. J. (1991). Anthropometric characteristics as discriminators of body-building success. *Journal of Sports Sciences, 9,* 23–32.

Fujita, S., Dreyer, H. C., Drummond, M. J., Glynn, E. L., Volpi, E., & Rasmussen, B. B. (2009). Essential amino acid and carbohydrate ingestion before resistance exercise does not enhance postexercise muscle protein synthesis. *Journal of Applied Physiology, 106,* 1730–1739.

Giada, F., Zuliani, G., Baldo-Enzi, G., Palmieri, E., Volpato, S., Vitale, E. et al. (1996). Lipoprotein profile, diet and body composition in athletes practicing mixed and anaerobic activities. *Journal of Sports Medicine and Physical Fitness, 36,* 211–216.

Gibala, M. J., Interisano, S. A., Tarnopolsky, M. A., Roy, B. D., MacDonald, J. R., Yarasheski, K. E. et al. (2000). Myofibrillar disruption following acute concentric and eccentric resistance exercise in strength-trained men. *Canadian Journal of Physiology and Pharmacology, 78,* 656–661.

Goston, J. L., & Correia, M. I. (2010). Intake of nutritional supplements among people exercising in gyms and influencing factors. *Nutrition, 26,* 604–611.

Grandjean, A. C. (1989). Macronutrient intake of US athletes compared with the general population and recommendations made for athletes. *American Journal of Clinical Nutrition, 49* (5 suppl.), 1070–1076.

Grunewald, K. K., & Bailey, R. S. (1993). Commercially marketed supplements for bodybuilding athletes. *Sports Medicine, 15,* 90–103.

Haff, G. G., Koch, A. J., Potteiger, J. A., Kuphal, K. E., Magee, L. M., Green, S. B. et al. (2000). Carbohydrate supplementation attenuates muscle glycogen loss during acute bouts of resistance exercise. *International Journal of Sport Nutrition and Exercise Metabolism, 10,* 326–339.

Haff, G. G., Schroeder, C. A., Koch, A. J., Kuphal, K. E., Comeau, M. J., & Potteiger, J. A. (2001). The effects of supplemental carbohydrate ingestion on intermittent isokinetic leg exercise. *Journal of Sports Medicine and Physical Fitness, 41,* 216–222.

Haff, G. G., Stone, M. H., Warren, B. J., Keith, R., Johnson, R. L., Nieman, D. C. et al. (1999). The effect of carbohydrate supplementation on multiple sessions and bouts of resistance exercise. *Journal of Strength and Conditioning Research, 13,* 111–117.

Hakkinen, K. (1993). Neuromuscular fatigue and recovery in male and female athletes during heavy resistance exercise. *International Journal of Sports Medicine, 14,* 53–59.

Hargreaves, M., Hawley, J. A., & Jeukendrup, A. (2004). Pre-exercise carbohydrate and fat ingestion: Effects on metabolism and performance. *Journal of Sports Sciences, 22,* 31–38.

Hartman, J. W., Moore, D. R., & Phillips, S. M. (2006). Resistance training reduces whole-body protein turnover and improves net protein retention in untrained young males. *Applied Physiology, Nutrition, and Metabolism, 31,* 557–564.

Heinemann, L., & Zerbes, H. (1989). Physical activity, fitness, and diet: Behavior in the population compared with elite athletes in the GDR. *American Journal of Clinical Nutrition, 49* (5 suppl.), 1007–1016.

Hespel, P., & Derave, W. (2007). Ergogenic effects of creatine in sports and rehabilitation. *Sub-cellular Biochemistry, 46,* 245–259.

Heymsfield, S. B., Chiracharyavej, T., Rhyu, I. J., Roongpisuthipong, C., Heo, M., & Pietrobelli, A. (2009). Differences between brain mass and body weight scaling to height: Potential mechanism of reduced mass-specific resting energy expenditure of taller adults. *Journal of Applied Physiology, 106,* 40–48.

Heyward, V. H., Sandoval, W. M., & Colville, B. C. (1989). Anthropometric, body composition and nutritional profiles of bodybuilders during training. *Journal of Applied Sport Science Research, 3,* 22–29.

Hildebrandt, T., Schlundt, D., Langenbucher, J., & Chung, T. (2006). Presence of muscle dysmorphia symptomology among male weightlifters. *Comprehensive Psychiatry, 47,* 127–135.

Hoffman, J. R., Cooper, J., Wendell, M., & Kang, J. (2004). Comparison of Olympic vs. traditional power lifting training programs in football players. *Journal of Strength and Conditioning Research, 18,* 129–135.

Huygens, W., Claessens, A. L., Thomis, M., Loos, R., Van Langendonck, L., Peeters, M. et al. (2002). Body composition estimations by BIA versus anthropometric equations in body builders and other power athletes. *Journal of Sports Medicine and Physical Fitness, 42,* 45–55.

Jackman, S. R., Witard, O. C., Jeukendrup, A. E., & Tipton, K. D. (2010). Branched-chain amino acid ingestion can ameliorate soreness from eccentric exercise. *Medicine and Science in Sports and Exercise, 42,* 962–970.

Jacobs, I., Kaiser, P., & Tesch, P. (1981). Muscle strength and fatigue after selective glycogen depletion in human skeletal muscle fibers. *European Journal of Applied Physiology and Occupational Physiology, 46,* 47–53.

Judge, L. W., Moreau, C., & Burke, J. R. (2003). Neural adaptations with sport-specific resistance training in highly skilled athletes. *Journal of Sports Sciences, 21,* 419–427.

Keogh, J. W., Hume, P. A., Pearson, S. N., & Mellow, P. (2007). Anthropometric dimensions of male powerlifters of varying body mass. *Journal of Sports Sciences, 25,* 1365–1376.

Keogh, J. W., Hume, P. A., Pearson, S. N., & Mellow, P. J. (2009). Can absolute and proportional anthropometric characteristics distinguish stronger and weaker powerlifters? *Journal of Strength and Conditioning Research, 23,* 2256–2265.

Khosla, T. (1968). Unfairness of certain events in Olympic Games. *British Medical Journal, 4* (5623), 111–113.

Kiningham, R. B., & Gorenflo, D. W. (2001). Weight loss methods of high school wrestlers. *Medicine and Science in Sports and Exercise, 33,* 810–813.

Kleiner, S. M., Bazzarre, T. L., & Litchford, M. D. (1990). Metabolic profiles, diet, and health practices of championship male and female bodybuilders. *Journal of the American Dietetic Association, 90,* 962–967.

Kleiner, S. M., Calabrese, L. H., Fiedler, K. M., Naito, H. K., & Skibinski, C. I. (1989). Dietary influences on cardiovascular disease risk in anabolic steroid-using and nonusing bodybuilders. *Journal of the American College of Nutrition, 8,* 109–119.

Koopman, R., Beelen, M., Stellingwerff, T., Pennings, B., Saris, W. H., Kies, A. K. et al. (2007). Coingestion of carbohydrate with protein does not further augment postexercise muscle protein synthesis. *American Journal of Physiology: Endocrinology and Metabolism, 293,* E833–E842.

Koopman, R., Manders, R. J., Jonkers, R. A., Hul, G. B., Kuipers, H., & van Loon, L. J. (2006). Intramyocellular lipid and glycogen content are reduced following resistance exercise in untrained healthy males. *European Journal of Applied Physiology, 96,* 525–534.

Kraft, J. A., Green, J. M., Bishop, P. A., Richardson, M. T., Neggers, Y. H., & Leeper, J. D. (2010). Impact of dehydration on a full body resistance exercise protocol. *European Journal of Applied Physiology, 109,* 259–267.

Kulik, J. R., Touchberry, C. D., Kawamori, N., Blumert, P. A., Crum, A. J., & Haff, G. G. (2008). Supplemental carbohydrate ingestion does not improve performance of high-intensity resistance exercise. *Journal of Strength and Conditioning Research, 22,* 1101–1107.

Lamar-Hildebrand, N., Saldanha, L., & Endres, J. (1989). Dietary and exercise practices of college-aged female bodybuilders. *Journal of the American Dietetic Association, 89,* 1308–1310.

Lambert, C. P., & Flynn, M. G. (2002). Fatigue during high-intensity intermittent exercise: Application to bodybuilding. *Sports Medicine, 32,* 511–522.

Lambert, C. P., Flynn, M. G., Boone, J. B. J., Michaud, T. J., & Rodriguez-Zayas, J. (1991). Effects of carbohydrate feeding on multiple-bout resistance exercise. *Journal of Strength and Conditioning Research, 5,* 192–197.

Lenn, J., Uhl, T., Mattacola, C., Boissonneault, G., Yates, J., Ibrahim, W. et al. (2002). The effects of fish oil and isoflavones on delayed onset muscle soreness. *Medicine and Science in Sports and Exercise, 34,* 1605–1613.

Leveritt, M., & Abernethy, P. J. (1999). Effects of carbohydrate restriction on strength performance. *Journal of Strength and Conditioning Research, 13,* 52–57.

Loucks, A. B., Kiens, B., & Wright, H. (2011). Energy availability in athletes. *Journal of Sports Sciences.*

MacDougall, J. D., Ray, S., Sale, D. G., McCartney, N., Lee, P., & Garner, S. (1999). Muscle substrate utilization, and lactate production during weightlifting. *Canadian Journal of Applied Physiology – Revue Canadienne de Physiologie Appliquee, 24,* 209–215.

Maestu, J., Eliakim, A., Jurimae, J., Valter, I., & Jurimae, T. (2010). Anabolic and catabolic hormones and energy balance of the male bodybuilders during the preparation for the competition. *Journal of Strength and Conditioning Research, 24,* 1074–1081.

Manore, M. M., Barr, S. I., & Butterfield, G. E. (2000). Joint Position Statement: Nutrition and athletic performance. American College of Sports Medicine, American Dietetic Association, and Dietitians of Canada. *Medicine and Science in Sports and Exercise, 32,* 2130–2145.

Matsumoto, K., Koba, T., Hamada, K., Sakurai, M., Higuchi, T., & Miyata, H. (2009). Branched-chain amino acid supplementation attenuates muscle soreness, muscle damage and inflammation during an intensive training program. *Journal of Sports Medicine and Physical Fitness, 49,* 424–431.

Maughan, R. J., Greenhaff, P. L., & Hespel, P. (2011). Risks and rewards of dietary supplement use by athletes. *Journal of Sports Sciences.*

Mettler, S., Mitchell, N., & Tipton, K. D. (2010). Increased protein intake reduces lean body mass loss during weight loss in athletes. *Medicine and Science in Sports and Exercise, 42,* 326–337.

Miller, P. C., Bailey, S. P., Barnes, M. E., Derr, S. J., & Hall, E. E. (2004). The effects of protease supplementation on skeletal muscle function and DOMS following downhill running. *Journal of Sports Sciences, 22,* 365–372.

Miller, S. L., Tipton, K. D., Chinkes, D. L., Wolf, S. E., & Wolfe, R. R. (2003). Independent and combined effects of amino acids and glucose after resistance exercise. *Medicine and Science in Sports and Exercise, 35,* 449–455.

Mitchell, J. B., DiLauro, P. C., Pizza, F. X., & Cavender, D. L. (1997). The effect of preexercise carbohydrate status on resistance exercise performance. *International Journal of Sport Nutrition, 7,* 185–196.

Moore, D. R., Robinson, M. J., Fry, J. L., Tang, J. E., Glover, E. I., Wilkinson, S. B. et al. (2009). Ingested protein dose response of muscle and albumin protein synthesis after resistance exercise in young men. *American Journal of Clinical Nutrition, 89,* 161–168.

Morrison, L. J., Gizis, F., & Shorter, B. (2004). Prevalent use of dietary supplements among people who exercise at a commercial gym. *International Journal of Sport Nutrition and Exercise Metabolism, 14,* 481–492.

Nieper, A. (2005). Nutritional supplement practices in UK junior national track and field athletes. *British Journal of Sports Medicine, 39,* 645–649.

Norton, K., & Olds, T. (2001). Morphological evolution of athletes over the 20th century: Causes and consequences. *Sports Medicine, 31,* 763–783.

Oppliger, R. A., Case, H. S., Horswill, C. A., Landry, G. L., & Shelter, A. C. (1996). American College of Sports Medicine position stand: Weight loss in wrestlers. *Medicine and Science in Sports and Exercise, 28* (6), ix–xii.

Pascoe, D. D., Costill, D. L., Fink, W. J., Robergs, R. A., & Zachwieja, J. J. (1993). Glycogen resynthesis in skeletal muscle following resistive exercise. *Medicine and Science in Sports and Exercise, 25,* 349–354.

Peiser, B., & Reilly, T. (2004). Environmental factors in the summer Olympics in historical perspective. *Journal of Sports Sciences, 22,* 981–1001; discussion 1001–1002.

Philen, R. M., Ortiz, D. I., Auerbach, S. B., & Falk, H. (1992). Survey of advertising for nutritional supplements in health and bodybuilding magazines. *Journal of the American Medical Association, 268,* 1008–1011.

Phillips, S. M. (2004). Protein requirements and supplementation in strength sports. *Nutrition, 20,* 689–695.

Phillips, S. M., Tang, J. E., & Moore, D. R. (2009). The role of milk- and soy-based protein in support of muscle protein synthesis and muscle protein accretion in young and elderly persons. *Journal of the American College of Nutrition, 28,* 343–354.

Phillips, S. M., & Van Loon, L. J. (2011). Dietary protein for athletes: From requirements to optimal adaptation. *Journal of Sports Sciences.*

Richardson, D. P., Wayler, A. H., Scrimshaw, N. S., & Young, V. R. (1979). Quantitative effect of an isoenergetic exchange of fat for carbohydrate on dietary protein utilization in healthy young men. *American Journal of Clinical Nutrition, 32,* 2217–2226.

Ronsen, O., Sundgot-Borgen, J., & Maehlum, S. (1999). Supplement use and nutritional habits in Norwegian elite athletes. *Scandinavian Journal of Medicine and Science in Sports, 9,* 28–35.

Roy, B. D., & Tarnopolsky, M. A. (1998). Influence of differing macronutrient intakes on muscle glycogen resynthesis after resistance exercise. *Journal of Applied Physiology, 84,* 890–896.

Saunders, M. J., Kane, M. D., & Todd, M. K. (2004). Effects of a carbohydrate-protein beverage on cycling endurance and muscle damage. *Medicine and Science in Sports and Exercise, 36,* 1233–1238.

Schulz, L. O., & Schoeller, D. A. (1994). A compilation of total daily energy expenditures and body weights in healthy adults. *American Journal of Clinical Nutrition, 60,* 676–681.

Sharp, C. P., & Pearson, D. R. (2010). Amino acid supplements and recovery from high-intensity resistance training. *Journal of Strength and Conditioning Research, 24,* 1125–1130.

Sheppard, H. L., Raichada, S. M., Kouri, K. M., Stenson-Bar-Maor, L., & Branch, J. D. (2000). Use of creatine and other supplements by members of civilian and military health clubs: A cross-sectional survey. *International Journal of Sport Nutrition and Exercise Metabolism, 10,* 245–259.

Shimomura, Y., Inaguma, A., Watanabe, S., Yamamoto, Y., Muramatsu, Y., Bajotto, G. et al. (2010). Branched-chain amino acid supplementation before squat exercise and delayed-onset muscle soreness. *International Journal of Sport Nutrition and Exercise Metabolism, 20,* 236–244.

Sobal, J., & Marquart, L. F. (1994). Vitamin/mineral supplement use among athletes: A review of the literature. *International Journal of Sport Nutrition, 4,* 320–334.

Sugiura, K., Suzuki, I., & Kobayashi, K. (1999). Nutritional intake of elite Japanese track-and-field athletes. *International Journal of Sport Nutrition, 9,* 202–212.

Sundgot-Borgen, J., & Garthe, I. (2011). Elite athletes in aesthetic and weight-class sports and the challenge of weight and body composition. *Journal of Sports Sciences.*

Swinton, P. A., Lloyd, R., Agouris, I., & Stewart, A. (2009). Contemporary training practices in elite British powerlifters: Survey results from an international competition. *Journal of Strength and Conditioning Research, 23,* 380–384.

Tang, J. E., & Phillips, S. M. (2009). Maximizing muscle protein anabolism: The role of protein quality. *Current Opinion in Clinical Nutrition and Metabolic Care, 12,* 66–71.

Tarnopolsky, M. A., MacDougall, J. D., & Atkinson, S. A. (1988). Influence of protein intake and training status on nitrogen balance and lean body mass. *Journal of Applied Physiology, 64,* 187–193.

Tesch, P. A., Colliander, E. B., & Kaiser, P. (1986). Muscle metabolism during intense, heavy-resistance exercise. *European Journal of Applied Physiology and Occupational Physiology, 55,* 362–366.

Tipton, K. D., Elliott, T. A., Cree, M. G., Aarsland, A. A., Sanford, A. P., & Wolfe, R. R. (2007). Stimulation of net muscle protein synthesis by whey protein ingestion before and after exercise. *American Journal of Physiology: Endocrinology and Metabolism, 292,* E71–E76.

Tipton, K. D., Rasmussen, B. B., Miller, S. L., Wolf, S. E., Owens-Stovall, S. K., Petrini, B. E. et al. (2001). Timing of amino acid-carbohydrate ingestion alters anabolic response of muscle to resistance exercise. *American Journal of Physiology: Endocrinology and Metabolism, 281,* E197–E206.

van der Ploeg, G. E., Brooks, A. G., Withers, R. T., Dollman, J., Leaney, F., & Chatterton, B. E. (2001). Body composition changes in female bodybuilders during preparation for competition. *European Journal of Clinical Nutrition, 55,* 268–277.

van Erp-Baart, A. M., Saris, W. H., Binkhorst, R. A., Vos, J. A., & Elvers, J. W. (1989). Nationwide survey on nutritional habits in elite athletes. Part I. Energy, carbohydrate, protein, and fat intake. *International Journal of Sports Medicine, 10* (suppl. 1), S3–S10.

van Loon, L. J., Saris, W. H., Kruijshoop, M., & Wagenmakers, A. J. (2000). Maximizing postexercise muscle glycogen synthesis: Carbohydrate supplementation and the application of amino acid or protein hydrolysate mixtures. *American Journal of Clinical Nutrition, 72,* 106–111.

Volek, J. S., Forsythe, C. E., & Kraemer, W. J. (2006). Nutritional aspects of women strength athletes. *British Journal of Sports Medicine, 40,* 742–748.

Walberg, J. L., & Johnston, C. S. (1991). Menstrual function and eating behavior in female recreational weight lifters and competitive body builders. *Medicine and Science in Sports and Exercise, 23,* 30–36.

Walberg-Rankin, J., Edmonds, C. E., & Gwazdauskas, F. C. (1993). Diet and weight changes of female bodybuilders before and after competition. *International Journal of Sport Nutrition, 3,* 87–102.

Warren, G. L., Park, N. D., Maresca, R. D., McKibans, K. I., & Millard-Stafford, M. L. (2010). Effect of caffeine ingestion on muscular strength and endurance: A meta-analysis. *Medicine and Science in Sports and Exercise, 42,* 1375–1387.

Withers, R. T., Noell, C. J., Whittingham, N. O., Chatterton, B. E., Schultz, C.G., & Keeves, J. P. (1997). Body composition changes in elite male bodybuilders during preparation for competition. *Australian Journal of Science and Medicine in Sport, 29,* 11–16.

Zehnder, M., Muelli, M., Buchli, R., Kuehne, G., & Boutellier, U. (2004). Further glycogen decrease during early recovery after eccentric exercise despite a high carbohydrate intake. *European Journal of Nutrition, 43,* 148–159.

Zello, G. A. (2006). Dietary reference intakes for the macronutrients and energy: Considerations for physical activity. *Applied Physiology, Nutrition, and Metabolism, 31,* 74–79.

Nutrition for power sports: Middle-distance running, track cycling, rowing, canoeing/kayaking, and swimming

TRENT STELLINGWERFF[1], RONALD J. MAUGHAN[2], & LOUISE M. BURKE[3]

[1]Nestlé Research Centre, Lausanne, Switzerland, [2]School of Sport, Exercise and Health Sciences, Loughborough University, Loughborough, UK, and [3]Department of Sports Nutrition, Australian Institute of Sport, Belconnen, ACT, Australia

Abstract

Contemporary training for power sports involves diverse routines that place a wide array of physiological demands on the athlete. This requires a multi-faceted nutritional strategy to support both general training needs – tailored to specific training phases – as well as the acute demands of competition. Elite power sport athletes have high training intensities and volumes for most of the training season, so energy intake must be sufficient to support recovery and adaptation. Low pre-exercise muscle glycogen reduces high-intensity performance, so daily carbohydrate intake must be emphasized throughout training and competition phases. There is strong evidence to suggest that the timing, type, and amount of protein intake influence post-exercise recovery and adaptation. Most power sports feature demanding competition schedules, which require aggressive nutritional recovery strategies to optimize muscle glycogen resynthesis. Various power sports have different optimum body compositions and body weight requirements, but increasing the power-to-weight ratio during the championship season can lead to significant performance benefits for most athletes. Both intra- and extracellular buffering agents may enhance performance, but more research is needed to examine the potential long-term impact of buffering agents on training adaptation. Interactions between training, desired physiological adaptations, competition, and nutrition require an individual approach and should be continuously adjusted and adapted.

Introduction

While some sports emphasize the exclusive development of strength or endurance, several sports require high power output for success. Power is the rate at which work is performed or energy is produced. Most elite power sport athletes can sustain very high power outputs (20 kcal · min^{-1}; 500 W) at greater than 100% of maximal oxygen uptake ($\dot{V}O_{2max}$), over races lasting up to 10 min (Table I), which result in post-exercise blood lactate concentrations in excess of 20 mmol · L^{-1}. Accordingly, these athletes utilize the continuum of energy systems to supply adenosine triphosphate (ATP) to meet their energy demands, and are completely reliant upon endogenously stored fuel. To fully develop all energy systems, elite power athletes undertake a modern periodized training approach that features a high volume of training during aerobic development and high-intensity training during the competition phase, coupled with strength training. The demanding competition schedules of power athletes and the complexities of micro- and macro-training cycles

result in nutritional challenges that can be best addressed through a periodized nutritional approach.

Only a few previous reviews have focused on the complexities of power sport athletes (Maughan et al., 1997; Stellingwerff, Boit, & Res, 2007a). The focus of the current article is to outline nutrition recommendations during training and competition, specific to power-based athletes involved in events of 1–10 min duration, including middle-distance running, track cycling, rowing, canoeing/kayaking, and swimming. In this review, we provide practical nutrition recommendations based on modern scientific data for acute and chronic training and competitive situations. We also highlight body composition considerations and supplements that are relevant to power athletes.

Fuel utilization and energy systems in power sports

A brief overview of energy systems and fuel utilization will set the structure for subsequent

Table I. Differences in energy source provision in power-based sporting events.

Event time range	Event example	Approx. % $\dot{V}O_{2max}$	% Energy contribution		
			Phospho	Glycolysis	Oxidative
0.5 to 1 min	400-m running; individual cycling time-trial (500 m or 1 km); 100-m swimming disciplines	~150	~10	~47–60	~30–43
1.5 to 2 min	800-m running; 200-m swimming disciplines; 500-m canoe/kayak disciplines	113–130	~5	~29–45	~50–66
3 to 5 min	1500-m running; cycling pursuit; 400-m swimming disciplines; 1000-m canoe/kayak disciplines	103–115	~2	~14–28	~70–84
5 to 8 min	3000-m running; 2000-m rowing	98–102	<1	~10–12	~88–90

Note: Phospho = phosphagen breakdown; Glycolysis = non-oxidative glycolysis (anaerobic metabolism); Oxidative = oxidative phosphorylation (aerobic metabolism). Data adapted from Spencer and Gastin (2001).

nutritional recommendations. Table I outlines the approximate fractional energy contribution across a range of event lengths for the three energy systems that provide ATP, namely: (1) phosphagen breakdown, (2) non-oxidative glycolysis ("anaerobic" glycolysis), and (3) oxidative phosphorylation ("aerobic" metabolism). Carbohydrate provides the majority of the fuel for exercise intensities above 75% $\dot{V}O_{2max}$, and is a fuel for both non-oxidative glycolysis and oxidative phosphorylation. In contrast, fat is metabolized exclusively via oxidative phosphorylation. Oxidative phosphorylation provides the bulk of ATP provision during low-intensity exercise, primarily utilizing Type I muscle fibres. However, during exercise of increasing intensity, when ATP production from oxidative phosphorylation cannot match the rate of ATP hydrolysis, the shortfall in ATP supply is met by substrate level phosphorylation. This system provides energy via phosphagen utilization and the metabolism of muscle glycogen and plasma glucose, via the glycolytic pathway, with lactate formation. During moments of high energy demand, there is an increased activation of Type IIa muscle fibres, which have both a high oxidative and glycolytic capacity. At very high workloads, Type IIb muscle fibres become activated to maintain the high demand for ATP provision via glycolysis and phosphagen breakdown, leading to the extreme levels of lactate production associated with many power sport events. Therefore, power athletes have several highly developed energy-producing pathways that utilize different blends of phosphagen, carbohydrate, and/or fat, coupled with greater muscle buffering capacity, to handle a range of different metabolic demands during varying exercise intensities. This understanding of the different energy systems and the fuels required to produce ATP must be taken into consideration when making nutrition recommendations.

Nutrition for training

Periodized nutrition for the yearly training programme

Although the concept of training periodization has been around since the 1950s, the concept of coupling training with nutrition and body composition periodization is just starting to gain scientific awareness (Stellingwerff et al., 2007a). Periodization is defined as the purposeful sequencing of different training units (macro- and micro-training cycles and sessions), so that athletes can attain the desired physiological readiness for optimum on-demand performances (Bompa & Carrera, 2005). Traditional periodization sequences training into the four main macro-cycles of "general preparation phase", "specific preparation phase", "competition phase", and "transition phase". However, the training stimuli during these different phases can differ drastically in terms of intensity and volume. Therefore, the types of fuels and the amount of energy that are used to generate the required ATP during these phases need to be addressed through a periodized nutritional approach (Table 1; Figure 1). General macronutrient and energy intake recommendations for athletes when training and in competition are covered by Burke and colleagues (Burke, Hawley, Wong, & Jeukendrup, 2011), Loucks and co-workers (Loucks, Kiens, & Wright, 2011), and Phillips and Van Loon (2011), but further recommendations specific to power athletes will be made in this review.

General macronutrient and energy intake recommendations. During most of the training season, adequate energy must be consumed to support the training volume and intensity. For example, the training load of elite swimmers can involve individual swim practices lasting more than 3 h with over 10,000 m covered, and daily energy needs are calculated to be about 3000–6800 kcal · day^{-1} for males and about 1500–3300 kcal · day^{-1} for females (Van Handel,

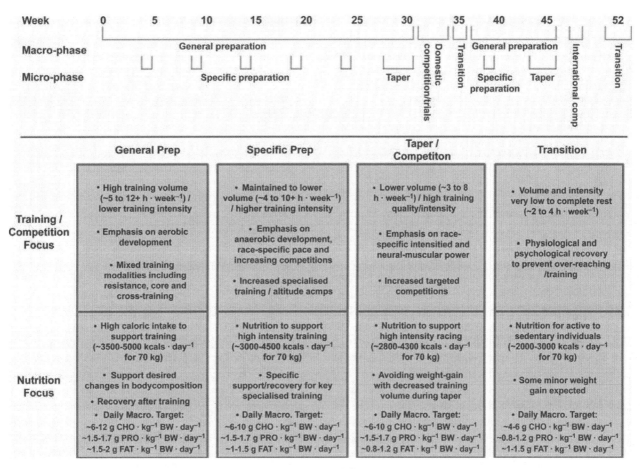

Figure 1. Overview of general nutrition recommendations during different yearly training phases for power athletes. Nutrition recommendations for a 70–kg power sport athlete. Prep, preparation; CHO, carbohydrate; FAT, fat; PRO, protein; kcal, nutritional calorie. Adapted from Burke et al. (2001), Tarnopolsky (1999), and Tipton and Wolfe (2004).

Cells, Bradley, & Troup, 1984). Many power athletes undertake 9–14 training sessions each week, with workouts from about 30 min to 3 h in duration, including resistance and plyometric/neuromuscular training several times per week. Dietary intake studies typically find that female athletes report substantially lower energy intake per kilogram of body weight (BW) than male athletes: ~ 40 kcal $\cdot$ kg BW$^{-1} \cdot$ day^{-1} for females versus ~ 55 kcal $\cdot$ kg BW$^{-1} \cdot$ day^{-1} for males (Burke, Cox, Cummings, & Desbrow, 2001). Lower daily energy and carbohydrate intake in females may be due to greater under-reporting on dietary surveys, lower energy/carbohydrate requirements due to lower training volumes and intensities than their male counterparts, or a combination of these factors.

Many athletes aspire to be at competition target body weight or body composition year round, which is physiologically and psychologically challenging. During the transition phase, most athletes take a period of rest for both mental and physical recovery in which training volume and intensity are generally very low. Some weight gain during this phase is natural, and due to the diminished or non-existent training, energy intake during this phase/day should be reduced towards nutritional recommendations that are similar to those of the general public (Figure 1).

Dietary carbohydrate intake recommendations. The seminal paper by Bergstrom and colleagues (Bergstrom, Hermansen, Hultman, & Saltin, 1967) showed that a high carbohydrate diet led to augmented glycogen stores, translating into a longer time to exhaustion than after a low carbohydrate diet. Conversely, extremely low carbohydrate diets (3–15% carbohydrate) have uniformly been shown to impair both high-intensity and endurance-based performance (Coggan & Coyle, 1991; Maughan & Poole, 1981). The amount of carbohydrate that is oxidized during exercise depends on both exercise intensity and duration, with carbohydrate oxidation providing the majority of ATP when exercising above 75% $\dot{V}O_{2peak}$. Owing to high exercise intensities during the specific preparation and competition phases, the relative dependency on carbohydrate-based ATP provision increases throughout yearly training macro-cycles. However, given the large training volumes during the general preparation phase, the absolute requirement for carbohydrate is high, thus carbohydrate-rich foods must provide the majority of the energy provision throughout the training year (Figure 1).

An examination of dietary studies of power-based sports, albeit usually of sub-elite populations, shows that male athletes typically report daily carbohydrate intakes averaging approximately $8–9 \text{ g} \cdot \text{kg BW}^{-1} \cdot \text{day}^{-1}$, which is within the recommended range, while the apparent intake of females is considerably lower at $\sim 5.5 \text{ g} \cdot \text{kg BW}^{-1} \cdot \text{day}^{-1}$ (Burke et al., 2001). It is absolutely clear that low pre-exercise muscle glycogen concentrations result in reduced high-intensity performance over a cycling test lasting about 5 min (Maughan & Poole, 1981), and that constantly training in an energy and carbohydrate depleted state may compromise immune function, training staleness, and burnout. Therefore, depending on individual training volume and intensity, a habitually high carbohydrate diet of about $6–12 \text{ g} \cdot \text{kg BW}^{-1} \cdot \text{day}^{-1}$, with females on the lower end and males on the higher end of the range, is recommended to maintain immune function, recover glycogen storage, and reduce over-reaching (Figure 1). Several studies have shown the potential beneficial effects of training with low/restricted carbohydrate availability during specific training sessions (reviewed by Burke et al., 2011). However, this approach remains controversial in terms of performance outcomes, and appears more applicable to endurance athletes than power athletes.

Dietary protein intake recommendations. Few studies have examined the protein needs of power sport athletes, as most recommendations have been made for either pure strength- or endurance-trained athletes. However, the daily protein requirement is probably based on the quantity and quality of training rather than the specific sport discipline. During stable training periods, protein intake greater than $1.7 \text{ g} \cdot \text{kg BW}^{-1} \cdot \text{day}^{-1}$ has been shown to lead to increased protein oxidation. Therefore, it is suggested that elite athletes who undertake a large and intense training load will meet their protein requirements with an intake of $1.5–1.7 \text{ g} \cdot \text{kg BW}^{-1} \cdot \text{day}^{-1}$ (Figure 1; Tarnopolsky, 1999). Dietary surveys of westernized athletes have consistently shown that athletes who consume more than $3000 \text{ kcal} \cdot \text{day}^{-1}$ most likely consume protein at or above these levels. However, beyond satisfying the current daily protein intake recommendations, emerging evidence strongly suggests that the timing, type, and amount of protein consumed over the day, and in relation to exercise sessions, will have a marked effect on the efficacy of the protein to increase protein synthesis and optimize post-exercise recovery.

Dietary fat intake recommendations. Although the majority of dietary fuel for power sport athletes is in the form of carbohydrate, fat also serves many important roles and is a vital fuel source during endurance training. Skeletal muscle can store nearly the energy equivalent of glycogen in the form of intramuscular triacylglyceride, which is a viable fuel source during prolonged moderate-intensity exercise up to about 85% $\dot{V}O_{2\text{max}}$ (Stellingwerff et al., 2007b). The general preparation phase features considerable amounts of endurance training where endogenous fats are a significant source of fuel (Figure 1). The amount of dietary fat required for daily intramuscular triacylglyceride repletion after prolonged ($>2 \text{ h}$) endurance training has been estimated at $2 \text{ g} \cdot \text{kg BW}^{-1} \cdot \text{day}^{-1}$ (Decombaz, 2003), while fat intakes greater than this may compromise muscle glycogen recovery and muscle tissue repair by displacing the intake of adequate amounts of dietary carbohydrate and protein. At certain times of the year, such as the competition phase, fat intake may be limited to reduce total energy intake to achieve body composition optimization. However, throughout all training phases, some dietary fat is always needed to aid absorption of fat-soluble vitamins and to provide substrate for hormone synthesis, as well as for cellular membrane and myelin sheath integrity.

Fuelling and fluids during training

Since power sport events last only a few minutes, there is no opportunity for fuelling (carbohydrate) and fluid intake during competition. However, given that some training sessions during the general preparation phase can approach 2 h in length, there is ample opportunity to benefit from carbohydrate and fluid intake during training. Current recommendations for carbohydrate are set to $30–60 \text{ g} \cdot \text{h}^{-1}$ for athletes during exercise, with greater amounts for exercise exceeding 2 h. For an overview of current recommendations on carbohydrate and fluid intake during training, see Burke et al. (2011), Jeukendrup (2011), and Shirreffs (2011).

Some power sports feature highly technical components (e.g. swim stroke technique). Consequently, carbohydrate intake during training can not only assist in providing energy, but also neuromuscular support via the attenuation of cognitive fatigue, which can reduce technical errors and enhance skill development, as previously demonstrated in team sport models (Currell, Conway, & Jeukendrup, 2009). The high intensity of power sport training sometimes prevents the ingestion of carbohydrate and fluids during training due to associated gastro-intestinal problems. However, several recent papers have shown that carbohydrate mouth-washing alone (for about 12 s every 7–10 min), without carbohydrate consumption, improved one-hour time-trial performance (Carter, Jeukendrup, & Jones, 2004), with the mechanism involving the activation of reward-related brain regions (Chambers, Bridge, & Jones, 2009). Anecdotal reports have demonstrated successful utilization of carbohydrate mouth-washing during rests within high-intensity interval training sessions as a way to stimulate the quality and performance of the training, while circumventing any negative gastrointestinal side-effects associated with fluid intakes during this type of session (unpublished observations). However, whether carbohydrate mouth-washing improves high-intensity repeated sprint interval performance remains to be confirmed in a well-controlled study.

Nutrition strategies to optimize recovery

Given the diversity of training and competition that power athletes undertake, an individualised post-training nutritional recovery approach needs to be implemented. Table II illustrates the different training and competition situations that will dictate different specific recovery needs and, consequently, different nutritional recommendations. The primary focus for power athletes is the recovery of muscle energy stores (primarily glycogen) and the synthesis of new proteins. Although fat consumption plays a fundamentally important role in the general diet, it remains to be shown whether increased fat intake during recovery results in a beneficial recovery profile.

Glycogen resynthesis. Since muscle glycogen is the primary fuel for power athletes, and clear evidence suggests that low pre-exercise muscle glycogen concentrations result in reduced high-intensity performance (Maughan & Poole, 1981), glycogen resynthesis after training or competition is of utmost importance. In short, 1.2–1.5 g carbohydrate $\cdot$ kg BW^{-1} ingested soon after exercise will optimize muscle glycogen re-synthesis, and when carbohydrate is consumed at this level the effect of added protein will be negligible, as further covered by Burke et al. (2011). However, specific to power sport athletes, several studies have shown an approximately 20% higher muscle glycogen concentration concomitant with increased total muscle creatine stores after creatine supplementation (20 g $\cdot$ day^{-1} for 5 days) in combination with exercise (Robinson, Sewell, Hultman, & Greenhaff, 1999; Van Loon et al., 2004). Furthermore, a recent report has shown that high-dose creatine (20 g $\cdot$ day^{-1}), in combination

with carbohydrate, caused a glycogen super-compensation effect within 24 h (Roberts et al., 2004). However, creatine intake in combination with carbohydrate did not affect the very short-term (<6 h) glycogen resynthesis rate (Robinson et al., 1999). Van Loon et al. (2004) also demonstrated that high-dose creatine (20 g $\cdot$ day^{-1}) over 6 days augmented muscle glycogen stores, but this effect was not maintained over a further 37 days when participants were placed on low-dose creatine (2 g $\cdot$ day^{-1}). However, this low-dose creatine protocol did not maintain augmented total creatine stores compared with the 6-day creatine loading phase. Taken together, it appears that a high creatine loading dose is needed to augment glycogen stores concomitantly with creatine stores, and this effect may be seen already by 24 h after supplementation. However, given that high-dose creatine intake may cause a 2–3% increase in body weight, the potential benefits of ~20% higher muscle glycogen need to be weighed against the potential negative performance effects of body weight gain on an individual and sport-specific basis.

Protein synthesis. The details of the role that specific proteins and their timing play in enhancing post-exercise muscle protein synthesis is covered elsewhere in this issue (Phillips & Van Loon, 2011). Although it has yet to be clearly established whether more or less protein is needed to optimize acute protein synthesis for athletes of varying muscle mass, given the huge diversity in body weights among power athletes, a body weight-corrected dose of ~0.3 g protein $\cdot$ kg BW^{-1} might be a prudent way to describe the optimum post-exercise protein dose (Table II). However, more studies are needed to examine nutritional timing of protein throughout the day, and in particular around exercise, to better elucidate the optimum timing for recovery and adaptation. Nevertheless, it can currently be concluded that protein and carbohydrate should be ingested in close temporal proximity to the exercise bout to maximize the anabolic response to training.

Nutrition for competition

Many power sports feature challenging competition schedules that require specific and timely nutrition recommendations. For example, when exceptional swimmer Michael Phelps won eight gold medals at the 2008 Beijing Olympics, he raced 20 times over nine consecutive days, and five of those days featured three races each. Even when power sport athletes compete in a single event, major competitions typically schedule heats or rounds to qualify for the final; recovery after each race will be the key to the

Table II. Recommendations for recovery nutrition across different training and competition situations for power-athletes.

	Specific type of training/race situation			
	Long aerobic/endurance training	Intense short duration or prolonged resistance circuit training	Technical drills/short duration resistance training	Situations of short recovery (<4 h)
Exercise characteristics	• Prolonged aerobic exercise (>1 h) of easier intensity • Primarily oxidative metabolism (FAT and CHO)	• High-intensity training of shorter durations (~20–40 min) • Primarily non-oxidative glycolytic metabolism (primarily CHO)	• Low volume of explosive movements • Primarily glycolytic and phosphagen metabolism (PCr + CHO)	• Multiple races or training sessions on the same day
Training objective	• Enhance oxidative enzymes, fat metabolism and endurance • Energy replacement (FAT and CHO)	• Enhance glycolytic enzymes, buffering capacity & lactate tolerance & muscular power • Energy replacement (primarily CHO)	• Sub-maximal and maximal muscular strength, technique and economy development • Energy needs are low	• N/A – specific to the training and racing demands • Some energy replacement (primarily CHO)
Specific recovery needs	• Carbohydrate intake of primary importance for glycogen re-synthesis • Protein needed for muscle recovery and re-modelling	• Carbohydrate intake of primary importance for glycogen resynthesis • Protein needed for muscle recovery and re-modelling	• Lower carbohydrate intake needs (some glycogen resynthesis needed) • Protein needed for muscle recovery and re-modelling	• Carbohydrate intake of primary importance for glycogen re-synthesis • Focus on foods that are GI tolerable for subsequent exercise (minimize FAT and PRO intakes)
Macronutrient recommendations (within first ~2 h)	• CHO: ~1.2–1.5 g·kg BW^{-1} • PRO: ~0.3 g·kg BW^{-1} • FAT: ~0.2–0.3 g·kg BW^{-1}	• CHO: ~1.2–1.5 g·kg BW^{-1} • PRO: ~0.3 g·kg BW^{-1} • FAT: minimal requirements	• CHO: ~0.5–1.0 g·kg BW^{-1} • PRO: ~0.3 g·kg BW^{-1} • FAT: minimal requirements	• CHO: ~1.2–1.5 g·kg BW^{-1} • PRO: minimal requirements • FAT: minimal requirements
Practical example for 70-kg athlete	• 750 mL carbohydrate sports drink, with protein recovery bar, and ~300 ml milk	• Individual mini-veggie and meat pizza, ~300 ml juice, and 1 piece of fruit	• Fruit smoothie (~300 ml: skimmed milk, yogurt, fruit + protein powder) and 1 piece of fruit	• 750 mL carbohydrate sports drink and/or high carbohydrate food snacks (e.g. sports bar, crackers, cookies, etc.)

Note: Nutrition recommendations adapted from Burke et al. (2001), Moore et al. (2009), Tarnopolsky (1999), and Tipton and Wolfe (2004). BW = body weight; CHO = carbohydrate; GI = gastrointestinal; PCr = phosphagen; PRO = protein.

ultimate outcome. In combination with the recovery recommendations above, some competition-based practical suggestions are highlighted in Table II and below:

- Before a championship, evaluate several individualized pre-competition meal options that are convenient, readily available, and feel "right" for the athlete (no gastrointestinal discomfort). These meals should be high in carbohydrate ($1–4 \text{ g} \cdot \text{kg BW}^{-1}$), lower in protein and fat, and consumed 1–6 h before competition (Burke et al., 2011).
- Meals at dining-hall buffets can feature a large variety of food choice, but for some this can cause over-eating. Athletes should select serving sizes and food choices that are appropriate to their needs (including considerations of reduced energy expenditure during tapering phases) rather than being influenced by the eating practices of other athletes or the foods available. Recording body weight daily can help athletes make sure they are on track.
- Due to the short race lengths, hydration is normally not an issue for power athletes except when faced with multiple races per day. Athletes should aim for 400–600 ml of a sport drink and/or water with electrolytes in the 1–2 h before competition, unless they are sure that they are well hydrated (Shirreffs, 2011).
- Many athletes consume small carbohydrate-based snacks and sports drinks 1–3 h before a competition warm-up. When travelling, athletes should try to pack some convenient and favourite non-perishable snacks from home, taking into consideration any customs requirements regarding the transport of food.
- It is vital to plan ahead to ensure that suitable post-competition foods and fluids are immediately available to optimize post-competition recovery. Carbohydrate-rich foods and fluids with a medium to high glycaemic index at $1.0–1.5 \text{ g carbohydrate} \cdot \text{kg BW}^{-1}$ for the first 4 h should be the target (Burke et al., 2011). Practical considerations may include food choices that can be suitably stored or prepared, or consumed in challenging circumstances and in spite of reduced appetite. The busy competition schedules of many athletes must often accommodate warm-downs, drug testing, media appearances, and other activities that can interfere with the opportunity to eat.
- Due to the usual competition venue and travel constraints, it is often difficult to get a normal meal immediately after competition. Sports nutrition products can provide convenience and meet many of these initial carbohydrate

and protein needs until a normal meal can be consumed.

Body composition considerations for power sport athletes

Although other articles in this issue (Loucks et al., 2011; Sundgot-Borgen & Garthe, 2011) review the topic of altered energy balance in athletes, some specific considerations for power athletes will be addressed here. For many athletes, achieving very low body fat and an increased power-to-weight ratio can lead to significant performance increases. Furthermore, different power sports will dictate different optimum body composition and body mass requirements. For example, despite the fact that 2000-m rowers (less weight-dependent) and 1500-m runners (fully weight-dependent) both compete with a similar sustained power over about 3.5–6.0 min, the types of body composition that dictate success are fundamentally different between these sports. Rowers are taller, stronger, and heavier than middle-distance runners and have a lower relative aerobic capacity (although absolute values of $\dot{V}O_{2\text{max}}$ are higher in heavyweight rowers). There is a wide range of normative data in elite power-based athletes, with body fat values of 5–10% for males and 8–15% for females, and swimmers generally having 4–8% higher body fat than endurance-matched runners (Fleck, 1983).

Achieving *extremely* low body fat is less important in weight-supported power sports, such as rowing or track cycling, where high absolute power outputs are more important for performance, than in more weight-dependent power sports, such as middle-distance running. Like training, body composition should also be periodized throughout the year. Although much research needs to be done to further examine what optimum yearly fluctuations in body weight and body fat might be, the practical experience of the authors has shown that changes of around 3–5% of body weight or percent body fat throughout the year appear to be ideal. This allows athletes to be at a slightly higher and healthier body weight and body fat percentage for the majority of the training year, while still being close enough to more easily achieve target body composition for the peak competition phase. Athletes should be at competition performance body weight and body composition for only short periods of time, as aspiring to be in peak body composition year round by chronically restricting energy availability results in an increased risk of injury and sickness, as well as a myriad of other associated negative health and performance effects.

Very few scientific data have been published on elite athletes and body composition, as most previous studies involving negative energy balance have been conducted in untrained individuals. However, recent data in trained individuals suggest that through aggressive exercise and dietary protein periodization, muscle mass can be maintained while losing body weight during a one-week period featuring a 40% negative energy balance (Mettler, Mitchell, & Tipton, 2010). In this study, participants utilized a higher daily protein diet (~ 2.3 g $\cdot$ kg BW^{-1} $\cdot$ day^{-1}) with resistance exercise to lose significant weight (~ 1.5 kg), of which nearly 100% was fat loss rather than muscle loss. Therefore, a combined approach of slightly decreasing energy intake (~ 500 kcal), while either maintaining or slightly increasing energy expenditure, is the best approach to optimizing body composition over an approximately 3–6 week period prior to the targeted competitive season (Figure 1; O'Connor, Olds, & Maughan, 2007). Therefore, during periods of negative energy balance in elite athletes aspiring to lose weight, it has been proposed to raise the daily protein intake to $\sim 35\%$ of daily needs, or about 1.5–2.5 g $\cdot$ kg BW^{-1} $\cdot$ day^{-1}, which appears to assist in lean tissue preservation (Phillips, 2006). Ultimately, an individualized approach needs to be taken and extremely low body fat values should be maintained for only short periods of time. It is also recommended that athletes undertake body fat and body weight reduction under the supervision of an expert dietitian/physiologist.

Ergogenic supplements for power sports

Most power sports are fuelled primarily by glycolysis (Table I), resulting in a large production of lactate and hydrogen ions (H$^+$). These large increases in H$^+$ can cause decreases in muscle pH, from resting values of ~ 7.1 down to ~ 6.4 at exhaustion. Although fatigue is multi-factorial, the primary causes of exhaustion during intense exercise lasting 1 to 10 min involves limitations imposed by non-oxidative glycolysis, as well as negative consequences resulting from the associated muscular acidosis and ionic disturbances. This drop in muscular pH has been shown to negatively affect metabolic processes, including disturbances of the creatine-phosphagen equilibrium, limiting the resynthesis of phosphagen, as well as the inhibition of glycolysis and the muscle contraction process itself (Hultman & Sahlin, 1980).

During high-intensity exercise, many different innate metabolic processes and physico-chemical properties contribute to both intracellular and extracellular buffering capacity in attempts to maintain intramuscular pH, with intramuscular carnosine and plasma bicarbonate playing primary roles. Accordingly, there are two supplements that power athletes can potentially utilize to augment buffering capacity, and potentially improve performance: (1) the pro-longed supplementation of β-alanine to increase muscle carnosine content to enhance intracellular buffering, and (2) the acute supplementation of sodium citrate or bicarbonate to enhance extracellular buffering. As of 2010, these substances are not on the World Anti-Doping Agency's prohibited substances list, and for further general information on the risk and rewards of dietary supplements, see the review by Maughan and colleagues (Maughan, Greenhaff, & Hespel, 2011).

Intracellular buffering: Carnosine

Carnosine (β-alanyl-L-histidine) is a cytoplasmic dipeptide found at high concentrations in skeletal muscle and in particular Type II fibres (Artioli, Gualano, Smith, Stout, & Lancha, 2010; Derave, Everaert, Beeckman, & Baguet, 2010). Higher concentrations have been found in sprinters and rowers than in marathon runners (Parkhouse & McKenzie, 1984). Carnosine is a potent intramuscular buffer due to its nitrogen-containing imidazole ring, which can buffer H$^+$ ions with a pKa of 6.83, thus slowing the decline in pH during intense exercise. Supporting this mechanism is recent evidence showing that 4 weeks of β-alanine supplementation reduced the decline of blood pH during intense exercise (Baguet, Koppo, Pottier, & Derave, 2010). The contribution of normal muscle carnosine to total intracellular muscle buffering capacity has been suggested to be $\sim 7\%$, but can reach $\sim 15\%$ after β-alanine supplementation (Harris et al., 2006).

Harris and colleagues (2006) were the first to show increases in muscle carnosine after prolonged β-alanine supplementation in humans. All subsequent supplementation studies have shown a significant increase in muscle carnosine concentrations utilizing approximately 3–6 g of β-alanine per day over 4–8 weeks (Derave et al., 2010). On average, this has led to a significant (40–50%) increase in muscle carnosine. A direct linear correlation has also been shown between the amount of β-alanine consumed (total grams) and the percent increase in muscle carnosine ($R = 0.569$; $P < 0.01$; unpublished observations). The washout of augmented skeletal muscle carnosine is slow, with an estimated washout time of 10–15 weeks after a $\sim 50\%$ increase in muscle carnosine (Baguet et al., 2009; Stellingwerff et al., 2010).

Although some studies have not found enhanced performance resulting from prolonged β-alanine supplementation, several well-controlled studies have demonstrated significant high-intensity (about 1–6 min) performance benefits using both cycling and rowing protocols, as well as showing improved isokinetic knee-extension performance (Artioli et al., 2010; Derave et al., 2010). Studies not demonstrating positive performance effects are most likely due to inadequate β-alanine dosing, not using well-trained and motivated participants, or being under-powered and/or using inappropriately designed performance tests in which acid–base perturbations are not limiting the outcome. Taken together, the emerging data reveal that consumption of about 3–6 g β-alanine $\cdot$ day^{-1} over 4–8 weeks (for a total β-alanine intake of >120 g) will result in an increase of muscle carnosine of about 40–50%, and, given a correctly designed performance test, will lead to positive anaerobic performance outcomes in intense exercise lasting 1–6 min. At this point, it remains to be established whether prolonged β-alanine supplementation can enhance weight training, sprint (<15 s) or endurance (>20 min) performance.

Extracellular buffering: Sodium bicarbonate and citrate

During intense exercise, lactate and H$^+$ are transported out of the muscle via monocarboxylate transporters (primarily MCT-4) to the extracellular space. Since hydrogen ions are transported against a concentration gradient, any mechanism to increase the rate of H$^+$ release from the muscle will help maintain muscle pH and delay fatigue. One such mechanism is an increase in the plasma bicarbonate (HCO$_3$–) pool, which combines with the H$^+$ to form carbonic acid (H$_2$CO$_3$), which in turn dissociates to form carbon dioxide and water. Supplementation of sodium bicarbonate (NaHCO$_3$) can lead to increased plasma bicarbonate and increased buffering by improving the rate of H$^+$ release from active skeletal muscle.

A series of studies throughout the 1980s found that the optimum dosing regimen to augment the blood's buffering capacity is via the supplementation of NaHCO$_3$ (~ 300 mg $\cdot$ kg BW^{-1}; ~ 20 g) in the 1–3 h before a high-intensity event (about 1–6 min; McNaughton, 2000). However, there is a high degree of individual tolerance and variability, as ingestion of water with the NaHCO$_3$ causes a 1–2% increase in body weight and can cause significant gastrointestinal upset in $\sim 50\%$ of individuals. This can be partially circumvented by supplementing the active dose of NaHCO$_3$ in multiple gelatin capsules, with significantly less water (Galloway & Maughan, 1996). A recent study that systematically manipulated the timing and type of bicarbonate supplementation protocols (capsules versus powder) found that the most effective strategy to increase plasma bicarbonate concentrations involved the use of bicarbonate capsules consumed in serial doses over a period of 120–150 min before exercise and co-ingested with a high-carbohydrate meal or snack (Carr, Slater, Gore, Dawson, & Burke, 2011).

When utilizing the ideal NaHCO$_3$ dosing regimen, there appears to be a small but significant effect of NaHCO$_3$ to improve intense exercise performance in situations lasting from about 1 to 5 min or during repeated sprints, with less pronounced effects on single sprints (<50 s) or longer exercise duration (>5 min). The only meta-analysis conducted examining the performance effects of NaHCO$_3$ found that supplementation resulted in a performance effect that was 0.44 standard deviations better than the control trial (Matson & Tran, 1993). An improvement of 0.44 of the standard deviation would result in a modest ~ 0.8 s improvement over a race of about 1 min 45 s (e.g. 800 m), which for world-class athletes is within the worthwhile range of improvement. Nevertheless, there are many inconsistencies in the literature regarding whether NaHCO$_3$ can improve performance, with the main reasons including studies that did not use an optimum performance test, bicarbonate dose, negative individual gastrointestinal responses, or were drastically under-powdered. Sodium citrate ingestion appears to result in lower buffering and performance effects than sodium bicarbonate (Van Montfoort, Van Dieren, Hopkins, & Shearman, 2004). Furthermore, in the studies that have monitored body weight, it appears that both NaHCO$_3$ and citrate cause a small (about 1–2%) increase in body weight, which could potentially diminish performance benefits in events that are more weight dependent (running) versus less weight dependent (cycling, rowing). Taken together, athletes and coaches need to experiment with NaHCO$_3$ in practice and low key competitions to ascertain individual water retention, body weight gains, and gastrointestinal effects, before use in major championships.

New horizons for buffers: Buffer combinations and training effects

Given the different mechanisms involved in intra- and extracellular buffering, it could be hypothesized that an additive effect on buffering and performance could be found with chronic β-alanine supplementation, coupled with acute pre-exercise NaHCO$_3$ supplementation. Indeed, this was found in a recent report, in which cycling capacity at 110% of maximum power was improved to a greater extent with a combined buffering approach than with acute NaHCO$_3$ or chronic β-alanine supplementation alone (Sale et al., 2010).

Also, a previous study found positive effects of utilizing acute NaHCO$_3$ supplementation before intense interval training (three times a week for 8 weeks) in moderately trained females (Edge, Bishop, & Goodman, 2006). In this study, the group supplemented with NaHCO$_3$ had larger training improvements in lactate threshold and endurance capacity performance than the control training group. These findings suggest ways of how to acutely induce the most favourable level of muscular acidosis (H^+ accumulation) during training by altering training intensities or altering muscular acidosis via supplementation of intra- and extracellular buffers, resulting in optimal chronic training adaptations. However, currently the data are too limited to make recommendations regarding the use of buffers and training adaptation.

Conclusions

The variety in training sessions and the yearly periodized training programmes with power athletes result in considerable challenges and planning to optimize the nutritional impact of general daily nutrition, recovery nutrition, and supplement interventions. Accordingly, the interactions between training, competition, and nutrition need to be approached on an individual basis and should be continuously adjusted and adapted. Nevertheless, since the training and competition physiology of power sport athletes span the entire continuum of energy systems, these athletes provide a unique opportunity to study different nutrition and training approaches.

References

Artioli, G. G., Gualano, B., Smith, A., Stout, J., & Lancha, A. H. Jr., (2010). Role of beta-alanine supplementation on muscle carnosine and exercise performance. *Medicine and Science in Sports and Exercise*, 42, 1162–1173.

Baguet, A., Koppo, K., Pottier, A., & Derave, W. (2010). Beta-alanine supplementation reduces acidosis but not oxygen uptake response during high-intensity cycling exercise. *European Journal of Applied Physiology*, 108, 495–503.

Baguet, A., Reyngoudt, H., Pottier, A., Everaert, I., Callens, S., Achten, E. et al. (2009). Carnosine loading and washout in human skeletal muscles. *Journal of Applied Physiology*, 106, 837–842.

Bergstrom, J., Hermansen, L., Hultman, E., & Saltin, B. (1967). Diet, muscle glycogen and physical performance. *Acta Physiologica Scandinavica*, 71, 140–150.

Bompa, T. O., & Carrera, M. (2005). *Periodization training for sports: Science-based strength and conditioning plans for 17 sports* (2nd edn.). Champaign, IL: Human Kinetics.

Burke, L. M., Cox, G. R., Cummings, N. K., & Desbrow, B. (2001). Guidelines for daily carbohydrate intake: Do athletes achieve them? *Sports Medicine*, 31, 267–299.

Burke, L. M., Hawley, J. A., Wong, S. H. S., & Jeukendrup, A. E. (2011). Carbohydrates for training and competition. *Journal of Sport Sciences*, 29, S17–S27.

Carr, A. J., Slater, G. J., Gore, C. J., Dawson, B., & Burke, L. M. (2011). Effect of sodium bicarbonate on [HCO3–], pH and gastrointestinal symptoms. *International Journal of Sport Nutrition and Exercise Metabolism*, 21, 189–194.

Carter, J. M., Jeukendrup, A. E., & Jones, D. A. (2004). The effect of carbohydrate mouth rinse on 1-h cycle time trial performance. *Medicine and Science in Sports and Exercise*, 36, 2107–2111.

Chambers, E. S., Bridge, M. W., & Jones, D. A. (2009). Carbohydrate sensing in the human mouth: Effects on exercise performance and brain activity. *Journal of Physiology*, 587, 1779–1794.

Coggan, A. R., & Coyle, E. F. (1991). Carbohydrate ingestion during prolonged exercise: Effects on metabolism and performance. *Exercise and Sport Sciences Reviews*, 19, 1–40.

Currell, K., Conway, S., & Jeukendrup, A. E. (2009). Carbohydrate ingestion improves performance of a new reliable test of soccer performance. *International Journal of Sport Nutrition and Exercise Metabolism*, 19, 34–46.

Decombaz, J. (2003). Nutrition and recovery of muscle energy stores after exercise. *Sportmedizin und Sporttraumatologie*, 51, 31–38.

Derave, W., Everaert, I., Beeckman, S., & Baguet, A. (2010). Muscle carnosine metabolism and beta-alanine supplementation in relation to exercise and training. *Sports Medicine*, 40, 247–263.

Edge, J., Bishop, D., & Goodman, C. (2006). Effects of chronic $NaHCO_3$ ingestion during interval training on changes to muscle buffer capacity, metabolism, and short-term endurance performance. *Journal of Applied Physiology*, 101, 918–925.

Fleck, S. J. (1983). Body composition of elite American athletes. *American Journal of Sports Medicine*, 11, 398–403.

Galloway, S. D., & Maughan, R. J. (1996). The effects of induced alkalosis on the metabolic response to prolonged exercise in humans. *European Journal of Applied Physiology and Occupational Physiology*, 74, 384–389.

Harris, R. C., Tallon, M. J., Dunnett, M., Boobis, L., Coakley, J., Kim, H. J. et al. (2006). The absorption of orally supplied beta-alanine and its effect on muscle carnosine synthesis in human vastus lateralis. *Amino Acids*, 30, 279–289.

Hultman, E., & Sahlin, K. (1980). Acid–base balance during exercise. *Exercise and Sport Sciences Reviews*, 8, 41–128.

Jeukendrup, A. (2011). Nutrition for endurance sports: Marathon, triathlon, and road cycling. *Journal of Sport Sciences*, 29, S91–S99.

Loucks, A. B., Kiens, B., & Wright, H. H. (2011). Energy availability in athletes. *Journal of Sport Sciences*, 29, S7–S15.

Matson, L. G., & Tran, Z. V. (1993). Effects of sodium bicarbonate ingestion on anaerobic performance: A meta-analytic review. *International Journal of Sport Nutrition*, 3, 2–28.

Maughan, R. J., Greenhaff, P. L., & Hespel, P. (2011). Dietary supplements for athletes: Emerging trends and recurring themes. *Journal of Sport Sciences*, 29, S57–S66.

Maughan, R. J., Greenhaff, P. L., Leiper, J. B., Ball, D., Lambert, C. P., & Gleeson, M. (1997). Diet composition and the performance of high-intensity exercise. *Journal of Sports Sciences*, 15, 265–275.

Maughan, R. J., & Poole, D. C. (1981). The effects of a glycogen-loading regimen on the capacity to perform anaerobic exercise. *European Journal of Applied Physiology and Occupational Physiology*, 46, 211–219.

McNaughton, L. R. (2000). Bicarbonate and citrate. In R.J. Maughan (Ed.), *Nutrition in sport* (pp. 393–404). Oxford: Blackwell.

Mettler, S., Mitchell, N., & Tipton, K. D. (2010). Increased protein intake reduces lean body mass loss during weight loss in athletes.*Medicine and Science in Sports and Exercise*, 42, 326–337.

Moore, D. R., Robinson, M. J., Fry, J. L., Tang, J. E., Glover, E. I., Wilkinson, S. B. et al. (2009). Ingested protein dose response of muscle and albumin protein synthesis after resistance exercise in young men. *American Journal of Clinical Nutrition*, 89, 161–168.

O'Connor, H., Olds, T., & Maughan, R. J. (2007). Physique and performance for track and field events. *Journal of Sports Sciences*, 25, S49–S60.

Parkhouse, W. S., & McKenzie, D. C. (1984). Possible contribution of skeletal muscle buffers to enhanced anaerobic performance: A brief review. *Medicine and Science in Sports and Exercise*, *16*, 328–338.

Phillips, S. M. (2006). Dietary protein for athletes: From requirements to metabolic advantage. *Applied Physiology, Nutrition and Metabolism*, *31*, 647–654.

Phillips, S. M., & Van Loon, L. J. C. (2011). Dietary protein for athletes: From requirements to optimum adaptation. *Journal of Sport Sciences*, *29*, S29–S38.

Roberts, P. A., Fox, J., Jones, S. W., Peirce, N., Casey, A., & Greenhaff, P. L. (2004). The time-course of creatine mediated augmentation of skeletal muscle glycogen storage following exhaustive exercise in man. *Journal of Physiology*, *555P*, C59.

Robinson, T. M., Sewell, D. A., Hultman, E., & Greenhaff, P. L. (1999). Role of submaximal exercise in promoting creatine and glycogen accumulation in human skeletal muscle. *Journal of Applied Physiology*, *87*, 598–604.

Sale, C., Saunders, B., Hudson, S., Sunderland, C. D., Wise, J. A., & Harris, R. C. (2010). Effect of beta-alanine supplementation, with and without sodium bicarbonate, on high-intensity cycling capacity. *Medicine and Science in Sports and Exercise*, *42*, S930.

Shirreffs, S. M., & Sawaka, M. N. (2011). Fluid and electrolyte needs for training, competition and recovery. *Journal of Sports Sciences*, *29*, S39–S46.

Spencer, M. R., & Gastin, P. B. (2001). Energy system contribution during 200- to 1500-m running in highly trained athletes. *Medicine and Science in Sports and Exercise*, *33*, 157–162.

Stellingwerff, T., Anwander, H., Egger, A., Buehler, T., Kreis, R., Boesch, C. et al. (2010). The effect of two β-alanine dosing protocols on muscle carnosine synthesis and washout.*Medicine and Science in Sports and Exercise*, *42*, S929.

Stellingwerff, T., Boit, M. K., & Res, P. (2007a). Nutritional strategies to optimize training and racing in middle-distance athletes. *Journal of Sports Sciences*, *25*, S17–S28.

Stellingwerff, T., Boon, H., Jonkers, R. A., Senden, J. M., Spriet, L. L., Koopman, R. et al. (2007b). Significant intramyocellular lipid use during prolonged cycling in endurance trained males as assessed by three different methodologies. *American Journal of Physiology: Endocrinology and Metabolism*, *292*, E1715–E1723.

Sundgot-Borgen, J., & Garthe, I. (2011). Elite athletes in aesthetic and Olympic weight-class sports and the challenge of body weight and body composition. *Journal of Sports Sciences*, *29*, S101–S114.

Tarnopolsky, M. A. (1999). Protein metabolism in strength and endurance activities. In D. R., Lamb & R. Murray (Eds.), *Perspectives in exercise science and sports medicine: The metabolic basis of performance in exercise and sport* (Vol. 12, pp. 125–164). Carmel, IN: Cooper Publishing Group.

Tipton, K. D., & Wolfe, R. R. (2004). Protein and amino acids for athletes. *Journal of Sports Sciences*, *22*, 65–79.

Van Handel, P. J., Cells, K. A., Bradley, P. W., & Troup, J. P. (1984). Nutritional status of elite swimmers. *Journal of Swimming Research*, *1*, 27–31.

Van Loon, L. J., Murphy, R., Oosterlaar, A. M., Cameron-Smith, D., Hargreaves, M., Wagenmakers, A. J. et al. (2004). Creatine supplementation increases glycogen storage but not GLUT-4 expression in human skeletal muscle. *Clinical Science*, *106*, 99–106.

Van Montfoort, M. C., Van Dieren, L., Hopkins, W. G., & Shearman, J. P. (2004). Effects of ingestion of bicarbonate, citrate, lactate, and chloride on sprint running. *Medicine and Science in Sports and Exercise*, *36*, 1239–1243.

Nutrition for endurance sports: Marathon, triathlon, and road cycling

ASKER E. JEUKENDRUP

School of Sport and Exercise Sciences, University of Birmingham, Birmingham, UK

Abstract

Endurance sports are increasing in popularity and athletes at all levels are looking for ways to optimize their performance by training and nutrition. For endurance exercise lasting 30 min or more, the most likely contributors to fatigue are dehydration and carbohydrate depletion, whereas gastrointestinal problems, hyperthermia, and hyponatraemia can reduce endurance exercise performance and are potentially health threatening, especially in longer events (>4 h). Although high muscle glycogen concentrations at the start may be beneficial for endurance exercise, this does not necessarily have to be achieved by the traditional supercompensation protocol. An individualized nutritional strategy can be developed that aims to deliver carbohydrate to the working muscle at a rate that is dependent on the absolute exercise intensity as well as the duration of the event. Endurance athletes should attempt to minimize dehydration and limit body mass losses through sweating to 2–3% of body mass. Gastrointestinal problems occur frequently, especially in long-distance races. Problems seem to be highly individual and perhaps genetically determined but may also be related to the intake of highly concentrated carbohydrate solutions, hyperosmotic drinks, as well as the intake of fibre, fat, and protein. Hyponatraemia has occasionally been reported, especially among slower competitors with very high intakes of water or other low sodium drinks. Here I provide a comprehensive overview of recent research findings and suggest several new guidelines for the endurance athlete on the basis of this. These guidelines are more detailed and allow a more individualized approach.

Introduction

Endurance sports are becoming increasingly popular and more people are running half marathons, marathons, ultramarathons, half Ironmans, and even Ironman competitions, lasting anywhere between 2 h and 17 h. Many events are organized to encourage people to take up endurance sports and events of 30 min to 2 h, which are more manageable for the novice athlete, are also rapidly increasing in popularity. For the purpose of this review, endurance exercise will therefore refer to events lasting 30 min or more as defined in the PASSCLAIM document (Saris et al., 2003). PASSCLAIM was an initiative of the European Commission with the aim to develop a set of methods and procedures for assessing the scientific support for function-enhancing and health-related claims for foods and food components.

This review focuses on areas of sports nutrition that have developed significantly in the last 5 years. Other areas, where developments have been relatively slow, will be reviewed and summarized and the reader will be referred to recent review articles.

Physiological demands and nutritional demands of endurance sports

Muscle glycogen and blood glucose are the most important substrates for the contracting muscle (Romijn et al., 1993). Fatigue during prolonged exercise is often associated with muscle glycogen depletion and reduced blood glucose concentrations (Jeukendrup, 2004) and, therefore, high pre-exercise muscle and liver glycogen concentrations are believed to be essential for optimal performance, although it is unlikely that any of these factors *alone* limits prolonged exercise performance.

In addition to glycogen depletion, dehydration can also impair endurance performance (for a review, see Sawka et al., 2007). Sweat losses occur because there is the need to dissipate the heat that is generated during exercise. Therefore, the nutritional challenge is to prevent major dehydration (>2–3%) and thus contribute to the prevention of fatigue (Shirreffs, 2011). This recommendation is in line with the most recent guidelines by the American College of Sports Medicine stating that dehydration of more than

2–3% of body weight should be prevented but also warns against drinking in excess of sweating rate (Sawka et al., 2007) to prevent hyponatraemia.

Pre-competition

Carbohydrate loading. The effect of high-carbohydrate diets and elevated muscle glycogen on exercise performance has been summarized in a review by Hawley and colleagues (Hawley, Schabort, Noakes, & Dennis, 1997), and despite this review being published in 1997, it is still up to date. It was suggested that super-compensated muscle glycogen levels can improve performance (i.e. time to complete a predetermined distance) compared with low to normal glycogen (non-supercompensated) by 2–3% in events lasting more than 90 min. There seems to be little or no performance benefit of supercompensated muscle glycogen when the exercise duration is less than 90 min.

Well-trained endurance athletes can achieve glycogen supercompensation without the need for the depletion phase prior to loading (Burke, Hawley, Wong, & Jeukendrup, 2011). Furthermore, the amount of dietary carbohydrate needed to provide the high carbohydrate availability needed to recover glycogen stores on a daily basis or promote glycogen loading depends on the duration and intensity of the athlete's exercise programme. Such requirements can vary from around 5 to $12 \text{ g} \cdot \text{kg}^{-1} \cdot \text{day}^{-1}$ depending on the athlete and their activity. It should be noted that even if a higher carbohydrate intake can achieve higher glycogen stores, this might not always result in better performance. For example, in one study (Coyle, Jeukendrup, Oseto, Hodgkinson, & Zderic, 2001) increasing the carbohydrate intake from $10 \text{ g} \cdot \text{kg}^{-1}$ to almost $13 \text{ g} \cdot \text{kg}^{-1}$ resulted in an increase of muscle glycogen but had no effect on endurance performance. Another consideration for some athletes is that glycogen storage is associated with weight gain as a result of water retention (approximately 3 g per gram of glycogen) and this may not be desirable in some cases.

Carbohydrate ingestion <60 min before exercise. Although the consumption of a high-carbohydrate diet in the days before exercise as well as ingestion of carbohydrate meals 3–4 h before exercise (Hargreaves, Hawley, & Jeukendrup, 2004) can have positive effects on exercise performance, it has been suggested that the intake of carbohydrate 30–60 min before exercise may adversely affect performance (Foster, Costill, & Fink, 1979). Glucose ingestion in the hour before exercise can result in hyperglycaemia and hyperinsulinaemia, which is often followed by a rapid decline in blood glucose 15–30 min after the onset of exercise (Foster et al., 1979; Koivisto, Karonen, & Nikkila, 1981), referred to as reactive or rebound hypoglycaemia. The fall in blood glucose is most likely the result of an increased muscle glucose uptake as well as a reduced liver glucose output. In addition, hyperinsulinaemia following carbohydrate ingestion inhibits lipolysis and fat oxidation (Foster et al., 1979; Koivisto et al., 1981) and this may lead to more rapid muscle glycogen depletion. Therefore, pre-exercise carbohydrate feedings in the hour before exercise may have the potential to impair performance. However, only two studies have found reduced performance capacity, while the majority of studies have reported no change or an improvement in performance following pre-exercise carbohydrate ingestion (Jeukendrup & Killer, 2011). Furthermore, a rebound hypoglycaemia in the early stage of exercise seems to be of little functional significance, as it does not affect exercise performance (Jeukendrup & Killer, 2011). This suggests that there is no need to avoid carbohydrate intake in the hour before exercise.

It is interesting to note that rebound hypoglycaemia occurs in some triathletes but not in others (Jentjens & Jeukendrup, 2002). Kuipers and colleagues (Kuipers, Fransen, & Keizer, 1999) suggested that rebound hypoglycaemia in trained triathletes is related to a high insulin sensitivity. However, we have shown that trained individuals who developed rebound hypoglycaemia did not have better glucose tolerance compared with individuals who did not show rebound hypoglycaemia (Jentjens & Jeukendrup, 2002). It is therefore unlikely that insulin sensitivity plays an important role in the prevalence of rebound hypoglycaemia in trained athletes. It may be argued that there are some athletes who are very "sensitive" to low blood glucose levels and for them exercise-induced hypoglycaemia may be a major contributor to fatigue. These metabolic disturbances may be attenuated by choosing pre-exercise carbohydrate sources with a low glycaemic index because these result in more stable blood glucose and insulin responses during subsequent exercise (Jentjens & Jeukendrup, 2003; Wee, Williams, Gray, & Horabin, 1999). Another approach to minimize the glycaemic and insulinaemic responses during exercise is to delay carbohydrate feeding until 5–15 min before the start of the activity (Moseley, Lancaster, & Jeukendrup, 2003). Of note, the metabolic and performance effects of carbohydrate ingestion shortly before exercise (<15 min) are very similar to those observed when carbohydrate is fed during activity.

An intriguing observation is that there is no clear relation between hypoglycaemia (blood glucose $<3.5 \text{ mmol} \cdot \text{L}^{-1}$) and symptoms of hypoglycaemia (Jeukendrup & Killer, 2011). Symptoms are often reported in the absence of true hypoglycaemia and low plasma glucose concentrations are not always associated with symptoms. This finding is not new, however. In 1979, Foster and colleagues noted that reported symptoms did not match serum glucose concentrations in a cohort of individuals who consumed glucose before exercise. Further attention to this issue is warranted.

In conclusion, the advice to avoid carbohydrate feeding in the hour before exercise is unfounded. Some athletes may develop symptoms similar to those of hypoglycaemia, even though they are not always linked to low glucose concentrations. Most importantly, rebound hypoglycaemia does not appear to affect performance. To minimize symptoms of hypoglycaemia, an individual approach may be desirable, which could include ingesting carbohydrate just before exercise or during warm-up and selection of low-to-moderate glycaemic index carbohydrates. The effects of pre-exercise carbohydrate feeding are discussed in more detail in a recent review (Jeukendrup & Killer, 2011).

Fluid ingestion before exercise. As discussed earlier, dehydration can compromise exercise performance and it is therefore important to start exercise in a euhydrated state. When hydrating prior to exercise "the individual should slowly drink beverages (for example, ~5–7 mL/kg BW [body weight]) at least 4 h before the exercise task. If the individual does not produce urine, or the urine is dark or highly concentrated, s/he should slowly drink more beverage (for example, another ~3–5 mL/kg) about 2 h before the event" (Sawka et al., 2007).

It is believed that athletes who have difficulty drinking sufficient amounts of fluid during exercise or who lose body water at high rates (i.e. during exercise in hot conditions) may benefit from hyperhydration. Hyperhydration has been suggested to improve thermoregulation and exercise performance, especially in the heat (for a review, see van Rosendal, Osborne, Fassett, & Coombes, 2010). However, attempting to hyperhydrate with fluids that expand the extra- and intracellular spaces (e.g. water and glycerol solutions) will greatly increase the risk of having to void during competition (Latzka et al., 1998). There is also a risk that hyperhydration can substantially dilute and lower plasma sodium prior to exercise, thereby increasing the risk of dilutional hyponatraemia, if fluids are replaced aggressively during exercise (Montain, Cheuvront, & Sawka, 2006). Finally, it must be noted that plasma expanders or hyper-hydrating agents like glycerol are banned by the World Anti-Doping Agency.

During competition

Carbohydrate ingestion during exercise and performance. Although the exact mechanisms are still not completely understood, it has been known for some time that carbohydrate ingestion during exercise can increase exercise capacity and improve exercise performance (for reviews, see Jeukendrup, 2008, 2010). In general, during exercise longer than 2 h, the effects of carbohydrate are mainly metabolic.

However, carbohydrate ingestion during exercise has also been demonstrated to improve exercise performance even when the exercise is of high intensity ($>75\%$ $\dot{V}O_{2max}$) and relatively short duration (~ 1 h), and it has become clear that the underlying mechanisms for the ergogenic effect during this type of activity is not metabolic but may reside in the central nervous system. Carbohydrate mouth rinses have been shown to result in similar performance improvements (Jeukendrup & Chambers, 2010). This would suggest that the beneficial effects of carbohydrate feeding during exercise are not confined to its conventional metabolic advantage but may also serve as a positive afferent signal capable of modifying motor output (Gant, Stinear, & Byblow, 2010). These effects are specific to carbohydrate and are independent of taste (Chambers, Bridge, & Jones, 2009). The receptors in the oral cavity have not yet been identified and the exact role of various brain areas is not clearly understood. Further research is warranted to fully understand the separate taste transduction pathways for simple and complex carbohydrates and how these differ between mammalian species, particularly in humans. However, it has been convincingly demonstrated that carbohydrate is detected in the oral cavity by unidentified receptors and this can be linked to improvements in exercise performance (for a review, see Jeukendrup & Chambers, 2010). New guidelines suggested here take these findings into account (Table I).

These results suggest that it is not necessary to ingest large amounts of carbohydrate during exercise lasting approximately 30–60 min and a mouth rinse with carbohydrate may be sufficient to obtain a performance benefit (Table I). In most conditions, the performance effects with the mouth rinse have been similar to ingesting the drink, so there does not seem to be a disadvantage of taking the drink, although occasionally athletes may complain of gastrointestinal distress when taking on board too much fluid. Of course when the exercise is more prolonged (2 h or more), carbohydrate becomes a very important fuel and it is essential to ingest carbohydrate. As will be discussed below, larger amounts of carbohydrate may be required for more prolonged exercise.

Different carbohydrates ingested during exercise may be utilized at different rates (Jeukendrup, 2010) but until a landmark publication in 2004 (Jentjens, Moseley, Waring, Harding, & Jeukendrup, 2004), it was believed that carbohydrate ingested during

Table I. Recommendations for carbohydrate (CHO) intake during different endurance events.

Event	CHO required for optimal performance and minimizing negative energy balance	Recommended intake	CHO type	Single carbohydrate (e.g. glucose)	Multiple transportable carbohydrates (e.g. glucose : fructose)
<30 min	None required	–	–	–	–
30–75 min	Very small amounts	Mouth rinse	Most forms of CHO	●	●
1–2 h	Small amounts	Up to 30 g · h^{-1}	Most forms of CHO	●	●
2–3 h	Moderate amounts	Up to 60 g · h^{-1}	Forms of CHO that are rapidly oxidized (glucose, maltodextrin)	○	●
>2.5 h	Large amounts	Up to 90 g · h^{-1}	Only multiple transportable CHO		●

Note: ●, optimal; ○, OK, but perhaps not optimal. These guidelines are intended for serious athletes, exercising at a reasonable intensity (>4 kcal · min^{-1}). If the (absolute) exercise intensity is below this, the figures for carbohydrate intake should be adjusted downwards.

exercise could only be oxidized at a rate no higher than 1 g · min^{-1} (60 g · h^{-1}) independent of the type of carbohydrate. This is reflected in guidelines published by the ACSM, which recommends that athletes should take between 30 and 60 g of carbohydrate during endurance exercise (>1 h) (Sawka et al., 2007) or 0.7 g ·kg^{-1} · h^{-1} (Rodriguez, Di Marco, & Langley, 2009).

It appears that exogenous carbohydrate oxidation is limited by the intestinal absorption of carbohydrates. It is believed that glucose uses a sodium dependent transporter SGLT1 for absorption that becomes saturated at a carbohydrate intake around 60 g · h^{-1}. When glucose is ingested at this rate and another carbohydrate (fructose) that uses a different transporter is ingested simultaneously, oxidation rates that were well above 1 g · min^{-1} (1.26 g · min^{-1}) (Jentjens et al., 2004) can be observed. A series of studies followed in an attempt to work out the maximal rate of exogenous carbohydrate oxidation. In these studies, the rate of carbohydrate ingestion was varied and the types and combinations of carbohydrates varied. All studies confirmed that multiple transportable carbohydrates resulted in (up to 75%) higher oxidation rates than carbohydrates that use the SGLT1 transporter only (for reviews, see Jeukendrup, 2008, 2010). Interestingly, such high oxidation rates could not only be achieved with carbohydrate ingested in a beverage but also as a gel (Pfeiffer, Stellingwerff, Zaltas, & Jeukendrup, 2010a) or a low-fat, low-protein, low-fibre energy bar (Pfeiffer, Stellingwerff, Zaltas, & Jeukendrup, 2010b).

Carbohydrate during exercise and performance: dose–response. Very few well-controlled dose–response studies on carbohydrate ingestion during exercise and exercise performance have been published. Most of the older studies had serious methodological issues that made it difficult to establish a true dose–response relationship between the amount of carbohydrate ingested and performance. The conclusion seemed to be that you needed a minimum amount of carbohydrate (probably about 20 g · h^{-1} based on one study) but it was assumed that there was no dose–response relationship (Rodriguez et al., 2009).

Evidence is accumulating for a dose–response relationship between carbohydrate ingestion rates, exogenous carbohydrate oxidation rates, and performance. In one recent carefully conducted study, endurance performance and fuel selection were assessed during prolonged exercise while ingesting glucose (15, 30, and 60 g · h^{-1}) (Smith et al., 2010b). Twelve participants cycled for 2 h at 77% $\dot{V}O_{2peak}$ followed by a 20-km time-trial. The results suggest a relationship between the dose of glucose ingested and improvements in endurance performance. The exogenous glucose oxidation increased with ingestion rate and it is possible that an increase in exogenous carbohydrate oxidation is directly linked with, or responsible for, exercise performance.

In a large-scale multi-centre study, Smith et al. (2010a) also investigated the relationship between carbohydrate ingestion rate and cycling time-trial performance to identify a range of carbohydrate ingestion rates that would enhance performance. In their study, across four research sites, 51 cyclists and triathletes completed four exercise sessions consisting of a 2-h constant-load ride at a moderate to high intensity. Twelve different beverages (consisting of glucose:fructose in a 2:1 ratio) were compared, providing participants with 12 different carbohydrate doses raging from 10 to 120 g carbohydrate per hour during the constant-load ride. At all four sites, a common placebo that was artificially sweetened, coloured, and flavoured and did not contain carbohydrate was provided. The order of the beverage treatments was randomized at each site (three at each site). Immediately after the constant-load ride, participants completed a computer-simulated 20-km time-trial as quickly as possible. The ingestion of carbohydrate significantly improved performance in a dose-dependent manner and the authors concluded that the greatest performance enhancement was seen at an ingestion rate between

60 and 80 g carbohydrate per hour. Based on the studies above, carbohydrate intake recommendation for more prolonged exercise can be formulated and are listed in newly proposed guidelines in Table I. Please note that these guidelines for carbohydrate intake during exercise are expressed in grams per hour of exercise and that these figures are not corrected for body mass.

Effect of body weight. In the most recent position statement by the American Dietetics Association (ADA) and ACSM (Rodriguez et al., 2009), advice with respect to carbohydrate intake during exercise is expressed in $g \cdot kg \, BW^{-1}$. The rationale for this was unclear, as there appears to be no correlation between body mass and exogenous carbohydrate oxidation (Jeukendrup, 2010). The reason for this lack of correlation between body weight and exogenous carbohydrate oxidation is probably that the limiting factor is carbohydrate absorption and absorption is largely independent of body mass. It is likely, however, that the absorptive capacity of the intestine is modified by carbohydrate content of the diet, as it has been shown in animal studies that intestinal transporters can be upregulated with increased carbohydrate intake. Since exogenous carbohydrate is independent of body mass or muscle mass, but dependent on absorption and to some degree the absolute exercise intensity (at very low absolute intensities, low carbohydrate rates may also restrict exogenous carbohydrate oxidation), the advice given to athletes should be in absolute amounts. These results clearly show that there is no rationale for expressing carbohydrate recommendations for athletes per kilogram body mass (Table I).

In summary, individual differences in exogenous carbohydrate oxidation exist, although they are generally small. These differences are not related to body mass but more likely to a capacity to absorb carbohydrates. This in turn could be diet related.

Carbohydrate intake in real-life events. In a study by Kimber and colleagues (Kimber, Ross, Mason, & Speedy, 2002), the average carbohydrate intake during an Ironman distance triathlon was $1.0 \, g \cdot kg \, BW^{-1} \cdot h^{-1}$ in female triathletes and $1.1 \, g \cdot kg \, BW^{-1} \cdot h^{-1}$ in male triathletes. They achieved these carbohydrate intakes by ingesting very large amounts of carbohydrate during cycling (approximately $1.5 \, g \cdot kg \, BW^{-1} \cdot h^{-1}$). Most of the intake occurred during the cycling leg, where intake was almost three times as high as during the running leg. In male athletes, carbohydrate intake was positively correlated with finish time but this relationship could not be confirmed in females. In a large study of endurance events, Pfeiffer et al. (2011a) demonstrated wide variation in carbohydrate intake re-

ported by athletes between and within events, with the highest intakes in cycling and triathlon events and the lowest in marathons. Pfeiffer et al. also found that in Ironman races carbohydrate intake was related to finish time, with greater carbohydrate intake correlating with better performance.

Different advice for different endurance sports. With carbohydrate feeding during cycling, it has repeatedly been shown that muscle glycogen breakdown is unaffected. During running, however, there are suggestions that muscle glycogen breakdown is reduced in particular in type I muscle fibres (Tsintzas, Williams, Boobis, & Greenhaff, 1995). Therefore, carbohydrate feeding results in improved performance in cycling and running, although the mechanism by which this occurs may not necessarily be the same. This issue is discussed in more detail in an excellent review by Tsintzas and Williams (1998). Exogenous carbohydrate oxidation appears to be similar in cycling and running (Pfeiffer, Stellingwerff, Zaltas, Hodgson, & Jeukendrup, 2011b), suggesting that the advice for cyclists and runners should not be different.

Training the gut. Since the absorption of carbohydrate limits exogenous carbohydrate oxidation, and exogenous carbohydrate oxidation seems to be linked with exercise performance, an obvious potential strategy would be to increase the absorptive capacity of the gut. Anecdotal evidence in athletes would suggest that the gut is trainable and that individuals who regularly consume carbohydrate or have a high daily carbohydrate intake may also have an increased capacity to absorb it. Intestinal carbohydrate transporters can indeed be upregulated by exposing an animal to a high carbohydrate diet (Ferraris, 2001). To date, there is limited evidence in humans. In a recent study, Cox et al. (2010) investigated whether altering daily carbohydrate intake affects substrate oxidation and in particular exogenous carbohydrate oxidation. It was demonstrated that exogenous carbohydrate oxidation rates were higher after the high carbohydrate diet ($6.5 \, g \cdot kg \, BW^{-1} \cdot day^{-1}$; $1.5 \, g \cdot kg \, BW^{-1}$ provided mainly as a carbohydrate supplement during training) for 28 days compared with a control diet ($5 \, g \cdot kg \, BW^{-1} \cdot day^{-1}$). This study provided evidence that the gut is indeed adaptable and this can be used as a practical method to increase exogenous carbohydrate oxidation. We recently suggested that this may be highly relevant to the endurance athlete and may be a prerequisite for the first person to break the 2-h marathon barrier (Stellingwerff & Jeukendrup, 2011).

Maintaining fluid balance during exercise. To prevent large fluid losses, perhaps the best advice is for endurance athletes to weigh themselves to assess fluid losses during training and racing and limit weight losses to 2–3% during exercise lasting more than 90 min. In the absence of such planning, concrete advice is difficult since differences between individuals, race distances, course profiles, and environmental conditions will confound any suggestions. The addition of sodium and carbohydrate to sports drinks is widely recommended to enhance the absorption of water.

Although hypertonic solutions tend to delay water absorption in the intestine (Rehrer, Brouns, Beckers, & Saris, 1994) and energy density is perhaps the most important factor dictating gastric emptying rates (Brouns, Senden, Beckers, & Saris, 1995; Noakes, Rehrer, & Maughan, 1991), the use of multiple transportable carbohydrates can help to maintain high rates of gastric emptying and improve the delivery of fluid (Jeukendrup & Moseley, 2010). Although difficult to draw firm conclusions in almost every study, we have also seen better tolerance of the drinks with multiple transportable carbohydrates compared with a single carbohydrate at these high intake rates ($>1 \text{ g} \cdot \text{min}^{-1}$).

In summary, a balance must be struck between the goals of maintaining hydration status and providing carbohydrate to the working muscle. The rate of fluid absorption is closely related to the carbohydrate content of the drink with high carbohydrate concentrations compromising fluid delivery, although multiple transportable carbohydrates can remove some of this impaired fluid delivery. In all cases, a drink should contain sodium (10–30 mmol · L^{-1}) (Maughan, 1998) for optimal fluid absorption and prevention of hyponatraemia.

Caffeine

Caffeine is one of the most common supplements used in endurance sports. It is an alkaloid xanthine derivative (1, 3, 7-trimethylxanthine) found in, and added to, a wide variety of foods, beverages, and sports nutrition products. Caffeine has been consumed in various foods and beverages for centuries due to its perceived work-enhancing (ergogenic) and alertness effects. A large number of studies have reported improvements in endurance performance (for reviews, see Graham, 2001; Tarnopolsky, 1994) and the ergogenic properties of caffeine are generally accepted. The International Olympic Committee (IOC) previously had caffeine on the banned substance list with urinary concentrations greater than 12 mg · L^{-1} considered a doping infraction; however, the Word Anti-Doping Agency removed caffeine from the banned substance list in 2004 and placed it on the monitoring list.

Although habitual consumption of caffeine may down-regulate many of the physiological effects (tachyphylaxis; attenuated acute ingestion induced rise in heart rate or blood pressure; attenuation of lipolytic effects), the ergogenic effects of caffeine are similar in both non-habitual and habitual caffeine consumers (Van Soeren, Sathasivam, Spriet, & Graham, 1993). In line with these findings, a recent study showed that 4 days of caffeine withdrawal had no effect on the ergogenic effect of caffeine during a time-trial lasting approximately 1 h (Irwin et al., 2011).

The vast majority of the studies that reported ergogenic effects used caffeine doses in the range 3–6 mg · kg^{-1} taken approximately 1 h before exercise. More recently, studies have reported that much lower doses of caffeine (1.0–2.0 mg · kg^{-1}), especially when taken later during an endurance exercise task, have also enhanced performance (Cox et al., 2002).

Caffeine is absorbed with a time to peak plasma concentration of 30–90 min and half-life of about 5 h. Therefore, an effective strategy might be to ingest a dose close to 3 mg · kg^{-1} 60 min before the start of exercise followed by 1 mg · kg^{-1} every 2 h after that. However, even when only taken late in exercise, caffeine can still be effective (Cox et al., 2002).

Gastrointestinal problems

There is a very high prevalence of gastrointestinal complaints during exercise among long-distance runners, triathletes, and athletes involved in other types of strenuous long lasting exercise (Rehrer et al., 1992), with studies reporting a prevalence of between 10% and 95% depending on the event, the environmental conditions, and methodology used to assess gastrointestinal distress. Pfeiffer et al. (2011a) reported severe gastrointestinal distress ranging from 4% in marathon running and cycling up to 32% in Ironman races. In a recent study, Pfeiffer and colleagues (Pfeiffer, Cotterill, Grathwohl, Stellingwerff, & Jeukendrup, 2009) demonstrated that there was a strong correlation between gastrointestinal symptoms and having a history of gastrointestinal symptoms, perhaps suggesting that some people are more prone to develop gastrointestinal distress and there might be a genetic component to these problems.

The most frequently reported symptoms include dizziness, nausea, stomach or intestinal cramps, vomiting, and diarrhoea. Rehrer et al. (1992) reported a link between nutritional practices and gastrointestinal complaints during a half Ironman distance triathlon. It was found that gastrointestinal problems were more likely to occur with the ingestion of fibre, fat, protein, and concentrated carbohydrate solutions during the triathlon. In particular, beverages with a very high osmolality seemed to be responsible for some of the reported complaints.

Symptoms are often mild and may not even affect performance. Some of the symptoms, however, can be very serious and will not only affect performance but are health threatening. For example, marathon runners and long-distance triathletes occasionally have blood loss in faeces in the hours following a marathon. Schaub and colleagues (Schaub, Spichtin, & Stalder, 1985) observed epithelial surface changes known to occur during ischaemia upon colonoscopic inspection of one such triathlete following a marathon and suggested that ischaemia of the lower gastro-intestinal tract induced the problems. Øktedalen et al. (1992) reported increased intestinal permeability after a marathon, indicating damage to the gut and impaired gut function. Despite the high prevalence of symptoms, mild or severe, the aetiology of these gastrointestinal complaints in endurance athletes is still incompletely understood.

Hyponatraemia

Hyponatraemia has occasionally been reported in long-distance triathletes (Speedy et al., 1999). This appears to be most common among slow competitors in triathlons and ultra-marathon races and probably arises due to loss of sodium in sweat coupled with very high intakes of water or other low sodium drinks (Noakes, Goodwin, Rayner, Branken, & Taylor, 1985). The symptoms of hyponatraemia are similar to those associated with dehydration and include mental confusion, weakness, and fainting. Such symptoms are usually seen at serum sodium concentrations of 126–130 mmol $\cdot$ L^{-1}. Below 126 mmol $\cdot$ L^{-1}, seizures, coma, and death may occur.

Endurance athletes may develop hyponatraemia without displaying the symptoms. Hyponatraemia may occur in a state of euhydration or even dehydration but is generally associated with fluid overload (Speedy et al., 1999). To prevent hyponatraemia, athletes need to be informed about the potential dangers of drinking too much water or sodium-free beverages. One study showed no evidence that sodium ingestion significantly influenced changes in plasma sodium concentration or plasma volume more than fluid replacement alone (Speedy, Thompson, Rodgers, Collins, & Sharwood, 2002). The authors therefore suggested that sodium supplementation was not necessary to prevent the development of hyponatraemia in these athletes. In a modelling paper, Montain et al. (2006) suggested that electrolyte replacement should be considered only as part of the preventive process; most important is the avoidance of excessive fluid intake.

Conclusion

To optimize endurance exercise, carbohydrates and fluids play an important role, both before and during exercise. Starting with high muscle glycogen concentrations and being euhydrated is important, which can be achieved by high carbohydrate consumption and adequate drinking. An individualized nutritional strategy can be developed that aims to deliver carbohydrate to the working muscle at a rate that is dependent on the absolute exercise intensity as well as the duration of the event. Higher carbohydrate intakes may result in better performance and the ingestion of multiple transportable carbohydrates will allow very high carbohydrate oxidation rates and superior performance. Endurance athletes should attempt to minimize dehydration and limit body mass losses through sweating to 2–3% of body mass. Other issues in endurance sports include gastrointestinal problems, which are highly individual but can be minimized by talking certain nutritional precautions. Hyponatraemia has occasionally been reported but can be avoided in almost all cases by avoiding overdrinking.

References

Brouns, F., Senden, J., Beckers, E. J., & Saris, W. H. (1995). Osmolarity does not affect the gastric emptying rate of oral rehydration solutions. *Journal of Parenteral and Enteral Nutrition*, *19*, 403–406.

Burke, L. M., Hawley, J. A., Wong, S. H. S., & Jeukendrup, A. (2011). Carbohydrates for training and competition. *Journal of Sports Sciences*.

Chambers, E. S., Bridge, M. W., & Jones, D. A. (2009). Carbohydrate sensing in the human mouth: Effects on exercise performance and brain activity. *Journal of Physiology*, *587*, 1779–1794.

Cox, G. R., Clark, S. A., Cox, A. J., Halson, S. L., Hargreaves, M., Hawley, J. A. et al. (2010). Daily training with high carbohydrate availability increases exogenous carbohydrate oxidation during endurance cycling. *Journal of Applied Physiology*, *109*, 126–134.

Cox, G. R., Desbrow, B., Montgomery, P. G., Anderson, M. E., Bruce, C. R., Macrides, T. A. et al. (2002). Effect of different protocols of caffeine intake on metabolism and endurance performance. *Journal of Applied Physiology*, *93*, 990–999.

Coyle, E. F., Jeukendrup, A. E., Oseto, M. C., Hodgkinson, B. J., & Zderic, T. W. (2001). Low-fat diet alters intramuscular substrates and reduces lipolysis and fat oxidation during exercise. *Amerian Journal of Physiology: Endocrinology and Metabolism*, *280*, E391–E398.

Ferraris, R. P. (2001). Dietary and developmental regulation of intestinal sugar transport. *Biochemistry Journal*, *360*, 265–276.

Foster, C., Costill, D. L., & Fink, W. J. (1979). Effects of preexercise feedings on endurance performance. *Medicine and Science and Sports*, *11*, 1–5.

Gant, N., Stinear, C. M., & Byblow, W. D. (2010). Carbohydrate in the mouth immediately facilitates motor output. *Brain Research*, *1350*, 151–158.

Graham, T. E. (2001). Caffeine, coffee and ephedrine: Impact on exercise performance and metabolism. *Canadian Journal of Applied Physiology*, *26* (suppl.), S103–S119.

Hargreaves, M., Hawley, J. A., & Jeukendrup, A. (2004). Pre-exercise carbohydrate and fat ingestion: Effects on metabolism and performance. *Journal of Sports Sciences*, *22*, 31–38.

Hawley, J. A., Schabort, E. J., Noakes, T. D., & Dennis, S. C. (1997). Carbohydrate loading and exercise performance: An update. *Sports Medicine*, *24*, 73–81.

Irwin, C., Desbrow, B., Ellis, A., O'Keeffe, B., Grant, B., & Leveritt, M. (2011). Caffeine withdrawal and high intensity endurance cycling performance. *Journal of Sports Sciences, 29*, 509–515.

Jentjens, R. L., & Jeukendrup, A. E. (2002). Prevalence of hypoglycemia following pre-exercise carbohydrate ingestion is not accompanied by higher insulin sensitivity. *International Journal of Sport Nutrition and Exercise Metabolism, 12*, 398–413.

Jentjens, R. L., & Jeukendrup, A. E. (2003). Effects of pre-exercise ingestion of trehalose, galactose and glucose on subsequent metabolism and cycling performance. *European Journal of Applied Physiology, 88*, 459–465.

Jentjens, R. L., Moseley, L., Waring, R. H., Harding, L. K., & Jeukendrup, A. E. (2004). Oxidation of combined ingestion of glucose and fructose during exercise. *Journal of Applied Physiology, 96*, 1277–1284.

Jeukendrup, A. E. (2004). Carbohydrate intake during exercise and performance. *Nutrition, 20*, 669–677.

Jeukendrup, A. (2008). Carbohydrate feeding during exercise. *European Journal of Sport Science, 8*, 77–86.

Jeukendrup, A. E. (2010). Carbohydrate and exercise performance: The role of multiple transportable carbohydrates. *Current Opinion in Clinical Nutrition and Metabolic Care, 13*, 452–457.

Jeukendrup, A. E., & Chambers, E. S. (2010). Oral carbohydrate sensing and exercise performance. *Current Opinion in Clinical Nutrition and Metabolic Care, 13*, 447–451.

Jeukendrup, A. E., & Killer, S. (2011). The myths surrounding pre-exercise carbohydrate feeding. *Annals of Nutrition and Metabolism, 57* (suppl. 2), 18–25.

Jeukendrup, A. E., & Moseley, L. (2010). Multiple transportable carbohydrates enhance gastric emptying and fluid delivery. *Scandinavian Journal of Medicine and Science in Sports, 20*, 112–121.

Kimber, N. E., Ross, J. J., Mason, S. L., & Speedy, D. B. (2002). Energy balance during an ironman triathlon in male and female triathletes. *International Journal of Sport Nutrition and Exercise Metabolism, 12*, 47–62.

Koivisto, V. A., Karonen, S. L., & Nikkila, E. A. (1981). Carbohydrate ingestion before exercise: Comparison of glucose, fructose, and sweet placebo. *Journal of Applied Physiology, 51*, 783–787.

Kuipers, H., Fransen, E. J., & Keizer, H. A. (1999). Pre-exercise ingestion of carbohydrate and transient hypoglycemia during exercise. *International Journal of Sports Medicine, 20*, 227–231.

Latzka, W. A., Sawka, M. N., Montain, S. J., Skrinar, G. S., Fielding, R. A., Matott, R. P. et al. (1998). Hyperhydration: Tolerance and cardiovascular effects during uncompensable exercise-heat stress. *Journal of Applied Physiology, 84*, 1858–1864.

Maughan, R. J. (1998). The sports drink as a functional food: Formulations for succesful performance. *Proceedings of the Nutrition Society, 57*, 15–23.

Montain, S. J., Cheuvront, S. N., & Sawka, M. N. (2006). Exercise associated hyponatraemia: Quantitative analysis to understand the aetiology. *British Journal of Sports Medicine, 40*, 98–105; discussion 198–105.

Moseley, L., Lancaster, G. I., & Jeukendrup, A. E. (2003). Effects of timing of pre-exercise ingestion of carbohydrate on subsequent metabolism and cycling performance. *European Journal of Applied Physiology, 88*, 453–458.

Noakes, T. D., Goodwin, N., Rayner, B. L., Branken, T., & Taylor, R. K. N. (1985). Water intoxication: A possible complication during endurance exercise. *Medicine and Science in Sports and Exercise, 17*, 370–375.

Noakes, T. D., Rehrer, N. J., & Maughan, R. J. (1991). The importance of volume in regulating gastric emptying. *Medicine and Science in Sports and Exercise, 23*, 307–313.

Øktedalen, O., Lunde, O. C., Opstad, P. K., Aabakken, L., & Kvernebo, K. (1992). Changes in gastro-intestinal mucose after long-distance running. *Scandinavian Journal of Gastroenterology, 27*, 270–274.

Pfeiffer, B., Cotterill, A., Grathwohl, D., Stellingwerff, T., & Jeukendrup, A. E. (2009). The effect of carbohydrate gels on gastrointestinal tolerance during a 16-km run. *International Journal of Sport Nutrition and Exercise Metabolism, 19*(5), 485–503.

Pfeiffer, B., Stellingwerff, T., Hodgson, A. B., Randell, R., Poettgen, K., Res, P. et al. (2011a). Nutritional intake and gastrointestinal problems during competitive endurance events. *Medicine and Science in Sports and Exercise* (DOI: 10.1249/MSS.0b013e31822dc809).

Pfeiffer, B., Stellingwerff, T., Zaltas, E., Hodgson, A. B., & Jeukendrup, A. E. (2011b). Carbohydrate oxidation from a drink during running compared with cycling exercise. *Medicine and Science in Sports and Exercise, 43*, 327–334.

Pfeiffer, B., Stellingwerff, T., Zaltas, E., & Jeukendrup, A. E. (2010a). CHO oxidation from a CHO gel compared with a drink during exercise. *Medicine and Science in Sports and Exercise, 42*, 2038–2045.

Pfeiffer, B., Stellingwerff, T., Zaltas, E., & Jeukendrup, A. E. (2010b). Oxidation of solid versus liquid CHO sources during exercise. *Medicine and Science in Sports and Exercise, 42*, 2030–2037.

Rehrer, N. J., Brouns, F., Beckers, E. J., Frey, W. O., Villiger, B., Riddoch, C. J. et al. (1992). Physiological changes and gastrointestinal symptoms as a result of ultra-endurance running. *European Journal of Applied Physiology, 64*, 1–8.

Rehrer, N. J., Brouns, F., Beckers, E. J., & Saris, W. H. M. (1994). The influence of beverage composition and gastrointestinal function on fluid and nutrient availability during exercise. *Scandinavian Journal of Medicine and Science in Sports, 4*, 159–172.

Rodriguez, N. R., Di Marco, N. M., & Langley, S. (2009). American College of Sports Medicine position stand: Nutrition and athletic performance. *Medicine and Science in Sports and Exercise, 41*, 709–731.

Romijn, J. A., Coyle, E. F., Sidossis, L. S., Gastaldelli, A., Horowitz, J. F., Endert, E. et al. (1993). Regulation of endogenous fat and carbohydrate metabolism in relation to exercise intensity. *American Journal of Physiology: Endocrinology and Metabolism, 265*, E380–E391.

Saris, W. H., Antoine, J. M., Brouns, F., Fogelholm, M., Gleeson, M., Hespel, P., & Stich, V. (2003). PASSCLAIM – physical performance and fitness. *European Journal of Nutrition, 42* (suppl. 1), I50–I95.

Sawka, M. N., Burke, L. M., Eichner, E. R., Maughan, R. J., Montain, S. J., & Stachenfeld, N. S. (2007). American College of Sports Medicine position stand: Exercise and fluid replacement. *Medicine and Science in Sports and Exercise, 39*, 377–390.

Schaub, N., Spichtin, H. P., & Stalder, G. A. (1985). Ischämische Kolitis als Ursache einer Darmblutung bei Marathonlauf? *Schweizerische Medicin Wochenschrift, 115*, 454–457.

Shirreffs, S. (2011). Fluid and electrolyte needs for training, competition and recovery. *Journal of Sports Sciences*.

Smith, J. W., Zachwieja, J. J., Horswill, C. A., Pascoe, D. D., Passe, D., Ruby, B. C. et al. (2010a). Evidence of a carbohydrate dose and prolonged exercise performance relationship. *Medicine and Science in Sports and Exercise, 42* (5), 84.

Smith, J. W., Zachwieja, J. J., Peronnet, F., Passe, D. H., Massicotte, D., Lavoie, C. et al. (2010b). Fuel selection and cycling endurance performance with ingestion of [13C]glucose: Evidence for a carbohydrate dose response. *Journal of Applied Physiology, 108*, 1520–1529.

Speedy, D. B., Noakes, T. D., Rogers, I. R., Thompson, J. M., Campbell, R. G., Kuttner, J. A. et al. (1999). Hyponatremia in ultradistance triathletes. *Medicine and Science in Sports and Exercise, 31*, 809–815.

Speedy, D. B., Thompson, J. M., Rodgers, I., Collins, M., & Sharwood, K. (2002). Oral salt supplementation during ultra-distance exercise. *Clinical Journal of Sport Medicine, 12*, 279–284.

Stellingwerff, T., & Jeukendrup, A. E. (2011). Authors' reply to Viewpoint by Joyner et al. entitled "The Two-Hour Marathon: Who and When?" *Journal of Applied Physiology, 110*, 278–293.

Tarnopolsky, M. A. (1994). Caffeine and endurance performance. *Sports Medicine, 18*, 109–125.

Tsintzas, K., & Williams, C. (1998). Human muscle glycogen metabolism during exercise: Effect of carbohydrate supplementation. *Sports Medicine, 25*, 7–23.

Tsintzas, O. K., Williams, C., Boobis, L., & Greenhaff, P. (1995). Carbohydrate ingestion and glycogen utilisation in different muscle fibre types in man. *Journal of Physiology, 489*, 243–250.

van Rosendal, S. P., Osborne, M. A., Fassett, R. G., & Coombes, J. S. (2010). Guidelines for glycerol use in hyperhydration and rehydration associated with exercise. *Sports Medicine, 40*, 113–129.

Van Soeren, M. H., Sathasivam, P., Spriet, L. L., & Graham, T. E. (1993). Caffeine metabolism and epinephrine responses during exercise in users and nonusers. *Journal of Applied Physiology, 75*, 805–812.

Wee, S. L., Williams, C., Gray, S., & Horabin, J. (1999). Influence of high and low glycemic index meals on endurance running capacity. *Medicine and Science in Sports and Exercise, 31*, 393–399.

Elite athletes in aesthetic and Olympic weight-class sports and the challenge of body weight and body composition

JORUNN SUNDGOT-BORGEN & INA GARTHE

Department of Sports Medicine, Norwegian School of Sport Sciences, Oslo, Norway

Abstract

The use of dieting, rapid weight loss, and frequent weight fluctuation among athletes competing in weight-class and leanness sports have been considered a problem for years, but the extent of the problem and the health and performance consequences have yet to be fully examined. Most studies examining these issues have had weak methodology. However, results from this review indicate that a high proportion of athletes are using extreme weight-control methods and that the rules of some sports might be associated with the risk of continuous dieting, energy deficit, and/or use of extreme weight-loss methods that can be detrimental to health and performance. Thus, preventive strategies are justified for medical as well as performance reasons. The most urgent needs are: (1) to develop sport-specific educational programmes for athletic trainers, coaches, and athletes; (2) modifications to regulations; and (3) research related to minimum percentage body fat and judging patterns.

Introduction

Elite athletes often embody the concept of physical perfection. However, not all athletes have, or believe that they have, bodies that are adapted to the optimal paradigm of their specific sport. Such athletes often experience pressure to achieve this "ideal" body type (Drinkwater, Loucks, Sherman, Sundgot-Borgen, & Thompson, 2005; Sundgot-Borgen & Torstveit, 2010). Also, athletes competing in aesthetic sports such as gymnasts, divers, and figure skaters, experience greater pressure to reduce weight than athletes competing in sports in which leanness and/or a specific weight are considered less important for performance (de Bruin, Oudejans, & Bakker, 2007). In addition to the socio-cultural demands placed on males and females to achieve and maintain an ideal body shape, elite athletes are also under pressure to improve performance and conform to the requirements of their sport. They are evaluated by coaches and judges on an almost daily basis (Nattiv et al., 2007; Sundgot-Borgen, 1994). Weight-class athletes have a certain weight to obtain before competition as a requirement of the sport. These factors may lead to dieting, the use of extreme weight-control methods, disordered eating behaviours, and impaired health

and performance (Drinkwater et al., 2005; Nattiv et al., 2007; Oppliger, Steen, & Scott, 2003; Slater et al., 2005a). Data on the relationship between sport participation, use of extreme weight-control methods, and their effect on health and performance are inconsistent, varying by sport, level of athletic performance, and the methodology used in different studies. Consequently, it is difficult to draw conclusions that can be adopted in elite aesthetic and weight-class sports as a whole. However, associations between athletes, extreme dieting behaviours, and eating problems have been demonstrated through the development of specific terms, including weight cycling, anorexia athletica, and the female athlete triad (Drinkwater et al., 2005; Nattiv et al., 2007; Sundgot-Borgen, 1994; Sundgot-Borgen & Torstveit, 2004; Torstveit & Sundgot-Borgen, 2005).

To achieve fast weight loss, athletes use a number of extreme methods and place their health at risk. There have even been deaths among athletes representing sports in which rapid weight reduction and extreme dieting are common. A judo medallist died of a heart attack probably triggered by an extreme rapid weight-loss regimen while preparing for the 1996 Atlanta Olympic Games. Furthermore, three collegiate wrestlers died probably related to extreme dehydration methods to make weight in 1997. However, to our knowledge, none of the international federations in Olympic weight-class sports has implemented programmes aiming to discourage athletes from engaging in harmful weight-loss procedures. At present, the patterns of dieting and rapid weight loss among athletes competing in sports in which extreme leanness or a low weight is considered important for performance seem to be as common and inappropriate as those reported many years ago (Artioli et al., 2010a). Also, more athletes competing in leanness and weight-class sports compared with other sports meet the criteria for clinical eating disorders (Rosendahl, Bormann, Aschenbrenner, Aschenbrenner, & Strauss, 2009).

Dieting

No general guidelines for energy intake by athletes exist, but minimum intakes corresponding to 45 and 50 $kcal \cdot kg^{-1}$ body mass for females and males, respectively, have been suggested for athletes who exercise > 90 $min \cdot day^{-1}$ (Economos, Bortz, & Nilson, 1993).

The energy and nutrient intakes of weight-class athletes are not well-documented, but based on available data and practical experience there is no doubt that energy intake is below the recommended level at least during the competitive season (see Table I). Possible reasons for low energy intake include: restrictive eating behaviour; lack of knowledge of the energy cost, and thus needs, of high training volume; the additional energy needed for growth and development (if applicable) (Nattiv et al., 2007). On a continuum, dieting may include low energy availability, including healthy dieting (such as lowering energy intake by a modest amount per day to achieve gradual weight loss) and use of extreme weight loss methods such as extreme restrictive diets (< 30 $kcal \cdot kg^{-1}$ fat free mass $\cdot day^{-1}$) (Loucks, in press), fasting, passive (e.g. sauna, hot baths) or active (e.g. exercise with sweat suits) dehydration, laxatives, diuretics, vomiting, and excessive exercise (Table II). On this continuum, athletes struggle with body image, weight fluctuation, eating behaviours, and performance issues. The female athlete triad refers to the interrelationship between energy availability, menstrual function, and bone mineral density. This triad may have clinical manifestation including eating disorders, functional hypothalamic amenorrhoea, and osteoporosis (Nattiv et al., 2007).

Dieting to win

For many athletes, it is desirable to have a high lean body mass and low body fat mass to achieve a high power-to-weight ratio. Some sports require horizontal (e.g. running and long jump) or vertical (e.g. high jump and gymnastics) movements of the body where excessive fat mass is considered a disadvantage. A high fat mass decreases efficiency of movement and could therefore affect performance negatively. A high lean body-to-fat mass ratio is also desirable in sports for aesthetic reasons (e.g. figure skating and rhythmic gymnastics). Judges and coaches are influenced by athletes' body type, while athletes experience pressure to diet (de Bruin et al., 2007). In sports with weight categories such as wrestling, judo, and lightweight rowing, athletes aim to gain a competitive advantage by obtaining the lowest possible body weight with greatest possible strength, power, and endurance.

Athletes in weight-class sports believe that weight loss is a necessary part of the sport, and few question the weight loss methods used (Hall & Lane, 2001; Marquart & Sobal, 1994). They often compete in a weight class below their natural body weight (Oppliger et al., 2003; Steen & Brownell, 1990) and therefore start to diet due to their experience of the specific body weight/composition demands in their sport. In some sports, the weight-class system and/or the weight categories and weigh-in timing and procedure during competitive events may lead athletes to use extreme weight-loss methods. Today, some sports (e.g. tae kwondo and wrestling) have few weight classes separated by many kilograms, a long wait between the weight-in and the start of competition (which makes it possible to reduce larger amounts of weight), and only one weigh-in during tournaments. Thus, for many athletes weight concerns, dieting, and the use of extreme weight-loss methods become the focus of their athletic existence and some may be diagnosed with a clinical eating disorder (Matejek et al., 1999; Sundgot-Borgen, 1993; Torstveit, Rosenvinge, & Sundgot-Borgen, 2008). Also, some younger athletes may unknowingly slip into becoming eating disordered if they are not aware of the energy demands of their increased training loads when following identical strategies as their training peers.

Prevalence of dieting and use of extreme weight-loss methods

Although a number of studies have reported suboptimal energy and nutrient intake among athletes competing in aesthetic and weight-class sports, the prevalence in athletes representing aesthetic and weight-class sports is not known. Most athletes use a combination of methods, but the methods most frequently used by weight-class athletes are reduced energy and fluid intake, fasting, increased training, and dehydration (passive and active) (Table II).

Table I. Reported intake of energy and macronutrients for aesthetic and weight-class athletes.

Study	Population (n), age (years), body weight (kg)	Method/time in season	Mean (±s) daily energy intake, kcal · day⁻¹ (kcal · kg⁻¹)	Carbohydrate E% (g · kg⁻¹)	Protein E% (g · kg⁻¹)	Fat E%
Ebine et al. (2000)	Japanese female elite synchronized swimmers ($n=9$), 16–21 years, 52.5 ± 2.7 kg	7-days self-reported dietary records and doubly labelled water. Period during moderate-intensity training	2128 ± 395 (41)	N.A.	N.A.	N.A.
Ziegler et al. (1999)	US national figure skaters ($n=18$ females, 19 males), 11–18 years, ♀: 46.5 ± 7.1 kg, ♂: 63.6 ± 8.9 kg	4-days self-reported dietary record	♀: 1536 ± 620 (33), ♂: 2365 ± 869 (37)	♀: 56 (4.6), ♂: 52 (4.8)	♀: 16 (1.3), ♂: 18 (1.7)	♀: 29, ♂: 31
Ziegler et al. (2005)	US female international figure skate teams ($n=123$), 17.0 ± 2.1 years, 59 kg	3-days self-reported dietary record	1552 ± 45 (26)	62 (4.1)	14 (0.9)	24
Sundgot-Borgen (1996)	High-level Norwegian modern rhythmic gymnasts ($n=12$), 13–20 years, 33–58 kg	3-days self-reported dietary record	1703 (1200–2374)	N.A.	N.A.	N.A.
Ziegler et al. (2001)	US figure skaters ($n=81$ females, 80 males), 12–28 years, ♀: 47.8 ± 6.3 kg, ♂: 65.2 ± 8.9 kg	3-days self-reported dietary record. Training camps in Colorado between 1988 and 1995	♀: 1545 (33), ♂: 2329 (36)	♀: 60 ± 10 (5.0), ♂: 57 ± 7 (5.1)	♀: 16 ± 4 (1.3), ♂: 15 ± 3 (1.3)	♀: 25 ± 9, ♂: 30 ± 7
Cupisti et al. (2000)	Rhythmic gymnasts of the Italian national team ($n=20$), 14–18 years, 46.7 ± 5.1 kg	3-days self-reported dietary record and clinical interview	1315 ± 97 (29)	52.8 ± 6.5 (3.7)	15.2 ± 1.5 (1.0)	31 ± 5.7
Jonnalagadda et al. (1998)	US female national artistic gymnasts ($n=28$), 12–19 years, 47 kg	3-days self-reported dietary record	1306 ± 270 (27)	67 (4.6)	18 (1.2)	16
Kirchner et al. (1995)	US female collegiate gymnasts ($n=26$), 20 years, 54 kg	Food frequency questionnaire	1377 ± 549 (25)	52 (3.3)	15.5 (1.0)	31
Chen et al. (1989)	Chinese elite gymnasts ($n=5$ females, 4 males), 18–21 years, ♀: 45 kg, ♂: 59 kg	3–5 days weighed dietary record	♀: 2286 ± 334 (51), ♂: 3311 ± 55 (55)	♀: 42 (5.4), ♂: 43 (6.1)	♀: 16 (2.1), ♂: 18 (2.6)	♀: 42, ♂: 38
Garthe et al. (2009)	Norwegian elite weight-class athletes ($n=5$ females, 5 males), 18–32 years, ♀: 64 kg, ♂: 74 kg	4-days weighed dietary record. Weight-stable period before weight-loss intervention	♀: 1931 ± 732 (31), ♂: 2478 ± 715 (33)	♀: 34 (3.0), ♂: 52 (4.7)	♀: 13 (1.2), ♂: 18 (1.6)	♀: 25, ♂: 30

N.A. = data not available.

Table II. The most frequently used weight-loss methods among weight-class athletes expressed as a percentage.

Study	Method and athletes that regularly lose weight	Age began losing weight (years) (mean ± s)	Weight lost (kg) (mean ± s)	Sauna/heat room	Rubber suit	Fluid restriction	Food restriction	Fasting	Laxatives	Diuretics	Spitting	Vomiting	Excessive exercise	Gradual dieting
Steen and Brownell (1990)	Closed-ended questionnaire, male college wrestlers, $n=63$ (89%)	14.0 ± 2.0	4.4 ± 2.1* 7.2 ± 3.2**	78	90	95	93	73	7	3	—	2	—	—
Oppliger et al. (2003)	Closed-ended questionnaire, male college wrestlers, $n=741$ (84%)	13.7 ± 3.4	5.3 ± 2.8**	32	6	21	46	8	3 #	3 #	9	2 #	75	80
Alderman et al. (2004)	Structured interview, male NWC wrestlers, $n=45$	—	5.3**	56	49	—	—	—	11	11	—	0	91	—
Slater at al. (2005a)	Closed-ended questionnaire, male lightweight rowers, $n=58$ (92%), female lightweight rowers, $n=42$ (94%)	—	♂: 6.0**	♂ 33	♂ 41	♂ 21	♂ 78	♂ 7	♂ 11	—	—	♂ 0	♂ 33	♂ 59
Artioli et al. (2010a)	Closed-ended questionnaire, male judo athletes, $n=607$; female judo athletes, $n=607$, (89%) §	12.6 ± 6.1	♀: 4.5 ** 1.6 ± 1.6* 4.0 ± 3.1**	♀ 58 (a) 29 (b) 55	♀ 29 (a) 30 (b) 40	♀ 88 (a) 29% (b) 55%	♀ 94 (a) 19 (b) 41	♀ 12 (a) 12 (b) 24	♀ 68 (a) 3 (b) 8	(a) 2 (b)6	(a) 19 (b) 28	♀0 (a) 0 (b)2	♀ 53 (a) 62 (b) 25	♀ 94 (a) 18 (b) 35

( ) = Percentage of athletes that regularly lose weight.
— = Not reported in the study.
* Usual weight loss.
** Most weight lost.
# One time per month or more.
NWC = National Wrestling Championship.
§ Male and female data are merged due to no significant differences between the sexes.
(a) = Always.
(b) = Sometimes.

Up to 94% of athletes competing in weight-class sports report dieting and use of extreme weight-control methods to make weight prior to competition (Table II). Among athletes representing leanness and aesthetic sports it is more common to observe disordered eating behaviour and clinical eating disorders. When reviewing studies on the prevalence of clinical eating disorders by clinical evaluation, there is a significantly higher prevalence of eating disorders in both male and female elite athletes representing leanness/weight-class sports than elite male and female athletes representing sports with less focus on leanness/weight: the prevalence is 40–42% in aesthetic and 30–35% in weight-class sports for females and 17–18% in weight-class and 22–42% in gravitational sports for male elite athletes compared with 5% and 16% in ball-game sports and 4% and 17% in technical sports for male and females, respectively (Rosendahl et al., 2009; Sundgot-Borgen & Torstveit, 2010)

Weight-class athletes lose up to 13% of body weight, but most of these athletes usually lose 3–6% frequently during the season (Table II). Athletes in the lightweight categories practise more extreme weight-loss behaviour than athletes in the middle- or heavyweight categories (Oppliger et al., 2003). It has also been reported that athletes start losing weight as early as age 9–14 years (Alderman, Landers, Carlson, & Scott, 2004; Steen & Brownell, 1990) and that there seems to be an association between the age at which athletes start losing weight and the severity of weight-management behaviour (Artioli et al., 2010a). Most studies investigating the use of extreme weight-loss methods and clinical eating disorders show that athletes under-report both the use of extreme weight-loss methods and presence of eating disorders (Nattiv et al., 2007; Sundgot-Borgen & Torstveit, 2010). The prevalence of the triad components among female athletes in weight and aesthetic sports is high (Torstveit & Sundgot-Borgen, 2005). The triad components are not well studied in male athletes, but in a population of male cyclists 25% and 9% were diagnosed with osteopenia and osteoporosis, respectively (Smathers, Bemben, & Bemben, 2009). However, further research in male and female athletes is needed to explore the mechanisms and prevalence of the three components.

Performance consequences

The effect of weight loss on performance depends on the athlete's initial percentage of body fat, the magnitude of the weight loss, and the strategy used for weight loss and recovery (Table III). Most athletes reduce the amount of strength training in the weight-loss period prior to competition in favour of more sport-specific/competition training. Reduced stimulus for muscle growth combined with negative energy balance is likely to cause a reduction in lean body mass and may therefore impair strength and performance (Koral & Dosseville, 2009; Koutedakis et al., 1994).

Since most studies on the effect of extreme weight loss have methodological weaknesses such as small samples, undefined performance level, unclear and uncontrolled diet and recovery regimes/strategies, and questionable test parameters with regard to a specific performance test, it is difficult to draw conclusions regarding the effect of extreme dieting and its effect on performance. Nevertheless, the results indicate that muscle endurance and prolonged aerobic and anaerobic work, such as most combat sports and rowing, are likely to be impaired by rapid weight loss. To what extent seems to depend on the time from weigh-in to competition and the recovery strategy used. For example, Slater et al. (2005b) found minimal impairment of 2000-m rowing after rapid weight loss with an aggressive nutritional intervention during recovery. However, that may not apply to combat athletes due to the characteristics of the sport (e.g. rapid movements) and possible gastrointestinal discomfort with high volume intake. Other studies indicate that a less aggressive nutritional recovery also prevents performance impairment in an interval-related performance (Fogelholm, Koskinen, Laakso, Rankinen, & Rukonen, 1993; Hall & Lane 2001). Athletes report symptoms such as dizziness, hot flashes, nausea, headache, and nose bleeds after rapid weight loss (Alderman et al., 2004) and report that extreme weight-loss methods may decrease performance. Considering that most athletes have 2–3 h to recover, they should carefully consider the amount of weight lost by the rapid method and have an optimal recovery strategy after weigh-in. Although the intention is to lose body water over 1–7 days, it is unavoidable to lose some fat mass and muscle mass during fasting or extremely low energy intake (Artioli et al., 2010b). When it comes to gradual weight loss, there are very few studies available. Both Koutedakis et al. (1994) and Koral and Dosseville (2009) reported loss of lean tissue as well as fat mass, while lean tissue was reported by Garthe and colleagues (Garthe, Raastad, Refsnes, Koivisto, & Sundgot-Borgen, 2009) to be stable or increased during the weight-loss period. This result is most likely due to the additional strength training during weight loss, stimulating lean tissue growth while in a moderate negative energy balance. Gradual weight loss seems to be the method with least impairment of performance in these athletes. Interestingly, studies indicate that some athletes may even improve performance during weight loss when using a gradual approach (Fogelholm et al., 1993; Garthe et al., 2009; Koutedakis et al., 1994).

Table III. Rapid and gradual weight loss and the effect on performance.

Reference and participants	Methods (% loss of body weight)	Recovery strategy	Performance testing/physical indicators of performance	Effect on performance	Comments
Rapid weight loss					
Webster et al. (1990) (male intercollegiate wrestlers, n = 7)	Dehydration (4.9%) using exercise in a rubberized sweat suit over 36 h	—	Strength (5 repetitions of chest press, shoulder press, knee flexion and extension), anaerobic power, aerobic peak capacity, and lactate threshold	↓	Impairment in all test parameters. Although athletes had 36 h to lose weight, all of the weight loss occurred within 12 h before testing
Horswill et al. (1990) (male wrestlers, n = 12)	2 × weight loss (6%) by energy and fluid restriction over 4 days (one with low CHO intake and one with high CHO intake)	—	Arm cranking ergometer. Eight bouts of 15-s maximal effort intervals with 30 s of easy pace between	↑ ↓	Performance maintained with the high CHO diet and impaired with the low CHO diet. Performance decreased more the second time of weight loss
Burge et al. (1993) (male and female elite lightweight rowers, n = 8)	Weight loss (5.2%) by energy and fluid restriction combined with exercise over 24 h	2 h recovery period with an intake of 1.5 L water	Rowing ergometer time trial (2000 m)	↓	Performance was impaired by 9%
Fogelholm et al. (1993) (male wrestlers, n = 7; judo athletes, n = 3)	Weight loss (6%) by energy and fluid restriction over 2.4 days	5 h recovery period with *ad libitum* intake of food and fluid	Sprint (30-m run), anaerobic power (1-min Wingate test), and vertical jump height with extra load	↑	Athletes regained 55% of body weight during recovery time
Filaire et al. (2000) (male judo athletes, n = 11)	Weight loss (4.9%) by self-selected energy and fluid restriction over 7 days (~30% reduction in energy, CHO, and fluid intake)	—	Handgrip strength, 30-s and 7-s jump tests	↑ ↓	Performance remained unchanged for left arm strength and 7-s jump test but was impaired for right arm strength and 30-s jump test
Smith et al. (2000) (male amateur boxers, n = 7)	Dehydration (3.8%) by low-intensity exercise for ~2 h in hot environment	—	Simulated boxing-related task with 3 × 3 min rounds with 1 min rest between on a boxing ergometer	↓	One athlete improved performance whereas mean reduction in performance was 27% for the other athletes
Smith et al. (2001) (male amateur boxers, n = 8)	Repeated (2 days between) weight loss (3%) by energy (1000 kcal · day⁻¹) and fluid restriction (1.0 ml · day⁻¹)	—	Repeated (2 days between) simulated boxing-related task with 3 × 3 min rounds with 1 min rest between on a boxing ergometer	↑	Performance tended to be lower in both bouts but did not reach statistical significance due to large individual differences
Hall and Lane (2001) (male amateur boxers, n = 16)	Weight loss (5.2%) by energy and fluid restriction over one week (self-selected weight-loss strategy)	2 h recovery with both food and fluid intake (self-selected recovery strategy)	4 × 2 min circuit training session with 1 min recovery between rounds	↑	Athletes failed to reach their subjective expected level of performance after weight loss
Slater et al. (2005b) (male and female	Weight loss (4.3%) by energy and fluid restriction over 24 h	Aggressive nutritional	4 rowing ergometer time trials (2000 m) separated by 48 h in	↓	Performance was impaired by 0.7% during thermoneutral

(Continued)

Table III. (*Continued*)

Reference and participants	Methods (% loss of body weight)	Recovery strategy	Performance testing/physical indicators of performance	Effect on performance	Comments
competitive rowers, $n=17$		recovery strategies in 2 h (2.3 g CHO · kg⁻¹, 34 mg Na · kg⁻¹, 28.4 ml fluid · kg⁻¹)	thermoneutral and hot environments		trials and 1.1% during hot trials when trials were merged
Degoutte et al. (2006) (male judo athletes, $n=10$)	Weight loss (5%) by self-selected energy and fluid restriction over 7 days	—	Handgrip strength, maximal strength, 30-s rowing task, and simulated competition (5 × 5 min bouts)	↓	Energy intake was reduced by 4 MJ · day⁻¹ during weight loss
Slater et al. (2006) (male and female competitive rowers, $n=17$)	Weight loss (3.9%) by energy and fluid restriction and increased training load over 24 h	Aggressive nutritional recovery strategies in 2 h (2.3 g CHO · kg⁻¹, 34 mg Na · kg⁻¹, 28.4 ml fluid · kg⁻¹)	Three on-water rowing time trials (1800 m) separated by 48 h	↑	Environmental conditions were cool, showing slight variations. There was a non-significant increase in time of 1.0 s
Artioli et al. (2010b) (male judo athletes, $n=14$)	Weight loss (5%) by self-selected energy and fluid restriction over 7 days, $n=7$ (control group, $n=7$)	4 h recovery period with *ad libitum* intake of food and fluid. Regained 51% of reduced weight	Specific judo exercise, number of repeated attacks (10 s, 20 s, 30 s, with 10 s rest between), followed by 5 min rest and a 5-min judo combat and three bouts of upper-body Wingate test	↑ ←	Performance remained unchanged in specific judo exercise (number of attacks). Both control and intervention groups saw a slight improvement in Wingate test
Gradual weight loss Fogelholm et al. (1993) (male wrestlers, $n=7$; judo athletes, $n=3$)	Weight loss (5%) by energy restriction over 3 weeks	—	Sprint (30-m run), anaerobic power (1-min Wingate test), and vertical jump height with extra load	↑ ←	Performance remained unchanged except for vertical jump, which improved by 6–8%
Koutedakis et al. (1994) (female elite lightweight rowers, $n=6$).	Weight loss (6%) by energy restriction over 8 weeks	—	$\dot{V}O_{2max}$ respiratory anaerobic threshold, upper body anaerobic peak power and mean power outputs, knee flexor and extensor and isokinetic peak torques	↑ →	Performance remained unchanged except for a decrease in respiratory anaerobic threshold and knee flexor. 50% of weight lost as fat-free mass
Koutedakis et al. (1994) (female elite	Weight loss (7.4%) by energy restriction over 16 weeks	—	Maximal rowing ergometer test and upper-body Wingate test	↑ ←	Improved performance in respiratory anaerobic threshold,

(*Continued*)

Table III. (*Continued*)

Reference and participants	Methods (% loss of body weight)	Recovery strategy	Performance testing/physical indicators of performance	Effect on performance	Comments
lightweight rowers, $n = 6$			(VO_{2max}) anaerobic threshold, peak power and mean power outputs); isokinetic knee flexion and extension		knee flexion, VO_{2max} and upper body anaerobic peak power. 50% of weight lost as fat-free mass
Koral and Dosseville (2009) ($n = 10$ male and 10 female elite judo athletes)	Weight loss (4%) by self-selected energy and fluid restriction over 4 weeks	—	Countermovement jump, squat jump, 5-s repetitions of judo movements, 30-s repetition of judo movements, rowing with additional loads	↑ ↓	Performance remained unchanged for squat jump, countermovement jump, and judo movement repetitions over 5 s, while impaired for 30-s judo movements
Garthe et al. (2009) (male and female elite athletes, $n = 13$)	Weight loss (5.6%) by controlled diet intervention combined with strength training over 9 weeks	—	Countermovement jump, 1-RM squat, bench press, bench pull, and 40-m sprint	↑ ←	Improved performance in all parameters except for 40-m sprint, which was unchanged Energy intake was reduced by 19% while lean body mass increased by 2%
Garthe et al. (2009) (male and female elite athletes, $n = 11$)	Weight loss (5.5%) by controlled diet intervention combined with strength training over 5 weeks.	—	Countermovement jump, 1-RM squat, bench press, bench pull, and 40-m sprint	↑ ←	Performance remained unchanged except for an improvement in 1-RM squat. Energy intake was reduced by 30%

— = No recovery strategy. ↓ = Impaired performance. ↑ = Improved performance.

Health consequences

Dehydration

In a dehydrated state, plasma volume is reduced and peripheral blood flow and sweating rate diminish. This impairs thermoregulatory function and may lead to risks to the athlete's health (Shirreffs, Armstrong, & Cheuvront, 2004). Thus, dehydration combined with exercise in a rubber suit/sweat suit or sauna, common methods of weight loss, makes heat dissipation difficult and can even be fatal.

Inadequate intake of macro- and micronutrients

Very low energy intake and fasting place the athletes at risk of inadequate intake of carbohydrate (CHO), essential fatty acids, and protein (Table I). Reduced carbohydrate intake will result in glycogen depletion, fatigue, and inadequate recovery between training sessions (Burke, Kiens, & Ivy, 2004). Furthermore, a reduced protein intake is likely to cause a greater loss of lean tissue during weight loss (Mettler, Mitchell, & Tipton, 2010). During weight loss there is also an increased risk for suboptimal intake of calcium and iron and other micronutrients (Filaire, Maso, Degoutte, Jouanel, & Lac, 2000; Fogelholm et al., 1993; Heyward, Sandoval, & Colville, 1989). Although this is not likely to cause problems in the short term, repeated weight-loss periods during the season may lead to compromised vitamin and mineral status.

Cognitive function and psychological factors

Dehydration and severe energy restriction will lead to a general feeling of fatigue and is likely to result in an increased perception of effort (Horswill, Hickner, Scott, Costill, & Gould, 1990). Athletes undergoing rapid weight loss have shown an increase in anger, fatigue, tension, and anxiety as well as impaired short-term memory (Choma, Sforzo, & Keller, 1998; Degoutte et al., 2006; Filaire et al., 2000; Hall & Lane, 2001; Steen & Brownell, 1990). Some athletes experience this increased anger as performance-enhancing, and thus as an essential part of the pre-competition preparation (Steen & Brownell, 1990).

Increased stress and impaired immune function

Heavy training loads combined with low energy intake or low carbohydrate intake increase the risk of chronic fatigue, injuries and oxidative stress, and may impair immune function (Burke et al., 2004; Gleeson, Nieman, & Pedersen, 2004; Nattiv et al., 2007; Yanagawa et al., 2010), which, in the long term, can lead to more frequent episodes of injuries and illness for the athlete.

Metabolic changes

It has been stated that weight-cycling athletes have lower metabolic rate than athletes with no history of weight-cycling (Brownell, Steen, & Wilmore, 1987; Steen, Oppliger, & Brownell, 1998). However, longitudinal studies show that metabolic rate decreases during the season but rises to baseline values post-season, suggesting that the decrease in metabolic rate is not permanent (Melby, Schmidt, & Corrigan, 1990). These changes may be reversible, but frequent dieting may have long-term consequences. From practical experience, weight-class athletes who have used extreme methods for years experience increasing difficulties in "making weight" and have to use more and more aggressive methods to reach their competitive weight. Whether this is a result of metabolic changes or other physiological, biological or psychological factors is unknown.

Long-term effect

For athletes, the stress of constantly denying hunger, obsession about food, agonizing over body weight, and fearing high body weight is mentally exhausting. Moreover, this preoccupation interferes with the athlete's daily activities as well as his or her training and competition. Longer periods with low energy availability, with or without disordered eating, can impair health and physical performance (Nattiv et al., 2007). Medical complications involve the cardiovascular, endocrine, reproductive, skeletal, gastrointestinal, renal, and central nervous systems (Nattiv et al., 2007).

Disordered eating, hormonal changes, and low bone density

Dieting athletes may slip into disordered eating, which in turn can lead to a serious eating disorder, disruption of the normal menstrual cycle, and eventually an imbalance in bone remodelling leading to low bone mass, osteopenia or osteoporosis. Although any one of these problems can occur in isolation, the emphasis on weight loss among at-risk individuals can start a cycle in which all three diseases occur in sequence. The female athlete triad has been described elsewhere (Drinkwater et al., 2005; Nattiv et al., 2007). The consequences of low energy availability, amenorrhoea, and imbalance in bone remodelling are more severe for the adolescent athlete, since imbalance in bone remodelling hinders high peak bone mass, stature, and the development of the reproductive system. Although most research into the triad and its components has been done exclusively in females, some studies indicate that male athletes also are at risk for these problems.

Both reduced testosterone levels as a consequence of low percent body fat (Karila et al., 2008) and low bone mineral density (competitive cyclists and long-distance runners) have been reported (Hetland, Haarbo, & Christiansen, 1993; Smathers et al., 2009).

Athletes restricting energy intake, whether inadvertently or by intent, could be considered as at risk for disordered eating. However, it is not necessarily dieting *per se* that triggers disordered eating or an eating disorder, but whether dieting is guided or not (Sundgot-Borgen & Torstveit, 2010). Controlled weight-loss intervention in elite athletes seems not to increase the risk for disordered eating or eating disorders when guided by a professional sports nutritionist (Garthe et al., 2009). Also, although weight-class athletes are considered to be at special risk for developing eating disorders, this disturbed eating behaviour and use of extreme weight-loss methods may exist only in-season (Dale & Landers, 1999; Steen & Brownell, 1990). Eating disorder risk factors considered to be specific to athletes are: personality factors, pressure to lose weight leading to restricted eating and/or frequent weight cycling/fluctuation, body dissatisfaction, early start of sport-specific training, injuries, symptoms of overtraining, and the impact of coaching behaviour.

Growth and maturation

Aesthetic-sports training starts early, at pre-school age, and quickly becomes intense, frequent, and long lasting, always with a view to maintaining minimal subcutaneous body fat. Inadequate energy and nutrient intakes during the growth period, however, could result in delayed pubertal development and retarded growth (Soric, Misigoj-Durakovic, & Pedisic, 2008). Delayed menarche, bone growth retardation, reduced height, weight and body fat have been reported in gymnasts (Weimann, Witzel, Schwidergall, & Böhles, 2000) and even short-term weight loss may have marked effects on blood biochemistry and hormonal parameters (Karila et al., 2008). This may constitute a special health risk for the adolescent athlete with repeated weight loss during the season. Even though it may take months, studies show that there seems to be a catch-up effect when it comes to growth of bone and lean body mass after a weight-reduction period in young athletes (Caine, Lewis, O'Connor, Howe, & Bass, 2001; Roemmich & Sinning, 1997). It has been reported that eating disorders are associated with sport-specific training at a young age (Sundgot-Borgen, 1994). Some children start practising sports by the age of 3 or 4 years. At the age of 5–7 years, girls competing in aesthetic sports report greater weight concerns than girls in non-aesthetic sports and girls not involved in sports (Davison, Earnest, & Birch, 2002). However, controlled studies concerning the long-term effect of frequent dieting and weight fluctuation on growth and development are lacking.

Practical implications

Considering the possible detrimental effect of extreme dieting and rules and regulations on performance and health effects, continuous preventive and educational work is needed and further research is warranted. Since extreme dieting and eating disorders are almost part of the culture within the aesthetic and weight-class sports, the recommendations for these sports will be more related to how to prevent extreme dieting, how to optimize energy and nutrient intake, and finally education about how to "approach" athletes who need or want to diet and or change body competition to enhance performance.

Recommendations

There is a lack of sports-specific guidelines for energy intake and the need for macro- and micronutrients for athletes competing in gymnastics, diving, figure skating, synchronized swimming, and weight-class sports. However, from practical experience we know that energy intake varies a great deal during the season and on whether the athlete is dieting/cutting weight or not. As shown in Table I, dietary intake among female gymnasts and figure skaters is characterized by low energy intake, considered the estimated energy requirement, as well as a modest carbohydrate and protein intake. However, due to low body weight, most gymnasts have adequate macronutrient intakes. In addition, they report intake of some micronutrients such as iron, zinc, and calcium below the recommended daily allowance. Under-reporting and under-eating are common errors of measurement in self-reported dietary intake and thus such data should be interpreted with caution (Magkos & Yannakoulia, 2003).

The lack of documentation makes it difficult to recommend specific guidelines for energy intake and intakes of macro- and micronutrients for the different aesthetic and weight-class athletes. Since the greatest challenge is low energy intake and increased risk of nutritional deficiencies and hormonal disturbances, it should be emphasized that the athlete should consume sufficient energy to avoid menstrual irregularities (Loucks, in press). A frequent meal pattern and optimal recovery strategies between training sessions may reduce fatigue during training sessions and may possibly help optimizing body composition over time (Deutz, Benardot, Martin, & Cody, 2000). If the diet plan is set to maintain a low body weight, it should aim to have a relatively high protein intake (1.4–1.8 g · kg^{-1}) to maintain lean body mass and to induce thermogenic and satiety effects (Karst, Steiniger, Noack, & Steglich, 1984; Mettler et al., 2010). Carbohydrate requirements vary for different sports, but both aesthetic and weight-class sports (except for light-weight rowing) can relate to the general recommendation for the non-endurance athlete (ACSM, 2009). Weight-class sports such as lightweight rowing, wrestling, boxing, and judo have relatively high energy demands during both training and competitions and rely on both aerobic and anaerobic energy metabolism. Diving, gymnastics, and figure skating involve more short-duration high-intensity bouts with plenty of rest between exercises and often have long training bouts (up to 4 h) with modest total energy expenditure (Deutz et al., 2000). Thus, both categories can be categorized as carbohydrate-dependent sports and should aim for a carbohydrate intake corresponding to 5–7 g · kg^{-1} (ACSM, 2009; Burke et al., 2004). However, on low-energy diets some athletes may have carbohydrate intakes corresponding to 4 g · kg^{-1}, and for some athletes that may be adequate, depending on the type and duration of exercise. Since carbohydrate and protein are considered to be important macronutrients for athletes, diets to maintain a low body weight are often low in fat. However, it is not recommended to have a diet containing less than 15–20% of fat.

There is special concern for adolescent athletes when it comes to the dieting culture in some sports. Due to the expected consequences related to restrictive eating, menstrual dysfunction, and loss of bone mass, it is the authors' opinion that adolescent athletes should not diet except for when medically indicated.

Education

To decrease the high number of athletes representing weight-class and leanness sports that are dieting and using extreme weight-loss methods, there is a need for education among athletes, trainers, coaches, and parents. The educational part should include optimization of eating behaviour and energy intake, and healthy body image and body composition. Also, elite athletes who need to reduce weight or change body composition should be advised appropriately.

Information and guidelines

Sports governing organizations and federations should give support to their coaches and provide education for coaches and athletes regarding health and performance-enhancing nutrition behaviour, disordered eating/eating disorders, and the female athlete triad. Each federation should have position statements with guidelines related to optimizing

nutrition and body composition and reducing harmful weight-loss methods

De-emphasize weight

The athlete's weight and body composition should not be measured unless there are well-founded health and/or performance reasons. For elite athletes, weight and body composition are important performance variables as well as a necessity in some of the practical work. However, dieting and weight issues should never be a theme from the coach, but should be presented according to the athlete's wish. In such cases, the coach should take the athlete's initiative seriously and refer to professional help. In this respect, the possibility of increasing weight and a change of weight class should also be discussed with the athlete. The focus should be on performance enhancement via non-dieting strategies: improved nutrition, improved health, mental and psychological approaches, and physical aspects.

Avoid unnecessary dieting

Coaches should avoid telling an athlete to lose weight. Most weight-class athletes and those competing in leanness sports are fit and lean, but want to reduce weight to further enhance performance. In such cases, the coach and health care team (nutritionist/dietitian, exercise physiologist or physician) should motivate the athlete to improve strength and power and compete in a higher weight class. Health-care providers should educate athletes and coaches that weight loss does not necessarily lead to improved athletic performance. Furthermore, since athletes are eager to perform, it is important to inform them about side-effects of under-eating and abnormal eating behaviour. If the coach is concerned about an athlete's eating behaviour, body image, and/or weight or body fat level, the athlete should be referred to a sports nutritionist or health care specialist for further evaluation and consultation.

Recommendations for appropriate weight loss/change in body composition

For athletes who should lose weight for medical or performance reasons, the following recommendations are offered:

- The weight goal should be based on objective measurements of body composition (e.g. DXA, ultrasound, sum of skinfold with protocol from International Society for the Advancement of Kinanthropometry (ISAK)). A thorough screening including weight history, menstrual history for females, nutritional status, and questions regarding motivation, thoughts and feelings about body image, body weight and food should be done. If there is a history of disordered eating/eating disorders, a more intense and longer follow-up is suggested.

- The weight-loss period should be undertaken during the off-season to avoid interference with competitions and sport-specific training loads.
- A dietary registration should be the basis for the diet plan. If the athlete has a history of amenorrhoea or other indicators of low bone mineral density, an objective measure of bone mineral density is warranted (e.g. DXA). A blood test should be taken and if it indicates any specific micronutrient needs (e.g. iron, vitamin B12), these should be provided and biochemical changes monitored. A multi-vitamin/mineral supplement and omega-3 fatty acids should be provided during the weight-loss period to ensure sufficient micronutrient intake and essential fat intake.
- The athlete should consume sufficient energy to avoid menstrual irregularities and aim for a gradual weight loss corresponding to ~ 0.5 kg per week. To induce a weight loss of 0.5 kg per week, an energy deficit of ~ 500 kcal$\cdot$day^{-1} is needed, but there are individual differences. This can be achieved by reducing energy intake, increasing energy expenditure, or a combination of the two.
- A sports nutritionist/dietitian should plan individual nutritionally adequate diets. The diet plan should aim at a protein intake corresponding to 1.4–2.0 g$\cdot$kg^{-1}, a carbohydrate intake corresponding to 4–6 g$\cdot$kg^{-1}, and 15–20% fat. Emphasize recovery meals containing carbohydrates and protein within 30 minu after training to optimize recovery and include dairy food sources to meet the recommended dietary intake of calcium. To avoid extra energy by adding a recovery meal it can be recommended to "time" the meals so that the recovery meal is one of the planned meals during the day.
- Strength training should be included during the weight-loss period to alleviate the negative consequences on lean body mass and performance.
- Lower limits of percent body fat of 5% for male athletes and 12% for female athletes have been suggested (Fogelholm, 1994; Heyward & Wagner, 2004). However, individual evaluation should be undertaken. An *ad hoc* IOC working group is currently looking at body composition measurements and body fat cut-off values and will provide guidelines for the appropriate percentage body fat values for male and female athletes, as well as the most valid method(s) to

measure body composition in athletes. Change in body composition should be monitored on a regular basis including a period of at least 2 months after the weight or body fat goal has been reached to detect any continued or unwarranted losses or weight fluctuations.

- Weight-class athletes with frequent competitions during most of the calendar year are encouraged to be no more than approximately 3% above competition weight and to lose no more than 2% of body mass in rapid weight loss (dependent on time from weigh-in to competition and recovery strategies) to avoid large weight fluctuations and impaired performance. Athletes in sports with fewer competitions and a more defined on- and off-season should seek out the most important events to reach their competition weight and to allow a higher fat mass and body weight for periods with larger training loads and fewer competitions.
- Normal-weight athletes under the age of 18 should be discouraged to lose weight.

Modification of regulations

1. In sports such as wrestling and tae kwondo, it would be more difficult for competitors to rapidly lose a great amount of weigh if a daily weigh-in and a delay of only 2–3 h from weigh-in to competition could be implemented.
2. The sport federations should have the same weight categories at national and international competitions, and more weight categories, especially in the low- and middleweight classes, should be implemented.
3. Accepting weight allowance (e.g. 1–2 kg over weight limit) during the season in some of the smaller tournaments might reduce the frequency of weight loss.
4. Organizers should make sure that the weight scale used for weigh-in is professionally calibrated.
5. There is a need for a "competition certificate" where athletes must have a minimum percentage body fat and a safe hydration level. However, there is a need for research to decide the minimum percentage of body fat and most valid and reliable methods for measuring body fat percentage and hydration status.

Summary

There is no hard evidence for the causal effect of the use of extreme weight-control methods and the development of eating disorders. However, the prevalence of the use of extreme weight-loss methods and disordered eating is higher among elite athletes competing in sports focusing on leanness and or a specific weight, compared with that seen in athletes competing in sports less focused on weight and/or leanness. Since the use of these methods is a risk to both performance and health, proper prevention strategies are necessary. First, education programmes to increase athletes', coaches', and parents' awareness about the risks associated with a long period of dieting and energy deficit and the use of extreme weight-loss methods, how to implement healthy nutrition practices, and the use of recommended weight-loss strategies are important and should be part of any preventive programme. Furthermore, the coaches, leaders, and medical staff of teams together with parents must be able to recognize athletes who are abusing extreme methods to make weight and symptoms indicating risk for eating disorders. Lastly, modifications of regulations in some of the weight-class sports are needed.

References

Alderman, B. L., Landers, D. M., Carlson, J., & Scott, J. R. (2004). Factors related to rapid weight loss practices among international-style wrestlers. *Medicine and Science in Sports and Exercise, 36*, 249–252.

American College of Sports Medicine (2009). Position stand: Nutrition and athletic performance. *Medicine and Science in Sports and Exercise, 41*, 709–731.

Artioli, G. G., Gualano, B., Franchini, E., Scagliusi, F. B., Takesian, M., Fuchs, M. et al. (2010a). Prevalence, magnitude, and methods of rapid weight loss among judo competitors. *Medicine and Science in Sports and Exercise, 42*, 436–442.

Artioli, G. G., Iglesias, R. T., Franchini, E., Gualano, B., Kashiwagura, D. B., Solis, M. Y. et al. (2010b). Rapid weight loss followed by recovery time does not affect judo-related performance. *Journal of Sports Sciences, 28*, 21–32.

Brownell, K. D., Steen, S. N., & Wilmore, J. H. (1987). Weight regulation practices in athletes: Analysis of metabolic and health effects. *Medicine and Science in Sports and Exercise, 6*, 546–560.

Burge, C. M., Carey, M. F., & Payne, W. R. (1993). Rowing performance, fluid balance, and metabolic function following dehydration and rehydration. *Medicine and Science in Sports and Exercise, 25*, 1358–1364.

Burke, L. M., Kiens, B., & Ivy, J. L. (2004). Carbohydrates and fat for training and recovery. *Journal of Sports Sciences, 22*, 15–30.

Caine, D., Lewis, R., O'Connor, P., Howe, W., & Bass, S. (2001). Does gymnastics training inhibit growth of females? *Clinical Journal of Sports Medicine, 11*, 260–270.

Chen, J. D., Wang, J. F., Li, K. J., Zhao, J. W., Wang, S. W., & Jiao, Y. (1989). Nutritional problems and measures in elite and amateur athletes. *American Journal of Clinical Nutrition, 49*, 1084–1089.

Choma, C. W., Sforzo, G. A., & Keller, B. A. (1998). Impact of rapid weight loss on cognitive function in collegiate wrestlers. *Medicine and Science in Sports and Exercise, 30*, 746–749.

Cupisti, A., D'Alessandro, C., Castrogiovanni, S., Barale, A., & Morelli, E. (2000). Nutrition survey in elite rhythmic gymnasts, *Journal of Sports Medicine and Physical Fitness, 40*, 350–355.

Dale, K. S., & Landers, D. M. (1999). Weight control in wrestling: Eating disorders or disordered eating? *Medicine and Science in Sports and Exercise, 31*, 1382–1389.

Davison, K. K., Earnest, M. B., & Birch, L. L. (2002). Participation in aesthetic sports and girls weight concerns at ages 5 and 7 years. *International Journal of Eating Disorders, 31*, 312–317.

de Bruin, A. P., Oudejans, R. R. D., & Bakker, F. C. (2007). Dieting and body image in aesthetic sports: A comparison of Dutch female gymnasts and non-aesthetic sport participants. *Psychology of Sport and Exercise, 8*, 507–520.

Degoutte, F., Jouanel, P., Bègue, R. J., Colombier, M., Lac, G., Pequignot, J. M. et al. (2006). Food restriction, performance, biochemical, psychological, and endocrine changes in judo athletes. *International Journal of Sports Medicine, 27*, 9–18.

Deutz, R. C., Benardot, D., Martin, D. E., & Cody, M. M. (2000). Relationship between energy deficits and body composition in elite female gymnasts and runners. *Medicine and Science in Sports and Exercise, 32*, 659–668.

Drinkwater, B., Loucks, A., Sherman, R., Sundgot-Borgen, J., & Thompon, R. (2005). International Olympic Committee Medical Commission Working Group: Women in sport. Position stand on the female athlete triad. Retrieved from http://multimedia. olympic.org/pdf/en_report_917. pdf.

Ebine, N., Feng, J. Y., Homma, M., Saitoh, S., & Jones, P. J. (2000). Total energy expenditure of elite synchronized swimmers measured by the doubly labeled water method. *European Journal of Applied Physiology, 83*, 1–6.

Economos, C. D., Bortz, S. S., & Nilson, M. E. (1993). Nutritional practices of elite athletes: Practical recommendations. *Sports Medicine, 16*, 381–399.

Filaire, E., Maso, F., Degoutte, F., Jouanel, P., & Lac, G. (2000). Food restriction, performance, psychological state and lipid values in judo athletes. *International Journal of Sports Medicine, 22*, 454–459.

Fogelholm, M. (1994). Effects of bodyweight reduction on sports performance. *Sports Medicine, 4*, 249–267.

Fogelholm, M. G., Koskinen, R., Laakso, J., Rankinen, T., & Rukonen, I. (1993). Gradual and rapid weight loss: Effects on nutrition and performance in male athletes. *Medicine and Science in Sports and Exercise, 25*, 371–377.

Garthe, I., Raastad, T., Refsnes, P. E., Koivisto, A., & Sundgot-Borgen, J. (2009). Is it possible to maintain lean body mass and performance during energy-restriction in elite athletes? *Medicine and Science in Sports and Exercise, 41*, 9.

Gleeson, M., Nieman, D. C., & Pedersen, B. K. (2004). Exercise, nutrition and immune function. *Journal of Sports Sciences, 22*, 115–125.

Hall, C. J., & Lane, A. M. (2001). Effects of rapid weight loss on mood and performance among amateur boxers. *British Journal of Sports Medicine, 35*, 390–395.

Hetland, M. L., Haarbo, J., & Christiansen, C. (1993). Low bone mass and high bone turnover in male long distance runners. *Journal of Clinical Endocrinology and Metabolism, 77*, 770–775.

Heyward, V. H., Sandoval, W. M., & Colville, B. (1989). Anthropometric, body composition and nutritional profiles of bodybuilders during training. *Journal of Applied Sport Science Research, 3*, 22–29.

Heyward, V. H., & Wagner, D. R. (2004). *Applied body composition assessment* (2nd edn.). Champaign, IL: Human Kinetics.

Horswill, C. A., Hickner, R. C., Scott, J. R., Costill, D. L., & Gould, D. (1990). Weight loss, dietary carbohydrate modifications, and high intensity physical performance. *Medicine and Science in Sports and Exercise, 22*, 470–476.

Jonnalagadda, S. S., Bernadot, D., & Nelson, M. (1998). Energy and nutrient intakes of the United States national women's artistic gymnastics team. *International Journal of Sport Nutrition, 8*, 331–344.

Karila, T. A., Sarkinnen, P., Martinnen, M., Seppälä, T., Mero, A., & Tallroth, K. (2008). Rapid weight loss decreases serum testosterone. *International Journal of Sports Medicine, 29*, 872–877.

Karst, H., Steiniger, J., Noack, R., & Steglich, H. D. (1984). Diet-induced thermogenesis in man: thermic effects of single proteins, carbohydrates and fats depending on their energy amount. *Annals of Nutrition and Metabolism, 28*, 245–252.

Kirchner, E. M., Lewis, R. D., & O'Connor, P. J. (1995). Bone mineral density and dietary intake of female college gymnasts. *Medicine and Science in Sports and Exercise, 27*, 543–549.

Koral, J., & Dosseville, F. (2009). Combination of gradual and rapid weight loss: Effects on physical performance and psychological state of elite judo athletes. *Journal of Sports Sciences, 27*, 115–120.

Koutedakis, Y., Pacy, P. J., Quevedo, R. M., Millward, D. J., Hesp, R., Boreham, C. et al. (1994). The effect of two different periods of weight-reduction on selected performance parameters in elite lightweight oarswomen. *International Journal of Sports Medicine, 15*, 472–477.

Loucks, A. (in press). Energy availability in athletes. *Journal of Sports Sciences.*

Magkos, F., & Yannakoulia, M. (2003). Methodology of dietary assessment in athletes: Concepts and pitfalls. *Current Opinion on Clinical Nutrition and Metabolic Care, 6*, 539–549.

Marquart, L. F., & Sobal, J. (1994). Weight loss beliefs, practices and support systems for high school wrestlers. *Journal of Adolescent Health, 15*, 410–415.

Matejek, N. E., Weimann, C., Witzel, G., Molenkamp, S., Schwidergall, S., & Bohles, H. (1999). Hypoleptinaemia in patients with anorexia nervosa and in elite gymnasts with anorexia athletica. *International Journal of Sports Medicine, 20*, 451–456.

Melby, C. L., Schmidt, W. D., & Corrigan, D. (1990). Resting metabolic rate in weight-cycling collegiate wrestlers compared with physically active, noncycling control subjects. *American Journal of Clinical Nutrition, 52*, 409–414.

Mettler, S., Mitchell, N., & Tipton, K. D. (2010). Increased protein intake reduces lean body mass loss during weight loss in athletes. *Medicine and Science in Sports and Exercise, 42*, 326–337.

Nattiv, A., Loucks, A. B., Manore, M. M., Sanborn, C. F., Sundgot-Borgen, J., & Warren, M. P. (2007). The female athlete triad. Special Communications: Position stand. *Medicine and Science in Sports and Exercise, 39*, 1867–1882.

Oppliger, R. A., Steen, S. A., & Scott, J. R. (2003). Weight loss practices of college wrestlers. *International Journal of Sports Nutrition and Exercise Metabolism, 13*, 29–46.

Roemmich, J. N., & Sinning, W. E. (1997). Weight loss and wrestling training: Effects on growth-related hormones. *Journal of Applied Physiology, 82*, 1760–1764.

Rosendahl, J., Bormann, B., Aschenbrenner, K., Aschenbrenner, F., & Strauss, B. (2009). Dieting and disordered eating in German high school athletes and non-athletes. *Scandinavian Journal of Medicine and Science in Sports, 19*, 731–739.

Shirreffs, S. M., Armstrong, L. E., & Cheuvront, S. N. (2004). Fluid and electrolyte needs for preparation and recovery from training and competition: Carbohydrates and fat for training and recovery. *Journal of Sports Sciences, 22*, 57–63.

Slater, G. J., Rice, A. J., Sharpe, K., Mujika, I., Jenkins, D., & Hahn, A. G. (2005a). Body-mass management of Australian lightweight rowers prior to and during competition. *Medicine and Science in Sports and Exercise, 37*, 860–866.

Slater, G. J., Rice, A. J., Sharpe, K., Tanner, R., Jenkins, D., Gore, C. J. et al. (2005b). Impact of acute weight loss and/or thermal stress on rowing ergometer performance. *Medicine and Science in Sports and Exercise, 37*, 1387–1394.

Slater, G. J., Rice, A. J., Tanner, R., Sharpe, K., Jenkins, D., & Hahn, A. G. (2006). Impact of two different body mass management strategies on repeat rowing performance. *Medicine and Science in Sports and Exercise, 38*, 138–146.

Smathers, A. M., Bemben, M. G., & Bemben, D. A. (2009). Bone density comparisons in male competitive road cyclists and untrained controls. *Medicine and Science in Sports and Exercise, 41*, 290–296.

Smith, M. S., Dyson, R., Hale, T., Hamilton, M., Harrison, J. H., & McManus, P. (2000). The effects in humans of rapid loss of body mass on a boxing related task. *European Journal of Applied Physiology, 83*, 34–39.

Smith, M., Dyson, R., Hale, T., Hamilton, M., Kelly, J., & Wellington, P. (2001). The effect of restricted energy and fluid intake on simulated amateur boxing performance. *International Journal of Sports Nutrition and Exercise Metabolism, 11*, 238–247.

Soric, M., Misigoj-Durakovic, M., & Pedisic, Z. (2008). Dietary intake and body composition of prepubescent female aesthetic athletes. *International Journal Sports Nutrition and Exercise Metabolism, 18*, 343–354.

Steen, S. N., & Brownell, K. D. (1990). Pattern of weight loss and regain in wrestlers: Has the tradition changed? *Medicine and Science in Sports and Exercise, 22*, 762–768.

Steen, S. N., Oppliger, R. A., & Brownell, K. D. (1998). Metabolic effects of repeated weight loss and regain in adolescent wrestlers. *Journal of the American Medical Association, 260*, 47–50.

Sundgot-Borgen, J. (1993). Prevalence of eating disorders in elite female athletes. *International Journal of Sports Nutrition, 3*, 29–40.

Sundgot-Borgen, J. (1994). Risk and trigger factors for the development of eating disorders in female elite athletes. *Medicine and Science in Sports and Exercise, 4*, 414–419.

Sundgot-Borgen, J. (1996). Eating disorders, energy intake, training volume and menstrual function in high-level modern rhythmic gymnasts. *International Journal of Sports Nutrition, 2*, 100–109.

Sundgot-Borgen, J., & Torstveit, M. K. (2004). Prevalence of eating disorders in elite athletes is higher than in the general population. *Clinical Journal of Sports Medicine, 14*, 25–32.

Sundgot-Borgen, J., & Torstveit, M. K. (2010). Aspects of disordered eating continuum in elite high-intensity sports. *Scandinavian Journal of Medicine and Science in Sports, 20*, 112–121.

Torstveit, M. K., Rosenvinge, J., & Sundgot-Borgen, J. (2008). Prevalence of eating disorders and the predictive power of risk factor models in female elite athletes: A controlled study. *Scandinavian Journal of Medicine and Science in Sports, 18*, 108–118.

Torstveit, M. K., & Sundgot-Borgen, J. (2005). The female athlete triad exists in both elite athletes and controls. *Medicine and Science in Sports and Exercise, 37*, 1449–1459.

Webster, S., Rutt, R., & Weltman, A. (1990). Physiological effects of a weight loss regimen practiced by college wrestlers. *Medicine and Science in Sports and Exercise, 22*, 229–234.

Weimann, E., Witzel, C., Schwidergall, S., & Böhles, H. J. (2000). Peripubertal perturbations in elite gymnasts caused by sport specific training regimes and inadequate nutritional intake. *International Journal of Sports Medicine, 21*, 210–215.

Yanagawa, Y., Morimura, T., Tsunekawa, K., Seki, K., Ogiwara, T., Kotajima, N. et al. (2010). Oxidative stress associated with rapid weight reduction decreases circulating adiponectin concentrations. *Endocrine Journal, 57*, 339–345.

Ziegler, P. J., Kannan, S., Jonnalagadda, S. S., Krishnakumar, A., Taksali, S. E., & Nelson, J. A. (2005). Dietary intake, body image perceptions, and weight concerns of female US international synchronized figure skating teams. *International Journal of Sports Nutrition and Exercise Metabolism, 15*, 550–566.

Ziegler, P. J., Nelson, J. A., Barratt-Fornell, A., Fiveash, L., & Drewnowski, A. (2001). Energy and macronutrient intakes of elite figure skaters. *Journal of the American Dietetic Association, 101*, 319–325.

Ziegler, P. J., Nelson, J. A., & Jonnalagadda, S. S. (1999). Nutritional and physiological status of U.S. national figure skaters. *International Journal of Sport Nutrition, 9*, 345–360.

Sport-specific nutrition: Practical strategies for team sports

FRANCIS E. HOLWAY[1] & LAWRENCE L. SPRIET[2]

[1]Nutrition, Club Atlético River Plate, Buenos Aires, Argentina and [2]Human Health and Nutritional Sciences, University of Guelph, Guelph, Ontario, Canada

Abstract

Implementation of a nutrition programme for team sports involves application of scientific research together with the social skills necessary to work with a sports medicine and coaching staff. Both field and court team sports are characterized by intermittent activity requiring a heavy reliance on dietary carbohydrate sources to maintain and replenish glycogen. Energy and substrate demands are high during pre-season training and matches, and moderate during training in the competitive season. Dietary planning must include enough carbohydrate on a moderate energy budget, while also meeting protein needs. Strength and power team sports require muscle-building programmes that must be accompanied by adequate nutrition, and simple anthropometric measurements can help the nutrition practitioner monitor and assess body composition periodically. Use of a body mass scale and a urine specific gravity refractometer can help identify athletes prone to dehydration. Sports beverages and caffeine are the most common supplements, while opinion on the practical effectiveness of creatine is divided. Late-maturing adolescent athletes become concerned about gaining size and muscle, and assessment of maturity status can be carried out with anthropometric procedures. An overriding consideration is that an individual approach is needed to meet each athlete's nutritional needs.

Introduction

Delivering optimum nutrition to team sport athletes presents unique challenges in that several cultural, economic, and psychological factors may interfere with the process (Burke, 2007). Nutrition support personnel must use an array of social skills that complement those that are nutrition-specific in the daily interaction with team players and coaching and medical staff. Common-sense judgement and knowledge of the sport's cultural environment must accompany decisions weighing the emotional and physiological gains and losses in situations of conflict. Establishing nutrition policies and procedures on hydration, supplementation, nutritional recovery, and physique assessment that can be implemented on a daily basis is critical to the success of nutrition interventions, since the sports dietitian may have to work with up to 30–40 team-sport athletes simultaneously.

Structure of team sports

Team sports may be classified as field or court (indoor) (Burke, 2007). Field games can be subdivided into: (1) strength-and-power sports, such as American gridiron football, rugby union, and rugby league; (2) more endurance-based sports, such as soccer, field hockey, Australian and Gaelic football, and lacrosse; and (3) batting sports, such as cricket, baseball, and softball. Nutritional requirements for training and competition are determined by the rules of each sport, which vary in playing arena size, duration and frequency of matches, season length, training phase, number of players, and substitutions allowed. Position-specific tasks and physique requirements, weather characteristics, as well as playing level, gender, and age issues further affect nutrient requirements. Throughout team sports, the overriding characteristic is the pattern of intermittent activity between bursts of high-intensity play followed by rest pauses or periods of low activity – the stop-and-go sports (Gabbett, King, & Jenkins, 2008; Hoffman, 2008; Reilly & Borrie, 1992). This pattern taxes both the aerobic system (carbohydrate and fat) and the so-called anaerobic systems (phosphagen and anaerobic glycolysis), highlighting carbohydrate intake as a dietary priority because it is a fuel for both energy systems (Burke, Loucks, & Broad, 2006). Strength-and-power team sport athletes tend to cover less running distance, with frequent bursts of short sprints ending in contact, with additional energy spent in scrimmaging and tackling bouts (Duthie, Pyne, & Hooper, 2003). Players in endurance-based field sports usually cover the greatest distances during games, with estimates of ~10 km (Mohr, Krustrup, & Bangsbo, 2003) and up to 15 km or more in Australian Rules Football (Gray & Jenkins, 2010). A significant portion of the distance is covered at high speeds, placing a burden on glycogen repletion and hydration strategies (Burke, 1997). Batting sports, although not very demanding in energy requirements, may require players to spend many hours in the sun during summer months, shifting attention to hydration concerns (Soo & Naughton, 2007). Maintaining adequate glucose to fuel the brain for attention and decision-making is also a concern in these sports, thus carbohydrate intake during games would also be helpful (Winnick et al., 2005). Court sports are characterized by smaller playing arenas, games of shorter duration, and frequent substitutions. This allows players to play 2–3 games on consecutive days, but with the encumbrance of spending much time travelling and in hotels. This disrupts the normal routine including nutrition, with the possibility of glycogen and fluid depletion over successive daily efforts. Training routines during the competitive calendar are generally less exhausting than actual matches, but during pre-season training, when twice-daily sessions are commonplace, physical exertion is very high.

Dietary intake of team sport athletes

Unique to team sports is the fact that no two games are alike (Gregson, Drust, Atkinson, & Salvo, 2010), which creates problems for scientists trying to measure nutritional strategies to increase performance, a scenario where standardization of effort conditions is important (Hopkins, Hawley, & Burke, 1999). Therefore, much of the team sport information for optimizing performance must be drawn from studies with exertion protocols that do not resemble competitive play, and sports practitioners must also rely on inference, experience, and rudimentary trial-and-error. Perhaps a good starting point is to analyse the dietary intake of team sport athletes published in the last 30 years (Tables I and II), taking into consideration the limitations of such surveys (Magkos & Yannakoulia, 2003). Weighted averages for energy intake are 15.3 MJ $\cdot$ day^{-1} (3660 kcal) and 8.6 MJ $\cdot$ day^{-1} (2064 kcal) for males ($n = 819$) and females ($n = 283$) respectively. The mean macronutrient percentages for carbohydrates, proteins, and fats are 49, 17, and 34% for males and 50, 15, and 35% for females respectively. It can be seen that pre-season intakes are greater than in-season intakes; that larger athletes consume more energy, and that, in general, carbohydrate intake at around 49% energy is below some past recommendations of 55–65% (Clark, 1994). Relative to body mass, male team sport athletes reported eating an average of 5.6 ± 1.3 g $\cdot$ kg^{-1} $\cdot$ day^{-1} carbohydrates, and females 4.0 ± 0.7 g $\cdot$ kg^{-1} $\cdot$ day^{-1} (Tables I and II), which are again below expert committee recommendations of 6–10 g $\cdot$ kg^{-1} $\cdot$ day^{-1} (Rodriguez, DiMarco, & Langley, 2009a, 2009b). In fact, only a few studies report carbohydrate intakes above 8 g $\cdot$ kg^{-1} $\cdot$ day^{-1}, and only in soccer players (Hickson, Johnson, Schrader, & Stockton, 1987; Jacobs, Westlin, Karlsson, Rasmusson, & Houghton, 1982; Rico-Sanz, 1998). In women team athletes, the highest carbohydrate intake of 5.2 g $\cdot$ kg^{-1} $\cdot$ day^{-1} was also reported for a group of soccer players (Clark, Reed, Crouse, & Armstrong, 2003). The published literature (Burke, Cox, Culmmings, & Desbrow, 2001) as well as on-field experience in working with team sport athletes indicates that these averages seem to be appropriate amounts, coinciding with the FIFA/FMARC 2006 soccer recommendation of 5–7 g $\cdot$ kg^{-1} $\cdot$ day^{-1} (Consensus Statement, 2006). Unfortunately, data are lacking for some sports such as rugby union and cricket, and there is a need to collect data on the dietary intake of athletes on match days, since most of the published data relate to training days.

Size, physique, and body composition issues

Strength-and-power athletes are usually very large and muscular, endurance-based players are smaller and carry little body fat, batting sport team members tend to be tall and powerful, and court sports like basketball, volleyball, handball, and netball are characterized by tall and muscular participants, except players in futsal (indoor soccer), who resemble their field counterparts but are shorter. Athletes have been increasing in size during the last century, as sport becomes more competitive (Nevill, Holder, & Watts, 2009; Olds, 2001; Yamamoto, Yamamoto, Yamamoto, & Yamamoto, 2008), leading to exercise and nutritional strategies to increase muscle mass.

Position-specific anthropometric reference standards for elite athletes in each sport are useful for athlete profiling (Holway & Garavaglia, 2009) and decision-making regarding dietary intervention. The sports dietitian must bear in mind that there may be a normal 3–4% variation in body fat concomitantly with each training macro-cycle (Gore, 2000), and

Table I. Reported energy and macronutrient intakes of male team sport athletes.

Sport	Level	Country	n	Mass (kg)	Energy (MJ)	Energy (kcal)	CHO (g)	CHO ($g \cdot kg^{-1}$)	CHO (%)	PRO (g)	PRO ($g \cdot kg^{-1}$)	PRO (%)	FAT (g)	FAT (%)	Reference	Survey method	Notes
Aussie rules	professional	Australia	15		13.6	3250	410	4.7	48	138	1.6	21	116	31	Wray et al. (1994)		
Aussie rules	professional	Australia	10		14.0	3346	489	5.9	57	148	1.8	19	88	24	Grahan & Jackson (1998)		
Aussie rules	professional	Australia	40	86.2	13.2	3155	415	4.8	52	139	1.6	18	104	29	Schockman (1999)	4-day	
baseball	professional	USA	11		19.5	4654	523		45	219		18	195	37	Grandjean (1989)	3-day	
baseball	college	USA	13	89.4	13.2	3161									Malinauskas (2007)		
basketball	college	USA	8		16.3	3886	421		43	152		16	169	39	Short & Short (1983)	3-day	season
basketball	college	USA	13		23.3	5571	584		42	212		15	254	41	Short & Short (1983)	3-day	season
basketball	college	USA	16	83.0	14.9	3561	437	5.3	47	159		17	139	34	Nowak et al. (1988)	3-day	
basketball	professional	USA	11		17.1	4076	448		44	160		15	189	41	Grandjean (1989)	3-day	
basketball	professional	Spain	16	96.0	17.9	4278	380		45	211		19	211	36	Schröder et al. (2000)	24-h	
basketball	professional	Spain	55	93.0	17.7	4230		4.6	40		2.3	20		39	Schröder et al. (2004)		
football	college	USA	33	96.0	20.4	4871	550	5.7	44	201	2.0	16	208	38	Short & Short (1983)	3-day	offensive
football	college	USA	23	94.0	20.3	4840	528	5.6	43	191	2.0	16	218	41	Short & Short (1983)	3-day	defensive
football	college	USA	11	108.1	15.0	3593	329	3.0	39	190	1.8	22	158	39	Hickson et al. (1987)	3-day	other positions
football	professional	USA	30		16.0	3826			45			16		39	Grandjean (1989)	3-day	linemen
football	professional	USA	25		16.6	3961			48			16			Grandjean (1989)	3-day	
football	college	USA	35	99.0	15.9	3793	443	4.5	45	157	1.6	17	130	35	Millard-Stafford et al. (1989)	3-day	
football	college	USA	28	110	13.8	3293	392	3.6	53	169	1.5	22	103	23	Cole et al. (2005)	3-day	
gaelic	county	Ireland	12	83.0	12.5	2995	432		52	120		16	86	26	Reeves & Collins (2003)	3-day	
gaelic	club	Ireland	13	80.9	12.2	2907	360		49	105		14	96	30	Reeves & Collins (2003)	3-day	
hockey	elite	Holland	8	75.0	13.9	3322	365	4.9	42	105	1.4	22	132	36	van Erp-Baart et al. (1989)	4-day	
hockey	elite	USA	8		15.6	3721	343	4.2	39	156	1.9	18	155	39	Grandjean & Ruud (1994)		
lacrosse	college	USA	10		17.5	4173	542		46	140		14	145	40	Short & Short (1983)	3-day	pre-season
lacrosse	college	USA	10		15.5	3709	398		43	154		17	130	40	Short & Short (1983)	3-day	season
rugby league	professional	Australia	18	98.4	18.0	4309		6.0	52		1.9	18		23	Lundy et al. (2006)	4-day	forwards

(Continued)

Table I. (*Continued*).

Sport	Level	Country	n	Mass (kg)	Energy (MJ)	Energy (kcal)	CHO (g)	CHO ($g \cdot kg^{-1}$)	CHO (%)	PRO (g)	PRO ($g \cdot kg^{-1}$)	PRO (%)	FAT (g)	FAT (%)	Reference	Survey method	Notes
rugby league	professional	Australia	16	85.5	17.3	4142		6.0	49		2.1	18		27	Lundy et al. (2006)	4-day	backs
soccer	professional	Sweden	15	74.0	20.7	4947	596	8.1	47	170	2.3	14	217	29	Jacobs et al. (1982)	3-day	
soccer	college	USA	8		12.4	2961	320		43	113		16	135	41	Short & Short (1983)	3-day	
soccer	college	USA	17	72.0	18.7	4469	596	8.3	52			14		34	Hickson et al. (1987)	3-day	conditioning
soccer	college	USA	8	72.0	15.9	3805	487	6.8	52			16		32	Hickson et al. (1987)	3-day	season
soccer	college	USA	9	72.0	12.8	3057	306	4.2	42			16		42	Hickson et al. (1987)	3-day	season
soccer	elite	Holland	20	74.5	14.5	3466	420	5.6	47	111	1.5	18	134	35	van Erp-Baart et al. (1989)	4-day	
soccer	professional	Italy	33	76.0	12.8	3062	449	5.9	56						Caldarone et al. (1990)	3-day	
soccer	professional	Denmark	7	77.0	15.7	3752	426	5.5	46	144	1.9	16	152	38	Bangsbo et al. (1992)	3-day	
soccer	professional	Italy	16	74.0	13.4	3212	454	6.1	57	86	1.2	19	90	24	Schena et al. (1995)	3-day	
soccer	professional	Italy	25	71.0	15.3	3647	532	7.4	56						Zuliani et al. (1996)	4-day	
soccer	professional	Scotland	26	80.1	11.0	2629	354	4.4	51	103	1.3	16	93	32	Maughan (1997)		
soccer	professional	Scotland	25	74.6	12.8	3059	397	5.3	48	108	1.4	14	118	35	Maughan (1997)		
soccer	Olympic	Puerto Rico	8	63.0	16.5	3948	526	8.3	53	143	2.3	14	142	32	Rico-Sanz (1998)	3-day	pre-season
soccer	professional	Japan	7	70.0	13.0	3107									Ebine et al. (2002)	3-day	
soccer	professional	UK	21	74.0	12.8	3066	437	5.9	57	115	1.6	1	94	28	Reeves & Collins (2003)	3-day	
soccer	professional	Brazil	15	83.9	12.4	2961			59			20		26	do Prado (2006)		centre backs
soccer	professional	Brazil	28	70.8	8.3	1989			52			19		34	do Prado (2006)		midfielders
soccer	professional	Brazil	8	83.9	16.3	3903			57			13		30	do Prado (2006)		goalkeepers
soccer	professional	Brazil	18	72.1	15.2	3641			54			18		30	do Prado (2006)		strikers
soccer	professional	Brazil	17	69.7	14.1	3361			52			19		26	do Prado (2006)		last defenders

Note: CHO = carbohydrate, PRO = protein.
Adapted from Burke (2007).

Table II. Reported energy and macronutrient intakes of female team sport athletes.

Sport	Level	Country	n	Mass (kg)	Energy (MJ)	Energy (kcal)	CHO (g)	CHO (g·kg⁻¹)	CHO (%)	PRO (g)	PRO (g·kg⁻¹)	PRO (%)	FAT (g)	FAT (%)	Reference	Survey method	Notes
basketball	college	USA	9	71.0	13.6	3250	379	5.3	46	108	1.5	14	145	40	Short & Short (1983)	3-day	
basketball	college	USA	13	68.0	8.4	2003									Hickson et al. (1986)	24-h	
basketball	college	USA	10	72.0	7.2	1728	229	3.2	51	68			63		Nowak et al. (1988)	3-day	
basketball	college	USA	9	70.0	7.5	1797	227	3.3	48	69	1.0	15	52	26	Risser et al. (1990)	24-h	
handball	elite	Holland	8	63.2	9.0	2151	251	4.0	45	76	1.2	14	101	42	van Erp-Baart et al. (1989)	4-day	
handball		Turkey	10	62.0	7.3	1745	229	3.7	53	51	0.8	12	68	35	Ersoy (1995)	3-day	
hockey	elite	Holland	9	62.1	9.0	2151	264	4.3	46	42	1.0	19	85	35	van Erp-Baart et al. (1989)	4-day	
hockey	college	USA	8	60.0	8.2	1955	228	3.8	47	76	1.3	16	84	39	Tilgner & Schiller (1989)	3-day	
hockey	college	USA	9	64.0	6.4	1518	213	3.4	54	57	0.9	15	45	27	Nutter (1991)	3-day	season
hockey	college	USA	9	64.0	6.0	1432	213	3.0	54	57	0.9	16	47	30	Nutter (1991)	3-day	post-season
lacrosse	college	USA	7		9.3	2228	257		50	89		16	95	35	Short & Short (1983)	3-day	
netball	elite	Australia	10	66.1	11.0	2619		4.8	47		1.7	17		33	Heaney et al. (2010)		
soccer	college	USA	14	61.6	9.6	2297	320	5.2	55	87	1.4	15	75	29	Clark et al. (2003)	3-day	season
soccer	college	USA	14	61.6	7.8	1871	263	4.3	57	59	1.0	13	66	31	Clark et al. (2003)	3-day	post-season
soccer	elite	USA	11		8.4	2015			55			15		30	Mullinix et al. (2003)	3-day	
soccer	college	USA	15	59.0	8.5	2022				71	1.3	14			Gropper et al. (2003)	3-day	
soccer	elite	UK	16	61.5	8.0	1904	252	4.1	54	74	1.2	17	55	29	Martin et al. (2006)	3-day	
softball	college	USA	6	66.0	7.7	1828				64	1.0	14			Gropper et al. (2003)	3-day	
softball	elite	Australia	14	74.8	9.0	2144		3.3	44		1.2	18		32	Heaney et al. (2010)		
volleyball	college	USA	11		10.3	2455	314		49	103		16	95	34	Short & Short (1983)	3-day	season
volleyball	college	USA	7		7.6	1819	244		53	61		13	69	34	Short & Short (1983)	3-day	season
volleyball	elite	Holland	9	66.0	9.4	2247	263	4.0	46	73	1.1	17	92	37	van Erp-Baart et al. (1989)	4-day	
volleyball	college	USA	12	66.0	6.7	1609	216	3.3	51	70	1.1	17	54	30	Risser et al. (1990)	24-h	
volleyball	elite	Greece	8	64.6	9.8	2346			50			13		39	Hassapidou & Manstrantoni (2001)		
volleyball	elite	Greece	16	66.0	8.5	2020	228	3.5	45	67	1.0	15	98	41	Papadopoulou et al. (2002)	3-day	
volleyball	elite	Australia	8	70.0	10.8	2574		4.1	44		1.6	17		36	Heaney et al. (2010)		

Note: CHO = carbohydrate, PRO = protein.
Adapted from Burke (2007).

must not stress competition levels of body composition at all times during the year. Furthermore, there are always exceptions to the rule, where players who do not conform to size and body composition standards still perform well. Detailed tables are not always easy to find or are non-existent or limited in information. However, when available, the sports dietitian can measure height, weight and, depending on time and equipment available, anthropometric skinfolds as proxies for adiposity, skinfold-corrected girths for muscle mass, and breadths and lengths for skeletal structure (Norton & Olds, 1996). High-technology body composition assessment apparatus such as dual-energy X-ray absorptiometry machines and plethysmography chambers are good for research settings but usually beyond the budget of most sports nutrition practitioners, and are not transportable. Low-cost bioimpedance analysis equipment suffers from the limitation that it estimates body composition rather than measures it, as can be deducted from the multiple-regression equations it uses (Lukaski, Johnson, Bolonchuk, & Lykken, 1985). Notwithstanding the need for practice, standardization and assessment of error or measurement, anthropometry can provide an inexpensive, transportable tool to objectively assess up to 40 variables related to body dimensions.

If an athlete must change his or her size and body composition, it must be realized that change takes time, and that these modifications must take place preferably away from the competitive season when they might interfere with tapering or sport-specific technical skills. Some sports such as professional soccer have long competition seasons that complicate the process of implementing body composition changes, thus it is advantageous if these changes take place in the youth divisions. Other sports like power-and-strength team sports allow several months per year for an improvement in muscle mass. In some positions in gridiron football, the amount of body mass (including large quantities of skeletal muscle and body fat) required to perform better might be harmful to the player's health (Jonnalagadda, Rosenbloom, & Skinner, 2001; Tucker et al., 2009), although not all authors agree (Allen, Vogel, Lincoln, Dunn, & Tucker, 2010). This presents an ethical dilemma for the sports dietitian, but it is the reality of sport.

Nutrition for training and competition

Coaches working with team sports usually plan three macro-cycles each year for their teams, consisting of pre-season training (lasting from 3 weeks in soccer to 4–5 months in rugby, for example), competition, and off-season or transition phase. Athletes in pre-season training may have high energy needs that double their resting energy requirements for twice-daily training, while during the competitive period they require less (Clark et al., 2003). Many teams stage pre-season training at a camp or residence setting away from home, and weekly-cycle menu planning is important, not only to help the athletes recover from intense training, but also because food can become one of the few sources of gratification during a tough training regimen. In our experience, we have found that: (1) menu plans that are very low in fat encourage junk-food smuggling (junk food to be eaten in dormitories); (2) if menus are too high in fruit and fibre, many gastro-intestinal episodes may occur; (3) athletes tend to prefer a more repetitive food schedule of familiar foods as opposed to abundant variety; (4) many day-to-day grievances are channelled through complaints about the menu; (5) after a week, complaints reach a peak and it is best to plan a different meal activity, like staging a hamburger and fries outdoor cookout or visiting a restaurant and eating ice-cream for dessert.

Energy expenditure and carbohydrate requirements on match days tend to be higher than on weekly training days (Burke et al., 2006), but in our experience we find that team sport athletes tend to eat less on these days because of game stress and/or the travel and match schedule altering the normal eating pattern. In sports where games are played once a week, athletes have sufficient time to recover nutritionally during the week, but some sports may play for three days in a row, with matches lasting several hours and away from home (Burke, 1995). In these instances, progressive fluid and glycogen depletion may hamper performance in the latter days of competition, thus aggressive strategies to promote adequate fluid and carbohydrate are imperative (Reilly & Ekblom, 2005). Circumstances are more difficult when travelling (on the road) where the proper selection of eating venues and menu choices must include good sources of high-carbohydrate, low-fat choices (Burke, 2007). Snacking can be a very effective way to aid nutritional recovery.

Studies on glycogen depletion in team sport athletes are scarce and difficult to carry out because coaches would rather avoid match-day distractions but one available study reported a marked glycogen depletion pattern (Bangsbo, Iaia, & Krustrup, 2007). This must be put into perspective when addressing the carbohydrate needs of weekly training as team sport members do not, on a daily basis, need the amount of carbohydrates that they would on a match day or that an endurance athlete requires. A high-carbohydrate diet can best be left for the day before a match (Williams & Serratosa, 2006), and this strategy would have to be compensated by a lower intake of protein and, more especially, fats, lest the total energy intake exceed requirements. Since the training load is tapered prior to matches, maintaining a normal carbohydrate intake can also result in adequate glycogen synthesis and subsequent super-compensation to cover match requirements.

Pre-match meals are a highly individual matter, with some stressed athletes needing a low-bulk liquid meal supplement, and others not being able to tolerate any food. In general, an easily digestible meal supplying carbohydrate sources, eaten 2–4 h before a game, seems to be the best alternative (Williams & Serratosa, 2006). Some teams prefer to add low-fat protein source to provide more satiety, but it is suggested that high-fibre foods be avoided to prevent gastrointestinal discomfort and that high-fat foods also be avoided as they may delay digestion (Williams & Serratosa, 2006). Fluid intake, like water or sports beverages, is encouraged at this stage and leading up to game time (Burke, 2007). During matches, fluid and glycogen losses can be replaced via the administration of sports beverages, and aided by other easily digested carbohydrate sources such as sports gels and bars (Mujika & Burke, 2010). This strategy can aid performance in the latter stages of the game (Williams & Serratosa, 2006), but game rules may restrict the occasions for fluid and carbohydrate intake; however, it is recommended that athletes take advantage of half-time and game-stoppage opportunities to drink and/or eat. The amount of fluid and carbohydrate recommended varies according to type of sport, positional role, weather conditions, and inter-individual differences.

Following matches, nutritional recovery strategies can start at the training table in the locker room, and include sports drinks, carbohydrate-dense drinks and/or gels, energy bars, and fruit, followed by a carbohydrate-rich meal a couple of hours later (Ryan, 2005). Ideally, co-ingestion of protein with $1.2 \text{ g} \cdot \text{kg}^{-1} \cdot \text{day}^{-1}$ carbohydrate as soon as possible after the match has been shown to accelerate protein synthesis (Howarth, Moreau, Phillips, & Gibala, 2009), and so foods and/or supplements containing both macronutrients benefit recovery (Beelen, Burke, Gibala, & van Loon, 2010). Replacement of lost fluids should aim to match amounts lost during training and competition (Rodriguez et al., 2009a, 2009b). A free day usually follows match-days in most football codes, which also allows athletes to recover further, but court and batting sports usually have two or three games on successive days, whereby recovery nutrition is indispensable. It is important that enough carbohydrates are eaten on this day, which is not very hard to accomplish with normal meals provided, as they include starches, fruits, and vegetables. However, in practice we find that many athletes eat far too little on these days or indulge in high-fat foods, preferring to sleep more or rest psychologically from a sports menu.

Dietary planning

In the process of converting energy and macronutrients into food and portions that the athlete can relate to and understand, a common problem surfaces with team sport players: if the carbohydrate dose is calculated as $7\text{–}8 \text{ g} \cdot \text{kg}^{-1} \cdot \text{day}^{-1}$, these foods also cover much of the protein requirement and leave little room. Male team sport athletes prefer to eat between 1.2 and $2.3 \text{ g} \cdot \text{kg}^{-1}$ protein daily (Tables I and II), amounts that would not allow a high carbohydrate intake on a moderate energy budget. This conundrum between sports science research and practice needs to be bridged with more modest daily carbohydrate recommendations, such as $5\text{–}7 \text{ g} \cdot \text{kg}^{-1} \cdot \text{day}^{-1}$ for team sport athletes during the competitive season. During pre-season training, these amounts can be surpassed, as energy expenditure is higher, and perhaps on game-day or the preceding day a higher-carbohydrate/lower-protein diet can be implemented. To improve athletes' understanding of portion sizes, it is useful, when circumstances permit, to employ or weigh with small inexpensive electronic kitchen scales for a few days the prescribed foods and/or to use food models.

Nutrition education strategies can be implemented at several levels, from individual counseling to team talks, fact sheets, and supermarket tours, although being present at meal venues and interacting with athletes is also effective in delivering information.

Assessing and implementing hydration strategies

In the most rudimentary conditions, weighing athletes before and after practice and identifying those exceeding 2% weight loss, a level beyond which performance can be hampered (Rodriguez et al., 2009a, 2009b), can yield important information on fluid losses. Going a step further, simple urine specific gravity (USG) measurements with a hand-held refractometer can be used to assess hydration status (Volpe, Poule, & Bland, 2009). Many athletes are known to show up for practice or games in a hypohydrated state (Burke & Hawley, 1997; Maughan & Shirreffs, 2010). Where there is more time, consuming ~600 mL of water or sports drink will bring the athlete into the euhydrated zone within 30–45 min (Palmer, Logan, & Spriet, 2010). Urine specific gravity data can be plotted against published percentile standards of hydration (Armstrong et al., 2010) and players prone to dehydration can be identified. In our experience, baseline USG values for players can be obtained from regular training sessions and be used to assess hydration status where inter-individual differences exist and may not always conform to established standards.

Other techniques to assess hydration status include the use of urine colour charts (Armstrong et al., 1998), although urine colour may be confounded by intake of vitamin supplements. While it may be difficult to measure team members on match day, because coaches prefer to avoid any distractions, these data can be valuable and in our experience are often different from data obtained at friendly matches and training sessions. Sweat losses can be high when games are played in hot climates (Kurdak et al., 2010). We have found that game-day stress may alter players' drinking practices, leading to over- or under-hydration. Drinking at half-time varies widely, with some players drinking two cans of energy drink and some tentatively sipping water. Nevertheless, most adapt comfortably to half a litre or more of sports beverages. Team sports without a formal half-time break such as baseball can take advantage of time off the field to refuel with fluids. Sports teams with limited funding have had success preparing their own homemade sports drink with sugar and/or maltodextrin, table salt, water, and a flavouring agent. To identify heavy salt sweaters, training with dark-coloured clothing can be used to identify contrasting white salt stains. More sophisticated methods include the application of sweat patches to assess the extent of electrolyte loss (Shirreffs, Sawka, & Stone, 2006). Although still an issue of debate, some authors suggest that increasing salt intake may help some athletes prone to cramping (Eichner, 2007). Lastly, availability of drinking opportunities and accessibility of drinking bottles are helpful strategies in providing fluids to athletes (Murray, 2006).

Supplements and ergogenic aids in team sports

The most popular and beneficial supplements for team sports in our experience are sports beverages (Rodriguez et al., 2009a, 2009b) and caffeine (Spriet & Gibala, 2004). Creatine is also popular among team sport athletes but a controversial item to both scientists (Hespel, Maughan, & Greenhaff, 2006; Lemon, 2002) and practitioners. Creatine alone or combined with protein powders is very popular in strength-and-power sports, although some players complain about tight muscles or muscle tears when on creatine, in spite of published evidence to the contrary (Greenwood, Kreider, Greenwood, & Byars, 2003a; Greenwood et al., 2003b). As a strategy to prevent unwanted purported side-effects, European professional soccer teams sometimes supplement creatine in low doses of $2–3 \text{ g} \cdot \text{day}^{-1}$, avoiding the acute loading phase of 20 g daily for 5 days (R. Maughan, personal communication). Until further research clears many of the controversial anecdotal reports regarding this supplement, it is best to individualize creatine supplementation,

targeting only players who acknowledge benefits without mischief, and to educate and advise athletes about the potential risks versus benefits.

Youth team sport athletes

Among youth athletes, one of the main concerns of parents, coaches, and managers is when a player fails to grow at the pace of his or her team-mates. The most common underlying reason is that this young athlete may be a late maturing adolescent in a competitive youth sport where a high incidence of success for early maturing athletes prevails. Assessment of maturity status using simple anthropometric measures such as height, weight, sitting height together with decimal age (Mirwald, Baxter-Jones, Bailey, & Beunen, 2002) can aid when deciphering whether a growth problem exists or whether it is a case of late maturation. In 13- to 15-year-old soccer players, we (F. Holway, unpublished data) have found that that a difference of up to 10 kg of muscle mass can co-exist within stage two of the Tanner maturation scale (Tanner, 1981); hence we find this method of maturity assessment lacks the resolving power to identify differences in size and strength in these young athletes. Another growing concern in young athletes is overweight and obesity. Ironically, excessive intake of starches and sugars is one of the causes (Speiser et al., 2005); thus the recommendation for a high-carbohydrate diet in youth athletes must perhaps be placed in the context of the energy and carbohydrate demands of training and match-play schedules.

Conclusions

Nutrition for team sports requires knowledge of the sport-specific physiology of training and competition coupled with social skills to be able to implement dietary recommendations within the framework of a multi-professional sport science and medicine group and coaching staff. An over-riding reality, even when working with team sport athletes, is that an individual approach is needed to meet each athlete's nutritional and hydration needs.

References

Allen, T. W., Vogel, R. A., Lincoln, A. E., Dunn, R. E., & Tucker, A. M. (2010). Body size, body composition, and cardiovascular disease risk factors in NFL players. *Physician and Sportsmedicine*, 38, 21–27.

Armstrong, L. E., Pumerantz, A. C., Fiala, K. A., Roti, M. W., Kavouras, S. A., Casa, D. J. et al. (2010). Human hydration indices: Acute and longitudinal reference values. *International Journal of Sport Nutrition and Exercise Metabolism*, 20, 145–153.

Armstrong, L. E., Soto, J. A., Hacker, F. T., Jr., Casa, D. J., Kavouras, S. A., & Maresh, C. M. (1998). Urinary indices during dehydration, exercise, and rehydration. *International Journal of Sport Nutrition, 8,* 345–355.

Bangsbo, J., Iaia, F. M., & Krustrup, P. (2007). Metabolic response and fatigue in soccer. *International Journal of Sports Physiology and Performance, 2,* 111–127.

Bangsbo, J., Norregaard, L., & Thorsoe, F. (1992). The effect of carbohydrate diet on intermittent exercise performance. *International Journal of Sports Medicine, 13,* 152–157.

Beelen, M., Burke, L. M., Gibala, M. J., & van Loon, L. J. (2010). Nutritional strategies to promote postexercise recovery. *International journal of Sport Nutrition and Exercise Metabolism, 20,* 515–532.

Burke, L. (1995). Practical issues in nutrition for athletes. *Journal of Sports Sciences, 13* (suppl.), S83–S90.

Burke, L. M. (1997). Fluid balance during team sports. *Journal of Sports Sciences, 15,* 287–295.

Burke, L. (2007). *Practical sports nutrition.* Chicago, IL: Human Kinetics.

Burke, L. M., Cox, G. R., Culmmings, N. K., & Desbrow, B. (2001). Guidelines for daily carbohydrate intake: Do athletes achieve them? *Sports Medicine, 31,* 267–299.

Burke, L. M., & Hawley, J. A. (1997). Fluid balance in team sports: Guidelines for optimal practices. *Sports Medicine, 24,* 38–54.

Burke, L. M., Loucks, A. B., & Broad, N. (2006). Energy and carbohydrate for training and recovery. *Journal of Sports Sciences, 24,* 675–685.

Caldarone, G., Tranquilli, C., & Giampietro, M. (1990). Assessment of the nutritional state of top level football players. In G. Santilli (Ed), *Sports medicine applied to football* (pp. 133–141). Rome: Instituto Dietician Scienza della Sport del Coni.

Clark, K. (1994). Nutritional guidance to soccer players for training and competition. *Journal of Sports Sciences, 12* (suppl.), S43–S50.

Clark, M., Reed, D. B., Crouse, S. F., & Armstrong, R. B. (2003). Pre- and post-season dietary intake, body composition, and performance indices of NCAA division I female soccer players. *International Journal of Sport Nutrition and Exercise Metabolism, 13,* 303–319.

Cole, C. R., Salvaterra, G. F., Davis, J. E., Jr., Borja, M. E., Powell, L. M., Dubbs, E. C. et al. (2005). Evaluation of dietary practices of National Collegiate Athletic Association Division I football players. *Journal of Strength and Conditioning Research, 19,* 490–494.

Consensus Statement (2006). Nutrition for football: The FIFA/F-MARC Consensus Conference. *Journal of Sports Sciences, 24,* 663–664.

do Prado, W. F. (2006). Anthropometric profile and macronutrient intake in professional Brazilian soccer players according to their position. *Revista Brasileira de Medicina Esporte, 12* (2), 52e–55e.

Duthie, G., Pyne, D., & Hooper, S. (2003). Applied physiology and game analysis of rugby union. *Sports Medicine, 33,* 973–991.

Ebine, N., Rafamantanantsoa, H. H., Nayuki, Y., Yamanaka, K., Tashima, K., Ono, T. et al. (2002). Measurement of total energy expenditure by the doubly labelled water method in professional soccer players. *Journal of Sports Sciences, 20,* 391–397.

Eichner, E. R. (2007). The role of sodium in "heat cramping". *Sports Medicine, 37,* 368–370.

Ersoy, G. (1995). Nutrient intake and iron status of Turkish female handball players. In C. V. Kies & J. A. Driskell (Eds.), *Sports nutrition: Minerals and electrolytes* (pp. 59–64). Boca Raton, FL: CRC Press.

Gabbett, T., King, T., & Jenkins, D. (2008). Applied physiology of rugby league. *Sports Medicine, 38,* 119–138.

Gore, C. J. (Ed) (2000). *Physiological tests for elite athletes.* Champaign, IL: Human Kinetics.

Graham, L. A., & Jackson, K. A. (1998). *The dietary micronutrient intake of elite Australian rules footballers: Is there a need for supplementation?* Unpublished manuscript prepared for Flinders University, Adelaide, Australia.

Grandjean, A. C. (1989). Macronutrient intake of US athletes compared with the general population and recommendations made for athletes. *American Journal of Clinical Nutrition, 49* (suppl), 1070–1076.

Grandjean, A. C., & Rudd, J. S. (1994). Energy intake of athletes. In M. Harries, C. Williams, W. D. Stanish, & L. J. Micheli (Eds), *Oxford textbook of sports medicine* (pp. 53–65). New York: Oxford University Press.

Gray, A. J., & Jenkins, D. G. (2010). Match analysis and the physiological demands of Australian football. *Sports Medicine, 40,* 347–360.

Greenwood, M., Kreider, R. B., Greenwood, L., & Byars, A. (2003a). Cramping and injury incidence in collegiate football players are reduced by creatine supplementation. *Journal of Athletic Training, 38,* 216–219.

Greenwood, M., Kreider, R. B., Melton, C., Rasmussen, C., Lancaster, S., Cantler, E. et al. (2003b). Creatine supplementation during college football training does not increase the incidence of cramping or injury. *Molecular and Cellular Biochemistry, 244,* 83–88.

Gregson, W., Drust, B., Atkinson, G., & Salvo, V. D. (2010). Match-to-match variability of high-speed activities in premier league soccer. *International Journal of Sports Medicine, 31,* 237–242.

Gropper, S. S., Sorrels, L. M., & Blessing, D. (2003). Copper status of collegiate female athletes involved in different sports. *International Journal of Sport Nutrition, Exercise and Metabolism, 13,* 343–357.

Hassapidou, M. N., & Manstrantoni, A. (2001). Dietary intakes of elite female athletes in Greece. *Journal of Human Nutrition and Dietetics, 14,* 391–396.

Heaney, S., O'Connor, H., Gifford, J., & Naughton, G. (2010). Comparison of strategies for assessing nutritional adequacy in elite female athletes' dietary intake. *International Journal of Sport Nutrition and Exercise Metabolism, 20,* 245–256.

Hespel, P., Maughan, R. J., & Greenhaff, P. L. (2006). Dietary supplements for football. *Journal of Sports Sciences, 24,* 749–761.

Hickson, J. F., Jr., Johnson, C. W., Schrader, J. W., & Stockton, J. E. (1987). Promotion of athletes' nutritional intake by a university foodservice facility. *Journal of the American Dietetic Association, 87,* 926–927.

Hickson, J. F., Schrader, J., & Trischler, L. C. (1986). Dietary intakes of female basketball and gymnastics athletes. *Journal of the American Dietetic Association, 86,* 251–253.

Hoffman, J. R. (2008). The applied physiology of American football. *International Journal of Sports Physiology and Performance, 3,* 387–392.

Holway, F. E., & Garavaglia, R. (2009). Kinanthropometry of Group I rugby players in Buenos Aires, Argentina. *Journal of Sports Sciences, 27,* 1211–1220.

Hopkins, W. G., Hawley, J. A., & Burke, L. M. (1999). Design and analysis of research on sport performance enhancement. *Medicine and Science in Sports and Exercise, 31,* 472–485.

Howarth, K. R., Moreau, N. A., Phillips, S. M., & Gibala, M. J. (2009). Coingestion of protein with carbohydrate during recovery from endurance exercise stimulates skeletal muscle protein synthesis in humans. *Journal of Applied Physiology, 106,* 1394–1402.

Jacobs, I., Westlin, N., Karlsson, J., Rasmusson, M., & Houghton, B. (1982). Muscle glycogen and diet in elite soccer players. *European Journal of Applied Physiology and Occupational Physiology, 48,* 297–302.

Jonnalagadda, S. S., Rosenbloom, C. A., & Skinner, R. (2001). Dietary practices, attitudes, and physiological status of collegiate freshman football players. *Journal of Strength and Conditioning Research*, 15, 507–513.

Kurdak, S. S., Shirreffs, S. M., Maughan, R. J., Ozgunen, K. T., Zeren, C., Korkmaz, S., Yazici, Z., Ersoz, G., Binnet, M. S., & Dvorak, J. (2010). Hydration and sweating responses to hot-weather football competition. *Scandinavial Journal of Medicine, Science and Sports*, 20 (Suppl. 3), 133–139.

Lemon, P. W. (2002). Dietary creatine supplementation and exercise performance: Why inconsistent results? *Canadian Journal of Applied Physiology*, 27, 663–681.

Lukaski, H. C., Johnson, P. E., Bolonchuk, W. W., & Lykken, G. I. (1985). Assessment of fat-free mass using bioelectrical impedance measurements of the human body. *American Journal of Clinical Nutrition*, 41, 810–817.

Lundy, B., O'Connor, H., Pelly, F., & Caterson, I. (2006). Anthropometric characteristics and competition dietary intakes of professional rugby league players. *International Journal of Sport Nutrition and Exercise Metabolism*, 16, 199–213.

Magkos, F., & Yannakoulia, M. (2003). Methodology of dietary assessment in athletes: Concepts and pitfalls. *Current Opinion in Clinical Nutrition and Metabolic Care*, 6, 539–549.

Malinauskas, B. M., Aeby, V. G., Overton, R. F., Carpenter-Aeby, T., & Barber-Heidal, K. (2007). A survey of energy drink consumption patterns among college students. *Nutrition Journal*, 31 (6), 35.

Martin, L., Lambeth, A., & Scott, D. (2006). Nutritional practices of national female soccer players: Analysis and recommendations. *Journal of Sports Science and Medicine*, 5, 130–137.

Maughan, R. J. (1997). Energy and macronutrient intakes of professional football (soccer) players. *British Journal of Sports Medicine*, 31, 45–47.

Maughan, R. J., & Shirreffs, S. M. (2010). Dehydration and rehydration in competitive sport. *Scandinavian Journal of Medicine and Science in Sports*, 20 (suppl. 3), 40–47.

Millard-Stafford, M., Rosskopf, L.B., & Sparling, P.B. (1989). Coronary heart disease: Risk profiles of college football players. *Physician and Sportsmedicine*, 17, 151–163.

Mirwald, R. L., Baxter-Jones, A. D., Bailey, D. A., & Beunen, G. P. (2002). An assessment of maturity from anthropometric measurements. *Medicine and Science in Sports and Exercise*, 34, 689–694.

Mohr, M., Krustrup, P., & Bangsbo, J. (2003). Match performance of high-standard soccer players with special reference to development of fatigue. *Journal of Sports Sciences*, 21, 519–528.

Mujika, I., & Burke, L. M. (2010). Nutrition in team sports. *Annals of Nutrition and Metabolism*, 57 (suppl. 2), 26–35.

Mullinix, M. C., Jonnalagadda, S. S., Rosenbloom, C. A., Thompson, W. R., & Kicklighter, J. R. (2003). Dietary intake of female U.S. soccer players. *Nutrition Research*, 23, 585–594.

Murray, B. (2006). Fluid, electrolytes, and exercise. In M. Dunford (Ed.), *Sports nutrition: A practice manual for professionals* (4th edn., pp. 94–115). Chicago, IL: American Dietetic Association.

Nevill, A., Holder, R., & Watts, A. (2009). The changing shape of "successful" professional footballers. *Journal of Sports Sciences*, 27, 419–426.

Norton, K., & Olds, T. (Eds.) (1996). *Anthropometrica: A textbook of body measurement for sports and health courses*. Sydney, NSW: UNSW Press.

Nowak, R. K., Knudsen, K. S., & Schulz, L. O. (1988). Body composition and nutrient intakes of college men and women basketball players. *Journal of the American Dietetic Association*, 88, 575–578.

Nutter, J. (1991). Seasonal changes in female athletes' diets. *International Journal of Sport Nutrition*, 1, 395–407.

Olds, T. (2001). The evolution of physique in male rugby union players in the twentieth century. *Journal of Sports Sciences*, 19, 253–262.

Palmer, M. S., Logan, H. M., & Spriet, L. L. (2010). On-ice sweat rate, voluntary fluid intake, and sodium balance during practice in male junior ice hockey players drinking water or a carbohydrate-electrolyte solution. *Applied Physiology, Nutrition and Metabolism*, 35, 328–335.

Papadopoulou, S. K., Papadopoulou, S. D., & Gallos, G. K. (2002). Macro- and micro-nutrient intake of adolescent Greek female volleyball players. *International Journal of Sport Nutrition and Exercise Metabolism*, 12, 73–80.

Reeves, S., & Collins, K. (2003). The nutritional and anthropometric status of Gaelic football players. *International Journal of Sport Nutrition and Exercise Metabolism*, 13, 539–548.

Reilly, T., & Borrie, A. (1992). Physiology applied to field hockey. *Sports Medicine*, 14, 10–26.

Reilly, T., & Ekblom, B. (2005). The use of recovery methods post-exercise. *Journal of Sports Sciences*, 23, 619–627.

Rico-Sanz, J. (1998). Body composition and nutritional assessments in soccer. *International Journal of Sport Nutrition*, 8, 113–123.

Risser, W. L., Lee, E. J., LeBlanc, A., Poindexter, H. B., Risser, J. M., & Schneider, V. (1990). Bone density in eumenorrheic female college athletes. *Medicine and Science in Sports and Exercise*, 22, 570–574.

Rodriguez, N. R., Di Marco, N. M., & Langley, S. (2009a). American College of Sports Medicine position stand: Nutrition and athletic performance. *Medicine and Science in Sports and Exercise*, 41, 709–731.

Rodriguez, N. R., DiMarco, N. M., & Langley, S. (2009b). Position of the American Dietetic Association, Dietitians of Canada, and the American College of Sports Medicine: Nutrition and athletic performance. *Journal of the American Dietetic Association*, 109, 509–527.

Ryan, M. (2005). Eating for training and recovery. In . *Performance nutrition for team sports* (pp. 87–103). Boulder, CO: VeloPress.

Schena, F., Pattini, A., & Mantovanelli, S. (1995). Iron status in athletes involved in endurance and prevalently anaerobic sports. In C. V. Kies & J. A. Driskell (Eds.), *Sports nutrition: Minerals and electrolytes* (pp. 65–76). Boca Raton, FL: CRC Press.

Schokman, C. P., Rutishauser, I. H., & Wallace, R. J. (1999). Pre- and postgame macronutrient intake of a group of elite Australian football players. *International Journal of Sport Nutrition*, 9, 60–69.

Schroder, H., Navarro, E., Tramullas, A., Mora, J., & Galiano, D. (2000). Nutrition antioxidant status and oxidative stress in professional basketball players: Effects of a three compound antioxidative supplement. *International Journal of Sports Medicine*, 21, 146–150.

Schroder, H., Terrados, N., & Tramullas, A. (2004). Risk assessment of the potential side effects of long-term creatine supplementation in team sport athletes. *European Journal of Nutrition*, 44, 255–261.

Shirreffs, S. M., Sawka, M. N., & Stone, M. (2006). Water and electrolyte needs for football training and match-play. *Journal of Sports Sciences*, 24, 699–707.

Short, S. H., & Short, W. R. (1983). Four-year study of university athletes' dietary intake. *Journal of the American Dietetic Association*, 82, 632–645.

Soo, K., & Naughton, G. (2007). The hydration profile of female cricket players during competition. *International Journal of Sport Nutrition and Exercise Metabolism*, 17, 14–26.

Speiser, P. W., Rudolf, M. C., Anhalt, H., Camacho-Hubner, C., Chiarelli, F., Eliakim, A. et al. (2005). Childhood obesity. *Journal of Clinical Endocrinology and Metabolism*, 90, 1871–1887.

Spriet, L. L., & Gibala, M. J. (2004). Nutritional strategies to influence adaptations to training. *Journal of Sports Sciences, 22,* 127–141.

Tanner, J. M. (1981). Growth and maturation during adolescence. *Nutrition Reviews, 39,* 43–55.

Tilgner, S. A., & Schiller, M. R. (1989). Dietary intakes of female college athletes: The need for nutrition education. *Journal of the American Dietetic Association, 89,* 967–969.

Tucker, A. M., Vogel, R. A., Lincoln, A. E., Dunn, R. E., Ahrensfield, D. C., Allen, T. W. et al. (2009). Prevalence of cardiovascular disease risk factors among National Football League players. *Journal of the American Medical Association, 301,* 2111–2119.

van Erp-Baart, A. M., Saris, W. H., Binkhorst, R. A., Vos, J. A., & Elvers, J. W. (1989). Nationwide survey on nutritional habits in elite athletes. Part I. Energy, carbohydrate, protein, and fat intake. *International Journal of Sports Medicine, 10* (suppl. 1), S3–S10.

Volpe, S. L., Poule, K. A., & Bland, E. G. (2009). Estimation of prepractice hydration status of National Collegiate Athletic Association Division I athletes. *Journal of Athletic Training, 44,* 624–629.

Williams, C., & Serratosa, L. (2006). Nutrition on match day. *Journal of Sports Sciences, 24,* 687–697.

Winnick, J. J., Davis, J. M., Welsh, R. S., Carmichael, M. D., Murphy, E. A., & Blackmon, J. A. (2005). Carbohydrate feedings during team sport exercise preserve physical and CNS function. *Medicine and Science in Sports and Exercise, 37,* 306–315.

Wray, N., Sherman, W. M., & Dernbach, A. R. (1994). *Comparison of nutritional attitudes and practices between elite and less professional Australian rules footballers.* Unpublished manuscript prepared for Flinders University, Adelaide, Australia.

Yamamoto, J. B., Yamamoto, B. E., Yamamoto, P. P., & Yamamoto, L. G. (2008). Epidemiology of college athlete sizes, 1950s to current. *Research in Sports Medicine, 16,* 111–127.

Zuliani, G., Baldo-Enzi, G., Palmieri, E., Volpato, S., Vitale, E., Magnanini, P. et al. (1996). Lipoprotein profile, diet and body composition in athletes practicing mixed and anaerobic activities. *Journal of Sports Medicine and Physical Fitness, 36,* 211–216.

Nutrition for winter sports

NANNA L. MEYER[1,2], MELINDA M. MANORE[3], & CHRISTINE HELLE[4]

[1]Beth-El College of Nursing and Health Sciences, University of Colorado, Colorado, USA, [2]Olympic Committee, Colorado Springs, Colorado, USA, [3]Department of Nutrition and Exercise Sciences, Oregon State University, Corvallis, Oregon, USA and [4]Olympiatoppen, The Norwegian Olympic and Paralympic Committee and Confederation of Sports, Oslo, Norway

Abstract

Winter sports are played in cold conditions on ice or snow and often at moderate to high altitude. The most important nutritional challenges for winter sport athletes exposed to environmental extremes include increased energy expenditure, accelerated muscle and liver glycogen utilization, exacerbated fluid loss, and increased iron turnover. Winter sports, however, vary greatly regarding their nutritional requirements due to variable physiological and physique characteristics, energy and substrate demands, and environmental training and competition conditions. What most winter sport athletes have in common is a relatively lean physique and high-intensity training periods, thus they require greater energy and nutrient intakes, along with adequate food and fluid before, during, and after training. Event fuelling is most challenging for cross-country skiers competing in long events, ski jumpers aiming to reduce their body weight, and those winter sport athletes incurring repeated qualification rounds and heats. These athletes need to ensure carbohydrate availability throughout competition. Finally, winter sport athletes may benefit from dietary and sport supplements; however, attention should be paid to safety and efficacy if supplementation is considered.

Introduction

Winter sports are pursuits played during the winter season on snow or ice. The Olympic movement included winter sports for the first time in Chamonix in 1924, with 258 participants from 16 nations. Today, winter sport Olympians are outnumbered by about one to four by summer Olympians. Nevertheless, the 2010 Vancouver Olympics reported the highest number of athletes and events at any one Winter Olympiad. This paper will first discuss the winter sport specific environment, altitude and cold, followed by an applied section emphasizing the specific nutrition issues faced by winter sport athletes.

Nutritional implications of altitude and cold

Winter sport athletes often encounter altitude and cold during competition or training. These athletes may also use a variety of strategies to promote acclimatization to higher elevations or to improve sea-level performance (Chapman, Stickford, & Levine, 2010). Winter sports conducted in an outdoor environment experience temperatures ranging from −25 to +5°C, while those performed indoors on ice have average temperatures of 5–10°C. Many winter sports are dependent on permanent snow located at higher altitude (glacier) or the southern hemisphere for sport-specific training in the summer and fall and for early-season competition. Glacier environments are located at moderate (2000–3000 m) to high (3000–5000 m) altitudes. In the winter, cold, altitude, and changing snow/ice conditions are characteristic of most competitive venues, as competitions typically occur at northern latitudes and altitudes between 500 m and 2000 m.

For several winter sports, the most challenging period of training occurs when athletes perform high-intensity training in the cold at altitude, on-snow or on-ice in late summer and early fall. Training under these conditions results in a compounding of environmental stresses and metabolic challenges that carry a number of nutritional implications.

Altitude

Upon ascent to altitude, energy expenditure increases. At 4300 m basal metabolic rate increases on average by 10–17% compared with sea level (Butterfield, 1999; Mawson et al., 2000). Altitude exposure is frequently accompanied by weight loss (Hoyt et al., 1994), averaging ~1.4 kg per week (Butterfield, 1996). At altitudes ≥3500 m, appetite suppression can also contribute to weight loss (Kayser, 1992). Weight loss as a result of an energy deficit increases the use of protein as metabolic fuel, leading to a negative nitrogen balance and loss of lean tissue (Kayser, Acheson, Decombaz, Fern, & Cerretelli, 1992). Matching energy intake to the increased energy requirement minimizes weight loss and maintains nitrogen balance at 4300 m, at least in controlled laboratory experiments (Butterfield et al., 1992; Mawson et al., 2000). In addition, carbohydrate supplementation in an energy-deficient state improves performance at altitude (Fulco et al., 2005). Thus, athletes training at altitude can probably maintain weight and preserve muscle mass if adequate energy and carbohydrate are consumed (Kayser et al., 1992).

Substrate utilization at high altitude shifts to greater use of blood glucose at rest and during exercise compared with sea level (Brooks et al., 1991a, 1991b), due to hypoxia increasing the expression of GLUT4 (Brooks et al., 1992). The predominant use of blood glucose, without a concomitant sparing effect of muscle glycogen (Green, Sutton, Young, Cymerman, & Houston, 1989), represents a challenge for athletes training in these environments, as glucose and glycogen quickly become a limiting fuel source. Metabolically, women respond differently to altitude than men, relying on fat as fuel to a greater extent at rest and during submaximal exercise, and women use less blood glucose and glycogen at altitude (Braun et al., 1998).

Early during exposure to altitude, plasma volume decreases, resulting in increased haemoglobin concentration. With continued exposure, red cell mass rises (Martin, Levett, Grocott, & Montgomery, 2010). Erythropoietin is responsible for the production and release of reticulocytes from bone marrow, which contributes to the increase in red cell mass, blood volume, and enhanced oxygen carrying capacity. Iron is an integral part of haemoglobin, so individuals with low iron stores have difficulty producing erythrocytes in sufficient quantity and maturity (Nielsen & Nachtigall, 1998). With altitude exposure, low iron stores will interfere with an effective haematological adaptation (Stray-Gundersen, Hochstein, deLemos, & Levine, 1992). Many winter sport athletes are naturally exposed to altitude, due to their reliance on snow for sport-specific training. Nordic skiers and long-track speed skaters frequently use live-high/train-low strategies, sleeping at moderate altitude (2000–2500 m) and training at lower elevations (1500 m) over the course of 3–4 weeks to optimize haematological adaptations and improve sea-level performance (Wilber, 2007). It is imperative to commence this training with adequate iron status.

Altitude exposure results in a reduction in total body water. Altitude-induced diuresis and reduced thirst during the initial hours at altitude may set the stage for dehydration. Furthermore, increased ventilation and the low humidity of atmospheric air lead to greater respiratory water loss at altitude. Respiratory water loss at altitude may be twice as high as at sea level; theoretical calculations for 24-h respiratory water loss approach $1 \; L \cdot day^{-1}$ in addition to fluids lost through sweat and urine (Milledge, 1992). Respiratory water loss can be as high as $1.9 \; L \cdot day^{-1}$ in men (Butterfield et al., 1992) and $850 \; mL \cdot day^{-1}$ in women (Mawson et al., 2000). Wilber (2004) suggested fluid intakes of $4\text{-}5 \; L \cdot day^{-1}$ in athletes training at altitude, while even higher recommendations may apply to cross-country skiers (Ekblom & Bergh, 2000.)

Cold

Work in the cold may increase energy requirements. Most of this increase depends on whether thermoregulation can maintain skin and core temperature via protective clothing, physiologic responses such as vasoconstriction and reduced blood flow to peripheral tissues, or metabolic heat production due to exercise (Castellani et al., 2006). Factors, in addition to ambient temperature, including wind chill, UV radiation, and humidity can influence the physiologic strain of defending core temperature in the cold (Sawka, Convertino, Eichner, Schnieder, & Young, 2000). When cold exposure is severe enough to elicit a shivering response, energy requirements rise, at least doubling metabolic heat production to maintain core temperature (Castellani et al., 2001). Few winter sport athletes experience shivering when training in the cold because they are able to maintain core temperature. Should shivering occur, however, carbohydrate oxidation is elevated (Vallerand, Zamecnik, & Jacobs, 1995). (For an excellent review, see Haman, Blondin, Imbeault, & Maneshi, 2010).

During exercise in cold environments, individuals often lose 3–8% of their body weight. Reasons for this include large sweat losses, respiratory water loss, cold-induced diuresis, impaired thirst, and limited access to fluids (Freund & Sawka, 1996) with few restrooms (Meyer et al., 1999), ultimately leading to voluntary hypohydration. Cold-induced fluid loss likely leads to greater water than solute loss (Costill, 1977), which can result in mild vasoconstriction and more severe and prolonged cold stress (O'Brien, Young, & Sawka, 1998). Few data are available on hypohydration and its effect on performance in the cold, but a recent study showed that a 3% hypohydration did not degrade endurance performance in the cold (Cheuvront, Carter, Castellani, & Sawka, 2005). Thus, while exercise in the cold can induce large fluid shifts, performance effects will depend on core and skin temperature.

Taken together, the data on altitude and cold suggest that winter sport athletes need to consider the cumulative effects of cold and altitude on energy expenditure, fuel selection, and fluid loss, while beginning training with good iron status. To evaluate the energy requirement of winter sport athletes at altitude and in the cold, estimates by Consolazio (1966) may be helpful: 45–55 kcal $\cdot$ kg^{-1} $\cdot$ day^{-1} for moderate physical activities and 53–68 kcal $\cdot$ kg^{-1} $\cdot$ day^{-1} for heavy physical activities. These values are in agreement with doubly-labelled water studies (Ekelund, Yngve, Westerterp, & Sjostrom, 2002; Sjödin, Andersson, Hogberg, & Westerterp, 1994) and 24-h activity records in winter sport athletes training intensely on snow and ice (N.L. Meyer, unpublished data; Meyer et al., 1999).

Most research on altitude is conducted at high elevations, with limited studies examining nutrition issues in winter sport athletes exposed to their training environments, such as live-high/train-low or live-low/train high intermittently. It should also be noted that elevations exceeding 3500 m may negatively affect sleep (Kinsman et al., 2005) and immune function (Mazzeo, 2005). Despite the fact that elite winter sport athletes are probably highly accustomed to these routines, individual variations and responses should be considered.

Some winter sports are performed indoors in ice arenas and/or at sea level. Nutritional implications for these athletes should centre on similar concepts of maintaining energy and carbohydrate availability and fluid balance.

Winter sport-specific nutrition issues

Physique of winter sport athletes

Winter sport athletes span the full spectrum of physiques, since sports are uniquely diverse in their physiological demand and movement patterns relative to gravity. Higher or longer jumps receive greater scores and/or technical merit, and jumping is facilitated by lightness and leanness (Monsma & Malina, 2005). In cross-country skiing, lighter skiers may have an advantage on a hilly and poorly gliding course, whereas heavier skiers may have an advan-

tage on a flat course. Cross-country skiing sprint events have shifted the focus to greater lean body mass, strength, and power (Larsson & Henriksson-Larsen, 2008). Alpine skiers, snowboarders, and sledding sport athletes can utilize gravity to their advantage in gaining speed.

Lean and muscular physiques are also common in ice hockey players (Montgomery, 1988) and speed skaters. As with other winter sports, the physiques of long-track speed skaters have changed, with athletes becoming leaner and more muscular (Meyer et al., 2004). There are a number of reviews that provide more information on physique in winter sports (Agostini, 2000; Foster, de Koning, Rundell, & Snyder, 2000; Meyer & Parker-Simmons, 2009; Orvanova, 1987).

Achieving and maintaining a low body weight and/or lean physique is an important issue in winter sports, but may come with severe health consequences. The effects of altitude and cold may compound suboptimal fuelling and result in glycogen depletion and hypoglycaemia, interfering with concentration and increasing injury risk, especially late during the day (Brouns, Saris, & Ten Hoor, 1986). Restrictive eating may also affect training adaptation and can negatively influence reproductive and bone health (Nattiv et al., 2007). While physique concerns and heightened risk of eating disorders exist in several winter sports, they are highest in figure skating, freestyle aerials, cross-country skiing, biathlon, and ski jumping/Nordic combined (N. L. Meyer, unpublished data; Torstveit & Sundgot-Borgen, 2005).

Training nutrition for winter sport athletes

This section will focus on training nutrition, highlighting the most important nutritional issues for winter sport athletes. For more information on training for winter sports, see Meyer and Parker-Simmons (2009).

1. MEETING HIGH ENERGY DEMANDS

Nordic sports. Of all winter sports athletes, cross-country skiers report the highest energy expenditures. At the extreme, a 50-km racer expends between 13 and 15 MJ (3107–3585 kcal) for the race. During intense, on-snow training, daily energy expenditure of cross-country skiers ranges from 20 to 25 MJ $\cdot$ day^{-1} (4780 to 5975 kcal $\cdot$ day^{-1}) (Ekblom & Bergh, 2000). Such high energy expenditures are due to the large muscle mass involved in cross-country skiing. Sjödin et al. (1994) studied male and female cross-country skiers during a one-week, on-snow training camp using doubly-labelled water. Energy expenditure ranged from 15.1 to 20.2 MJ $\cdot$ day^{-1} (3609 to 4838 kcal $\cdot$ day^{-1}) in females and

25.4 to 34.9 MJ · day^{-1} (6070 to 8341 kcal · day^{-1}) in males. Interestingly, these athletes maintained energy balance and body weight over the course of the study. Thus, athletes can meet high energy requirements by ingesting adequate quantities of food. Of interest is that daily energy intake did not correlate with training minutes. In fact, these athletes consumed an average of 335 kJ · kg^{-1} · day^{-1} (80 kcal · kg^{-1} · day^{-1}) with little day-to-day variability, despite changing intensity and volume (Sjödin et al., 1994). Thus, cross-country skiers should focus on ensuring high energy intakes throughout the duration of intense training camps, especially at altitude, to meet high energy demands.

Energy requirements differ greatly among Nordic sports. Ski jumpers have the lowest energy requirements (<8.4 MJ · day^{-1}; S. Parker-Simmons, unpublished data), whereas cross-country skiers have the highest, with Nordic combined athletes falling in the middle. Biathletes have high energy demands, similar to those of cross-country skiers, but they compete in shorter distances. However, biathletes are challenged by the task of concentration when aiming for targets during the shooting portion of the event and incur an additional energy cost from carrying a rifle weighing 3.5 kg (Rundell & Szmedra, 1998). Adjusting energy intake to meet variable energy demands poses difficulty to many athletes, particularly female skiers (Fogelholm et al., 1992). Sports dietitians should teach skiers how to prepare for and recover from training in environmental extremes through adequate energy and nutrient intakes.

Alpine, freestyle and snowboarding. Alpine, freestyle skiers (e.g. freestyle moguls), and snowboarders (e.g. alpine) are challenged with frequent travel and involuntary "sleep-high/train-high" conditions. Energy needs range from 188 to 230 kJ · kg^{-1} · day^{-1} (45 to 55 kcal · kg^{-1} · day^{-1}) for both men and women, not accounting for altitude and cold (Meyer & Parker-Simmons, 2009). Under shivering conditions and at altitude, energy expenditure likely exceeds 230 kJ · kg^{-1} · day^{-1} (55 kcal · kg^{-1} · day^{-1}). It is recommended to adjust resting energy expenditure to altitude and increase energy intake by an extra 200–300 kcal · day^{-1} (Butterfield, 1996). In addition, athletes' body weight, appetite, and sleep should be monitored. Energy demands within disciplines of skiing and snowboarding vary. Freestyle aerialists and halfpipe snowboarders cover a shorter course or focus on refining jumps and tricks; thus, energy expenditure is lower. These athletes often have little knowledge and skill to adjust energy and nutrient intakes to their periodized training plan (Meyer et al., 1999; N. L. Meyer, unpublished data).

Speed skating, ice hockey, and sledding. No data are available on energy expenditure in these sports except for long-track speed skating. Energy demands for training in speed skating are high. Using doubly-labelled water, daily energy expenditure in male junior long-track skaters ranged from 12.8 to 25.0 MJ · day^{-1} (3059 to 5975 kcal · day^{-1}), with an average of 16.8 ± 3.8 MJ · day^{-1} (4015 ± 908 kcal · day^{-1}). Exercise energy expenditure ranged from 3.4 to 13.0 MJ · day^{-1} (812 to 3107 kcal · day^{-1}) for high-volume endurance training and from 4 to 12 MJ · day^{-1} (956 to 2868 kcal · day^{-1}) for on-ice technique training (Ekelund et al., 2002). Energy expenditure is higher during the most intense training phase and will vary in speed skaters according to sprint, all-around (endurance), and short-track disciplines. For ice hockey and sledding, no data are currently available on energy expenditure.

2. Macronutrient needs: Carbohydrate

Carbohydrate requirements in winter sports will vary by sport, training/competition, and environmental conditions.

Nordic sports. Glycogen reserves may be a limiting factor in cross-country skiing. Glycogen stores decrease by 30–40% after a 10–15 km race and by nearly 100% after a 50-km race (Rusko, 2003). Cross-country skiers, Nordic combined athletes, and biathletes require daily repletion of carbohydrates. During intense training, daily carbohydrate intakes should be ≥ 6 g · kg^{-1} · day^{-1} and may need to exceed 10 g · kg^{-1} · day^{-1} (Sjödin et al., 1994). On average, Nordic skiers meet carbohydrate recommendations (Fogelholm et al., 1992; Sjödin et al., 1994). As training exceeds 1–2 h · day^{-1}, Nordic skiers are advised to use exogenous carbohydrates during exercise to maintain blood glucose concentration. Carbohydrate ingestion rates and forms (sport drinks, gels, and bars) similar to those recommended for cycling and running (30–60 and up to 90 g · h^{-1}) are adequate.

Alpine, freestyle, and snowboarding. Athletes in alpine, freestyle skiing (i.e. moguls), and snowboarding will also experience muscle glycogen depletion during on-snow training due to the intermittent nature, supra-maximal intensity, and environmental conditions. A day of giant slalom training reduces muscle glycogen content by 50% (Tesch, 1995; Tesch, Larsson, Eriksson, & Karlsson, 1978), with resynthesis of muscle glycogen dependent on carbohydrate intake (Nygaard et al., 1978). Significant blood occlusion and arterial oxygen desaturation occur during giant slalom skiing, with serum and muscle lactate concentrations after one run ranging from

6 to 15 mmol $\cdot$ L^{-1} and up to 24 mmol $\cdot$ kg^{-1} wet muscle, respectively (Ferguson, 2010; Szmedra, Im, Nioka, Chance, & Rundell, 2001). It is expected that alpine snowboarders experience similar responses, while mogul skiers show somewhat attenuated responses. Thus, these athletes should ingest greater quantities of carbohydrates during on-snow training, especially at altitude and in the cold. Unfortunately, athletes do not practise these recommendations (Meyer et al., 1999; Ronsen, Sundgot-Borgen, & Maehlum, 1999; Schena, Pattini, & Mantovanelli, 1995). While there may be an opportunity to resynthesize muscle glycogen during rest periods, carbohydrate intakes of 7–10 g $\cdot$ kg^{-1} $\cdot$ day^{-1} may be needed to replenish glycogen stores.

Changes in weather often interfere with training schedules on glaciers. Time trials require some winter sport athletes to train in thin body suits at temperatures around −15°C. Shivering thermogenesis can be a side-effect, increasing glycogen utilization and accelerating the onset of fatigue. One concern is that low glycogen stores may predispose an athlete to injury, since many skiing injuries occur late in the day (Brouns et al., 1986).

Coaches, staff, and athletes should be educated about the physiological effects of cold and altitude on food and fluid needs. It is common to see marginal intakes of sport drinks and foods when training at altitude (N. L. Meyer, unpublished data; Meyer et al., 1999). Training under such conditions should ensure that athletes receive carbohydrate-rich meals prior to exercise (Pitsiladis & Maughan, 1999) and carbohydrate and electrolyte-containing sport drinks (8–12% carbohydrate concentration; 15–30 g $\cdot$ h^{-1}) and foods during exercise (Galloway, Wootton, Murphy, & Maughan, 2001). While on the hill, warm, carbohydrate-containing fluids should be available at the start or finish of a run.

Speed skating, ice hockey, and sledding. For on-ice training, carbohydrate requirements will vary based on sport, training factors, and indoor ice conditions. In continuous and intermittent skating, rates of glycogen utilization are high (Green, 1978; Green, Daub, Painter, & Thomson, 1978). In long-track speed skating, energy contribution varies by event, with shorter events (≤1000 m) relying on more glycolytic than oxidative pathways. The low trunk position is a performance-limiting factor in speed skating (Van Ingen Schenau, de Koning, Bakker, & de Groot, 1996) that decreases blood flow to working muscles (Foster et al., 1999), leading to desaturation of haemoglobin and myoglobin (Rundell, Nioka, & Chance, 1997). Blood lactate accumulation is high in speed skaters (20 mmol $\cdot$ L^{-1}) (Foster & de Koning, 1999). Altitude and better ice conditions (e.g. Utah Olympic Oval in Salt Lake City) mean faster ice

times and skating turns at faster speeds, potentially increasing carbohydrate needs. Carbohydrate intake should be adjusted to the intensity and volume of training, with higher intakes (6–12 g $\cdot$ kg^{-1} $\cdot$ day^{-1}) recommended during high-intensity and/or high-volume periods during on-ice and dry-land training. A higher carbohydrate intake should also be the goal for short-track speed skaters during intense training due to the high frequency of training sessions per day. Ice hockey players also need more carbohydrates during intense training. This intense intermittent sport produces high lactate concentrations and reductions in muscle glycogen stores (Akermark, Jacobs, Rasmusson, & Karlsson, 1996; Green et al., 1978). Thus, carbohydrate recommendations should target at least 6 g $\cdot$ kg^{-1} $\cdot$ day^{-1}. In general, skaters do not meet carbohydrate needs during intense training (Houston & Green, 1976; N. L. Meyer, unpublished data). For sledding athletes, carbohydrate intake will depend on the discipline, runs taken, and dry-land training.

Long training sessions on ice are best supported by carbohydrate supplementation. Meyer and Parker-Simmons (2009) recommend athletes ingest at least 30 g of carbohydrate per hour, preferably in the form of a sport drink (5–8% carbohydrate with electrolytes), gels, and bars. Most skaters prefer liquid forms of carbohydrate that are easily ported on the ice. Recovery snacks and solid food are often preferred by athletes transitioning from ice to dry-land training.

Similar to summer sports, the type and timing of carbohydrate ingested should be adjusted to the duration, intensity, and frequency of training. More processed carbohydrate sources may be recommended after exercise to promote timely glycogen resynthesis, especially if several training sessions are planned in close succession. Frequent travel and exposure to altitude and cold may disrupt an athlete's regular bowel movement and cause constipation. Ingesting adequate fibre from fruits and vegetables, wholegrain breads, and cereals should also be part of the training diet.

For most winter sport athletes, replenishment of glycogen stores and repair of muscle tissue is of utmost importance. To ensure quick recovery after intense training in winter sport environments, it is recommended athletes ingest carbohydrates at a rate of 1.2–1.5 g $\cdot$ kg^{-1} $\cdot$ h^{-1} and begin carbohydrate feeding within the first 30 min. This should optimize performance in subsequent sessions, especially if multiple sessions are held. The addition of ∼15–20 g of protein promotes muscle protein repair and synthesis (see Phillips & Van Loon, 2011). This is especially important in winter sports with an endurance component, eccentric loading, and an emphasis on lean body mass and/or weight control.

Athletes on an energy budget (e.g. ski jumpers, freestyle aerialists) are advised to integrate recovery nutrition principles into their post-exercise meals. Recovery in winter sport is often delayed, because transportation, weather, drug testing, and press conferences can slow departure from the mountain. Athletes should be prepared for unexpected delays and have recovery foods with them.

Common to winter sports is that intense training phases coincide with changing seasons, travel, altitude and cold exposure, and an increased risk of illness. Considering the frequent cases of upper respiratory tract infections, injuries, mononucleosis, and signs of overtraining, especially observed in Nordic combined (Meyer & Parker-Simmons, 2009) and long-track speed skating (Foster & de Koning, 1999), the emphasis should be on meeting energy and macronutrient needs during this training period. Educating athletes on adjusting energy and carbohydrate to training intensity, and integrating fuelling strategies will promote training adaptation and maintain health. Sports dietitians, in collaboration with an interdisciplinary team, should monitor athletes using valid and reliable recovery parameters.

3. MACRONUTRIENT NEEDS: PROTEIN

Winter sport athletes need adequate dietary protein (~ 1.4–1.7 g $\cdot$ kg^{-1} $\cdot$ day^{-1}), especially when training intensity and/or volume increase and energy is restricted for weight loss. On average, most winter sport athletes get adequate protein (Fogelholm et al., 1992; Meyer et al., 1999; Schena et al., 1995; Sjödin et al., 1994). However, ski jumpers have low intakes (Rankinen et al., 1998). When exposed to environmental extremes, winter sport athletes who restrict energy intake or suffer from a loss of appetite should increase energy and carbohydrate but may also benefit from additional protein to preserve lean tissue (Kayser, 1992; Kayser et al., 1992).

4. MACRONUTRIENT NEEDS: FAT

Fat intake of winter sport athletes ranges from 25 to 40% of total energy intake (1.0 to 1.9 g $\cdot$ kg^{-1} $\cdot$ day^{-1}) (Meyer & Parker-Simmons, 2009). Fat intake may be higher in less experienced athletes with lower nutrition knowledge (Ronsen et al., 1999), in cross-country skiers during intense training (Sjödin et al., 1994), and in those sports where a low body weight is not a decisive performance factor (Meyer et al., 1999). Educating athletes on the amount and type of fat and how to balance training meals with flavourful oils, nuts, seeds, and fatty fish should be part of sport nutrition education. Winter sport athletes have similar fat needs to summer athletes, with the exception of the environmental factors; fat is an important energy source during rest

and submaximal exercise in the cold, but the effect of cold and altitude on glycogen depletion is probably of greater concern.

Fluid balance in winter sport environments

Some athletes use sport-specific training venues even when snow is not available (e.g. ski jumping, freestyle skiing, snowboarding). Nordic skiers and speed skaters use roller skis and inline skates on asphalt, respectively. Nordic combined and ski-jumping athletes compete in the European Summer Grand Prix and perform between 400 and 600 jumps, wearing winter suits. Thus, fluid requirements in the summer are elevated due to higher sweat rates (Meyer & Parker-Simmons, 2009). In winter sport environments, sweat rates are expected to be lower, but respiratory water loss and diuresis can be significant (O'Brien et al., 1998). Thus, assessing hydration status before the morning session (urine specific gravity) and estimating sweat rates during exercise to target fluid replacement are important strategies in winter sports.

Nordic sports. Nordic skiers competing in 15–30 km races typically lose 2–3% of body mass (Ekblom & Bergh, 2000). Seifert and colleagues (Seifert, Luetkemeier, White, & Mino, 1998) investigated the physiological effect of water versus sport drink ingestion during cross-country ski training in collegiate skiers. Results showed a 1.8% loss of body mass after 90 min of skiing. Sport drink-maintained plasma volume minimized urine output and led to lower ratings of perceived exertion compared with water. Therefore, ingesting fluids (especially sport drinks) during training sessions and races lasting longer than 15 km should maintain fluid balance. In addition, carbohydrates in sport drinks maintain glucose availability during prolonged exercise in the cold and/or altitude. Transporting a large volume of fluid onto the ski course and keeping the temperature of the beverages at 10–20°C is difficult. Warm sport drinks may be carried in leak-proof bottles with thermal covers (Meyer & Parker-Simmons, 2009).

Alpine, freestyle, and snowboarding. Little is known about fluid balance of skiers and snowboarders. In collegiate alpine skiers, fluid intake of 2 mL $\cdot$ kg^{-1} body mass, ingested after each slalom run (altitude: 2435–3045 m; temperature: <0°C), was compared with no fluid intake. In the fluid trial, total fluid intake was 1.2 L during 2 h of slalom training, which maintained body mass, whereas 0.6 kg was lost in the no-fluid trial. Urine output was lower, osmolality higher, and plasma volume changes significantly greater from baseline in the no-fluid trial (Seifert, Lutkemeier, White, Mino, & Miller, unpublished data). Thus, even in relatively short training sessions, fluid shifts do occur. Whether low fluid intakes and hypohydration affect skiing performance is unknown, but they may affect performance in subsequent sessions in warm climates. To support training intensity and prevent excessive dehydration in skiers and snowboarders, athletes are advised to ingest sport drinks with electrolytes at intervals of 15–20 min or as lift-rides and training infrastructure permit.

Hockey, speed skating, and sledding. Little is known about hydration levels and needs in speed skating and the sledding sports. Indoor cold exposure can lead to hypohydration (Rintamäki, Makinen, Oksa, & Latvala, 1995). In speed skating, the low trunk position and the inconvenience of interrupting training for the use of restroom facilities may keep athletes from drinking. Unpublished data (N. L. Meyer) for long- and short-track speed skating have shown that both hypohydration and weight loss as well as overhydration and weight gain, are risks that need to be monitored when training on ice. This situation may also apply to sledding athletes.

In ice hockey, sweat rates are high but heat dissipation difficult due to clothing (Green et al., 1978). Strategies to improve body cooling in ice hockey are to wear breathable fabrics, remove gloves and helmet during breaks, and to consume fluids. Recently, average sweat rates of $1.8 \ L \cdot h^{-1}$ (0.8% body mass loss) were measured in junior players, with a third of them losing more than 1% of body mass and more than half commencing practice hypohydrated (Palmer & Spriet, 2008). A subsequent study investigated the repeatability of field fluid testing in elite hockey players. Results showed that estimates of sweat loss, fluid intake, body mass loss, sweat salt concentrations, and salt loss were reliable. Furthermore, the study demonstrated that athletes who would normally drink water during practice, drank just as much sport drink when it was the only drink available (Palmer, Logan, & Spriet, 2010).

Micronutrient needs and supplement use

Winter sport athletes have unique micronutrient needs that are exacerbated when training is intense, integrates altitude and/or cold, and phases of energy restriction are imposed. The micronutrients of special interest for winter sport athletes are iron, antioxidants, and vitamin D. While the supplementation of certain micronutrients (e.g. iron and vitamin D) may be of benefit if status is low, ingestion of antioxidant supplements in the absence of elevated needs may be counterproductive. Winter sport athletes need to use caution when making decisions related to dietary and sport supplements due to the risk of contamination. Limited dietary/ sport supplements may benefit winter sport athletes. These include blood buffers, creatine, and caffeine.

Fuelling for competition

In many winter sports, training and competition are markedly different. While altitude and cold remain challenges throughout the winter, and are compounded by the effect of travel, energy, carbohydrate and fat needs are typically lower because races cover relatively short distances and there is adequate recovery time. Thus, pre-competition nutrition strategies are similar to those used in summer sports; athletes should consume easily digestible, carbohydrate-rich foods and adequate fluids in the days and hours before events. For cross-country skiing events (30–50 km), carbohydrate loading may be useful to maximize glycogen stores. A recent study also identified a potential performance effect from the ingestion of a carbohydrate supplement 45 min before a 20-km cross-country ski race (Francescato & Puntel, 2006).

Multiple events (e.g. long-track speed skating), heats (e.g. sprint cross-country skiing, snowboarding, short-track speed skating, sledding), or tournaments (e.g. ice hockey, curling) will require fuelling strategies aimed at maintaining carbohydrate availability. Furthermore, evening events can be challenging due to colder temperatures and shifts in meal patterns.

For the sport dietitian, ski jumping is particularly challenging since ski jumpers must keep body mass low during the competitive season. The length of time at which their competition weight can be maintained before energy levels, nutritional and immune status, and psychological health decline needs to be individually determined. Regular body composition testing, review of training logs, and experimentation at different weights are required. A few times per year, ski jumpers and Nordic combined athletes may carry out specific dietary manipulation (e.g. reduced energy intake, low-fibre/ residue, low sodium) to reduce competition weight. These approaches should minimize health and performance impacts (Meyer & Parker-Simmons, 2009).

Taken together, winter sport athletes need to be prepared to withstand the physiologic and energetic challenges of competition. Athletes should carry foods and fluids for fuelling throughout the course of competition. Foods consumed between runs should include easily digestible, carbohydrate-rich sources. Fluids should be provided by sport drinks or sweetened warm teas. If no fluids or carbohydrate-containing foods are available, the athlete may exhaust muscle glycogen stores and may be unable to maintain racing intensity. Most importantly, winter sport athletes need to focus on recovery, especially if repetitive racing occurs over several days or environmental conditions are severe.

Summary

Winter sports are unique in that they are undertaken under environmental extremes, which must be considered when planning nutrition programmes for the athletes' periodized training and competition season. Athletes at greatest risk for suboptimal nutrition are those with very high energy demands (e.g. cross-country skiing, Nordic combined, biathlon, and speed skating), those exposed to environmental extremes (e.g. alpine and freestyle skiing, snowboarding, cross-country skiing, biathlon, Nordic combined), and those focused on low body mass and fat (e.g. ski jumping, freestyle aerials, cross-country skiing).

References

Agostini, R. (2000). Alpine skiing. In B. L. Drinkwater (Ed.), *Women in sport* (pp. 613–625). Oxford: Blackwell Science.

Akermark, C., Jacobs, I., Rasmusson, M., & Karlsson, J. (1996). Diet and muscle glycogen concentration in relation to physical performance in Swedish elite ice hockey players. *International Journal of Sport Nutrition, 6*, 272–284.

Braun, B., Butterfield, G. E., Dominick, S. B., Zamudio, S., McCullough, R. G., Rock, P.B. et al. (1998). Women at altitude: Changes in carbohydrate metabolism at 4,300-m elevation and across the menstrual cycle. *Journal of Applied Physiology, 85*, 1966–1973.

Brooks, G. A., Butterfield, G. E., Wolfe, R. R., Groves, B. M., Mazzeo, R. S., Sutton, J. R. et al. (1991a). Increased dependence on blood glucose after acclimatization to 4,300 m. *Journal of Applied Physiology, 70*, 919–927.

Brooks, G. A., Butterfield, G. E., Wolfe, R. R., Groves, B. M., Mazzeo, R. S., Sutton, J. R. et al. (1991b). Decreased reliance on lactate during exercise after acclimatization to 4,300 m. *Journal of Applied Physiology, 71*, 333–341.

Brooks, G. A., Wolfel, E. E., Groves, B. M., Bender, P. R., Butterfield, G. E., Cymerman, A. et al. (1992). Muscle accounts for glucose disposal but not blood lactate appearance during exercise after acclimatization to 4,300 m. *Journal of Applied Physiology, 72*, 2435–2445.

Brouns, F., Saris, W. H., & Ten Hoor, F. (1986). Nutrition as a factor in the prevention of injuries in recreational and competitive downhill skiing: Considerations based on the literature. *Journal of Sports Medicine and Physical Fitness, 26*, 85–91.

Butterfield, G. E. (1996). Maintenance of body weight at altitude: In search of 500 kcal/day. In B. M. Marriott & S. J. Carlson (Eds.), *Nutritional needs in cold and in high-altitude environments* (pp. 357–378). Washington, DC: National Academy Press.

Butterfield, G. E. (1999). Nutrient requirements at high altitude. *Clinics in Sports Medicine, 18*, 607–621.

Butterfield, G. E., Gates, J., Fleming, S., Brooks, G. A., Sutton, J. R., & Reeves, J. T. (1992). Increased energy intake minimizes weight loss in men at high altitude. *Journal of Applied Physiology, 72*, 1741–1748.

Castellani, J. W., Stulz, D. A., DeGroot, D. W., Blanchard, L. A., Cadarette, B. S., Bradley, C. et al. (2001). Eighty-four hours of sustained operations after thermoregulation during cold exposure. *Medicine and Science in Sports and Exercise, 35*, 175–181.

Castellani, J. W., Young, A. J., Ducharme, M. B., Giesbrecht, G. G., Glickman, E., & Sallis, R. E. (2006). American College of Sports Medicine position stand: Prevention of cold injuries during exercise. *Medicine and Science in Sports and Exercise, 38*, 2012–2029.

Chapman, R. F., Stickford, J. L., & Levine, B. D. (2010). Altitude training considerations for the winter sport athlete. *Experimental Physiology, 95*, 411–421.

Cheuvront, S. N., Carter, R., III, Castellani, J. W., & Sawka, M. N. (2005). Hypohydration impairs endurance exercise performance in temperate but not cold air. *Journal of Applied Physiology, 99*, 1972–1976.

Consolazio, C. F. (1966). Nutrient requirements of troops in extreme environments. *Army Research and Development News Magazine,* 24 November.

Costill, D. L. (1977). Sweating: Its composition and effects on body fluids. *Annals of the New York Academy of Sciences, 301*, 160–174.

Ekblom, B., & Bergh, U. (2000). Cross-country skiing. In R. J. Maughan (Ed.), *Nutrition in sport* (Vol. 7, pp. 656–662): Oxford: Blackwell Science.

Ekelund, U., Yngve, A., Westerterp, K., & Sjostrom, M. (2002). Energy expenditure assessed by heart rate and doubly labeled water in young athletes. *Medicine and Science in Sports and Exercise, 34*, 1360–1366.

Ferguson, R. A. (2010). Limitations to performance during alpine skiing. *Experimental Physiology, 95*, 404–410.

Fogelholm, M., Rehunen, S., Gref, C. G., Laakso, J. T., Lehto, J., Ruokonen, I. et al. (1992). Dietary intake and thiamine, iron and zinc status in elite Nordic skiers during different training periods. *International Journal of Sport Nutrition, 2*, 351–365.

Foster, C., & de Koning, J. J. (1999). Physiological perspectives in speed skating. In H. Gemser, J. J. de Koning, & G. J. van Ingen Schenau (Eds.), *Handbook of competitive speed skating* (pp. 117–132). Lausanne: International Skating Union.

Foster, C., de Koning, J. J., Rundell, K. W., & Snyder, A. C. (2000). Physiology of speed skating. In W. E. Garrett, Jr. & D. T. Kirkendall (Eds.), *Exercise and sport science* (pp. 885–893). Philadelphia, PA: Lippincott Williams & Wilkins.

Foster, C., Rundell, K. W., Snyder, A. C., Stray-Gundersen, J., Kemkers, G., Thometz, N. et al. (1999). Evidence for restricted muscle blood flow during speed skating. *Medicine and Science in Sports and Exercise, 31*, 1433–1440.

Francescato, M. P., & Puntel, I. (2006). Does a pre-exercise carbohydrate feeding improve a 20-km cross-country ski performance? *Journal of Sports Medicine and Physical Fitness, 46*, 248–256.

Freund, B. J., & Sawka, M. N. (1996). Influence of cold stress on human fluid balance. In B. M. Marriott & S. J. Carlson (Eds.), *Nutritional needs in cold and in high-altitude environments* (pp. 161–180). Washington, DC: National Academy Press.

Fulco, C. S., Kambis, K. W., Friedlander, A. L., Rock, P. B., Muza, S. R., & Cymerman, A. (2005). Carbohydrate supplementation improves time-trial cycle performance during energy deficit at 4,300-m altitude. *Journal of Applied Physiology, 99*, 867–876.

Galloway, S. D., Wootton, S. A., Murphy, J. L., & Maughan, R. J. (2001). Exogenous carbohydrate oxidation from drinks ingested during prolonged exercise in a cold environment in humans. *Journal of Applied Physiology, 91*, 654–660.

Green, H. J. (1978). Glycogen depletion patterns during continuous and intermittent ice skating. *Medicine and Science in Sports*, 10, 183–187.

Green, H. J., Daub, B. D., Painter, D. C., & Thomson, J. A. (1978). Glycogen depletion patterns during ice hockey performance. *Medicine and Science in Sports*, 10, 289–293.

Green, H. J., Sutton, J., Young, P., Cymerman, A., & Houston, C. S. (1989). Operation Everest II: Muscle energetics during maximal exhaustive exercise. *Journal of Applied Physiology*, 66, 142–150.

Haman, F., Blondin, D. P., Imbeault, M. A., & Maneshi, A. (2010). Metabolic requirements of shivering humans. *Frontiers in Bioscience*, 2, 1155–1168.

Houston, M. E., & Green, H. J. (1976). Physiological and anthropometric characteristics of elite Canadian ice hockey players. *Journal of Sports Medicine and Physical Fitness*, 16, 123–128.

Hoyt, R. W., Jones, T. E., Baker-Fulco, C. J., Schoeller, D. A., Schoene, R. B., Schwartz, R. S. et al. (1994). Doubly labeled water measurement of human energy expenditure during exercise at high altitude. *American Journal of Physiology: Regulatory, Integrative and Comparative Physiology*, 266, R966–R971.

Kayser, B. (1992). Nutrition and high altitude exposure. *International Journal of Sports Medicine*, 13 (suppl.), S129–S132.

Kayser, B., Acheson, K., Decombaz, J., Fern, E., & Cerretelli, P. (1992). Protein absorption and energy digestibility at high altitude. *Journal of Applied Physiology*, 73, 2425–2431.

Kinsman, T. A., Gore, C. J., Hahn, A. G., Hopkins, W. G., Hawley, J. A., McKenna, M. J. et al. (2005). Sleep in athletes undertaking protocols of exposure to nocturnal simulated altitude at 2650 m. *Journal of Science and Medicine in Sport*, 8, 222–232.

Larsson, P., & Henriksson-Larsen, K. (2008). Body composition and performance in cross-country skiing. *International Journal of Sports Medicine*, 29, 971–975.

Martin, D. S., Levett, D. Z., Grocott, M. P., & Montgomery, H. E. (2010). Variation in human performance in the hypoxic mountain environment. *Experimental Physiology*, 95, 463–470.

Mawson, J. T., Braun, B., Rock, P. B., Moore, L. G., Mazzeo, R., & Butterfield, G. E. (2000). Women at altitude: Energy requirement at 4,300 m. *Journal of Applied Physiology*, 88, 272–281.

Mazzeo, R. S. (2005). Altitude, exercise and immune function. *Exercise Immunology Reviews*, 11, 6–16.

Meyer, N. L., Johnson, S. C., Askew, E. W., Lutkemeier, M. L., Bainbridge, C., Shultz, B. B. et al. (1999). Energy and nutrient intake of elite female alpine ski racers during the preparatory phase. *Medicine and Science in Sports and Exercise*, 31, S100.

Meyer, N. L., & Parker-Simmons, S. (2009). Winter sports. In L. M. Burke (Ed.), *Practical sports nutrition* (pp. 335–358). Champaign, IL: Human Kinetics.

Meyer, N. L., Shaw, J. M., Manore, M. M., Dolan, S. H., Subudhi, A. W., Shultz, B. B. et al. (2004). Bone mineral density of Olympic-level female winter sport athletes. *Medicine and Science in Sports and Exercise*, 36, 1594–1601.

Milledge, J. S. (1992). Salt and water control at altitude. *International Journal of Sports Medicine*, 13 (suppl.), S61–S63.

Monsma, D. V., & Malina, R. M. (2005). Anthropometry and somatotype of competitive female figure skaters 11–22 years: Variation by competitive level and discipline. *Journal of Sports Medicine and Physical Fitness*, 45, 491–500.

Montgomery, D. L. (1988). Physiology of ice hockey. *Sports Medicine*, 5, 99–126.

Nattiv, A., Loucks, A. B., Manore, M. M., Sanborn, C. F., Sundgot-Borgen, J., & Warren, M. P. (2007). American College of Sports Medicine position stand: The female athlete triad. *Medicine and Science in Sports and Exercise*, 39, 1867–1882.

Nielsen, P., & Nachtigall, D. (1998). Iron supplementation in athletes: Current recommendations. *Sports Medicine, 26*, 207–216.

Nygaard, E., Andersen, P., Nilsson, P., Eriksson, E., Kjessel, T., & Saltin, B. (1978). Glycogen depletion pattern and lactate accumulation in leg muscles during recreational downhill skiing. *European Journal of Applied Physiology and Occupational Physiology*, 38, 261–269.

O'Brien, C., Young, A. J., & Sawka, M. N. (1998). Hypohydration and thermoregulation in cold air. *Journal of Applied Physiology*, 84, 185–189.

Orvanova, E. (1987). Physical structure of winter sports athletes. *Journal of Sports Sciences*, 5, 197–248.

Palmer, M. S., Logan, H. M., & Spriet, L. L. (2010). On-ice sweat rate, voluntary fluid intake, and sodium balance during practice in male junior ice hockey players drinking water or a carbohydrate-electrolyte solution. *Applied Physiology, Nutrition, and Metabolism*, 35, 328–335.

Palmer, M. S., & Spriet, L. L. (2008). Sweat rate, salt loss, and fluid intake during an intense on-ice practice in elite Canadian male junior hockey players. *Applied Physiology, Nutrition, and Metabolism*, 33, 263–271.

Phillips, S. M., & Van Loon, L. J. (2011). Dietary protein for athletes: From requirements to optimal adaptation. Forthcoming in *Journal of Sports Sciences*.

Pitsiladis, Y. P., & Maughan, R. J. (1999). The effects of exercise and diet manipulation on the capacity to perform prolonged exercise in the heat and in the cold in trained humans. *Journal of Physiology*, 517, 919–930.

Rankinen, T., Lyytikainen, S., Vanninen, E., Penttila, I., Rauramaa, R., & Uusitupa, M. (1998). Nutritional status of the Finnish elite ski jumpers. *Medicine and Science in Sports and Exercise*, 30, 1592–1597.

Rintamäki, H., Makinen, T., Oksa, J., & Latvala, J. (1995). Water balance and physical performance in cold. *Arctic Medicine Research*, 54, 32–36.

Ronsen, O., Sundgot-Borgen, J., & Maehlum, S. (1999). Supplement use and nutritional habits in Norwegian elite athletes. *Scandinavian Journal of Medicine, Science and Sports*, 9, 28–35.

Rundell, K. W., Nioka, S., & Chance, B. (1997). Hemoglobin/myoglobin desaturation during speed skating. *Medicine and Science in Sports and Exercise*, 29, 248–258.

Rundell, K. W., & Szmedra, L. (1998). Energy cost of rifle carriage in biathlon skiing. *Medicine and Science in Sports and Exercise*, 30, 570–576.

Rusko, H. (2003). Training for cross-country skiing. In H. Rusko (Ed.), *Handbook of sports medicine and science – cross-country skiing* (pp. 62–100). Oxford: Blackwell Science.

Sawka, M. N., Convertino, V. A., Eichner, E. R., Schnieder, S. M., & Young, A. J. (2000). Blood volume: Importance and adaptations to exercise training, environmental stresses, and trauma/sickness. *Medicine and Science in Sports and Exercise*, 32, 332–348.

Schena, F., Pattini, A., & Mantovanelli, S. (1995). Iron status in athletes involved in endurance and in prevalently anaerobic sports. In C. V. Kies & J. A. Driskell (Eds.), *Sports nutrition: Minerals and electrolytes* (pp. 65–79). Boca Raton, FL: CRC Press.

Seifert, J. G., Luetkemeier, M. J., White, A. T., & Mino, L. M. (1998). The physiological effects of beverage ingestion during cross country ski training in elite collegiate skiers. *Canadian Journal of Applied Physiology*, 23, 66–73.

Sjödin, A. M., Andersson, A. B., Hogberg, J. M., & Westerterp, K. R. (1994). Energy balance in cross-country skiers: A study using doubly labeled water. *Medicine and Science in Sports and Exercise*, 26, 720–724.

Stray-Gundersen, J., Hochstein, A., deLemos, D., & Levine, B. D. (1992). Failure of red cell volume to increase to altitude exposure in iron deficient runners. *Medicine and Science in Sports and Exercise, 24*, S90.

Szmedra, L., Im, J., Nioka, S., Chance, B., & Rundell, K. W. (2001). Hemoglobin/myoglobin oxygen desaturation during Alpine skiing. *Medicine and Science in Sports and Exercise, 33*, 232–236.

Tesch, P. A. (1995). Aspects on muscle properties and use in competitive Alpine skiing. *Medicine and Science in Sports and Exercise, 27*, 310–314.

Tesch, P. A., Larsson, L., Eriksson, A., & Karlsson, J. (1978). Muscle glycogen depletion and lactate concentration during downhill skiing. *Medicine and Science in Sports, 10*, 85–90.

Torstveit, M. K., & Sundgot-Borgen, J. (2005). The female athlete triad: Are elite athletes at increased risk? *Medicine and Science in Sports and Exercise, 37*, 184–193.

Vallerand, A. L., Zamecnik, J., & Jacobs, I. (1995). Plasma glucose turnover during cold stress in humans. *Journal of Applied Physiology, 78*, 1296–1302.

Van Ingen Schenau, G. J., de Koning, J. J., Bakker, F. C., & de Groot, G. (1996). Performance-influencing factors in homogeneous groups of top athletes: A cross-sectional study. *Medicine and Science in Sports and Exercise, 28*, 1305–1310.

Wilber, R. (2004). *Altitude training and athletic performance.* Champaign, IL: Human Kinetics.

Wilber, R. L. (2007). Application of altitude/hypoxic training by elite athletes. *Medicine and Science in Sports and Exercise, 39*, 1610–1624.

Index

Page numbers in **bold** type refer to figures
Page numbers in *italic* type refer to tables